*Amid the Clouds and Mist*

China's Colonization of Guizhou,

1200–1700

Harvard East Asian Monographs 293

—

# *Amid the Clouds and Mist*
## China's Colonization of Guizhou,
### 1200–1700

John E. Herman

Published by the Harvard University Asia Center
Distributed by Harvard University Press
Cambridge (Massachusetts) and London 2007

Printed in the United States of America

The Harvard University Asia Center publishes a monograph series and, in coordination with the Fairbank Center for East Asian Research, the Korea Institute, the Reischauer Institute of Japanese Studies, and other faculties and institutes, administers research projects designed to further scholarly understanding of China, Japan, Vietnam, Korea, and other Asian countries. The Center also sponsors projects addressing multidisciplinary and regional issues in Asia.

Library of Congress Cataloging-in-Publication Data

Herman, John E., 1957–

    Amid the clouds and mist : China's colonization of Guizhou, 1200–1700 / John E. Herman.

        p. cm. -- (Harvard East Asian monographs ; 293)

    Includes bibliographical references and index.

    ISBN-13: 978-0-674-02591-2 (cl : alk. paper)

    1. Guizhou Sheng (China)--History. 2. Yi (Chinese people)--China--Guizhou Sheng--History. I. Title. II. Title: China's colonization of Guizhou, 1200–1700.

    DS793.K8H47 2007

    951'.3402--dc22

                                                                        2007014129

Index by the author

⊗    Printed on acid-free paper

Last figure below indicates year of this printing

16  15  14  13  12  11  10  09  08  07

# Acknowledgments

In the many years of researching and writing this book, I have benefited enormously from the advice and encouragement of several people, and it is now my pleasure to finally acknowledge them. First I must thank my teachers, R. Kent Guy and Chan Hok-lam. I am profoundly grateful for the wisdom and guidance (both professional and personal) they imparted to me. These two debts will never be repaid in full. I also want to thank Joe Esherick, Ralph Falconeri, Elizabeth Perry, and Steven Harrell for sharing their expertise on China and for prodding me to think beyond the late imperial period. I reserve special appreciation for the late Jack Dull, whose knowledge of ancient China far surpassed what he produced. And finally, I want to thank Daniel Chirot, Ray Jonas, and John Toews. They might not be experts in Chinese history, but they are scholars in the true sense of the word, and what they taught me about history informs everything I do.

The research for this book was conducted mostly in China, and I am indebted to a number of people there for sharing their knowledge and insights with me. In Beijing Wei Qingyuan, Luo Yuandao, and Yin Guoguang of People's University, Chen Yongling and Wang Zhonghan of the Central Minorities University, Li Sheyu of the Chinese Academy of Social Sciences, and Liu Ruzhong of China's National History Museum patiently tutored me on the history of late imperial China, the *tusi* institution of offices, China's expansion into the southwest, and, most critically, how to negotiate my way into and around Ming and Qing archives. In Taipei I want to thank Chen Chieh-hsien of National Taiwan University and Chuang Chi-fa of the National Palace Museum for their generous time and assistance. In Guizhou Mao Jianlin, Zhang Chengxia, and Liu Qinghua helped me make the most of my trips to Guiyang, Huaxi, Dafang, and Bijie. I also want to thank Norman and Ruth Geary for their warm hospitality in Huaxi, and for sharing their expertise in conducting fieldwork in Guizhou. In Shanghai Jin Guangyao and Chen Weiqing contributed invaluable assistance during the manuscript's final stages of preparation. To all, I thank you.

People who have read the manuscript at various stages include James Lee, C. Patterson Giersch, Leo Shin, Stevan Harrell, Evelyn Rawski, John Shepherd, Richard von Glahn, Susan Kennedy, and Beatrice Bartlett. I deeply appreciate your comments and criticisms. I also want to thank the two anonymous referees for the Harvard University Asia Center, to whom I am grateful for pointing out errors that might have otherwise made it into print. Many thanks also to the participants in forums at Harvard University, Dartmouth College, University of Michigan, University of Oregon, Virginia Commonwealth University, Lund University, Academia Sinica, Taipei, the Center for Chinese Studies, Taipei, People's University of China, Guizhou University, Guizhou Normal University, Fudan University, and the Association for Asian Studies, where parts of this book have been presented. Material for Chapter 2 first appeared in an essay titled "The Mongol Conquest of the Dali Kingdom: The Failure of the Second Front," in Nicola Di Cosmo, ed., *Warfare in Inner Asian History* (Leiden: E. J. Brill, 2002), 295–334, and is reprinted here with permission of the publisher. Naturally, I assume responsibility for the views expressed in this book and for any errors or misattributions it may contain.

Research for this book was made possible by generous support from the Joint Committee on Chinese Studies of the American Council of Learned Societies and the Social Science Research Council; the Pacific Cultural Foundation; the Center for Chinese Studies, Taipei; the Committee for Scholarly Communication with China; the An Wang Post-Doctoral Fellowship, Harvard University; and Virginia Commonwealth University. I also want to acknowledge the dedicated people at the following libraries and institutions: National Central Library, Taipei; National Palace Museum Archives, Taipei; Academia Sinica, Taipei; Center for Chinese Studies, Taipei; First Historical Archives, Beijing; National Library, Beijing; National Museum of History, Beijing; Guizhou University Library; Shanghai Municipal Library; Fudan University Library; Harvard-Yenching Library; Widener Library, Harvard University; and East Asia Library at the University of Washington. I give special thanks to the staff at the Guizhou Provincial Library in Guiyang for their willingness to accommodate my research trips on short notice.

Finally, for Tanya, Kyle, and Michael, who sacrificed time and tolerated long periods of separation, thanks are not enough. It is to you I dedicate this book.

J.E.H.

# Contents

# Maps and Figures

## Maps

## Figures

# Dates of Selected Eras

## Chinese Dynasties

| | |
|---|---|
| Shang | ca. 17th c.–ca. 11th c. BCE |
| Zhou | ca. 11th c.–221 BCE |
| Qin | 221–206 BCE |
| Han | 206 BCE–220 CE |
| Three Kingdoms | 220–80 |
| Southern and Northern Dynasties | 317–589 |
| Sui | 581–618 |
| Tang | 618–907 |
| Five Dynasties | 907–60 |
| Song | 960–1279 |
| Jin | 1115–1234 |
| Yuan | 1271–1368 |
| Ming | 1368–1644 |
| Qing | 1636–1912 |

## Kingdoms in the Southwest

| | |
|---|---|
| Mu'ege | ca. 300–1283 |
| Cuan | 338–737 |
| Nanzhao | 740–902 |
| Dali | 934–1253 |

# Weights and Measures

1 *jin* (catty) = 1.3 pounds or 0.6 kilograms

1 *li* = 0.36 miles or 0.576 kilometers

1 *mu* = 0.1647 acre or 0.0666 hectare

1 *shi* = 103.5 liters or 2.9 bushels (23.5 gallons). One *shi* of milled rice weighed approximately 175–95 pounds (80–89 kg).

*Amid the Clouds and Mist*

China's Colonization of Guizhou,

1200–1700

My eyes have gazed upon the empire's vast expanse,
And my heart has absorbed the landscape's peculiarities.
But Guizhou, far from well-traveled roads, is a true wilderness.
It is the strangest of all the places I have visited;
Its heights are magnificent and its depths treacherous.

Forgetting the burden of sense and cognition,
I have chanced on a hidden place where my footprints will remain unseen.
To this eerie place my heart and spirit are committed:
I remove vegetation on my way up the winding mountain path
And burn the thorny brush to clear an open hilltop.

Countless peaks are revealed before me here,
And assembled together in front and behind they are awesome.
I ascend to the highest point to gaze out into the distance,
Sensing how quickly the jagged summits disappear,
*Amid the clouds and mist*, assuming ten thousand shapes,
And with each image one sees an illusion never grasped in its entirety.

—Qian Bangqi, *Other Mountains*, ca. 1650

# Introduction

How did China's late imperial state(s) come to establish territorial sovereignty over the multicultural landscape that is southwest China today, the provinces of Guizhou, Yunnan, and the southern portion of Sichuan? At the beginning of the thirteenth century, the southwest was inhabited by an assortment of strikingly diverse cultures and ruled by a multitude of political entities. The vast majority of the region's polities were small, geographically confined units that came and went with violent regularity, yet there were a few exceptionally large kingdoms, which had, in some cases, ruled their respective territories for centuries. However, by the middle of the eighteenth century nearly all these polities, both large and small, had completely disappeared, and many of the region's cultures were moving rapidly toward extinction. China's military, political, sociocultural, and economic institutions were now firmly in control of the southwest, leaving only the most remote highlands and inaccessible valleys beyond the direct control of the Chinese state. One purpose of this book is to examine this span of roughly five hundred years, from 1200 to 1700, to see how China's three late imperial dynasties, the Yuan (1271–1368), Ming (1368–1644), and Qing (1636–1912), conquered, colonized, and assumed sovereign control over the southwest.[1]

Another objective of this book is to highlight the indigenous response to China's colonization of the southwest. Although it is true that the vast majority of the non-Han peoples did not possess a written script and therefore could not record for posterity the impact of the intrusive Chinese state/society on their daily lives, the Nasu Yi people of western Guizhou and eastern Yunnan did. The Nasu Yi are a sub-group of what the People's Republic of China refers to as the Yi national minority.[2] There are four linguistic subgroups of the Yi who have used a written script since at least the sixth century CE, if not earlier: the Northern Yi, or Nuosu, live primarily in southern Sichuan; the Eastern Yi, or Nasu, who are discussed in this book, reside in western Guizhou and northeast Yunnan; the Southern Yi, or Nisu, live in central and southern Yunnan; and the Southeastern Yi, which includes several subgroups, such as the Sani, Axi, Azhe, and Azha, live in central and southeastern Yunnan.[3]

The Yi language is part of the Tibeto-Burman family of languages. The traditional Yi script, also known as "Cuan script" and "Wei writing," is made up of characters that represent syllabic logographs, which means each character represents a syllable that is also a morpheme. There are between eight and ten thousand characters in classical Yi, but the core syllabary of modern Yi, developed in the 1970s, consists of 819 signs for syllables. The collection, translation, and publication of classical Yi texts began in earnest following the National Conference on Yi Language Work, held in Beijing in 1980. Since then, Yi scholars in China have provided historians with a wide range of historical texts that not only describe the religious, political, and social-economic institutions of the Yi of southwest China but also show in some measure how the Yi responded to China's colonization of the southwest frontier.[4]

This book, then, is organized around two interrelated narratives. The first narrative focuses on the late imperial Chinese state and its role in the military conquest and colonization of the southwest frontier. At times this narrative will present a wide-angle view of state policies toward the entire southwest—Yunnan, Guizhou, and southern Sichuan—but most often I will limit my focus to Guizhou province. The second narrative, which takes advantage of recently published Yi historical documents, tells the history of the Nasu Yi people in the southwest, examines how their Mu'ege kingdom (ca. 300–1283) dominated much of present-day Guizhou province for nearly a thousand years, and finally describes how the Nasu Yi responded to nearly five centuries of uninterrupted efforts to colonize their homeland.

## *Revisiting* China's March Toward the Tropics

"What are the underlying factors of the inexorable southward surge of the Han-Chinese that has swamped all the alien peoples and cultures in their path?"[5] This was the question Herold Wiens presented to his readers nearly half a century ago in his critically acclaimed book, *China's March Toward the Tropics*. The "inexorable southward surge," as Wiens saw it, was the result of successive waves of Han Chinese immigrants pushing south out of the political and cultural heartland of China, the "central plains" (*zhongyuan*), toward the sparsely inhabited and unexploited frontiers in the south. The first wave of immigrants escaped the violence, political instability, and natural disasters that plagued Western Jin (265–316) rule by settling in present-day Sichuan, Hubei, and Hunan.

The second wave, the product of political instability, inept rulership, and natural disasters, began during the Eastern Jin (317–420) and continued unabated to the sixth century with Han Chinese pushing south into the Yangzi River basin, northern Zhejiang, northern Jiangxi, and northern Fujian. The third wave of Han Chinese immigrants pressed even further south, into southern Jiangxi, Guangxi, and Guangdong during the Song (960–1279) period as North China recoiled in the face of foreign occupation, first at the hands of the Jurchen, whose Jin dynasty (1115–1234) controlled much of China north of the Huai River, and then in response to the Mongols, who defeated the Jin in 1234. According to Wiens, Chinese colonization of the southwest frontier did not begin until well after the Mongol conquest of the Dali kingdom (934–1253) in Yunnan in 1253, and then it was only a trickle as few Chinese dared venture into this alien, malaria-invested region. The demographic pressures afflicting eighteenth-century China, we are told, eventually pushed land-starved peasants from Hunan, Jiangxi, and Jiangsu to settle the southwest frontier of Yunnan and Guizhou, and it was this circumstance more than anything else that brought the southwest frontier within the fold of China proper (*neidi*).[6]

In each successive wave Han immigrants utilized their advanced agricultural know-how and technological acumen to exploit the frontier's natural resources and to transform inhospitable terrain. Swamps were drained, canals dug, and mountains terraced by settlers intent on

Map 1    Southwest China Today

reclaiming frontier land while the entrepreneurial among them established mining, logging, and agricultural enterprises. Moreover, Han settlers brought to the frontier social-cultural institutions unique to China proper, and once ensconced in the frontier these distinctly Chinese cultural beliefs and practices radiated out and influenced the indigenous peoples. In time, Wiens informs us, indigenes became indistinguishable from Han; in other words, the indigenes were assimilated into Chinese society, or sinicized (*hanhua*). This process of sinicization that Wiens saw operating in China's southern frontiers both pacified the savage, uncivilized frontier population and unified the frontier around common cultural characteristics, thereby eliminating differences between China and the frontier. In short, frontier territory was incorporated spatially following each wave of Han Chinese migration south, and it was unified internally through the acceptance of Chinese social, cultural, and economic institutions.

According to Wiens, Han immigrants were both pushed and pulled toward the southern frontiers. Warfare, natural disasters, and corrupt rule in China, and the lure of economic opportunities in a fertile, sparsely populated frontier unencumbered by state regulations, were the primary reasons given to explain China's march toward the tropics. On a few occasions, most notably during the reigns of Qin Shihuangdi (r. 221–210 BCE), Han Wudi (r. 141–87 BCE), and Hongwu (r. 1368–98), the Chinese state took the initiative in carving out territorial niches in the south for Han immigrants to settle. In each case armies were sent to pacify resistance, occupy vast tracts of frontier land, and set up military colonies in hopes of attracting additional Han settlers to the frontier. But for much of China's long history, we are told, the Chinese state played a secondary, if not inconsequential role in China's march south.

Another important feature of Wiens's study was the ethnographic descriptions of the more prominent indigenous non-Han peoples in the southern frontier. The intent of the ethnographic descriptions was to show that the southern frontiers were inhabited terrain, and Wiens's work does an admirable job in proving this point. However, his descriptions fail to move beyond simple declarative points to make the indigenes an integral part of the historical narrative.[7] It is as if indigenes, after having been introduced at the beginning of his study, wait passively in the south to be conquered and assimilated, or, as Wiens puts it, "swamped" by Chinese culture. In essence the indigenes appear as minor obstacles, more troubling afterthought than sympathetic victim of aggrandizement, and their token resistance to Han expansion seems oddly trivial and out of place. The action that propels the narrative forward comes entirely from China, and it is sustained by China.

The broad brushstrokes of the march thesis are fairly easy to discern: a history of China's organic migration southward, a firm conviction in the superiority of Chinese culture and the unquestioned sinicization of the south, the negligible role played by the Chinese state, and the absence of any serious attempt to incorporate the indigenous non-Han into the historical narrative. Although Wiens's explanation of China's expansion south is generally coherent and supported by Chinese sources, it is an account pieced together from assorted fragments and documentary evidence, and it is only one possible explanation of many that can be woven together from historical records.

## New Sources, New Narratives: The Nasu Yi of Guizhou

The march thesis is not the only "hegemonizing history" scholars have used to explain how the southern frontiers became an integral part of China.[8] After 1949 Chinese historians came to rely almost exclusively on the "objective" and "universal laws" of Marxism to analyze historical events and elucidate patterns of historical development. The social relations of production became the mantra for scholarly analysis, and it was (and in some quarters still is) believed that the only valid method of historical analysis begins with a rigorous investigation into how a society organizes its human resources for production. As soon as the historian determined the social relations to production, s/he instinctively classified the society according to the five stages of historical development (primitive, slave, feudal, capitalist, and socialist) first worked out by Lewis Henry Morgan in 1877 and adopted as "scientific" by Soviet historians during the 1920s and Chinese historians in the 1950s.[9] As a result, China's dynastic and predynastic histories, as well as the histories of many of the peoples living along China's periphery, have been cataloged according to this five-stage scale of historical development. Since Han scholars were convinced that they had entered the socialist stage of development following the communist revolution in 1949, they were equally certain that many of the non-Han living in the southwest were not nearly as advanced or as modern as Han Chinese.

By way of example, Chinese historians and ethnographers in the 1950s identified the Nuosu (Yi) society in southern Sichuan as a slave society because the predominant mode of production was, in their estimation, slave labor. But instead of adopting a diachronic mode of historical inquiry that takes the past and not the present as its starting point, many post-1949 Chinese studies of the Nuosu Yi betray a teleological obsession with the oppressive features of slave society, despite the fact that not all of the peoples identified as Yi could be linked to a slave mode of production. This contemporary snapshot of the Yi as a slave society not only unduly influenced the way historians approached the study of the Yi (if they were a slave society today, then they must have been a slave or primitive society earlier), but it also compelled Chinese historians to depict the Nuosu Yi as an unsophisticated, ancient, and barbaric people. The contrast to a modern, socialist China could not have been more striking. The Marx-Morgan paradigm froze the Nuosu Yi in time so that Nuosu Yi history appeared stagnant and entrenched in centuries of cruel immutability.[10]

The Marx-Morgan paradigm inhibited Han and non-Han scholars alike from offering a more informed history of the non-Han peoples living in China, and its ideological grip did not begin to fade until late 1978 with the emergence of Deng Xiaoping as China's paramount leader. Almost immediately Yi scholars began to organize research associations throughout the southwest in order to collect, translate, and publish Yi historical records. They pushed vigorously to have Yi language courses and Yi studies programs incorporated into the curricula of several universities in the southwest, so that a new generation of Yi and non-Yi scholars trained in Yi studies could carry on their work. In the past twenty-five years nearly one hundred volumes of Yi historical texts have been published (many of the published texts contain both the Yi script and Chinese translation), the number of scholarly journals devoted to the publication of articles on Yi history and society has increased tenfold, and several high-profile conferences have been organized both inside and outside China to bring together students of Yi history and culture. In short, the availability of Yi historical sources demands we rethink the China-centered paradigms that have claimed to describe not only the history of the Yi peoples (and all non-Han peoples in China for that matter) but also Chinese expansion into the southwestern frontier.[11]

For instance, instead of depicting Yi society as a caste-like society dominated by slaves, scholars have begun to describe traditional Yi society as both vertically differentiated by kin-based patrilineal clans, or patriclans, and horizontally layered according to an inflexible racial segregation (similar in many ways to how historians have described China's ancient Zhou [ca. 11th c.–221 BCE] society).[12] The towering presence of kin-based patriclans evokes images of a "forest of clans," in which one patriclan, because of its direct patrilineal ties to the six ancient ancestors, attained political-military primacy over subordinate branches.[13] There were slaves in Yi society, as there were in Chinese society at the time under discussion here, but there is an enormous difference between a "slave society" and a "society with slaves," as Ann Maxwell Hill has pointed out.[14]

Slaves were an identifiable feature of traditional Nasu Yi society in Guizhou, and they continued as a recognizable feature of Nasu Yi society until the fifteenth century, yet one would be hard pressed to declare unequivocally that the Nasu Yi society was a "slave society" prior to the fifteenth century. I do believe, however, that during the sixteenth century, as Ming China's colonization of the southwest expanded in scope and quickened in pace, the importance of slaves to the economic vitality of Nasu Yi society in Guizhou increased. Slaves became an important source of labor, and their ranks within Nasu Yi society swelled proportionately. In other words, Nasu Yi society in Guizhou came to resemble a slave society only after the political economy of the southwest changed under the weight of Ming colonialism.

## Ming China's Southwest Frontier

Prior to the nineteenth century, China's frontier policy was formulated first and foremost with the Central Eurasian steppe in mind, and its essential feature was the construction of defensive barriers to protect agrarian China from hostile nomadic neighbors. There were times when China's rulers sought to project military force into the steppe to create a forward buffer to China's defenses. When both offensive and defensive strategies were employed, China was relatively safe; however, when the offensive component was neglected, as was the case during much of the Ming dynasty, problems arose. Offensive and defensive strategies were utilized most effectively during the early decades of a new dynasty, when its vitality and martial vigor were most robust. In time, though, unanticipated domestic and international issues would weaken the dynasty's resolve to maintain the offensive component to its frontier policy, and rulers would come to rely increasingly on defensive measures.[15]

Arthur Waldron, in his examination of Ming frontier policy toward the Central Eurasian steppe, identifies three phases in the historical development of Ming strategic planning. First, from 1368 to 1449, the Ming military advanced repeatedly into the Central Eurasian steppe in an impressive display of offensive warfare. In particular, the third emperor of the Ming dynasty, Yongle (1360–1424, r. 1403–24), personally led several military campaigns into the steppe to destroy remnants of the Mongol confederation that still threatened Ming China. The second phase in frontier policy began in 1449 with the Tumu Incident. This marked a decided shift from an offensive strategy of high-profile and well-funded military campaigns into the northern steppe to a defensive strategy that emphasized wall construction. The most conspicuous feature of this phase was the building of the Great Wall. "After Tumu," Peter Perdue tells us, "the Ming rulers abandoned forward campaigns into the steppe. They found themselves on the defensive on all fronts, constantly warding off repeated attacks by many autonomous Mongol chieftains."[16] The third and final phase, according to Waldron, began in 1540 and lasted until the end of the dynasty in 1644, and it is distinguished by the completion of the Great Wall as a defensive barrier and the total abandonment of any offensive strategy.[17]

Students of Ming China have long noted that this shift to a strategic defensive posture following the Tumu Incident was so profound that its effects were felt not only in frontier policy but in virtually every phase of life in Ming China. The country's economic and social resources, not to mention political will, were mobilized to carry out one of the greatest construction projects known to man, the Great Wall.[18] As one noted authority on Ming China put it, "China turned inward after Tumu. It built a monstrous wall to keep the barbarians out and the Han [Chinese] in, and it remained inward looking and defensive until the nineteenth century. Understanding the siege mentality that afflicted China after Tumu is important for understanding why the country was unable to adequately respond to the West."[19] This post-Tumu shift in Ming China has been etched in stone by historians, but the edifice suffers from one indisputable flaw: throughout the entire span of the Ming dynasty the government carried out a massive colonizing project in the southwest frontier. There was no sign of a strategic defensive posture in the southwest; on the contrary, Ming policy toward the southwest was surprisingly consistent in its objective: the military conquest and civilian colonization of the frontier. By examining Ming colonization of the southwest frontier, this study hopes to shed new light on Ming frontier policy. I do this not with the intent to challenge the defensive posture on the northern steppe frontier, which would be foolish in my estimation, but to show that the Ming government oversaw several frontiers, not just the northern steppe, and that Ming officials charged with frontier planning were not nearly as constrained by the legacy of Tumu as some scholars have suggested.

Why did Ming China conquer and colonize the southwest frontier, and how did it accomplish this task? The answer to the first question is that the founding Ming emperor, Hongwu (Zhu Yuanzhang; 1328–98, r. 1368–98), sent his armies into the southwest to mitigate a strategic threat, secure control over the vast natural resources (primarily silver and copper) vital to China's economic recovery, and reclaim land formerly under Yuan dynasty control. In addition, he saw profits to be made by settling his soldier/farmer army on "uninhabited lands," which could then be enrolled on government tax registers. Subsequent Ming emperors replenished the Ming military garrisons in the southwest with new troops, and by the middle of the fifteenth century a sufficient security presence had been established in the southwest to encourage voluntary Han immigration to the region. As wave after wave of Han settled in the southwest, the frontier filled and closed, land was enrolled on tax registers, and Ming officials were appointed to govern the Han and non-Han populations. The expectation was that sufficient revenue could be generated in the frontier to compensate the large military presence and pay for civilian rule, and that what was left over could be remitted to the central government.

Understanding how the Ming colonized the southwest is less straightforward. In broad terms, students of empires and colonialism make a distinction between informal empires and formal empires. An informal empire is defined as the expanding power's attempt to exercise domination over territory through local collaborators, who themselves are legally independent but politically tied, generally through negotiated patron-client bonds, to the colonizing power. The informal empire has an abbreviated presence in the territory it is expanding into, and political, social-cultural, and economic institutions are still primarily a reflection of the interests of the indigenous elite. Formal empire, however, is characterized by a colonizing power that deploys troops, annexes territory, and then appoints its own officials to govern the annexed territory. In most cases the colonizing power relies on the assistance of local collaborators to extend its authority to local society, but it is clear that sovereignty is in the hands of the officials appointed by the colonial power.[20]

Prior to the Yuan dynasty, China's relationship with the inhabitants of the southwest can be characterized as that of an informal empire. China was unable (and unwilling) to effect any lasting military presence in the southwest, and its influence among the indigenous non-Han peoples was negligible. Furthermore, China was only one of several empires vying for influence in the region. The Mongol conquest of the Yunnan-based Dali kingdom in 1253 and then Song China in 1279 permanently altered China's relationship to the southwest: the Mongols eliminated many of China's rivals for imperial control of the southwest, and they effectively incorporated the southwest into the existing Chinese polity when they established the Yunnan Branch Secretariat. The Mongol conquest of the southwest had the psychological effect of altering Chinese perceptions of the southwest frontier: by the time of the Yuan-Ming transition in 1368, China's elites no longer considered the southwest an altogether alien, distant frontier beyond China's influence, and Ming officials seemed determined to exercise exclusive political control over the region and its inhabitants.

As was the case with most premodern empire builders, the Mongols sought to control people, not territory.[21] True, the Yuan military occupied and annexed territory in the southwest, and there were ample strategic and economic reasons for doing so, but Yuan officials were concerned first and foremost with winning the loyalty of the elites under their control. In the southwest, the Mongol innovation was to bestow upon the indigenous frontier elite official-sounding titles that signified a special negotiated relationship with the Mongol qan, or Yuan emperor. The native official, or *tusi*, was the client in this new patron-client relationship and as such the patron or qan exercised jurisdictional control over the client, not his/her territory.

When the Ming replaced the Yuan, it adopted the *tusi* office as part of its bureaucratic portfolio of offices, though its stature and place in the Ming bureaucracy was marginalized so as to distinguish the *tusi* office clearly from ordinary civilian offices. More important, during the Ming *tusi* offices were increasingly identified with territory, and as such this transformed the heretofore patron-client relationship into a patron-

client-territory relationship. In other words, during the Ming colonization of the southwest control of territory gradually replaced control of
people as an institutional means of imperial expansion; this study will
examine the *tusi* office as it relates to the transition from a negotiated
jurisdictional sovereignty (patron-client relationship) to territorial sovereignty (patron-client-territory relationship). China's transition from
informal to formal empire in the southwest was based in large measure
on institutional innovations introduced by the Yuan and adopted by
the Ming and Qing dynasties, most importantly, the *tusi* office.

It has been argued that the southwest frontier was not formally incorporated into the Chinese polity until the eighteenth century and
that the most aggressive phase of conquest and incorporation occurred
during the Yongzheng reign (1723–35) of the Qing dynasty.[22] One purpose of this study is to demonstrate just how aggressive and expansionistic the Ming dynasty was in the southwest. Building upon the Yuan
precedent, the Ming began its colonization of the southwest in the
1370s, and though its military strength waxed and waned, it was able to
eliminate the largest autonomous kingdoms in the southwest by the
early decades of the seventeenth century. By the time of the Ming-Qing
transition, what remained in the southwest were only a few small
autonomous polities, and the Rebellion of the Three Feudatories (*sanfan zhi luan*; 1673–81) did much to erase these from the landscape. In
short, the Yongzheng emperor's appointment of his trusted Manchu official Ortai (1680–1745) and the aggressive campaign against *tusi* offices
they initiated in the 1720s in the southwest should be seen as the end
point, not the beginning, of China's colonization of the southwest.

## *Ming Sinicization of the Southwest:*
## *A Different Perspective*

Past research on Chinese expansion into the southwest frontier has, due
to the wealth of Chinese historical records and the paucity of non-Han
Chinese texts, presented only China's perspective, the imperialist perspective. China's motives for colonizing the southwest frontier were
deemed noble and justifiable, and its scholar-officials struggled mightily
to bring civilization to the southwest. To them, the forces of modernity
radiated forth from China and attracted all who sought a better, more
civilized life. China's sophisticated political institutions, codified legal
system, and superior social-cultural institutions were destined to trans-

form the lawless southwest frontier and rescue the "barbarians" from their primitive existence. This "Confucian civilizing mission," as one scholar aptly described traditional Chinese representations of state/society expansion into the southwest, concealed the Ming military's role in the colonization of the southwest.

It is unrealistic to expect the entire complexity of a colonizing society, let alone its most advanced political and cultural institutions, to be present in a frontier setting. Representatives of China's elite culture were not the vanguard in the conquest of the southwest, even though they wrote about Chinese expansion into the southwest as a benevolent, civilizing project. Frontiers can be and generally are extraordinarily violent places where common ground between colonizer and colonized is both precious and ephemeral. Ming China's military annexation of the southwest was, if anything, an uninterrupted campaign of state-sponsored violence. The Ming state continually dispatched troops to the southwest to secure borders, subdue recalcitrant indigenes, and replenish the multitude of military garrisons, forts, and outposts established during the first decades of the Ming. Prior to the sixteenth century the Ming presence in the southwest was decidedly military, and even with the significant influx of Han immigrants in the sixteenth century the level of violence did not decrease; it increased. In short, Ming colonization of the southwest was not a "civilizing mission."

As mentioned above, the march thesis outlined by Wiens placed considerable weight on what he termed "the process of sinicization of the southern frontier." The word "sinicization" is the English translation of the Chinese characters *hanhua*, "to become Han," or "to be transformed into Han." For Wiens the process of sinicization is best seen in the unifying and transformative power of Chinese culture and in the seemingly inevitable process of non-Han acculturation and assimilation into Han. The sheer weight of the Chinese presence in the frontier and the prestige of their advanced cultural institutions encouraged the indigenous populations to adopt Chinese institutions as their own (acculturation), and in time the residual influence of the acculturation process would eventually transform the subjective values of the indigene so that s/he came to identify her/himself as Han Chinese (assimilation).[23]

If non-Han were to be transformed into Han, as the march thesis contends they were, then the process of sinicization would be successful only if institutions and offices created by Chinese state/society openly admitted the indigenous non-Han into positions of status. However, this was not the case. As this study will show, the non-Han peoples in the southwest were systematically prevented from acquiring the education needed to compete successfully in the triennial examinations, and as a consequence appointment to a routine political office in the Chinese bureaucracy was impossible. Police functions, judicial institutions, and military offices were likewise monopolized by Han immigrants. Han entrepreneurs dominated commercial enterprises in the southwest, and they controlled nearly all trade between the southwest and China proper. Occupations commonly defined as embodying high prestige and status were reserved exclusively for Han Chinese. The "cultural division of labor" Michael Hechter described in his study of Britain's colonial enterprise in Scotland, Wales, and Ireland was equally visible in Ming China's colonization of the southwest.[24]

The recent deluge of studies examining the concepts and phenomenon of ethnicity tend to agree that the creation of one's ethnic identity is a conditional construction acquired through sustained contact with others.[25] As Sow-theng Leong stated in his examination of the ethnohistory of the Hakka:

A cultural group "becomes ethnic" only when, in competition with another, these shared markers are consciously chosen to promote solidarity and mobilization, with the view of enhancing the group's share of societal resources or simply minimizing the threat to its survival.[26]

Ethnicity, then, is fundamentally defensive and transactional, and one's ethnic identity is ultimately the result of how one responds to a number of circumstances: for example, a real or perceived physical threat, like a military attack or the occupation of one's territory by an outside force; a challenge to one's socioeconomic way of life, possibly resulting from contact with a more economically developed society; and an assault on one's cultural institutions due to prolonged contact with a more advanced, cosmopolitan society.[27]

It is true that conditional and transactional processes surrounding the formation of ethnic identity might compel individuals to adapt culturally to the more powerful or advanced civilization and thus negate the creation of their own ethnic identity, but this can occur only if institutional barriers preventing fluid movement between diverse peoples and cultures do not exist, and if the expanding or more advanced power promotes policies with the intent to entice the indigenous peoples to adopt its cultural institutions. In regard to Ming expansion into the southwest, this study will show that non-Han acculturation and assimilation into Han civilization was exceedingly difficult, if not impossible, because the Ming state was unwilling to eliminate institutional barriers designed to protect Han dominance in the frontier. Ming officials were largely uninterested in "civilizing" or "transforming" the non-Han into Han, but their lack of interest did not prevent contemporary writers and later historians from using the "Confucian civilizing mission" as a rhetorical device to offer moral justification for the Ming colonial project in the southwest. The perception of the "Confucian civilizing mission" must be measured against the reality of the entire colonial project, which I intend to do in this book.

## Organization of the Book

The organization of this book is rather straightforward. In Chapter 1, I describe the origins of the Mu'ege kingdom and trace its expansion east into the Shuixi region of Guizhou over several centuries. I also discuss how the Nasu Yi leaders of the Mu'ege kingdom negotiated their way through the battlefields of the Tang-Nanzhao wars of the eighth and ninth centuries to extend Mu'ege control over much of present-day Guizhou province. In Chapter 2, I show how the Mongol conquest of Dali in 1253 and the subsequent Mongol subjugation of China in 1279 shattered Mu'ege isolation. The Mongols eventually conquered Mu'ege in 1283, which made it one of the last places in what is now China to succumb to Mongol rule, but Mongol control of Mu'ege was brief, as Mongol military campaigns into Southeast Asia continuously drained valuable resources away from the task of occupying Mu'ege. By the end of the thirteenth century, descendants of the former Mu'ege ruling elite, the Azhe patriclan, were back in control of nearly all of the territory formerly a part of the Mu'ege kingdom, though now the Azhe leadership governed Mu'ege territory both as the traditional rulers of Mu'ege and as *tusi* of the Yuan state.

I begin Chapter 3 with a description of the Mu'ege political economy during the Yuan-Ming transition in order to show how the Ming military conquest of the southwest in the 1380s and 1390s, and the subsequent Ming state/society colonization of the southwest, affected Nasu Yi rule of Shuixi. The strategic and economic importance of the southwest necessitated a Ming presence in the region, and its military superiority made conquest of the southwest possible. However, the exorbitant cost of financing permanent military and administrative control over this economically undeveloped region rendered Ming plans for annexation and incorporation impractical.

The description of the Ming military occupation of the southwest is followed in Chapter 4 by an analysis of the *tusi* offices used by the Ming state to extend its political influence into the southwest frontier. Due to the exorbitant costs and administrative difficulties associated with governing this frontier, the early Ming state, in an attempt to establish its hegemony over the multitude of indigenous leaders, consolidated the frontier *tusi* offices established by China's Mongol rulers during the Yuan dynasty into two categories, civilian and military, and incorporated these *tusi* offices into the Ming bureaucracy. This policy of political accommodation encouraged indigenous leaders to renounce loyalty to the Mongols and swear allegiance to the Ming throne, and in return they were bestowed *tusi* titles as Ming officials.

Unlike regular Ming officials, *tusi* officeholders enjoyed hereditary status, and they were expected to govern their domains as independent lords, albeit under Ming overlordship. *Tusi* offices, then, were a means of indirect rule that expressed a sense of negotiated joint community, political cooperation, and patron-client relations. The critical feature of *tusi* offices was the personal bond between ruler and subject, and the attendant jurisdictional sovereignty the Ming emperor enjoyed over the domains of those frontier leaders who accepted *tusi* status. Jurisdictional sovereignty symbolically asserted Ming rule of the heretofore independent frontier and provided the necessary ideological point of departure in the state's move toward complete annexation—*gaitu guiliu* (replacing *tusi* with state-appointed officials). In this sense, Ming expansion into and annexation of the southwest frontier should be seen as a transition from jurisdictional sovereignty to territorial sovereignty and from informal to formal empire, and this transition was embedded in the *tusi* office.

In Chapter 5, I shift my attention back to the Nasu Yi in Shuixi in order to show how they reacted to the presence of an increasingly intrusive Ming state/Chinese society. I examine the extent to which the expanding Chinese political economy influenced the Nasu Yi people in Shuixi, and I show how the Nasu Yi ruling elite took advantage of new economic opportunities to reconstitute its political-military authority. By the end of the sixteenth century, the Nasu Yi elite was once again asserting its political legitimacy as the inheritors of Mu'ege pride by challenging the presence of the Ming state in Guizhou. This Nasu Yi challenge to Ming authority culminated in the She-An Rebellion (1621–29), a turbulent Nasu Yi rebellion that nearly succeeded in driving the Ming out of the southwest altogether. Though Ming officials declared victory in 1629, the Ming state was an exhausted shell of its former self and altogether unable to govern the area as it had in years past. Members of the traditional Nasu Yi elite were once again granted *tusi* titles and asked to govern Shuixi on behalf of the Ming state, which they did. By this time, however, any claim of resurrecting the Mu'ege polity had been shorn of political legitimacy, and in its wake emerged a number of smaller, fragmented, and territorially discrete Nasu Yi domains.

In the final chapter, Chapter 6, I describe how Qing armies under Wu Sangui (1612–78) first occupied Shuixi during the campaigns against the Southern Ming (1644–62) and then replaced many of the territory's Ming *tusi* offices with Qing political units, prefectures, departments, and counties in a frantic effort to mobilize the economic resources of Shuixi to assist in Wu's consolidation of power over the southwest. The Qing defeat of Wu's forces in the Rebellion of the Three Feudatories launched the final phase in China's colonization of the southwest. The Kangxi emperor (1654–1722, r. 1661–1722) quickly maneuvered the Qing bureaucracy into a position whereby it reduced the autonomy *tusi* had enjoyed during the Ming. Kangxi also encouraged another wave of Han immigrants to settle in the southwest, and he challenged his officials in the southwest to build schools in urban and rural areas so that a Chinese education would be available to a broad section of the population. By the beginning of the eighteenth century, the emperor would note in one relevant edict on the southwest: "The Rebellion of the Three Feudatories destroyed the ability of the barbarians to resist us. The large and powerful barbarian leaders who challenged Ming rule are now gone. In recent years we have adopted policies that have transformed the barbarians into civilized men, and these policies have worked. I see no need to change course now."[28] Kangxi presided over the final chapter in China's long colonization of the southwest frontier, and it was his decision that brought the Azhe patriclan's political control of Shuixi to an end.

# I

## A Southern Kingdom, Mu'ege

Chinese historians have long considered the Yi and other Tibeto-Burman peoples in the southwest to be descendants of the ancient Qiang people first mentioned in classical sources at the end of the fifth century BCE. According to these sources, during the Warring States period (475–221 BCE) the Qiang abandoned their homelands in Eastern Tibet for less populated areas along China's northwestern corridor, in what today is the Gansu-Qinghai region. During the Han dynasty (206 BCE–220 CE), more than 150 different Qiang tribes living along China's western frontier were "granted permission" to settle within China to act as a military buffer between China and the increasingly combative Xiongnu of the Central Eurasian steppe. It is from Han sources that we first learn of a large-scale Qiang migration into the southwest, with Qiang tribes settling as far south as the Jinsha River in southern Sichuan. Subsequent Chinese documents describe how the Qiang initially lived high in the mountains of the southwest in territory conducive to their seminomadic lifestyle, but in time Qiang settlements could be found in the riverine lowlands throughout the southwest. In short, the traditional Chinese perspective on the origins of the Yi described them as descendants of the ancient Qiang people who migrated south from the Gansu-Qinghai region. Likewise, the cultural diversity noted among the Yi today is a result of what historians believe was a vertical migration from higher elevations to lowland river valleys and a horizontal migration that saw Qiang tribes fanning out and settling in virtually every corner of the southwest.[1]

In recent years a mounting body of archaeological evidence and a growing corpus of Yi historical texts have cast a critical light upon this traditional narrative. Many scholars today no longer consider the Yi to be descendants of the ancient Qiang. Instead, the Yi are now believed to be indigenous to the southwest. The impressive display of cultural diversity among the present-day Yi is still seen as the product of a series of dramatic vertical and horizontal migrations, just as the traditional Chinese scholarship noted; however, the northeast corner of present-day Yunnan province has consistently been identified as the place of origin for many of these migrations.[2] A few historians have countered the Yi textual argument by pointing out that the Yi migrations out of northeast Yunnan came long after the Qiang migrated into the Jinsha River valley, but these revisionist interpretations have withered under mounting archaeological evidence.

Several Paleolithic sites in central Yunnan have yielded pottery shards with writings linked to the ancient Yi script, and an astonishing number of archaeological sites in eastern Yunnan and western Guizhou have also offered up pottery incised with symbols that are strikingly similar to traditional Yi writing. Much of this pottery has been carbon-dated to the eighth century BCE, which means the pottery with ancient Yi inscriptions existed in several places throughout the southwest long before Han texts mentioned the Qiang migrations into the southwest.[3] One influential Yi scholar has even boasted that not only did the ancestors of the present-day Yi invent their own writing system about ten thousand years ago, but evidence from riverine excavation sites indicates that the ancestors of the Yi "subsisted primarily by rice cultivation supplemented by fishing and hunting, making theirs the earliest agricultural civilization [in present-day China proper]."[4]

Whereas recent archaeological discoveries make a strong case for viewing the Yi as indigenous to the southwest, or at least present in the southwest at the time the earliest Chinese sources were written, Yi historical texts are replete with elaborate "migration epics" describing how ancestors of the present-day Yi came to establish settlements throughout the southwest. Based on these migration epics, scholars have determined that when the size of the population exceeded the capacity of the land to sustain basic subsistence needs, the Yi initiated the practice of clan division and migration, and over time there emerged a "culture of migration," necessitating clan division and thus expansion. The Nasu Yi living in the Shuixi region of northwest Guizhou, for example, trace their ancestry back nearly one hundred generations to an individual named Dumu, who initiated just such a process of clan division and migration.[5]

According to Yi historical records, Dumu lived with his three wives among the Luyang Mountains in northeast Yunnan, in an area situated between the present-day cities of Huize, Xuanwei, and Dongchuan. Dumu's three wives provided him with six sons, and these six sons are referred to today by all Yi in the southwest as the six ancestors (*liuzu*), because each son became the founder of a patrilineal descent group that migrated out of the Luyang Mountains. In time these six patrilineal descent groups, whose surnames have been translated into Chinese as Wu, Zha, Nuo, Heng, Bu, and Mo, established fairly sophisticated polities in such areas as the Lake Dian region of Yunnan, the mountain recesses of southern Sichuan, and the Shuixi expanse of western Guizhou.[6] The genealogical records of several Yi patriclans make note of the fact that the migrations out of the Luyang Mountains were extraordinarily violent endeavors. Yi patriclans battled one another as well as non-Yi for control of fertile land, scarce water, and pristine pastureland. The history of the Nasu Yi settlement of the Shuixi region of northwest Guizhou in the third century CE, and the origins of the Mu'ege kingdom, which ruled much of present-day Guizhou from its headquarters in Shuixi, is one of the main focuses of this book. This history is intimately tied to the clan divisions and migratory patterns of the Mo patriclan.

## The Physical Setting: Shuixi

Today the Nasu Yi people of Guizhou reside in the harsh, inhospitable Shuixi region in northwest Guizhou. Shuixi is approximately 36,000 square kilometers in size and is bounded on all sides by a complex patchwork of natural barriers.[7] To the west are the Wumeng Mountains, the southern extreme of the vast Kunlun Mountains and the eastern edge of the Yunnan plateau. The highest peaks in the Wumeng Mountains average 2,700 meters, with Lu Jia Daying Mountain, located just west of the city of Weining, reaching 2,854 meters in elevation. To the north is another formidable geographic barrier, the Dalou Mountains. This mountain range originates amid the northern extension of the Wumeng Mountains in Yunnan and runs in a northeast direction across northern Guizhou. The tallest peak in the Dalou range is Baiyun Mountain, which rises nearly 1,950 meters. Also, along the northern edge of the Shuixi region is the Chishui River, a rapids-filled river that originates just north of the city of Zhenxiong in northeast Yunnan and winds across the northwest corner of Guizhou before emptying into the Yangzi River near the town of Hejiang in southern Sichuan.

The Wumeng Mountains also give rise to the sinuous Miaoling range. The Miaoling range enters northwest Guizhou west of the city of Weining and sweeps in a gentle southeast arc toward the city of Huishui in central Guizhou. As the Miaoling range reaches eastern Guizhou, it branches into four separate mountain ranges: the Fenghuang Mountains push south past the city of Duyun before entering Guangxi; the Jiuwan Dashan Mountains run in a southeasterly direction through the southeastern corner of Guizhou, passing just south of the city of Rongjiang and continuing into northwest Guangxi; the Leigong Mountains head east from the Miaoling Mountains into Hunan province; and the Fouding Mountains extend into northeast Guizhou. Although the Miaoling Mountains are an important geographical barrier along the southern extreme of Shuixi, these mountains were never considered the definitive southern boundary of the Shuixi region. This distinction was reserved for two fast-flowing rivers, the Sanfen and the Bei Pan.[8]

The Sanfen River forms in the course of the mountains surrounding Weining and rushes east through a series of precipitous gorges until it approaches the city of Puding. At Puding, the Sanfen turns north abruptly and crosses Guizhou in a northeasterly direction gaining in volume until it empties into the Yangzi River near the city of Fuzhou in southern Sichuan, approximately 1,100 kilometers from its point of origin. The Sanfen River, as it flows north from Puding, is commonly referred to as the Yachi River, and it is this stretch of the river that forms the easternmost boundary of the Shuixi region; however, at a point roughly halfway between the modern cities of Zunyi and Guiyang, the Yachi River becomes known by its more famous name, the Wu River.[9] The Bei Pan River is the other natural boundary of the Shuixi region, and it originates in the serrated eastern slope of the Wumeng Mountains, between the cities of Weining and Xuanwei. The Bei Pan River flows in a southeasterly direction through narrow ravines toward northwest Guangxi. In the Qin (221–206 BCE) and Han dynasties, the Bei Pan River was known as the Zangge River, and it formed an important transportation conduit linking the fertile Chengdu basin with the Red River valley of northern Vietnam. As the Bei Pan River

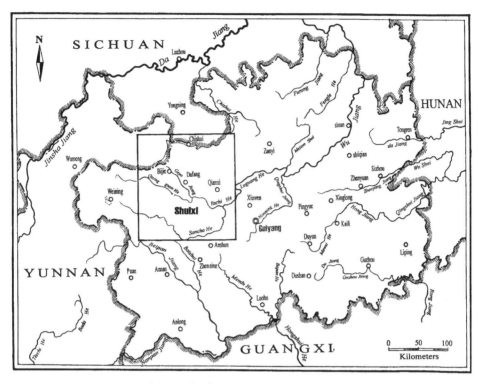

Map 2   Guizhou province, ca. 1700

approaches the Guizhou-Guangxi border, it merges with the Nan Pan
River, which originates in central Yunnan near the city of Kunming,
and these two rivers become the celebrated Hongshui River.[10]

Bounded on all sides by steep mountains and deep river canyons, the
Shuixi region reflects an impressive northwest-to-southeast slope in
Guizhou's terrain. Modern cities such as Weining, Hezhang, and Bijie,
located along the western fringe of the Shuixi region, are approximately
2,200 meters above sea level, whereas Qianxi, located near the Yachi
River in eastern Shuixi, is only 1,250 meters above sea level.[11] This decline in slope of nearly 1,000 meters extends over a distance of approximately 200 kilometers, which means the Shuixi region slopes downward
on an average 5 percent grade. The Liuchong River, which originates
west of Hezhang, flows through the center of the Shuixi region with such
force, again due to the slope of the terrain, that it has carved canyons
nearly 300 meters deep out of the easily dissolved limestone. This type
of natural erosion is representative of nearly all the river systems in

northwest Guizhou; thus, human settlement along Shuixi's rivers is limited to small, isolated, precariously situated enclaves.

Shuixi's complex system of mountain ranges, steep river valleys, and sloped terrain translates into a ruggedly dissected landscape. Nearly 95 percent of the Shuixi region is classified as mountain land, with the only significant exception being the relatively flat 20-kilometer-long by 10-kilometer-wide plain surrounding the city of Qianxi. Intensive wet-rice cultivation is practicable in only the handful of saturated limestone depressions scattered throughout the region.[12] Until recently agricultural production in Shuixi was restricted primarily to the cultivation of dry-farming cereals such as barley, millet, and oats, but during the summer months the Shuixi landscape is now blanketed with frail-looking corn-stalks. Bush beans, peanuts, soybeans, and tuber plants (taro and potatoes) are also cultivated.

Although Chinese outside Guizhou still refer to the province as an area where the sky is never clear for three consecutive days (*tian wu san ri qing*), where the ground is never level for three consecutive feet (*di wu san chi ping*), and where the people do not have three coins to rub together (*ren wu san fen yin*), the residents of Guizhou project the same colorful disdain toward the Shuixi region and its inhabitants. The high altitude of Shuixi results in a colder, drier, and windier weather pattern than what is experienced in other parts of Guizhou. According to recent provincial statistics, the city of Dafang, which lies in the heart of the Shuixi region, averages 210 frostless days per year, whereas areas in southeast Guizhou average more than 300 frostless days per year.[13] Snow, a common feature in Shuixi during the winter months, is virtually unknown in other parts of Guizhou. More striking, the average annual rainfall for the Shuixi region ranges between 700 and 900 millimeters, whereas central and southeast Guizhou receive an average annual rainfall of between 1,400 and 1,600 millimeters. The Shuixi region, due to its rugged terrain and inhospitable climate, has a reputation, at least in Guizhou, as a remote, backward region where drought, famine, and poverty are common.

## The Origins of the Mu'ege Kingdom

Recent Yi scholarship has determined that during the first and second centuries CE, the Heng, Bu, and Mo patriclans traveled east from the Luyang Mountains toward the Wumeng Mountains. The Heng quickly divided into two branches, with the first branch, identified as the

Wumeng, settling along the western slope of what would eventually become known in Chinese sources as the Wumeng Mountains. The Wumeng extended their control as far west as present-day Zhaotong, where the patriarch of the patriclan established his headquarters. The other branch of the Heng, the Chele, moved along the eastern slope of the Wumeng Mountains and settled north of the Chishui River. By the beginning of the Tang (618–907) dynasty, the Chele branch occupied the area from present-day Xuyong in southern Sichuan to Bijie in northwest Guizhou.[14]

Not long after migrating out of the Luyang Mountains, the Bu unexpectedly split into four branches, the Bole, Wusa, Azouchi, and Gukuge. The Bole branch was considered the preeminent branch of the Bu patriclan, and for this reason not only did the patriarch of the Bole branch demand deference from the other Bu branches, but his headquarters became the focus of Bu activity. The subordinate branches of the Bu, the Wusa, Azouchi, and Gukuge, routinely presented tribute to the patriarchs of the Bole in recognition of the Bole's superior stature, and in return the Bole organized lavish feasts, performed sacrifices to nature's many spirits, and appealed to deceased ancestors in hopes of bringing peace and prosperity to the patriclan's various constituents. Students of Yi history estimate that the Bole branch settled near the present-day city of Anshun in western Guizhou during the second half of the third century CE, possibly in response to the celebrated Shu Han (221–63) general Zhuge Liang's (181–234) invasion.[15]

The Wusa branch of the Bu patriclan settled near present-day Weining in western Guizhou, and, like the Wumeng example cited above, Weining was called Wusa in Chinese texts prior to the middle of the eighteenth century. The Azouchi branch settled in the Zhanyi area of eastern Yunnan, between the cities of Weining to the north and Qujing to the south, whereas the Gukuge branch remained near Dumu's original home territory in the Huize-Xuanwei-Dongchuan area of northeast Yunnan.[16] The shared genealogical ties and the recognized supremacy of the Bole branch meant that the geopolitical reach and economic influence of the Bole was not insignificant. The Bole leadership could command the other branches of the Bu patriclan to follow its lead in political and military matters, and it could utilize its economic wealth and control of vitally important horse markets to demand acquiescence to its policies.

The origins of the Mo who settled in Shuixi begin with Dumu's sixth son, Mujiji. Mujiji's direct descendants continued to reside in the

Dongchuan area of northeast Yunnan for several generations before acquiring the surname Mo. According to Yi genealogical accounts, Mujiji's tenth-generation descendant was a man named Shaoyamo, who, because it was the custom at this time for the son to adopt as his first name his father's second name (*fuzi lianming*, or father-and-son linked names), gave the name "Mo" to his eldest son, Moyade. It was also the custom among Mujiji's descendants to divide the patriclan every tenth generation, thus Moyade became the head of a new branch surnamed Mo. Nine generations later, custom again dictated that the three sons of Mujiji's nineteenth-generation descendant, Bi'ewu, form three new clans. Yi scholars estimate that during the Later Han period (25–220), Bi'ewu's eldest son, Wualou, led his patriclan, known later as the Awangren, into the Panxian-Puan area of southwest Guizhou and formed what Tang texts refer to as the Yushi kingdom.[17]

Nonetheless, the Huize-Xuanwei-Dongchuan area of northeast Yunnan remained home for a number of Mujiji's descendants. We know that during the third century CE, Mujiji's twenty-fourth-generation descendant, a man named Shaoyatuo, had two sons, Tuomangbu and Tuozahe, who apparently defied custom and split the patriclan prematurely. Tuomangbu led his followers north along the eastern slope of the Wumeng Mountains toward the present-day city of Zhenxiong, where his descendants established the Mangbu branch of the Mo. For his part, Tuozahe, also known as Huoji or Jihuo in Chinese texts, seized control of the commercial town of Luogen, near the present-day city of Bijie in western Guizhou. It was in Luogen in 225 CE that Zhuge Liang met Tuozahe and enlisted his support for the Shu Han campaign against "rebels" further south. Tuozahe reportedly supplied Zhuge's army with much-needed food, men, and horses, and in return Zhuge bestowed upon Tuozahe the hereditary title lord of Luodian (*Luodian junzhang*).

In Yi historical texts Tuozahe's descendants were known as the Azhe branch of the Mo patriclan (Azhe coming from the last character in Tuozahe's name). His descendants skillfully utilized their new political relationship with the Shu Han state to eliminate local resistance to their presence in Luogen. Within three generations of Tuozahe's meeting with Zhuge Liang, the Azhe had not only extended their control over the indigenous Pu people living in the mountainous Shuixi region but also abandoned the town of Luogen for Mugebaizhage, near the present-day city of Dafang in western Guizhou. It was here in the

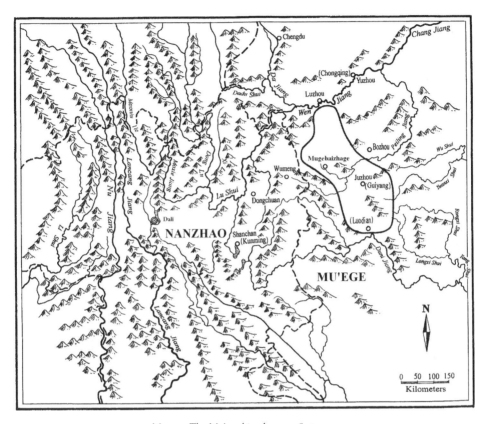

Map 3    The Mu'ege kingdom, ca. 800

Shuixi region of northwest Guizhou that Tuoazhe's great-grandson, Mowang, proclaimed the establishment of the Mu'ege kingdom. Mugebaizhage did not remain the political center of the Mu'ege kingdom for long, however. By the middle of the Tang dynasty, Chinese and Yi sources confirm the Azhe had relocated to a fortress on Shiren Mountain, near the present-day city of Guiyang in central Guizhou. From here Tuoazhe's descendants directed the affairs of a domain that was approximately one-half the size of present-day Guizhou province, and by the end of the Tang dynasty Mu'ege dominance had expanded to encompass nearly all of modern Guizhou.[18]

The existence of the large and expansive Mu'ege kingdom nestled away in the impenetrable terrain of China's southwest frontier went largely unnoticed in contemporary Chinese accounts. There were the occasional official-sounding titles bestowed upon the patriarch of the Azhe, but in large part Chinese attention remained fixated elsewhere. Admittedly since few literate Han dared travel to the southwest prior to the Tang dynasty, we should not expect to find many Chinese accounts of the Mu'ege kingdom, or of the Nasu Yi for that matter. In fact, Richard von Glahn's study of the Southern Lu region of Sichuan during the Song dynasty notes the paucity of reliable contemporary information on the Nasu Yi residing south of the frontier outpost of Luzhou.[19] Song officials in Luzhou were fearful of traveling south into the "dark forests of the *wuman* [black barbarians]," and they were mostly ignorant of the peoples south of the Chishui River.

It is because so few Chinese sources exist that recently published Yi historical texts are so important, for they illuminate an entirely new way of approaching the history of the southwest. We now know that during the last years of the Later Han dynasty ancestors of the present-day Yi migrated out of the Luyang Mountains and settled vast tracts of land in northeast Yunnan, southern Sichuan, and western Guizhou. Within a few hundred years of leaving the Luyang Mountains, these patriclans not only had conquered much of the territory that comprised eastern Yunnan and western Guizhou but also had erected an integrated network of semi-independent polities that shared common genealogical ties and cultural affinities. These Yi kingdoms occupied a strategically important place between China to the north and the Cuan (338–737), Nanzhao (740–902), and Dali kingdoms located to the south. During China's Period of Disunion (ca. 220–581), Mu'ege, Bole, Wumeng, Wusa, Chele, and Mangbu enjoyed closer ties with the Cuan kingdom than with the various states in China, but the demise of Cuan rule, the emergence of Tang rule in China, and the ascendance of a distinctly different ethno-cultural elite in the Nanzhao kingdom in Yunnan compelled the leaders of Mu'ege and the other Yi kingdoms to adapt and flexibly negotiate their way through the changing international order.

## Mu'ege During the Tang-Nanzhao Wars

The emergence of the Nanzhao kingdom during the eighth century was closely related to nearly three centuries of uninterrupted warfare between the Tang and Tibetan empires. According to Christopher I. Beckwith's study of the Tibetan empire, a succession of able and energetic leaders in Tibet forged a series of complex alliances with Tibetan noblemen to unify Tibet for the first time in history.[20] These alliances extended Tibetan rule to the Tarim Basin in the west, to western portions of present-day Gansu and Sichuan provinces in the east, and to parts of northwest Yunnan in the south. Tibet, Beckwith argues, was clearly the aggressor throughout much of Central Eurasia at this time, and Tang China, despite its own political and cultural preeminence, was forced to regard Tibet as a military equal. War between Tang China and Tibet seemed unavoidable.

During the first half of the eighth century, hostilities between Tibet and Tang China spilled into the southwest. Tibetan forays into Sichuan and western Yunnan had already paralyzed the Cuan kingdom, and Cuan soon disintegrated due to its inability to resist such encroachments. In a portion of western Yunnan heretofore unaffected by either Tibetan or Tang forces were six small kingdoms (*zhao*): Mengsui, Yuexi, Dengtan, Shilang, Langqiong, and Mengshe. Since the middle of the seventh century, these six kingdoms had tenaciously maintained their independence by feigning loyalty to Tibet, Tang China, and the Burmese kingdoms located to the south. In the first decades of the eighth century, the Mengshe kingdom, also known as Nanzhao, had begun to establish its military preeminence over the other five kingdoms.[21]

In 738 the Tang government, desperate to salvage some degree of influence in this strategic frontier following the collapse of Cuan, acknowledged the Nanzhao leader Pilege (r. 728–48) as the king of Yunnan (*Yunnan wang*).[22] Many of the Nasu Yi kingdoms described above were already sending "tribute missions" to the Nanzhao court. In 737, for example, the Mu'ege leadership sent a large delegation to Dali, the Nanzhao capital, along with horses, saddles, and woolen goods as gifts to the Nanzhao leader. In return, Pilege assured the Mu'ege envoys that they could continue to govern their territory free from Nanzhao interference, and that the Nanzhou court would grant them special administrative status as head of a tribal office (*bu*). Nanzhao asked only for military assistance in protecting its eastern borders, which Mu'ege readily agreed to provide. When terms of the Nanzhao-Mu'ege agreement were made known, the other Nasu Yi kingdoms in eastern Yunnan and western Guizhou, not to mention a host of non-Yi indigenous leaders, dispatched envoys to Dali and swore allegiance. In time, the Nanzhao court created thirty-seven tribal offices in those areas dominated by the Nasu Yi.[23]

Tang China now faced an astonishingly long military front stretching from the Nanzhao kingdom and its Nasu Yi allies in the south to the Kham region to the west, to the vast Kokonor expanse in the north. The death of Pilege in 748 did not ease tensions in the southwest. His son and successor, Ge Luofeng, was even less flattered by the presumptuous Tang title king of Yunnan. In an attempt to limit Tang influence in the southwest, Ge Luofeng convinced several influential Nasu Yi leaders to spurn Tang overtures. Tang China responded by launching two large military campaigns against Nanzhao, one in 751 and another in 754. The stated aim of both campaigns was to punish Nanzhao and its allies and, it was hoped, to "turn the barbarians" to the Tang cause in its fight against Tibet. Both campaigns failed to make it past Nanzhao's allies, the *wuman*—a Tang Chinese reference to the people residing roughly where the Mu'ege kingdom was located. As a consequence of these two failed military campaigns, any form of Tang presence in the region disappeared for several decades.

Apparently the Tang campaigns against Nanzhao's allies convinced Ge Luofeng that it was in his best interest to forge a strategic alliance with the Tibetans, which he did at the end of 754. The Tibetans officially recognized Ge Luofeng as the king of Nanzhao, and in return Ge provided military and financial assistance to the Tibetans in their war against Tang China.[24] The Tibetan-Nanzhao alliance endured for forty years, until Nanzhao leaders finally balked at the exorbitant Tibetan demands for Nanzhao assistance in fighting the Tang. As a result, in 794 Nanzhao severed its relations with Tibet and opened negotiations with Tang China.

While Tang China, Tibet, and Nanzhao warily eyed one another, the Azhe patrilineal clan continued to expand the geopolitical size of the Mu'ege kingdom. In the middle of the eighth century, just as relations between China and Nanzhao were beginning to deteriorate, the Azhe leaders relocated their political center to Shiren Mountain, near present-day Guiyang. According to the *Xi'nan Yizhi*, the Nasu credit Funazhi, Tuoazhe's eighteenth-generation descendant, with guiding the Azhe across the Yachi River into central Guizhou. From Shiren Mountain the Azhe oversaw a kingdom that included the entire Shuixi region of northwest Guizhou, as well as parts of present-day central, east, and southeast Guizhou. By the end of the eighth century, the modern cities of Longli, Duyun, and Luodian were all within the political scope of the Mu'ege kingdom. For its part, the Awangren patriclan continued to extend its authority throughout the Panxian-Puan area of southwest Guizhou (the Tang court referred to this area as the Yushi kingdom), thereby placing much of present-day Guizhou under the control of two powerful Nasu Yi kingdoms.[25]

Whereas Nanzhao leaders were content to forge ties with their Nasu Yi allies to the east, Mu'ege and Yushi, Tang officials advocated a more aggressive presence in Qian—Tang officials began using the word "Qian" to describe the area that is Guizhou today. Following a major institutional reform in 733, the Tang state remapped the entire Tang realm into fifteen circuits (*dao*), and as a result by the 770s a large portion of eastern Qian, a region heretofore outside Chinese jurisdiction, was hastily placed under the administrative umbrella of the Qianzhong circuit. On paper the Qianzhong circuit supervised ten commanderies (*jun*), each with an assortment of subcommandery civilian and military units: protectorates (*duhu fu*), area commands (*dudu fu*), prefectures (*zhou*), and districts (*xian*). The cartographic existence of the Qianzhong circuit gives the impression that all within the geopolitical boundaries of the circuit were administered directly by the Tang state, but this was not the case. Tang officials appointed to the Qianzhou Area Command, which was located along the Wujiang River near present-day Pengshui in southern Sichuan, were responsible for administering the political affairs of Qianzhong, and, as Tang accounts report, officials posted in Qianzhou rarely crossed the Wujiang River into Qianzhong.[26]

Instead, in the southern half of the Qianzhong circuit Tang officials negotiated a network of alliances with fifty-one local leaders in a manner similar to what the Nanzhao leadership had created with the Nasu Yi. By accepting Tang overlordship, these fifty-one leaders were given such titles as chief military commissioner (*dudu*), head protector (*duhu*), regional inspector (*cishi*), and village magistrate (*zhidong*). They were "assigned" to govern administrative units called prefectures, which, not surprisingly, configured exactly to the size of the territory already under their control. These frontier prefectures were part of what the Tang government called haltered-and-bridled prefectures (*jimi fuzhou*). The intent was to create an intermediate zone of vassals along China's frontier as a first line of defense against foreign attack, just as the Nanzhao leadership had done when it created the thirty-seven tribal offices among the Nasu Yi.[27]

Each indigenous leader was allowed to rule his/her area and population as s/he had prior to accepting haltered-and-bridled status. Household registers and land surveys were never demanded by the Tang state, nor were the haltered-and-bridled prefectures taxed like prefectures in

China proper. Moreover, leaders of the haltered-and-bridled prefectures did not present tribute (*gong*) to the Tang throne, though an abbreviated "tribute procedure" was hastily adopted to allow haltered-and-bridled leaders to visit the Qianzhou Area Command to purchase goods from Chinese merchants. The Tang state invested considerable energy in creating a buffer zone of haltered-and-bridled prefectures between itself and the Tibetan and Nanzhao empires, so much so that by the end of the seventh century Tang officials claimed to have negotiated into existence 856 haltered-and-bridled prefectures along China's western and southwestern frontiers.[28]

In territory beyond the haltered-and-bridled prefectures, particularly in the southwest portion of the Qianzhong circuit, Tang officials extended state recognition to a number of prominent families (*daxing*). These families, described collectively in Chinese texts as the Zangge clans (*Zangge daxing*), individually controlled much larger territories than did the haltered-and-bridled leaders and therefore provided an additional protective buffer for Tang China. The largest and most powerful family in the region, the Eastern Xie, controlled a sprawling domain that included parts of Xiangzhou, Manzhou, Juzhou, Zhuangzhou, and Yingzhou.[29] According to one Tang dynasty source, the lands controlled by the Eastern Xie were located several hundred kilometers west of Qianzhou and bordered territory under *wuman* (Mu'ege) control. In addition to the Eastern Xie, Tang officials courted such families as the Western Xie, Zhao, and Song and bestowed administrative titles, weapons, and money upon them in order to gain their allegiance.[30]

In one instance the head of the Eastern Xie, Xie Yuanshen, led a delegation of prominent families to meet with Tang officials in Qianzhou. Chinese sources described Xie Yuanshen as "a tall, dignified man who wore a crown made of black bear skin adorned with gold and silver ingots in the front, a felt cape draped over his shoulders, [and] fine-looking leather leg wrappings that extend up to his knees, and leather shoes."[31] In exchange for Xie's allegiance, Tang officials granted him and his direct descendants the hereditary title of regional inspector and placed his Yingzhou domain, now renamed Yingzhou prefecture, under the jurisdiction of the Qianzhou Area Command. Xie Longyu, head of the Western Xie clan, accompanied Xie Yuanshen to this meeting and reportedly offered his hosts the services of 10,000 of his best soldiers to fight Nanzhao. For this pledge Xie Longyu was granted the hereditary title Xiangzhou regional inspector as well as the historically significant title lord of the Yelang Commandery (*Yelang jun gong*), a reference to the Yelang kingdom, which existed in this region during the Han dynasty.[32]

Altogether the Tang government created seven Zangge clan prefectures (*Zangge daxing zhou*) directly adjacent to the Mu'ege and Yushi kingdoms.[33] This network of loyal frontier officials proved to be an adequate measure of protection for the Tang state when Nanzhao-Tibetan relations were strongest during the second half of the eighth century and even more so immediately following the resumption of Tang-Nanzhao relations in 794. In fact, in an effort to demilitarize the Tang-Nanzhao border, Tang officials in 814 ordered troops deployed by the Zangge clan prefectures to withdraw from the Tang-Nanzhao front and return home.[34]

The volatile nature of Tang-Nanzhao relations diminished as a consequence of the resumption of relations in 794. In the 820s, though, a quick succession of rulers in Nanzhao resulted in a change in Nanzhao foreign policy. The Nanzhao state promptly conquered the Pyu kingdom in northern Burma and then began to make threatening moves against allies of the Tang in the Qianzhong circuit. In response to an invigorated and expansionist Nanzhao state, Tang officials moved to create an additional zone of defense beyond the Zangge clan prefectures and haltered-and-bridled prefectures by adopting the model of dependent kingdoms (*shuguo*) first used by the Former Han (206 BCE–25 CE).[35]

Following the unexpected Nanzhao attack on Chengdu in 829, Tang officials learned that Agengawei, the patriarch of the Azhe patriclan and leader of the *wuman* (Mu'ege kingdom), was greatly disappointed in the belligerent actions of the Nanzhao leadership, and so they approached Agengawei with the hope of persuading him to ally with the Tang against Nanzhao.[36] Tang officials reported that Agengawei, who they identified as the "spirit master" (*guizhu*) of the Zangge kingdom ("Mu'ege" was never used in Chinese texts to identify the Azhe patriclan's kingdom, and "Spirit Kingdom of the Luo Clan," or *Luoshi gui guo*, was just coming into use in Chinese texts), possessed a large and highly skilled cavalry capable of traveling great distances quickly and had agreed to deploy his forces to assist the Tang military if Nanzhao armies encroached upon his kingdom or threatened Tang allies in Qian.[37]

To further solidify this new buffer between itself and the expansionistic Nanzhao kingdom, the Tang government in 846 bestowed on the Nasu Yi patriarch of the Bole patriclan the hereditary title of king of the Luodian kingdom (*Luodian guo wang*). In the same year, the Tang court recognized the patriarch of the Awangren patriclan as the king of the Yushi kingdom (*Yushi guo wang*); in the following year Tang officials granted the head of the Mangbu branch of the Azhe patriclan the title king of the Badedian kingdom (*Badedian guo wang*), which was located in the present-day Zhenxiong area of northeast Yunnan. These four kingdoms, Mu'ege, Luodian, Yushi, and Badedian, were situated to the west of the Zangge clan prefectures and haltered-and-bridled prefectures in the Qianzhong circuit, and they formed an additional defensive perimeter between Nanzhao-controlled territory to the southwest and Tang China.[38] In each case Chinese sources make reference to Tang officials presenting gifts to these kings (*wang*) and to the importance of allowing merchants from these kingdoms access to Chinese goods and services at nearby Chinese markets. Tang sources do not mention "tribute" as a part of the relationship between the Tang state and these four Nasu Yi kingdoms, an interesting omission in its own right.

As expected, these mid-ninth-century military alliances between the Tang state and these four Nasu Yi kingdoms resulted in some of the first Chinese descriptions of the people living in this part of the southwest. Fan Chuo, an official particularly deft at observation, described the ancestors of the present-day Nasu Yi in the following manner:

The men braid their hair, but the women allow their hair to fall loose and unbound. Upon meeting others, they exhibit no ritual decorum, neither bowing nor kneeling. Three or four translations are required before their speech is intelligible to Han [Chinese]. Cattle and horses are plentiful in this region, but silk and hemp are unknown. Both men and women wear cattle and sheep hides [as clothing]. . . . *Wuman* [black barbarians, or Yi elite] women wear a black woven cloth that drags on the ground when they walk, whereas *baiman* [white barbarians, or Yi commoners] women wear white woven garments that reach only to their knees.[39]

Fan noted that the *wuman* showed great respect for their ancestors and were awed by malevolent spirits inhabiting nature's mountains and rivers. For this reason the most influential person among the *wuman* was a political-religious figure called a "spirit master," who tamed the malevolent spirits and ruled over the many *wuman* tribes in western Guizhou and eastern Yunnan (Fan identified this area as Eastern Cuan, or the eastern half of the former Cuan kingdom).[40] Tang officials identified the paramount leader of the *wuman* as the "great spirit master" (*da guizhu*), whereas branches of the main patrilineal clan were led by "minor spirit masters" (*xiao guizhu*).[41] "Each year," Fan tells us, "every household is expected to bring oxen and sheep to the spirit master's residence to be offered as sacrifice. When the spirits arrive and depart the sacrificial festivities, the participants brandish their weapons, and this often leads to violence and blood feuds."[42] The imagery of "spirit masters" confronting malicious demons only enhanced the reputation of this frontier as a dark, mystical expanse possessed of supernatural spirits, poisonous plants, life-threatening diseases, and ferocious animals.

Fan also informs us that *wuman* society was a patrilineal society dominated by powerful patriclans whose rulership interspersed four exogamous groups: the *na* (aristocratic-warrior elite); the *quna* (commoners), who shared an ethnohistoric relationship with the *na* but were members of subordinate or inferior patriclans; the *sujie* (dependent farmers and craftspeople), a residual category of people who lived apart from the *na* and *quna*; and the *zesu* (house slaves), whose ranks were constituted of war captives. The *na* saw themselves as a "pure" or "unpolluted" people and placed strict prohibitions on the infusion of non-*na* blood. The *quna*, who made up the largest percentage of the *wuman* population, were seen as inferior to the *na* because their patriclans had been defeated by the more powerful *na* patriclans and because of their sustained contact with non-*na* peoples. The *sujie* and *zesu* were ethnically and culturally different from the *na* and *quna* and thus were seen as impure. Marriage between these four strata was (and in some cases still is) prohibited. Even those members of the *sujie* strata who could trace their ancestry to *na* and *quna* origins were prohibited from marrying non-*na* people. *Wuman* society, thus, followed the principle of strict endogamy to one's castelike stratum.

Initial Chinese descriptions of the *wuman* (Nasu Yi) aside, the Tang strategy of establishing an additional buffer zone of four dependent kingdoms between itself and Nanzhao proved fortuitous. In crafting these four dependent kingdoms, Tang officials had taken note of Nanzhao's expansionist ambitions since its withdrawal from Chengdu in 830. In 832, Nanzhao forces marched south into northern Burma and eliminated its vassal state, the Pyu kingdom. In the following year this same Nanzhao army fought its way into southern Burma, where it defeated the Michen kingdom. Late in the 830s, Nanzhao forces subjugated the kingdoms of Kunlun and Nuwang, located to the east and south of Nanzhao respectively, and in 846 a small Nanzhao force marched south along the Red River Valley and raided the Tang client state of Annam, in what is now northern Vietnam. An increasingly expansionistic Nanzhao was asserting itself as a regional power along Tang China's southern border.

Relations between Tang China and Nanzhao disintegrated in 859 with a change in leadership in both the Tang and the Nanzhao capitals and the stubborn insistence on the part of the Tang leadership on treating the new Nanzhao leader as its vassal.[43] Following Tang emperor Xuanzong's (Li Chen; 810–59, r. 846–59) death in 859, protocol required envoys be sent to neighboring states to inform them of the emperor's death and to remind them of the propriety of sending a diplomatic mission to the Tang capital to express condolences to the new Tang emperor, Yizong (Li Wen; 833–73, r. 859–73). When Tang envoys arrived in Nanzhao, they were met with contempt by Shilong, the king of Nanzhao. Shilong demanded the Tang envoys first offer their condolences to him out of respect for his recently deceased father, Fengyu. Moreover, Shilong demanded that the Tang envoys refer to him as the emperor (*huangdi*) of Nanzhao, not its king, which the Tang envoys were unwilling to do.[44]

To punish the Tang for its impropriety, Shilong ordered his finest troops to strike deep into China. Nanzhao forces attacked the Qianzhong circuit, pushing as far north as the town of Bozhou (modern Zunyi). The rapid thrust into Qianzhong exposed the fragile nature of the Tang defense network, four dependent kingdoms, seven Zangge clans, and countless haltered-and-bridled prefectures. When Tang officials discovered the attacking Nanzhao army included soldiers from each element of the Tang defensive network of allies, their doubts were confirmed and the betrayal was obvious. In response, the recently appointed Tang governor of Annam, Li Hu, tried to recapture Bozhou and remove Nanzhao forces from the Qianzhong circuit.[45]

As Li fought his way north to Bozhou, Shilong dispatched another Nanzhao force to attack the now lightly defended Tang garrison in Annam. The Nanzhao "emperor" also ordered his army to withdraw from Bozhou before Li's reached Bozhou, so as not to fully engage the Tang army. Instead, Shilong wanted Li to learn that Annam had fallen to Nanzhao troops, thereby demoralizing the Tang governor and compelling him to march quickly back to Annam to fight Nanzhao troops there. Li did return to Annam after securing Bozhou, but the campaigning from Annam to Bozhou, and then back, had the effect Shilong hoped for: the Tang military presence in both Qianzhong and Annam had been dramatically weakened.[46]

In 863, Shilong attacked Annam again, but this time nearly twenty thousand Nanzhao troops occupied the Red River Valley for three years before being pushed back north toward Nanzhao. Throughout the 860s Nanzhao armies roamed unhindered throughout the southwest, though their military activity seemed focused on southern Sichuan. In 869, Shilong amassed a huge force that once again reached the gates of Chengdu, and the city barely survived the siege.[47] When yet another large Nanzhao invasion of Qian, in 873, threatened the Chinese presence south of the Yangzi River, the Tang court issued a hastily crafted appeal to Han Chinese in North China to settle in the Qianzhong circuit in order to secure the territory from Nanzhao invaders.

In 876 Yang Duan answered the emperor's appeal and reportedly led nine branches of the Yang family from Shanxi into the northern portion of the Qianzhong circuit. Yang Duan boldly asserted that he hoped to settle the area and convert it into a line of defense to protect Tang China from the invading Nanzhao kingdom, as the emperor had requested. Within a year Yang had organized the growing Chinese settler population and sympathetic indigenes into a potent military force. By mid-877, Yang's hybrid army had driven the Nanzhao forces out of the Bozhou region, and with imperial blessings the Yang family was allowed to settle the Bozhou region and rule it as a personal domain. The Yang family would rule Bozhou as a personal fiefdom until the beginning of the seventeenth century—over seven hundred years![48]

At the end of the ninth century, the southwest frontier was still dominated by several independent states, and the Nanzhao kingdom was unmistakably the foremost political-military power in the southwest. It had developed a fairly elaborate bureaucracy to govern its own territory, and it negotiated political alliances with Tibet, Tang China, kingdoms in Burma, and a number of powerful local leaders in order to secure its own borders from attack. It inherited from its predecessor, Cuan, a desire to broaden its jurisdictional influence to include the Nasu Yi kingdoms, Mu'ege (Zangge), Luodian, Yushi, and Badedian, in the region known formerly as Eastern Cuan. Situated between Nanzhao to the south and Tang China to the north, these kingdoms had successfully maintained their political autonomy; they maintained cordial relations with both Nanzhao and Tang China.

Tang China, for its part, used its political, economic, and military stature to forge political ties with prominent local figures in the southwest frontier, just as the Cuan and Nanzhao kingdoms had done. The

Tang court negotiated with a number of local leaders to create hundreds of haltered-and-bridled prefectures in hopes of gaining the loyalty of non-Han Chinese leaders. To those indigenous leaders who controlled large tracts of land, the Tang bestowed noble titles and recognized their territories as dependent kingdoms. It also forged ties with prominent families, many of whom, such as the Xie, made dubious claim to Chinese descent. The Tang state was desperate to gain a measure of political influence in the increasingly militarized and strategically important frontier; however, the Qianzhong circuit proved to be an illusory cartographic representation and not a realistic extension of the Chinese state. Tang China laid claim to the Qianzhong circuit, but it did not exercise anything resembling territorial sovereignty over the circuit and its inhabitants. Instead, this circuit formed a defensive perimeter between a belligerent Nanzhao kingdom to the south and China proper, and it was home to a number of independent polities, many feigning allegiance to Tang China at the same time they allied with Nanzhao.

The Azhe patriclan's political maneuverings allowed the Mu'ege kingdom to sidestep many of the Tang-Nanzhao battles in the Qianzhong circuit, and by the end of the ninth century, as the expansionist energies of both Nanzhao and Tang China began to dissipate, its political leaders embarked on their own program of territorial conquest. From all appearances in the middle of the tenth century, Mu'ege was preparing to expand further east into Hunan and south into Guangxi. However, a resurgent Chinese military presence under Song leadership eventually brought Mu'ege expansion to a halt, but not before Mu'ege leaders staked claim, albeit briefly, to nearly all of modern Guizhou.

The collapse of the Tang and Tibetan empires at roughly the same time is an anomaly that interests few people besides historians. Whereas Tibet dissolved into a myriad of petty fiefdoms staunchly resistant to any reappearance of centripetal power, China in 960 overcame the centrifugal forces of the Five Dynasties Period (906–60) when the Later Zhou general Zhao Kuangyin (Song Taizu; 927–76, r. 960–76) founded the Song dynasty and set out to unify China. The Nanzhao kingdom also succumbed to many of the same forces that afflicted both the Tang and Tibetan empires at the beginning of the tenth century, but remnants of the Nanzhao elite were able to quickly reassemble fragments of the disintegrating kingdom and establish another centralized polity: the Dali kingdom.[49]

## The Song Prelude: Mu'ege Under Assault

Zhao made it known early in his reign that he hoped to establish cordial relations with the "multitude of tribes" in the southwest frontier. He was aware that Nanzhao armies had marched unobstructed throughout the region threatening Tang outposts, and he was determined to prevent the Dali kingdom's armies from doing the same. The Song emperor quickly granted high-ranking titles to powerful families who claimed Han descent, the Yang of Bozhou, the Song of Manzhou, the Tian of Sizhou, and the Long of Nanning, to name a few. After lengthy negotiations in 967, for example, Long Yanyao, patriarch of the Long family in Nanning, accepted terms presented him by Song officials. In addition to receiving such titles as regional inspector of Nanning prefecture, general who returned to virtue (*guide jiangjun*), and commissioner of the barbarian tribes (*fanluo shi*), Long was assured by Song officials that even though Nanning was now designated an official Song prefecture, the Song government would not appoint its own officials to the post of regional inspector, nor would the government dispatch Chinese military units to the region unless the Long family requested such assistance.[50]

According to Chinese sources, Long agreed to lead a delegation of family members and prominent retainers to the Song capital as a sign of vassalage to the Song emperor; however, Long's poor health and eventual death in 971 prevented the delegation from traveling to the Song capital. In 980 Long Yanyao's grandson, Long Qiongju, did lead a delegation of nearly 750 Long family members and retainers to the Song capital to express their condolences over the death of the Song emperor and to present a gift of five hundred Dali horses to the new Song emperor, Zhao Guangyi (Song Taizong; 939–97, r. 976–97). In 995 the Long patriarch, Long Hanyao, again visited the Song capital, during which the emperor requested that the Long delegation perform a dance according to the customs of Long's people. This performance so impressed the Song emperor that he granted Long two additional titles: general-in-chief who brings peace to distant corners of the realm (*ningyuan da jiangjun*) and prince who returned to civilization (*guihua wang*). The Song emperor also awarded minor imperial titles to twenty-four high-ranking members of Long's delegation.

Three years later, in 998, Long led another massive delegation to the Song court, ostensibly to pay his respects to the new emperor, Zhao

Dechang (Song Zhenzong; 968–1022, r. 998–1022), but in reality to gain access to Chinese markets. This delegation consisted of over a thousand Long family members and their retainers, and a thousand Dali and *wuman* (Nasu Yi) horses. As one Song official observed:

These horses possess a shape [that is] quite magnificent. They stand low with a muscular front, very similar to the shape of a chicken. The diaphragm is broad, shoulders thick, waist flat, and back round. They are trained to squat on their rear ends like a dog. They easily climb steep terrain on command and possess both speed and agility in chase. They have been raised on bitter buckwheat, so they require little to maintain. How could a horse like this not be considered a good horse?[51]

The Song emperor was so flattered by this generous gift of horses that he granted minor imperial titles to 130 members of this delegation and extended trading privileges at the capital markets for six additional days.[52]

The early Song rulers treated the Yang of Bozhou, the Song of Manzhou, and the Tian of Sizhou in the same manner, bestowing lofty hereditary titles on the patriarch of the family and investing family members and high-ranking retainers with minor imperial titles. In return these frontier leaders were granted the privilege of visiting the Song capital and meeting the emperor, which greatly enhanced their political stature among their own people. More important, they now had direct access to local Song officials and to Chinese goods and services. The one constant feature of these negotiations was the demand on the part of the frontier leader that he be granted regular access to Chinese markets (this is a feature very similar to what occurred between Central Eurasian leaders and China). Horses, saddles, cloth, and hemp were sold or exchanged for such Chinese products as tea, salt, wine, rice, and silk.

For the Azhe patriclan, Song diplomacy proved less accommodating, though no less effective. In 975 Zhao Kuangyin dispatched a communiqué to Pugui, the "great spirit master of the Spirit Kingdom of the Luo Clan," in hopes of convincing Pugui to acquiesce to Song overlordship.[53] The Song emperor knew Pugui had not claimed Han descent, nor would he, and it was probably for this reason that the emperor's letter appealed to Pugui's sense of dignity while also threatening his very existence:

I rely on justice to attract loyalty from China's neighbors, whereas tribal peoples [*manbo*] use force to gain followers. Only you [Pugui] in far-off Qian are willing to abide by our sense of justice. Regulations created by China's previous emperors demand that those who submit to our authority must present tribute to the court. As a result, frontier tribes who present tribute became quite successful, while our armies punish those unwilling to present tribute. Recently I ordered troops to assist the Yang of Bonan [Bozhou], an act that certainly frightened many of you in Qian. When my officials suggested I dispatch troops to your domain to punish you for not presenting tribute to my court, I said: "When people in remote areas refuse to submit to our authority, then our culture and sense of justice should be used to attract them. I do not believe using force can create loyalty." Not long after my troops returned from Bonan, I learned that you and your mother wanted to submit; therefore, I have written this edict announcing your allegiance. After you submit, you will be granted title and salary, and the land and people will remain under your family's control for generations to come. I will not break my promise. I announce this edict so that all will obey.[54]

Although we have no record of Pugui's response to the Song emperor's communiqué, Chinese sources indicate the Song court was not pleased with how the "great spirit master" replied, if he replied at all. In 976 Song military commanders ordered the Yang, Song, Tian, and Long families to mobilize their forces to attack Pugui's headquarters on Shiren Mountain. Long Hantang, Long Yanyao's son and successor, was to attack Pugui from the south, while Song Jingyang, the patriarch of the Song family and recently named regional inspector of Manzhou prefecture (present-day Kaiyang), attacked Shiren Mountain from the north. It was the Song family in Manzhou that had the most to gain from this military action. They had long coveted Pugui's territory east of the Yachi River, the fertile agricultural lands of Shuidong.[55]

The Song family rose to prominence in the Manzhou area of central Qian toward the end of the Tang dynasty, and by the beginning of the Song dynasty Song Jingyang's personal domain was bordered by Bozhou to the north, Sizhou to the east, and Pugui's Mu'ege kingdom to the south and west. What Song Jingyang's domain lacked in geographic size was made up for in agricultural production. The Song of Manzhou owned some of the most productive agricultural land in central Qian, and as such the Song family attracted Han immigrants from as far away as Sichuan and Hubei to settle in their domain. The Song state's orders to both the Song and the Long were to attack Pugui and drive him back across the Yachi River into Shuixi. As an incentive to attack Mu'ege, Song officials let it be known that the land and people the Song and Long families came into possession of during this military action could be kept as personal property.[56] Though the campaign against Mu'ege took nearly two years to complete and required the assistance of troops from Bozhou and Sizhou as well as of Song regulars stationed in Sichuan, Pugui and the *wuman* (Nasu Yi) elite were forced to retreat west into Shuixi, where they reestablished the political center of the Mu'ege kingdom in the city of Mugebaizhage—the ancient capital of Mu'ege and the present-day Dafang.[57]

Surprisingly, this confrontation between the Mu'ege kingdom and Song China and its local clients did not result in a permanent state of hostility. In 1042 the prefect of Luzhou (in Sichuan) wrote:

Control of the streams and grottoes [*xidong*] in the ten haltered-and-bridled prefectures [south of Luzhou] were heretofore bestowed by Tang and our [Song] officials. Now the *wuman* king [the patriarch of the Azhe], Degai, exercises control over much of the area [Shuixi] and he is very wealthy. He lives near the old Yaozhou prefecture, which was abolished long ago. But now, Degai would like to be named regional inspector of Yaozhou, so that he could use the office title to control the barbarians [*yizu*] in this area.[58]

Court officials granted Degai's request and ordered the reestablishment of Yaozhou, with Degai as its regional inspector. Despite the impressive sound of this title, Song officials never considered the regional inspector's title to be anything more than an honorific designation, especially since the characters *cishi* (regional inspector) had not been used to signify a bureaucratic post for centuries. The trade-off of granting an archaic bureaucratic title in return for the possibility to exert a modest degree of influence over the recipient's behavior was simply too enticing to pass up.

What mattered most to Degai, though, was not the title of regional inspector, which he certainly did not need to govern the *wuman*, but the trading privileges in Luzhou that receipt of this title granted. By way of example, in the spring of 1133 the leader of Mu'ege, Ayong, led a delegation of several thousand people, and approximately one thousand horses, down from the mountains of Shuixi to the city of Luzhou, where they spent two weeks selling horses and purchasing supplies. As was custom by this time, the Azhe sent large trade missions to Luzhou twice a year and several smaller missions periodically throughout the year. Chinese accounts inform us that the Luzhou merchants, as well as merchants from other parts of Sichuan, prepared months in advance for the two large trade missions from Shuixi.[59]

Moreover, the Luzhou prefect's report on Ayong's trade visit in 1133 indicated he faced the daunting task of reciting all of the titles bestowed upon the *wuman* spirit master and his predecessors as the trade delegation from Shuixi entered the gates of the city: chief of the Spirit Kingdom of the Luo Clan in northwest Qian (*Qian xibei Luoshi guiguo shouling*); grand military assistant to the southwest barbarians (*xi'nan fan wuyi dafu*); defense commissioner of Gui prefecture (*Guizhou fangyu shi*); chief inspector of the barbarian territory south of Luzhou (*Lu[zhou] nan yijie duda xunjian shi*); and grand military strategist, regional inspector of Yaozhou prefecture, and chief inspector for the barbarian tribes of the southwest (*wujing dafu zhongzhou cishi xi'nan fanbu da xunjian shi*).[60] Song officials rarely made reference in official texts to these bureaucratic titles granted to the leader of the Mu'ege kingdom; instead, contemporary Song texts identified the patriarch of the Azhe simply as the spirit master of the Luo clan, and the kingdom he ruled (Mu'ege) as the Spirit Kingdom of the Luo Clan.[61] Earlier terms like "lord of Luodian," the title bestowed upon Tuoazhe by the Shu Han court, and the "Zangge kingdom," which was used periodically throughout the Tang dynasty, disappeared altogether during the Song.[62]

Any attempt to forge a secure military buffer between Song China and the Dali kingdom required that the Song state follow the pattern established by the Tang. Haltered-and bridled prefectures were set up once again, as were cordial relations with powerful families who claimed (maybe fictitiously) to be Han. The Song government bestowed outdated bureaucratic titles, such as regional inspector, and granted trading privileges to powerful leaders in the southwest frontier in order to extend its influence into this strategically important region. The Song government also followed the Tang precedent and recognized the Bole patriclan as leaders of the Luodian kingdom, and the Mangbu patriclan as the head of the Badedian kingdom. For reasons not entirely clear Song officials decided to change the name of Yushi kingdom to Ziqi, but the Awangren patriclan remained in control of the kingdom. Despite the fact that the turbulent history of the Nanzhao invasion of Qian and Sichuan still resonated in the minds of Song officials, and that the Dali kingdom had given no indication that it might behave differently from its Nanzhao predecessors, the Song adopted the Tang model to protect its southwest frontier from an expanding Dali kingdom, and like the Tang it carried this out under the umbrella of negotiated alliances. Song China did not, nor could it, envision claiming sovereign control over territory in the southwest.[63]

While Song officials sought to create a zone of friendly clients in its southwest frontier Song military commanders worked tirelessly to defend North China from the Khitans, the Jurchens, and finally the Mongols. Beginning in the third decade of the thirteenth century, the emerging confederation of Mongols became engaged militarily with Song China, and for the next fifty years Mongol leaders were obsessive in their determination to conquer Song China. It just so happened that the Mongol path to Song defeat ran through the southwest, and in their way stood the Dali kingdom, the Mu'ege kingdom and their brethren *wuman* kingdoms, and the multitude of Song client polities.

2

———

# The Mongol Conquest of China's Southwest Frontier

In the summer of 1251 an assemblage of Mongol princes and high officials convened at Kode'u Aral, near the Kerulen River, to select the
forty-two-year-old Möngke (1209–59) as the next grand qan of the
Mongols.[1] This assemblage, known as a *quriltai*, was organized by Batu
(d. 1256), qan of the Golden Horde and son of Jochi (d. 1227), as well
as by Sorqaghtani Beki (d. 1252), Möngke's mother and influential
head of the Tolui lineage.[2] In addition to naming Möngke the grand
qan, the *quriltai* of 1251 affirmed Chinggis Qan's (1162–1227) adven-
turous mandate "to conquer every country in the world."[3] Batu and Sorqaghtani Beki sought to use Chinggis Qan's mandate to reassert the
political authority of the grand qan over the regional qans, who had by
this time acquired a considerable degree of political autonomy from the
previous grand qans, Ögödei (r. 1229–41) and Güyüg (r. 1246–48).[4] In
particular, Möngke and his supporters wanted to punish the leaders of
the powerful Chaghadai qanate for refusing to participate in the *quriltai*
of 1251 and for declining to recognize Möngke as grand qan.[5]

To accomplish this task, Möngke ordered his younger brothers,
Hülegü (d. 1265) and Qubilai (1215–94), to lead two critically important military campaigns. The first campaign was designed to isolate and
enclose the Chaghadai qanate. The intent of the second campaign was
to encircle Song China by opening a second front in the southwest. In
the summer of 1253, Hülegü broke camp and began an arduous five-

year campaign across Central Asia. Forced marches, bitter fighting, and rampant disease severely depleted Hülegü's army, but in February 1258 this stubborn Mongol commander willed his forces over the walls of Baghdad and defeated the Abbasid caliphate.[6] Hülegü immediately declared his political intentions by announcing the creation of the Ilqan qanate ("Ilqan" literally means "subservient qan," or, in this instance, "the qanate subservient to the grand qan").[7] With the Jochi family's Golden Horde qanate to the north, Hülegü's control of Persia (present-day Iran and Iraq) effectively blocked the Chaghadai qanate from expanding any further west and north. As Hülegü marched west across Central Asia toward Baghdad, Möngke looked to his other brother, Qubilai, to help solidify the grand qan's authority along the eastern front. Möngke wanted Qubilai to assist in the conquest of Song China.

In 1251 Möngke and his advisers understood that a direct frontal assault against Southern Song (1127–1279) forces could easily fail. Previous Mongol forays into Song territory had ended in failure, and now Song armies were concentrated along a defensive perimeter in anticipation of yet more Mongol raids from the north. During the 1240s Song forces often marched north from their defensive positions to challenge Mongol control of North China.[8] The grand qan's fragile control of North China and his apparent inability to conquer Song China reverberated throughout the Mongol empire as a sign of weakness. A risky offensive against Song China, if unsuccessful, could fracture the Mongol empire and undermine the authority of the grand qan.

Therefore, Möngke decided to outflank the entrenched Song armies by attacking China from the southwest. Opening a second front would force Song China to redeploy men and material away from its defensive perimeter in the north, thereby weakening its overall military posture. The main obstacle to Möngke's plan, aside from the adverse terrain and inhospitable weather his armies would face as they marched south, was the presence of the tenaciously independent Dali kingdom and *wuman* (Nasu Yi) kingdoms in the southwest. This chapter will examine the Mongol conquest of China's southwest frontier and the policies employed by the Mongols to incorporate the indigenous peoples of this region into the expanding Mongol empire. Although the Mongol presence in the southwest was brief, much of what they accomplished there became the cornerstone of the Ming colonization program.

## The Mongol Campaign Against Dali

In July 1252, Möngke selected Qubilai to lead the military campaign against the Dali kingdom.[9] Qubilai prepared meticulously for the Dali campaign. This was his first important military command, and at thirty-six years of age Qubilai was aware that a mistake at this critical juncture would seriously jeopardize any future political aspirations. Möngke also understood the gamble of relying on his untested and inexperienced brother to execute the logistically demanding Dali campaign, and for this reason he assigned one of the most battle-proven military commanders of his day, Uriyangqadai (d. 1272), to be commander-in-chief of the campaign. The son of Subötei, one of Chinggis Qan's most fearsome generals, Uriyangqadai had proven himself time and again in several campaigns in Central Eurasia, and his political alliance with Batu in 1251 assured the enthronement of Möngke as grand qan in 1251.[10] As expected Qubilai relied heavily on Uriyangqadai's military expertise in planning the Dali campaign. When Möngke received word that the Dali king had murdered the envoys he had sent to Dali to demand the king's surrender, he ordered Qubilai to begin the campaign in the summer of 1253.[11]

Qubilai partitioned his army into three columns. He gave command of the western column to Uriyangqadai and ordered him to march south from Lintao, in present-day Gansu, through the inhospitable Kham region of eastern Tibet toward Dali. Qubilai appointed Wang Dezhen (d. 1259) to lead the eastern column into Song-controlled portions of Sichuan.[12] As Wang's army marched south, it passed just west of Chengdu before reuniting briefly with Qubilai's middle column near the town of Jianchang, in southern Sichuan. Qubilai's middle column followed the mountain trails through Kham, placing his army at the forefront of the attack force. Qubilai anticipated that his column would engage the main Dali army along the Jinsha River, thus exposing Dali to attack from Uriyangqadai's army advancing from the northwest and from Wang's army arriving from the east. Following several skirmishes in which Dali forces repeatedly turned back Mongol raids across the Jinsha River, Qubilai's army crossed the Jinsha River in a daring nighttime raid and routed Dali defensive positions. With Dali forces in disarray, the three Mongol columns quickly converged on the city of Dali in late 1253.[13]

Rather than submit to the Mongols and accept Qubilai's terms, the king of Dali, Duan Xingzhi (d. 1273), abandoned Dali to the Mongols and fled east to the town of Shanchan (near present-day Kunming), where he rallied pro-Dali forces against the Mongol invasion. Since Möngke's primary objective was to attack Song China from the southwest, not to destroy the Dali kingdom and become mired in governing Dali directly, Duan's continued resistance proved a costly obstacle to Möngke's larger scheme. It took two years of fierce fighting in the Shanchan region before Uriyangqadai could announce the surrender of Duan and the end of Dali resistance in the region. By the end of 1255, however, Mongol forces were in possession only of the cities of Dali and Shanchan and the main road linking them. Territory east of the city of Shanchan was still under the control of pro-Dali forces, and resistance there received not only direct military aid from the Azhe, Awangren, Bole, Chele, Wumeng, Mangbu, and Wusa patriclans but also financial assistance from the Song state.[14]

Following a face-to-face meeting between Möngke and Duan in the first month of 1256, the grand qan bestowed upon the captive king a patent of investiture (*xinzhi*), three badges of authority (*paizi*), and an imperial seal (*yinxin*) and ordered him to return to Dali to rule his people as he had before the Mongol conquest, although now as a loyal subject of the Mongol qan. Qubilai had returned north to assist Möngke in planning the conquest of Song China, so Uriyangqadai was ordered to remain in the southwest to oversee Duan's rule of Dali and to push further east toward Song positions in China.[15]

Uriyangqadai worked quickly to solidify a Mongol presence in the southwest. By the middle of 1256 he had established nearly twenty military brigades (*wanhu fu*) throughout Dali proper and had dispatched military units east in preparation for attacking the town of Yushi, which was the center of the Awangren patriclan's Ziqi kingdom.[16] Uriyangqadai relied on trusted Mongols and Central Asians to fill the brigade commander (*wanhu*) positions, yet subbrigade battalions (*qianhu suo*) were staffed almost exclusively by members of the local elite.[17] In fact, in the region near the city of Shanchan a few of the new battalion commanders had previously held minor political posts under the Dali regime, though for the most part the newly appointed battalion heads had been low-ranking members of the local community prior to the arrival of the Mongols and had sided with the Mongols during the prolonged conflict. When Uriyangqadai showered land, slaves, livestock, political offices, and other rewards on individuals who had supported the Mongols in their campaign against Dali, he anticipated his actions would create a new elite to rival the old pro-Dali elite.

In the closing months of 1256, Mongol relations with their indigenous collaborators in Shanchan became strained when Uriyangqadai ordered many of these allies to lead the assault against what he described as territory inhabited by "spirit barbarians" (guiman), a clear reference to the wuman in eastern Yunnan and western Guizhou, the Azhe, Awangren, Bole, Chele, Wumeng, Mangbu, and Wusa.[18] Those who refused to participate in the campaign were "exterminated," according to a later account by a Yuan official. Song sources confirm that the Azhe informed Song officials in Luzhou that Mongol and Dali troops were moving east toward Yushi. In response, the Song court gave 10,000 taels of silver each to the Azhe, Awangren, and Bole patriclans to help shore up defensive fortifications, and the court ordered its client in Bozhou and Sizhou to dispatch forces to Yushi to resist the Mongols. The defensive buffer the founding Song emperor envisioned for the southwest frontier was being put to the test.[19]

Within a year these same Song allies were marching west into the Shanchan region in support of a large-scale rebellion against Mongol rule. Late in 1257, Uriyangqadai was inexplicably ordered to lead a military expedition south down the Red River Valley to attack the Tran dynasty in Annam. With Mongol troop strength in the Dali-Shanchan region precariously thin, a number of prominent indigenous leaders, such as Brigade Commander Sheliwei (d. 1274), attacked Mongol military installations throughout the Shanchan region. For over a decade indigenous leaders from the Shanchan region, with assistance from the Azhe, Awangren, Bole, Chele, Wumeng, Mangbu, and Wusa patriclans, battled Mongol forces and their Dali allies, and in a series of fierce encounters near the towns of Weichu and Yaoan in 1269 and 1270, they nearly displaced the Mongols from the southwest entirely. Not until 1274, after Mongol scouts ambushed and killed Sheliwei as he rode through the town of Dingyuan, did the Mongol-Dali alliance turn the tide in their war against the Shanchan resistance.[20]

By 1274 Qubilai, now grand qan of the Mongols, no longer considered control of the southwest vital to the conquest of Song China. A year earlier, Mongol forces had emerged victorious in the five-year battle for the city of Xiangyang, a strategic point located along the Han River. The Song had built the city of Xiangyang into an impenetrable fortress, or so they thought, in order to protect this critical area of the Yangzi River basin from Mongol attack. When initial attempts to destroy the city walls failed, Qubilai ordered engineers from Central Eurasia brought to China to construct large catapults to be used in the siege. Eventually, Xiangyang's fortifications were destroyed, and in March 1273 Lu Wenhuan (d. 1279), the esteemed Song commander of the city, surrendered.[21] The Song capital of Hangzhou was now exposed to a frontal attack, and within months Qubilai appointed Bayan (1237–95) to command the final Mongol assault against Song China. Bayan ordered his armies across the Yangzi River in January 1275: in 1276 he captured the Song capital, and by 1279 Song resistance near the southern port city of Canton had been crushed.[22]

## Sayyid 'Ajall Shams al-Din and Mongol Rule in the Southwest

Although Qubilai focused his attention on attacking Song China from the north, he was aware that control of the southwest could prevent Song patriots from using the region to continue their resistance. For this reason, in 1274 he appointed the able administrator Sayyid 'Ajall Shams al-Din (d. 1286) to the newly created post of manager of governmental affairs for the Yunnan Branch Secretariat (*xing zhongshu sheng pingzhang zhengshi*). By 1274 Sayyid 'Ajall, a Central Eurasian Muslim from the kingdom of Bukhara, had compiled an impressive record of political service to the Mongols, which made him a logical choice for this important endeavor.[23] According to the *Yuanshi*, Sayyid 'Ajall's assignment was fairly straightforward: solidify Mongol control of the southwest and integrate Yunnan politically with Yuan China and the Mongol empire.[24]

Sayyid 'Ajall's first task was to restore the Mongol military presence in Yunnan. He accomplished this by revitalizing many of the small-sized garrisons and outposts first established by Uriyangqadai. The main east-west highway connecting Dali and Shanchan was repaired, and an extensive network of seventy-eight postal relay stations (*yizhan*) was established from Dali in the west to the town of Shicheng (present-day Qujing) in the east.[25] Each postal station had a small militia made up of locals, a stable of fifty horses, food and accommodations for overnight guests, and a general store. Sayyid 'Ajall pressed the local population to provide each postal station with such necessities, and he issued patents to those individuals who assumed responsibility for managing the hostel, restaurant, store, and stable at each postal station. Initially, appointments to postal stations and the accompanying patents were negotiated for a specific length of time, usually for five years, but Sayyid 'Ajall soon realized that hereditary appointments to such posts would provide a measure of stability, and so he made postal station appointments hereditary.[26]

To govern this ethnically complex region, Sayyid 'Ajall abandoned Uriyangqadai's use of military brigades and instead established many of the same political units already in use in China proper, circuits (*dao*), routes (*lu*), superior prefectures (*fu*), prefectures (*zhou*), and districts (*xian*). Demographic, geographic (physical and cultural), and strategic features played important roles in determining where he established political units and which types of political unit he established throughout Yunnan. Nevertheless, his redrawing of the political map intensified the overall structure and pervasiveness of Mongol rule. It featured multiple layers of overlapping civilian jurisdictions that allowed Sayyid 'Ajall and the Mongols to exercise greater control over the mixed indigenous and immigrant population. Elizabeth Endicott-West recognized the increasing complexity of Yuan civilian rule when she noted how the "Yuan civilian government departed from earlier patterns and precedents in Chinese governmental history in the multiplicity of its levels of sub-metropolitan government and the sheer number of civilian officials staffing those units of government."[27] By way of example, Sayyid 'Ajall divided the Yunnan Branch Secretariat into ten circuits, each administered by either a pacification commissioner (*xuanwei shi*) or a pacification inspector (*xuanfu shi*). In time, many of these circuits became known simply as pacification commissions (*xuanwei si*) with place-name prefixes, for example, the Dali-Jinchi Pacification Commission.[28]

These circuits and pacification commissions regulated many administrative bodies, of which the route was the largest unit in a circuit.[29] The Yuan state generally made the distinction between "greater" (*shang*) and "lesser" (*xia*) routes, on the basis of the size of the population and the strategic location of the unit. The route was directly subordinate to both the branch secretariat and the circuit, but in frontier areas like Yunnan the pacification commissioner's authority was rarely challenged. His appointments to the two posts that managed route affairs, the route commander (*lu zongguan fu*) and the political resident or overseer (*darughachi*), were usually accepted without much interference from the head of the branch secretariat, known as the grand councilor (*chengxiang*).[30] Superior prefectures, prefectures, and counties were under the direct supervision of the route commander, and each administrative unit was assigned a *darughachi* along with a civilian official. In each case, both were appointed at the same rank, given the same salary, and allotted the same amount of office land. Any directive by an administrative unit had to be cosigned by the *darughachi* and his civilian counterpart.[31]

In the Shanchan area of central Yunnan, Sayyid 'Ajall adopted the administrative map of the former Dali kingdom to create eight routes: Zhongqing, Dengjiang, Lingan, Yuanjiang, Guangxi, Qujing, Wuding, and Weichu.[32] Each route supervised a mixture of superior prefectures, prefectures, and counties, but by and large the geopolitical landscape was dominated by a new bureaucratic post, the *tuguan*, or native official. *Tuguan* offices were introduced following Sayyid 'Ajall's conquest of the southwest. The Yuan state possessed neither the human resources nor the financial wherewithal needed to administer the southwest directly; therefore Sayyid 'Ajall ordered his route commanders and *darughachi* to meet with powerful local leaders in order to gain their allegiance. In exchange for sworn loyalty to the grand qan, the local leader was granted the title of *tuguan*, which made him an official representative of the Yuan state. *Tuguan* received the hereditary right to pass the *tuguan* office to their offspring, and they were assured by officials that the Yuan state would not intervene in the *tuguan*'s domestic affairs, that is unless the *tuguan* harbored criminals or acted in a decidedly anti-Yuan manner. This was Sayyid 'Ajall's innovative *tuqiu weiguan* policy, "to make officials out of native chieftains."[33]

According to records relating to the creation of *tuguan* offices in Kainan prefecture, as part of the Weichu route created by Sayyid 'Ajall in 1274, *tuguan* were ordered to register the land and population in their area with the Kainan prefect so that the area's land and labor taxes could be assessed. The Yuan assessment of land and labor taxes from *tuguan* offices was similar to what the Dali state demanded of its extrabureaucratic offices, and it was a clear departure from the Chinese model: the haltered-and-bridled prefectures were not taxed by the Chinese state.[34] In addition, *tuguan* were obligated to present tribute annually to the Yunnan Branch Secretariat, usually in the form of horses, precious metals, and finished goods. Naturally, *tuguan* were expected to maintain law and order in their areas of jurisdiction, but the Yuan state allowed them to do so according to local customs and refrained from imposing Yuan legal statutes to adjudicate cases. Finally, *tuguan* were ordered to deal firmly with anti-Yuan activity and provide military assistance to Yuan commanders when requested.[35]

To legitimize the political stature of the *tuguan* office, Sayyid 'Ajall and the Yuan court bestowed upon the *tuguan* such articles as a certificate of appointment (*gaochi*), which was to be publicly displayed in the *tuguan*'s administrative headquarters. When ordered to pay taxes or present tribute, the *tuguan* was required to verify his or her position by presenting this certificate to the route commander and *darughachi*. Yuan authorities also gave the *tuguan* a seal (*yinzhang*), so that s/he could issue orders on behalf of the Yuan state. A tiger-shaped tally (*hufu*) was granted to *tuguan* so s/he could maintain a large stable of horses for military purposes. If urgent military situations arose, the Yuan court would send imperial letters via courier and issue either gold or silver tallies (*jin yin ziyuan fu*) that authorized the *tuguan* to mobilize resources for military purposes.[36]

In conjunction with more centralized political rule, Sayyid 'Ajall sought to restore the economic vitality of this war-ravaged region. He published handbooks on farming techniques and livestock maintenance and issued seed, tools, and even livestock to indigenes and immigrants alike. He also dispatched teams of agricultural specialists to demonstrate advanced agricultural practices. In Shanchan, Sayyid 'Ajall oversaw the construction of dams and reservoirs, dredged rivers and canals for transport purposes, and drained disease-infested swamps as part of his ambitious land reclamation project. In his study of the history of Yunnan, Bai Shouyi gives a sense of the scope and innovation of Sayyid 'Ajall's construction projects:

In addition to overseeing the continued expansion of the military's land reclamation efforts, Shams al-Din [Sayyid 'Ajall] expended considerable energy in building water conservation projects. He ordered a team of engineers to construct an elaborate irrigation system in the Shanchan area. Prior to Sayyid 'Ajall's arrival, the rice paddies in Shanchan depended on an ancient irrigation system that flowed into and out of Lake Dian. All nearby rivers entered Lake Dian, but there was only one outlet, at Haikou. From Haikou to Anning there was one heart-shaped section of shoals, and the river frequently became obstructed with silt. Because the runoff was impeded, as soon as the rainy season arrived, the waters of Lake Dian flowed backward, often resulting in serious flooding. Sayyid 'Ajall appointed Zhang Lidao to supervise the renovations at Lake Dian.

First, to the area northeast of Shanchan Zhang looked into the source of the river and decided to concentrate his efforts on dredging the Panlong River. The Panlong had been in disrepair for many years, and the silt that had built up along the river shoals needed dredging. Zhang diverted the water coming from the Ninety-Nine Springs of Shaodian in the mountains in the northwest into the Panlong River, and as a result flooding on the upper reaches of Lake Dian was brought to an end.

Next, Sayyid 'Ajall ordered dikes built below Jinma Peak and water gates constructed along the Songhua River. The intent of this large-scale project was to dam the river for flood diversion. At the same time he ordered the construction of the Jinzhen canal, which traversed the Shanchan countryside for over 100 _li_. The width of the canal embankment varied between 12 feet and 16 feet. Along the length of the canal ten small water gates were constructed, as well as 360 culverts and ditch canals. In order to irrigate the elevated fields along the eastern portion of the canal, Sayyid 'Ajall built a series of water wheels designed to pump water uphill. To improve drainage along the lower reaches of Lake Dian, Sayyid 'Ajall dug the Baoxiang Canal and six other smaller canals and built water gates to better manage the flow of water. Under Sayyid 'Ajall's administration, every kind of water control technique available to him was carefully considered, and many of his construction projects are still in use today.[37]

In conjunction with these far-reaching political and economic reforms, Sayyid 'Ajall is credited with having established the first schools in Yunnan to use a distinctly Chinese curriculum. One can assume his extensive experience as an official in Yanjing (modern Beijing) influenced his decision to order the construction of schools in Yunnan.[38] He ordered arable land (_xuetian_) be set aside for each school so that it might be financially self-sufficient, and whenever possible Sayyid 'Ajall wanted Han hired as instructors. All told, Sayyid 'Ajall established fifty-five schools in Yunnan. Despite Qubilai's decree of 1282 ordering schools built in each of Yunnan's districts so that "they [the indigenous population] would know how to offer sacrifices to the ancient sages," only a handful of the schools established by Sayyid 'Ajall remained operational by the beginning of the fourteenth century.[39]

Once Sayyid 'Ajall began to extend his political reach beyond the core area of the former Dali kingdom (Dali and Shanchan) toward Sichuan to the north and Qian to the east, he soon found himself in contact with peoples reluctant to be governed by Yuan institutions. The limits of the branch secretariat's administrative reach and the necessity of expanding Mongol influence forced Sayyid 'Ajall to improvise. He did so by using the prestige of the offices of pacification commission and pacification inspector as currency to gain the allegiance of influential leaders, such as the patriarchs of the Azhe, Awangren, Bole, Chele, Wumeng, Mangbu, and Wusa patriclans. Those who accepted these Yuan offices were treated in a way analogous to *tuguan* offices. In return for an oath of allegiance to the grand qan, the indigenous leader as pacification commissioner or pacification inspector was granted immunity from Mongol interference in his or her territory, except of course when the leader requested Mongol military assistance.[40]

As a consequence, two types of pacification commissioners emerged in the southwest at this time: one supervised a circuit, was appointed directly by the grand councilor of the branch secretariat, and was an integral part of the subbranch bureaucracy; the other was a powerful indigenous leader given an honorary title primarily meant to gain his or her allegiance. For example, in order to secure safe travel along the main Sichuan-Yunnan highway (Bo circuit route) connecting Dali and Kunming with the Sichuan capital of Chengdu, Sayyid 'Ajall ordered his forces to go north to occupy the three large towns of Huichuan, Dechang, and Jianchang. These three towns, because of their location north of the Jinsha River, were spared much of the violence that engulfed Dali and Shanchan during the 1250s and 1260s. Before Mongol troops entered these towns, Sayyid 'Ajall designated each town a route, assigned route commanders and *darughachi* to them, and placed the entire region under the control of the newly formed Luoluosi Pacification Commission.[41] To placate the powerful patriclan leader whose territory surrounded the town of Jianchang, Sayyid 'Ajall offered him the post of Luoluosi pacification commissioner and granted him the right to nominate his own subordinates as *tuguan*. This negotiated agreement allowed Sayyid 'Ajall to open a previously dangerous stretch of the Sichuan-Yunnan highway without expending valuable military resources.

Within a few years, however, Sayyid 'Ajall betrayed this agreement by creating nearly twenty-five prefectures and conferring numerous *tuguan* offices upon influential indigenous leaders in the southern portion of the pacification commission. Even though nearly all of these prefectures were located well to the south of the pacification commissioner's personal domain, Sayyid 'Ajall had extended Mongol control as far north as Dechang by garrisoning troops along the Sichuan-Yunnan highway and ordering state farms (*tuntian*), both civilian (*mintun*) and military (*juntun*), to be established near each route headquarters. These state farms were primarily responsible for reclaiming lands and expanding agricultural production, but local records tell us that the Mongols also used the people enrolled in state farms to repair and maintain the highway, to build and repair government offices, postal stations, and outposts, and even to assist in policing the road.[42] By 1280, there were approximately five hundred households enrolled in the civilian farms near Huichuan and Dechang, and the population registers reveal that the majority of people in civilian farms were locals. The military farms, however, were made up primarily of troops drawn from the Shanchan region, and there are a few accounts of Han enrolled in Mongol military farms along the Sichuan-Yunnan highway.

Further to the east, Sayyid 'Ajall ordered his most capable military commander, Ailu (d. 1287), to lead a contingent of troops from Shicheng, soon to be renamed Qujing, north along the old Qin highway toward Luzhou. Sayyid 'Ajall knew this was a particularly dangerous assignment since Ailu would be leading his troops into Wusa territory, along the western edge of the Mu'ege kingdom.[43] As von Glahn pointed out, by the end of the twelfth century the town of Luzhou was the southernmost extension of the Song state, and Song officials considered it to be the last significant outpost of Chinese civilization before one entered the mysterious and uncharted world of the spirit masters. In this instance, though, Ailu was leading his forces in 1276 from south to north toward Luzhou in order to secure the road between Qujing and Luzhou for safe travel.[44]

Both Sayyid 'Ajall and Ailu knew that the people living near the Wumeng Mountains had received political appointments by the Dali state, and since the defeat of Dali they had stubbornly defended their independence from the Yuan. Moreover, Ailu was aware that of the "eight *wuman* tribes" inhabiting the region, three (the Wusa, Wumeng, and Mangbu) were related to the Azhe, Awangren, and Bole patriclans, and for this reason Ailu anticipated resistance from the local population as his army marched toward Wusa.[45] In preparation for the campaign, Sayyid 'Ajall had selected the town of Wusa to be a route headquarters, and he decided that Ailu would be its initial route commander. To quell the anticipated resistance, Sayyid 'Ajall authorized Ailu to dole out a liberal number of *tuguan* offices in the hopes that the importance of such an office, as well as the rapid collapse of the Song state, would convince the leaders of the eight *wuman* tribes to submit peacefully. Ailu proved an adept negotiator, for in less than two years Sayyid 'Ajall downgraded the Wusa route to the Wusa soldier/civilian command (*junmin zongguan fu*) and named the leader of the Wusa patriclan, Amou, to be the political-military authority in the area. This move was calculated to allow Ailu and his army to participate in the much-anticipated campaign against the recalcitrant Azhe, Awangren, and Bole patriclans planned for the following spring.[46]

## The Final Piece to the Yuan
## China Puzzle: Mu'ege

Although orders to invade the territory controlled by the Azhe, Awang-ren, and Bole patriclans were not announced until the middle of 1279, Qubilai had authorized the Tanzhou Branch Secretariat to send a re-connaissance mission into this part of Qian at the beginning of the year.[47] Liu Jichang (d. 1291), a suppression commissioner (*zhaotao shi*) assigned to the Liangwei circuit in the recently established Tanzhou Branch Secretariat, led a contingent of troops west along the Guizhou-Huguang (Qian-Xiang) highway.[48] This road bisected the intermediate zone that separated Song China from the Dali kingdom—the territory controlled by the Mu'ege, Luodian, and Yushi kingdoms. Liu's detach-ment encountered only sporadic resistance as it made its way through the eastern part of Qian; however, when Liu reached Xintian in the sixth month of 1279, he was ordered to halt his march and reinforce his position. By the middle of 1279, Liu's Tanzhou army was positioned along the eastern edge of the Mu'ege and Luodian kingdoms while Say-yid 'Ajall's Yunnan forces pressured Mu'ege from the west. It was at this time that Qubilai issued orders to secure control of the region and de-feat the *wuman* tribes.[49]

In compliance with Qubilai's orders, Liu employed the time-honored Mongol tactic of dispatching envoys ahead of the main army to intimi-date communities into surrendering. Liu knew that if he continued his march west along the main highway toward Yushi he would expose his army to attack from the hostile Bafan (Eight Barbarians) tribes located to the south of the road, as well as from Azhe troops situated to its north and from Bole and Awangren forces due west. Therefore, Liu decided inde-pendently to send envoys to meet with the preeminent political figure among the Bafan tribes, Wei Changsheng of the Da Longfan tribe, and with the patriarch of the Azhe patriclan, Acha (d. 1285).[50] Liu's envoys returned unharmed with news that both Wei and Acha had agreed to submit to Mongol rule. As part of the surrender procedure, Wei led a delegation of tribal leaders from Bafan to Liu's headquarters at Xintian and presented Liu with the land and population registers for the entire Bafan area. In return for peacefully agreeing to be a part of the grand qan's empire, Liu appointed each of the nine tribal leaders to the office of military commissioner (*anfu shi*) and ordered them to govern their respective localities as they always had, except they would now be officials of the Yuan state and vassals to the grand qan.[51]

Once Liu appointed the nine tribal leaders of the Bafan region to be military commissioners, he made them subordinate to the newly created Bafan Pacification Commission headquartered in Xintian.[52] Interestingly, Liu did not assign *darughachi* to these nine military commissions. He did not order the nine military commissioners to collect taxes on behalf of the Yuan state, and he did not impose Yuan legal institutions in the areas governed by the military commissioners. He did, however, order each military commissioner to present tribute to Yuan officials in Xintian every year.[53] In other words, the nine Bafan leaders were allowed to govern their respective areas just as they had prior to Liu's arrival. Moreover, they were authorized to appoint subordinates to *tuguan* offices just as Sayyid 'Ajall was doing in Yunnan at this time, thereby establishing a clear administrative hierarchy: the pacification commissioner was superior to the pacification inspector, who was superior to the military commissioner. *Tuguan* were subordinate to all the above.

Acha, too, surrendered to Liu in Xintian, yet the land and population registers he provided Liu represented only a fraction of the territory under his control. According to these registers, the 1,626 villages and 11,168 households were located east of the Yachi River in Shuidong (the Azhe were driven out of Shuidong at the beginning of the Song, and Acha was probably staking claim to Shuidong in anticipation that the territory would be returned to Mu'ege control), and his text failed to account for the vast Azhe-controlled territory of Shuixi located west of the Yachi River. Acha's deception succeeded, for Liu bestowed upon him the lofty title of Shunyuan (present-day Guiyang) pacification commissioner.[54] Unfortunately for Acha, this appointment to the post of pacification commissioner failed to insulate him and the Mu'ege kingdom from Ailu's soldiers in Wusa, or for that matter from the grand qan himself.

Sayyid 'Ajall and Ailu were still carrying out Qubilai's directive issued in mid-1279. Specifically, Qubilai ordered the Yunnan Branch Secretariat to pacify "Yixibuxue" (the Mongol term for both the Shuixi region in general and the town of Mugebaizhage) and to organize an army out of former Dali troops and attack the Mian kingdom (Burma).[55] In accordance with these orders, which were not countermanded following Acha's surrender to Liu in Xintian, by the end of 1279 Ailu had amassed an impressive army of approximately 25,000 troops, 6,000 of whom were identified as Mongol and Central Eurasian, in and around the city of Wusa.[56] A Mongol force of about 10,000 troops under the command of Yesudinger had taken up position to the south of the city of Luzhou, and the notorious Central Eurasian commander, Alihaya, had moved his personal cavalry of warriors, estimated to be 8,000 strong, into eastern Qian, despite assurances from Liu that his Tanzhou forces were firmly in control of the area.[57]

During the winter months of 1279–80, the armies from Yunnan and Sichuan did little more than provoke skirmishes with Azhe forces along the western edge of Mu'ege, but in the sixth month of 1280 Ailu launched his attack. As Ailu and Yesudinger's armies fought Mu'ege forces in the west, Liu and his subordinates in Xintian scrambled to determine what had precipitated the fighting. Liu ordered a military commander stationed in Bozhou, Li Dehui (1252–97), to send a delegation into Shuixi to meet with Acha.[58]

Five weeks later Li's envoys emerged from the mountains escorting a large delegation of Azhe officials and a gift of a thousand horses. Acha himself did not make the difficult journey to Bozhou due to ill health, but he did send two younger brothers and one son to deliver a letter to Li explaining his position. In the letter, Acha asserted that blame for the recent hostilities in Mu'ege be placed squarely on Ailu. Acha charged that the officials in Wusa had been tricked by Acha's longtime rival, Wusuonuo, the patriarch of the Wumeng patriclan, into believing that he would never accept Mongol overlordship. Acha's letter reminded Li that he had assisted Liu in convincing Wei, the powerful tribal leader among the Bafan, to submit to Mongol rule; that he had submitted to Mongol rule over a year earlier and had been appointed Shunyuan pacification commissioner; and finally, that he had never ordered his forces to threaten Ailu's position in Wusa.[59]

Li's discussions with Acha's brothers, son, and retainers convinced him that they were sincere. He forwarded the letter and information he collected from Acha's delegation to Liu in Xintian and to Qubilai. Even though a relatively minor military commander, Li nevertheless recommended that hostilities toward Mu'ege be suspended at once and that a

thorough investigation into the events in Wusa be ordered. Li also recommended that following Acha's death the Yuan state confer upon his
brother, Ali, the title of Yixibuxue-Shunyuan pacification inspector,
thereby placing much of the territory that had been the Mu'ege kingdom prior to its fight with the Song at the end of the tenth century
back under Azhe control. Clearly sympathetic to Acha's position, Li
downplayed Acha's failure to present himself personally in Bozhou,
which was considered a serious offense to Mongol protocol. Acha, according to Li's exculpatory report, was near death and the trip to
Bozhou would have surely killed him.[60]

Li's report clearly struck a nerve with Qubilai, for the grand qan berated Li for failing to make Acha conform to Mongol protocol and
submit personally to officials in Bozhou. Qubilai also chastised Li for
recommending that Acha's brother be appointed to a new office called
"Yixibuxue-Shunyuan pacification inspector" and, most important, for
suggesting that Mongol commanders in Yunnan and Sichuan were to
blame for the escalation of violence in the region. To clear Sayyid
'Ajall and Ailu of such accusations, Qubilai included in his communiqué a copy of the original orders he issued to Sayyid 'Ajall in mid-
1279 ordering Yunnan forces to attack Yixibuxue. Yet Qubilai, ever the
pragmatist, also presented his military commanders with an alternative
to war. He ordered Li to inform Acha that he had one month to surrender in person to Ailu in Wusa or face attack. To punctuate his demand,
Qubilai redeployed Alihaya's troops to Xintian and ordered a thousand
Mongol and Dongman (Barbarians of the Grottoes) troops to travel
along the trail from Bozhou to the border of Yixibuxue (the Mongol
name for Shuixi) to pressure Acha.[61]

In response to these provocative acts, Acha decided to resist rather
than meet Ailu in Wusa, which he probably concluded was a one-way
journey anyway. As a result, Yunnan forces under Ailu moved forward
from their positions in Wusa. While Sichuan forces under Yesudinger
attacked Mu'ege from the north, Bozhou forces led by the Yang patriclan attacked from their mountain enclave to the northeast, and Tanzhou forces under Alihaya, Tahai, and Manggudai consolidated Yuan
control over the Guizhou-Yunnan (Qian-Dian) highway between Xintian and Yushi before advancing north into Mu'ege.[62] Early in the campaign Qubilai ordered that all captured Azhe soldiers were to be sent to
the Mian front; but as the campaign wore on over the next year and a
half, many of the captured Mu'ege troops were instead incorporated

into the various Mongol army units and dispatched to Sichuan.[63] By mid-1282 Mongol forces had pushed far into the interior of Mu'ege and occupied the towns of Caoni, Yixibuxue, Pingchiande, Daguzhai, and Mopoleipo.[64]

Pockets of resistance continued to plague Mongol forces until the end of 1282, but by this time Yuan officials were well on their way toward carving the Mu'ege kingdom into several Yuan administrative units.[65] Eight prefectures were placed under the jurisdiction of three newly created routes: the Yixibuxue (present-day Dafang), Pingchiande (present-day Qianxi), and Mopoleipo (present-day Zhijin) Route Commands. A route commander, *darughaci*, and contingent of Mongol troops were assigned to each route, and these Yuan officials were authorized to anoint local figures as *tuguan*. The routes, prefectures, and *tuguan* jurisdictions were incorporated into the newly established Shunyuan Pacification Commission. One of the three heroes of the Mu'ege campaign, Suge, was appointed pacification commissioner, and the other two, Yesudaier and Yaocihai, were named chief military commander (*du yuanshuai*) and garrison commander (*zongling*), respectively.[66]

Suge, Yesudaier, and Yaocihai were commanders of Sichuan armies involved in the Mu'ege campaign, and their subordinates likewise filled important administrative posts throughout the newly created Yixibuxue unit. This meant that Chengdu, the administrative seat of the Sichuan Branch Secretariat, became responsible for rotating officials and troops into and out of Yixibuxue and for provisioning its personnel in the region. Clearly this was no easy task. Because Yunnan and Sichuan bore the brunt of responsibility for directing the Mian campaign, few Mongol troops were available to be stationed in Yixibuxue, and those troops who were assigned to Yixibuxue lacked even basic necessities such as food, clothing, and horses to carry out policing activities. For example, when two minor revolts broke out along the northern periphery of Yixibuxue during the early months of 1283, the Sanmao Incident and the Revolt in Nine Streams and Eighteen Grottoes (*jiuxi shiba dong*), Mongol commanders in Yixibuxue reported to Chengdu that disease, malnutrition, and the lack of adequate provisions prevented the garrison troops from suppressing even these two minor rebellions. Yaocihai, the garrison commander in Yixibuxue, sent a number of dispatches to Chengdu urgently requesting supplies, but when these were not forthcoming he improvised by exchanging Yixibuxue livestock for grain with military commanders from Tanzhou and Yunnan.[67]

Yuan officials in Chengdu were not intentionally abandoning their troops and officials in Yixibuxue. On the contrary, they were well aware of the dire circumstances of their garrison troops there, but there was very little they could do. Officials in Chengdu were under strict orders to mobilize and allocate all available resources in Sichuan for the Mian campaign. In the fourth month of 1283, officials in Chengdu had become so desperate for able-bodied men to fight in Mian that a general amnesty for criminals in Sichuan was declared, but only if they agreed to fight in Mian. As this explosive mix of exhausted troops, disgruntled civilians, freed prisoners, and military supplies filled the highways heading south from Sichuan to Yunnan and eventually the Mian front, the local people living along the roads heading south became easy targets for the raw and undisciplined recruits.

Violence along the main roads linking Yunnan to Chengdu forced Yuan officials to temporarily withdraw troops from Yixibuxue just to pacify the escalating hostility along the Sichuan-Yunnan highway and to hunt for deserters in Yunnan and Sichuan.[68] Consequently, almost immediately after Mongol forces defeated Mu'ege forces and occupied the remote, mountainous territory of Shuixi, they were compelled to withdraw their troops from the region. Yuan authorities in Chengdu had no other recourse but to turn over the day-to-day running of the administrative units to the local population, and they naturally relied on those surviving members of the *wuman* elite, the Azhe patriclan, to govern the region.

## Mu'ege Becomes a Pacification Commission

To deal with the growing level of anti-Mongol violence, Yuan officials decided in the fourth month of 1283 to concentrate Mongol and Central Asian forces in the main urban centers in the southwest and to rely on the local elite to govern the nonurban and nonstrategic areas of southern Sichuan, Yunnan, and the recently pacified Shuixi (Yixibuxue) region. As soon as this new directive was announced, Yesudaier, the chief military commander of the Shunyuan Pacification Commission, was sent back to Chengdu and placed in charge of the Sichuan provincial garrison. Chengdu had been under siege by rebel bands since the beginning of the year, and the number of Mongol troops stationed in Chengdu had dwindled to only a few hundred. Yesudaier was assigned to shore up Mongol control of Chengdu and eliminate bandit activity in the area. Yaocihai, the garrison commander in the town of Yixibuxue, replaced Yesudaier as Shunyuan's chief military commander, but before he assumed his new posting he was ordered to select a new garrison commander and train a new garrison force for the town. In doing so, he relied on the local population, which in this case meant the aristocratic-warrior Azhe and its affiliated branches. In addition, Yaocihai was asked to offer recommendations on how to reduce the onerous task of governing the entire Yixibuxue portion of the Shunyuan Pacification Commission.[69]

Following several months of discussions among Yaocihai, provincial leaders in Chengdu, and officials assigned to the Shunyuan Pacification Commission, Yaocihai was granted permission to enact a series of important reforms to Mongol control of Yixibuxue. First, Yaocihai ordered the removal of all Mongol troops from garrisons in the Shunyuan-Yixibuxue region and replaced them with a multiethnic force of local troops. Yaocihai personally selected the garrison commanders from among the local elite, and he allowed the commanders to build their own garrison units. Second, he detached the Yixibuxue region from Shunyuan Pacification Commission control and established an entirely independent Yixibuxue pacification inspector. Yaocihai appointed Ali, the younger brother of Acha, to be not only the pacification inspector of Yixibuxue but also the route commander of the Yixibuxue route. This dual appointment ensured that Ali and the Azhe patriclan would once again dominate the political landscape of Shuixi. Finally, Yaocihai withdrew Mongol forces from the Shuidong region east of the Yachi River and appointed Song Tianfu (d. 1307), a member of the Song family that defeated Pugui and occupied Shuidong at the beginning of the Song dynasty, to the post of Shunyuan battalion commander (*qianhu*), with authority over the entire Shuidong region, including the area formerly controlled by the Azhe patriclan as part of the Mu'ege kingdom.[70]

Notwithstanding Marco Polo's description of the "seven kingdoms of Karajang" ("Karajang" was Polo's term for the southwest) as a region in the throes of peace and prosperity, contemporary Yuan sources are unambiguous about the precarious state of Mongol control of the southwest during the last decades of the thirteenth century.[71] Because of the relentless banditry on the two main transportation routes linking Sichuan and Yunnan, the Sichuan Branch Secretariat experienced extreme difficulty in supplying Mongol forces in Yunnan, not to mention the Mongol troops fighting in the far south on the Mian front. Officials

in the Huguang Branch Secretariat seized upon this opportunity to propose in 1291 that Sichuan relinquish control of the Shunyuan Pacification Commission to the Huguang Branch Secretariat. Huguang officials
argued that it was better positioned to provide military supplies to
Mongol forces in Yunnan than was Sichuan, but to do so required Huguang control over Shunyuan. The Yuan government agreed and transferred control of Shunyuan from Sichuan to Huguang.[72]

Once in control of Shunyuan, Huguang authorities merged Shunyuan with Bafan, which it had controlled ever since Liu Jichang's campaign in central Qian in 1279, to form one large administrative unit
called the Shunyuan-Bafan Pacification Commission. The one justification given by Huguang officials for combining Shunyuan and Bafan was
that it would "create a more effective means to tax the indigenous
population and conscript soldiers."[73] It is also plausible, however, that
by combining Shunyuan and Bafan into one large political unit, Huguang officials hoped to make it difficult for the central government to
return Shunyuan to Sichuan control once hostilities in Yunnan ceased.
The revenue potential of the Shunyuan-Bafan region was enormous,
and it seems likely that officials in Huguang were interested primarily in
increasing Huguang's revenue base.[74]

The Shunyuan-Bafan Pacification Commission covered an enormous
geographic expanse in central Qian.[75] Shunyuan (Guiyang), the emerging commercial and political entrepôt in central Qian, was made the
administrative seat for the new pacification commission, the headquarters for the route command, and the site of the chief military commander. The administrative offices of the Bafan Pacification Commission were relocated to Shunyuan from Xintian, and the nine military
commissions (*anfu si*) of Bafan were also ordered to relocate their offices
to Shunyuan, something they were not required to do in Xintian. Below
the level of military commissioner, the Shunyuan-Bafan Pacification
Commission oversaw eleven native prefectures (*tu zhou*) and thirty-
nine barbarian native offices (*manyi zhangguan si*). Both the native prefectures and the barbarian offices were new to Qian, and the Yuan designed these offices to govern small, isolated indigenous populations. By
the end of the Yuan dynasty in 1368, there would be 208 barbarian
offices throughout Qian.[76]

For reasons not entirely clear, at the end of 1292 officials in Huguang
were ordered to take the additional step of incorporating the Yixibuxue
Pacification Inspector Commission into the Shunyuan-Banfan Pacifica-

tion Commission, thus forming the Shunyuan-Bafan-Yixibuxue Pacification Commission. In essence, Huguang officials had reconsolidated
the political unit that Sichuan authorities had created a decade earlier
and then, due to strategic reasons, were forced to disband. The geopolitical size of the Shunyuan-Bafan-Yixibuxue Pacification Commission encompassed nearly the same expanse of territory as that of the
former Mu'ege kingdom during the early years of the Song, and this fact
was not lost on Ali and the leaders of the Azhe patriclan.[77]

Though Mongol officials were not posted to Yixibuxue, we know the
actions of Yuan officials in and around Shunyuan greatly exacerbated
the already strained relations between Mongol forces and the region's
local elite. Particularly onerous were Mongol demands for military con-
scripts to fight in Yunnan. In the fifth month of 1300, Song Longjie,
the younger brother of the recently deceased Song Tianfu, and the
newly confirmed Shunyuan battalion head, warned his Mongol superiors that their brutal means of conscripting soldiers to fight in Yunnan
had created a level of hostility among the people that even he could no
longer restrain. According to Song Longjie,

> The Miao and Qilao complain bitterly to me that military officials have visited
> their villages for years taking the best young men away to fight in Dian [Yun-
> nan]. The new recruits are forced to shave their heads [in the Mongol style] and
> their faces are branded just like a criminal before they are led away, many never
> to be seen again. The Miao and Qilao have endured this cruelty for several
> years without any outbreak of violence, but now there are only a few men left
> and they would rather die here in their native villages than fight in far-off
> Yunnan. For this reason, conscript patrols are now killing those who refuse
> military service in their own villages. This is a dangerous time.[78]

The tension described by Song was in response to yet another mobilization order issued by the Yuan military early in 1300. This order
called for troops to be sent to the Yunnan frontier to subjugate the Babai xifu (Lanna) kingdom, located in what is present-day northern
Thailand.[79] The Yuan government had ordered the five branch secre-
tariats of Huguang, Jiangxi, Henan, Shaanxi, and Zhejiang to dispatch
20,000 troops each to Yunnan to assist in this military campaign. When
Liu Shen, the commander of the Huguang army, reached Shunyuan in
the fourth month of 1300, he ordered his field commanders to scour the
countryside for able-bodied men to serve as soldiers and porters. Liu also
demanded money, food, shelter, and fresh horses from the local population. For his part, Song was ordered to contribute 5,000 ounces of gold

to the Huguang army. Shejie, wife of the recently deceased Ali and mother to the infant heir to the office of Yixibuxue pacification commissioner, was instructed to provide Liu's personal staff with 3,000 ounces of gold and 3,000 of Shuixi's (Yixibuxue) finest horses. Instead of acquiescing to what they considered exorbitant demands, Song and Shejie attacked and easily routed the unsuspecting Huguang force.[80]

Information on what transpired in Shunyuan after the attack on Liu's army is rather sparse; however, we do know Yuan officials were unable (and possibly unwilling) to return to Shunyuan until 1308. To bring hostilities in Qian to an end, Yuan officials relied on negotiation, intimidation, and subterfuge. In dealing with Song Longjie, they approached his influential nephew Song Azhong and informed him that if he assisted them in capturing his uncle, the post of Shunyuan battalion head would be his. They also promised to refrain from sending Mongol troops into Shuidong following Song Longjie's capture. Song Azhong quickly obliged and handed Song Longjie over to the Yuan authorities in Shunyuan for execution. As for Shejie, Yuan officials approached Ali's younger brother and Shejie's brother-in-law, Ahua (d. 1335), and persuaded him to deliver Shejie to them in Shunyuan, after which he would be named Yixibuxue pacification inspector and Yixibuxue route commander. In the fifth month of 1308, Ahua brought a subdued Shejie to Shunyuan, where Yuan officials promptly executed her.[81]

One Yuan official very familiar with the negotiations to persuade Ahua to hand over Shejie was Li Jing. Li was a native of Hebei, and in 1301 he was appointed deputy pacification commissioner of Wusa and Wumeng, where he served for several years. From his headquarters in Wusa, Li managed this large administrative jurisdiction that included Wumeng, Dongchuan, and Mangbu. His primary responsibility in this area, however, was to mobilize local men and resources for the Lanna campaign, which the example of Liu Shen indicates was an exceedingly dangerous task.[82] Li's travels skirted the perimeter of the Azhe-controlled Yixibuxue Pacification Inspector Commission, and as a result he left several fascinating descriptions of the indigenous peoples of this region. The following representation by Li is of the Nasu Yi in Wusa:

The Luoluo [Nasu Yi] are also known as *wuman* [black barbarians]. Luoluo men either coil their hair into a topknot or shave their heads completely, and they like to pluck their facial hair. They carry two knives, one at each side, and enjoy fighting and killing. When a disagreement occurs between fathers, sons, and brothers, they do not hesitate to attack each other with weapons. Luoluo men consider fighting and killing a sign of valor. They prize horses with cropped tails, their saddles have no trappings, and their stirrups are carved from wood in the shape of a fish's mouth so that they are easy to put feet into.

The women wear their hair down, and their clothing is made of cotton. Wealthy women embroider their clothing with interesting designs and adorn themselves with jewelry, whereas commoners wear simple sheepskins. They ride horses sidesaddle. Unmarried girls wear large earrings and cut their hair at their eyebrows, and their skirts do not even cover their knees. Men and women, rich and poor, all wear felt caps and go barefoot and often go as long as one year without washing their face and hands.

It is the custom for husbands and wives not to see each other during the day but only sleep together at night. Children as old as ten years of age are likely to have never seen their fathers. Wives and concubines are not jealous of each other. Even the well-to-do do not use padding on their beds but instead just spread pine needles on the ground with only one mat and one cover. Marriages are arranged with the maternal uncle's family, but if a suitable partner cannot be found they can look elsewhere for a match. When someone falls ill, they do not use medicine but rely on a spirit master who uses chicken bones to divine good and evil fortunes. The tribal leader's orders are never questioned, and the spirit master is always at his side, and it is the spirit master who makes final decisions in all matters big and small.

All women who are about to get married must first have relations with the spirit master and then "dance" with the groom's brothers, and this custom is known as "making harmony." Only after ["making harmony"] can she marry. If one amongst the brothers refuses to go along with this custom, everyone will be disgusted with him and it will be considered a bad omen.

The first wife is known as the *naide*, and it is only her children who can inherit the father's position. If the *naide* does not have a son, or the son dies before he is married, they go ahead and arrange a wife for him anyway. Anyone can have relations with the wife, and any child born is considered the child of the deceased. If the tribal leader does not leave an heir, his wife's [the *naide*'s] daughter then becomes the leader. However, she then has no female attendants, only ten or more young male attendants, with whom she can have relations.[83]

Li wrote this description of the Luoluo in 1303 as part of his larger work, the *Yunnan zhilue*. The text was later revised and edited for popular dissemination in 1331, at which time it consisted of five sections in four chapters, geography, people, local customs, local products, and travel notes and poems. Unfortunately, only the introduction and those sections on people and local customs are extant. Nonetheless, what we can cull from Li's description affirms much of what has already been said about the ancestors of China's present-day Nasu Yi. They were an aristocratic-warrior people who gained status and prestige by demon-strating courage and valor in battle. They were skilled horsemen and -women, and the armor and weaponry they used in battle was of the highest quality. A spirit master dominated religious and secular life, and the status of women, at least those in the preeminent patriclan, appeared to be quite high. Although Li seemed slightly disturbed by Luo-luo hygiene and marriage customs, we can deduce from his description that the Yuan state would be much better off having the Luoluo as allies, not enemies. Yuan officials from the Huguang Branch Secretariat undoubtedly shared this sentiment when they decided to rely on Ahua and Song Azhong to maintain order in the Shuixi and Shuidong regions on behalf of the Yuan state.

During the twenty-seven-year period between his appointment as Yixibuxue pacification inspector in 1308 and his death in 1335, Ahua received an impressive collection of stately titles from the Yuan government. In large measure Ahua accumulated his titles and political power by providing timely military assistance to the Mongols. In the mid-1320s, for example, he responded to Yuan requests for military assistance nine times. The most serious instance was a Miao uprising in eastern Qian in 1326. The Miao had evidently severed the main highway in eastern Qian, making communication between Shunyuan officials and their superiors in Huguang impossible. Isolated and under siege, the authorities in Shunyuan turned to Ahua, who reportedly relieved Shunyuan by dispatching 10,000 troops to "pacify" the Miao in eastern Qian. Once the Guizhou-Huguang highway was reopened for passage, Ahua's troops retreated back across the Yachi River into Yixibuxue (Shuixi), to the delight (and probably the surprise) of Yuan officials in Shunyuan. For his efforts, Ahua was granted control of the Bafan Pacification Commission and awarded the lofty title of grand master, protector of the country, member of the imperial guard, chief military commissioner, and pacification commissioner of the Bafan frontier (*dafu huguo daiwei qinjun du zhihui Bafan yanbian xuanwei shi*).[84]

These titles paled in comparison to the titles granted to Ahua in 1330 following his support of yet another Mongol campaign in Yunnan. In that year he was awarded two titles, general of manifest courage (*zhaoyong da jiangjun*) and holder of the three-pearled tiger tally (*sanzhu hufu*), which had previously been granted to his father. For his outstanding service against *baiman* (Cuan) rebels in eastern Yunnan, Ahua was named vice minister of the Yunnan Branch Secretariat (*Yunnan xingsheng zoucheng*), though it was clear from another title he received at this time that he was not expected to take up residence in Zhongqing (Kunming). And finally, in 1331 Yuan authorities named Ahua the Shunyuan-Bafan-Yixibuxue pacification commissioner and charged him to govern an expanse of territory nearly equal in size to the Mu'ege kingdom during the last years of the Tang dynasty.[85] The Mongols conquered the Mu'ege kingdom in the 1280s, only to return it to the Azhe patriclan and the *na* aristocratic-warrior elite as hereditary *tuguan* officials in the 1330s.

The Mongol conquest of the southwest was a pivotal turning point in the history of the region, and of China's relationship to the southwest. In 1253 Mongol armies attacked the Dali kingdom in order to expose Song China's southern flank and quicken the demise of Song resistance. Mongol forces, however, struggled to consolidate their control over Dali, and they failed to make any significant headway in opening a southern front against the Song. The four Nasu Yi kingdoms, Mu'ege, Luodian, Yushi, and Badedian, along with several Song allies in the southwest frontier, such as the Yang of Bozhou, acted as a barricade against repeated Mongol advances toward Song China. It would take nearly thirty years and the defeat of Song forces by Mongol armies rushing south across the Yangzi River before Qubilai could subdue the four Nasu Yi kingdoms. By the close of the thirteenth century, many of the independent kingdoms that had existed for centuries in the southwest had been incorporated into the greater Mongol empire; yet, during the first decades of the fourteenth century it appears the Yuan state was transferring control of the region back to the indigenous elite.

Another important outcome of the Mongol conquest of the southwest was the creation of Yuan political boundaries, administrative jurisdictions, and institutional relationships that compelled China's political elite to view the southwest as a part of China. The appointment of Sayyid 'Ajall Shams al-Din to the newly formed Yunnan Branch Secretariat in 1274 defined the geopolitical sovereignty of the Yuan state to include Yunnan, and the political offices established by the Yuan throughout the southwest mirrored the bureaucratic structure found in China proper. Yuan territorial competence, in its broadest sense, now included the southwest, even if vast tracts of land between Yunnan and China proper remained beyond the direct control of the Yuan government.

Mongol control of the southwest was essentially structured around jurisdictions that were negotiated patron-client relationships. In a pre-

modern society such as Yuan China, a ruler's ability to control his territory decreases as distance from his court increases. If a ruler wishes to
extend the size of his kingdom, either by reclamation, negotiation, or
conquest, he is forced to develop strategies that enhance his prestige
and symbolic authority while not weakening his power. In a region as
far from the Yuan court as the southwest, the Yuan state mixed feudal
forms of political authority with piecemeal bureaucratic institutions to
exert political influence over the indigenous non-Han in the southwest.

For example, not long after Mongol armies entered Dali in 1253,
Qubilai ordered the ruling Dali king, Duan Xingzhi, to remain as the
political leader of his people. Duan presented himself as a vassal to the
Mongol qan and swore allegiance to the Mongols, and in return he and
his descendents were granted hereditary rights to the prominent political offices in Yunnan. The same was true for the Azhe in Mu'ege. After
Mongol forces occupied Mu'ege territory, a perilous shortage of competent officials forced the Yuan state to recruit members of the Azhe patriclan to staff the recently created Yuan political and military posts in
Shuixi. The Azhe also enjoyed hereditary control of these offices. In
fact, the majority of Yuan offices in the southwest were filled primarily
by the local elite. The Mongols defeated the independent polities on
the battlefield, but they proved unable to rule these areas despite the
creation of Yuan political units. In short, indigenous rule continued under the guise of Yuan institutions.

Here is the issue: tension exists between the jurisdictional notion of
sovereignty, as expressed in the political bond between qan and subject,
a bond easily understood by and recognizable to the indigenous elite,
and the territorial conception of sovereignty, symbolized by the creation of geopolitical boundaries and government offices, which informed
Chinese perceptions of the southwest and Chinese political discourse. It
is the latter that convinced China's elites to see the southwest as an integral part of China—what James Millward termed the "domestication"
of a frontier region—and from this point forward Chinese officials could
not contemplate withdrawal from the southwest.[86] Ming China's leaders
were determined to extend political control over the southwest, if for
no reason other than that the Yuan Mongols had. Unlike the Mongols,
the Ming promoted the rapid colonization of the southwest by Han settlers from China proper, and it is the Ming conquest and colonization of
the southwest that will comprise the remaining chapters in this book.

# 3

## Mu'ege During the Yuan-Ming Transition

With the death of Ahua in 1335, his eldest son, Aicui (d. 1382), inherited the political offices and prestigious titles bestowed upon his father by the Yuan state. Aicui maintained his allegiance to the multitude of Mongol qans during the turbulent last years of Yuan rule while often coordinating his actions with the powerful Mongol authorities in Yunnan. In 1371, however, Aicui recognized the futility of continuing his relationship with the Mongols and abruptly entered into direct negotiations with representatives of the newly formed Ming government. On February 21, 1372, the negotiations came to fruition as Aicui and Song Qin, the Shunyuan battalion head and political leader of the Shuidong region, pledged allegiance to the newly enthroned Chinese emperor Hongwu.[1]

Aicui, prior to his audience with Hongwu, surrendered his Yuan patent of investiture, the official paperwork accompanying his numerous Yuan titles, and his seal to the pacification commission. In return Hongwu bestowed upon Aicui the new title of Guizhou pacification commissioner. It was a reward of significant proportions: as Guizhou pacification commissioner Aicui was given political jurisdiction over the Shuixi, Shuidong, and Bafan regions. This pacification commission represented not only the reality of Aicui's political jurisdiction at the end of the Yuan dynasty but also the geopolitical extent of the Mu'ege kingdom at the beginning of the Song dynasty, and Hongwu was aware of this history, for his appointment notice references the expansive Luo kingdom during the Tang and Song dynasties.

For his allegiance Song Qin was appointed to the subordinate post of Guizhou vice pacification commissioner and ordered to cooperate fully with Aicui and his successors. The Ming emperor "lavished expensive gifts upon the southern barbarians chiefs" during their court audience, and he assured Aicui and Song that neither his military nor his civilian officials would be permitted to step foot in the pacification commission's jurisdiction (Shuixi and Shuidong), which included the town of Shunyuan, now renamed Guizhou (present-day Guiyang), where the pacification commission's headquarters was located. For both Aicui and Song, relations with the fledgling Ming government could not have started any better.

However, by the end of Hongwu's thirty-year reign in 1398, the relationship had soured, and the emperor's assurances of autonomy for these two frontier leaders had been largely forgotten. The Guizhou pacification commissioner still commanded unrivaled authority within his domain, but it was a domain now surrounded by a massive and permanent Ming military presence in the southwest. In the early 1380s the Ming military had commenced construction of a large garrison (*wei shihui shi si*) in the southern half of the "muddy, rat-infested town" of Guizhou, just opposite the pacification commission's headquarters, and Han Chinese civilians were now flooding into central Qian in order to provision the military units stationed there. Finally, in 1413 the Ming government annexed vast tracts of land in eastern Qian to create Guizhou province, thus sealing the fate of the heretofore autonomous pacification commission. This chapter will examine the roughly fifty-year period from the founding of the Ming dynasty in 1368 to the creation of Guizhou province in 1413 in order to illuminate both the motives behind the aggressive Ming expansion into the southwest and the impact of the Ming expansion on the Nasu Yi.[2]

## The Traditional Nasu
## Yi Administration of Shuixi

As Guizhou pacification commissioner Aicui was obligated to provide the Ming government with a genealogical history of his family, an outline of the geopolitical size of his domain, a brief explanation of how he came to control this territory, and a description of the people residing in his domain, including such noteworthy features as total population and ethnic diversity. Aicui duly noted in his report that the Mongols had created eight prefectures and three route commands in Shuixi in 1283, and that the spatial layout of the eight Yuan prefectures in Shuixi conformed almost exactly to the traditional Mu'ege institutions used to govern the region prior to the Mongol conquest.[3] Under Mu'ege rule the Shuixi-Shuidong region was partitioned into thirteen granary (*zexi*) units, and Aicui's ancestors had governed the territory by designating trustworthy branches of the patriclan to certain locales and by appointing competent individuals to posts in the granary unit.

Based on Aicui's recollection, after Yuan officials selected Ali, patriarch of the Azhe patriclan, to help staff offices in the eight prefectures and three route commands vacated by the Mongols, Ali selected individuals who either had held a position in a granary unit prior to Mongol occupation or were members of the *na* (aristocratic-warrior elite) where the granary unit and Yuan prefecture were located. In addition, Ali moved quickly to eliminate any trace of the Yuan prefectures and route commands and to resurrect the more familiar granary system to govern the population. In fact, the few early Ming accounts of the Shuixi-Shuidong region do reveal an awareness on the part of Ming officials of the existence of "native institutions" (*tuzhi*) used to govern the local population, and nowhere in these same Ming writings is there mention of a former Yuan administrative presence. Several recently published Nasu historical texts now provide us with richly detailed descriptions of the thirteen granary units first encountered by these early Ming officials.[4]

According to these texts, the territory west of the Yachi River (Shuixi) was divided into eleven granary units: Mukua, Fagua, Shuizhu, Jiale, Ajia, Dedu, Longkua, Duoni, Zewo, Yizhu, and Xiongsuo. To the east of the Yachi River were two additional granary units, Yude and Liumu. The person in charge of the granary unit was known as *zimo* (lit. "elder administrator"). In Chinese texts the *zimo* is often referred to as spirit master. Each *zimo* in Shuixi purportedly traced his ancestry back through Tuoazhe, the individual who was given the title lord of Luodian by the Shu Han general Zhuge Liang in 225 CE, to Mujiji and Dumu, the ancient ancestors who lived in the Luyang Mountains in northeast Yunnan during China's Warring States era. The *zimo*'s stature as political-religious leader also derived in large measure from the actions of more immediate ancestors who had played an important role in expanding the geopolitical size of the Mu'ege kingdom and in protecting the kingdom from outside forces. Based on records describing political succession, the deceased *zimo*'s eldest son by his wife was to inherit the *zimo* post, whereas siblings with demonstrated ability were appointed to other posts that formed the granary bureaucracy.

Directly subordinate to the *zimo* was the office of *muzhuo*. Generally, there were between three and four *muzhuo* posts in each granary unit, although the granary unit controlled directly by the main branch of the Azhe patriclan, the Mukua granary, had seven such *muzhuo* posts. A branch of the *zimo*'s patriclan usually controlled the *muzhuo* offices, and the eldest son of the deceased *muzhuo* inherited the post, but there are indications that staffing of this office was also based on individual ability. Some *muzhuo* domains were located in strategically important areas, such as near the Yachi River or along the old Qin highway that connected Chishui and Bijie, whereas others controlled important agricultural and grazing lands. The *zimo* had the authority to appoint individuals of demonstrated merit to these offices. Aicui, during his visit to Nanjing, informed his Ming counterparts that forty-eight officials (*tumu* in Chinese sources) governed the Shuixi region. This was a clear reference to the forty-seven *muzhuo* identified in Yi sources (see Appendix A).[5]

Further down the granary unit's administrative ladder were two influential posts, the *mayi* and *yixu* offices, to which capable individuals in either the *zimo*'s or the *muzhuo*'s patriclan were assigned. Both the *mayi* and *yixu* offices were civilian posts assigned with the responsibility of governing villages composed of people not related to the warrior aristocracy, the Azhe patriclan and various *na* branches that filled the *zimo* and *muzhuo* offices. The *mayi* was appointed to oversee the subordinate *quna*, or commoner, villages, whereas the *yixu* office was reserved primarily for the multiethnic *sujie* (dependent farmers and craftspeople) and *zesu* (house slaves), which consisted of Miao, Qilao, Longjia, Caijia, and Han villages scattered throughout the Shuixi region. According to seventeenth-century Nasu sources, *zimo* and *muzhuo* often appointed individuals to these posts who were not of the *na*; in other words, *quna*, Qilao, Miao, and Han were frequently appointed as *yixu* to govern their respective populations (see Appendix B).[6]

Regulations governing the granary system stipulated that individuals appointed to the *muzhuo, mayi,* and *yixu* posts maintain public security and organize labor teams for public works projects. Holders of these posts must also transmit grain tax to the *zimo*'s granary unit. These offi-

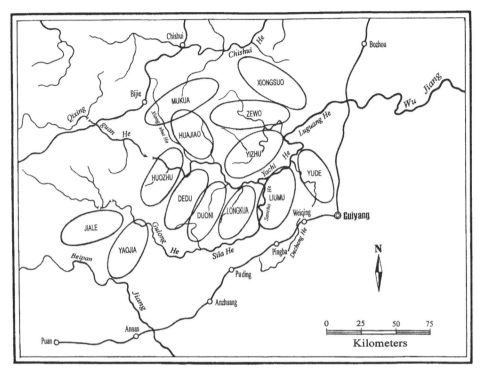

Map 4    The granary units in Shuixi and Shuidong

cials did not receive a salary from the *zimo* but instead were awarded a grant of land. This grant of land was not inconsequential when one considers that in the Shuixi-Shuidong region there were only forty-seven *muzhuo* posts. If these officials performed their tasks successfully, their sons were allowed to inherit the post. However, if their perform-ance proved unsatisfactory to the *zimo*, the individual would be required to step down from office and return control of the land to the *zimo*. At the beginning of the fifteenth century there were 13 *zimo*, 47 *muzhuo*, 120 *mayi*, and 1,200 *yixu* offices governing an estimated 7,000 villages in the Shuixi-Shuidong region.[7] Even though Chinese and Nasu Yi sources fail to provide census figures for the Shuixi-Shuidong region during the early years of the Ming, a comparison of the number of *yixu* offices with that of the *zimo*, *muzhuo*, and *mayi* posts would tend to sug-gest that the multiethnic dependent farmers and craftspeople and house slaves comprised the bulk of the population in Shuixi. But this type of analysis is misleading because we know that the *na* and *quna* lived in villages where the number of households was quite large, and the subordinate castes lived in villages with no more than a handful of households.

In addition to the territorial offices of *muzhuo*, *mayi*, and *yixu*, each *zimo* relied on a number of administrative appointees to assist him in the management of the granary unit. There were nine offices (*jiuzong*) that formed the *zimo*'s personal staff of advisers. Among this staff of advisers the *gengju*, *mokui*, and *zhuokui* participated in resolving important political and religious matters within the granary, with the *gengju*'s position superior to the others because this office also acted as regent for the infant heir to the *zimo*'s post. The *bumu*, *qimo*, and *beisuo* posts were responsible for managing the granary's economy, as well as overseeing the *zimo*'s staffing of the *yixu* posts, and the *gengju*, *mokui*, and *zhuokui* offices were consulted on appointments to the *mozhuo* posts and the *zimo*'s advisory staff. Finally, the *maxie*, *xiba*, and *heizha* offices were charged with supervising the granary's security, and this included the training of the *zimo*'s personal cavalry.[8] The *maxie* was the principal military adviser to the *zimo*, and he was authorized to assign the *xiba* and *heizha* to important military commands. For this reason, the *xiba* and *heizha* officials were often posted at strategic points throughout Shuixi and Shuidong.

To manage the day-to-day affairs of the granary unit, each of the thirteen *zimo* had a household staff consisting of nine officials (*jiuche*). Like the *zimo*'s advisory offices, the head officials of the household staff worked and resided near the *zimo*'s residence, but their duties often took them to other parts of the granary unit. The *zimo*, to manage his household affairs, draft correspondence, and issue decrees, relied on a personal secretary whose post was titled *amuche*. There were two offices that worked closely with the *amuche*: the *mushi*, which publicly announced decrees and proclamations issued by the *zimo*, and the *chengmu*, which served as the *zimo*'s recorder of important communiqués that came to his administrative headquarters.

The offices of *butu* and *zhuoyi* were jointly responsible for ensuring that proper etiquette and protocol were observed among the *na* (the purview of the *butu* post), and for communicating to the dependent farmers and craftsmen and house slave population what was expected of them in terms of proper etiquette and protocol when they came into contact with *na* (the responsibility of the *zhuoyi* office). The *baixiang* post was in charge of transportation-related affairs within the granary unit, such as road and bridge repairs, whereas the office of *baisu* handled the *zimo*'s courier system. The office of *chemo* instructed the *zimo* on the rituals to be observed in his sacrifices to gods and ancestors, and the *xiangmu* oversaw the preparation of utensils, vessels, and buildings used in religious ceremonies. Finally, the office of *yuanyue* trained and supervised the *zimo*'s personal bodyguards, and the *suwen* was the *zimo*'s personal instructor in the arts of war. The same granary regulations that applied to the *mozhuo*, *mayi*, and *yixu* offices also applied to the advisory and household posts. The *zimo* provided the holder of these posts with land and slaves to work the land (he did not issue a salary), and the *zimo* reserved the right to withdraw the appointment and grant it to someone else.[9]

The dependent farmers, craftsmen, and house slaves performed manual labor for the military aristocracy—the Azhe patriclan, its collateral branches, and *na*. The *quna*, *sujie*, and *zesu* were composed of subjugated Nasu, Miao, Qilao, Longjia, Caijia, and Han Chinese, and they lived in villages separated from the *na*.[10] In the political economy of the granary unit, the *na* regularly assigned specific labor tasks to specific castes and ethnic groups. For example, the Longjia were considered to be the best educated and most sophisticated of the subject population, and they were routinely given minor administrative posts in the *zimo*'s household staff, such as the office of *chengmu*. The Caijia were seen as skilled horsemen and adept at training horses, and therefore they often assisted the *na* in the stables. Since the Zhongjia (present-day Buyi) were regarded as better farmers than the Miao, Qilao, and Han Chinese, they were usually allocated the best farmland, whereas the latter groups were settled on the poorest land and given menial tasks.[11]

At the beginning of the fifteenth century animal husbandry was still the most important economic activity in the Shuixi region. Tang, Song, and Yuan sources are replete with tales of how proud *wuman* descended from the remote mountains of Shuixi at the head of a long train of excellent horses. They would remain at market for several days exchanging their horses for tea, salt, cloth, grain, and liquor before heading back into the "clouds and mist of the mountains."[12] The horse trade between the Azhe patriclan and Han merchants in Luzhou became so important during the Song and Yuan periods that Chinese texts referred to the Mu'ege kingdom by two names, Spirit Kingdom of the Luo Clan and Horse Kingdom (*Ma guo*). From the record of Aicui's discussions with Ming officials in 1372, we know it was very important to Aicui and the *na* in Shuixi that access to the Chinese market in Luzhou remain open and that trade restrictions be lifted, the latter a request to which Hongwu and his officials readily agreed. Horse breeding was the primary economic activity of the *na*, but sheep and cattle were also bred in large numbers and sold in the markets at Luzhou, Yushi, and Bole.[13]

By all accounts the agricultural regimen in the Shuixi region was still rather primitive at the end of the fourteenth century, and it appears to have been little more than a supplement to the more important economic activity of animal husbandry. The most common agricultural products in Shuixi were buckwheat, oats, and barley, but the mode of agricultural production was still slash-and-burn cultivation.[14] In 1382, as Ming military commanders led their units through the heart of Shuixi toward the town of Wusa, they included in reports that only slash-and-burn cultivation was practiced among the *wuman*. According to one eyewitness, "smoke billows from the fields as the barbarians [*man*] struggle to clear new ground with only wood and bamboo tools."[15]

However, in the more densely populated Shuidong region, wet-rice (*shuidao*) cultivation had become an important component in the overall agricultural regimen. There were relatively large tracts of level land in Shuidong, and the lower elevation and temperate climate made Shuidong one of only a handful of areas in central Qian where intensive agricultural cultivation could take place. The people living in this area were better able to harness the water from the river systems than were their counterparts in Shuixi because as the topography leveled off the steep ravines receded, thus allowing the construction of small canals to direct the water away from the rivers and toward the fields. As Ming forces entered Qian during the last decades of the fourteenth century, only local rice was sold at the markets in Guizhou. Ming military commanders complained bitterly that the quantity of rice was insufficient to meet the military's needs, and that it was inferior to the rice they were accustomed to in China proper. Buckwheat, oats, and barley were still the predominant grains sold in the markets in Shuidong, including the town of Guizhou.

## The Ming Enter Qian:
### Hongwu Meets She Xiang

Whereas it might seem that Ming officials enjoyed a decided advantage in their negotiations with Aicui and Song Qin, the reality was quite different. In 1371 the Ming military was exhausted. It had accomplished its primary task of driving the Mongols out of China, but the strategic concern over Yunnan loomed large. First, the Mongol prince of Liang, Basalawarmi, ruled much of Yunnan as a personal fiefdom, and his mere presence posed an unacceptable Mongol threat to the Ming state. Second, the Mongol creation of the Yunnan Branch Secretariat and its political incorporation with Yuan China compelled China's elites to see Yunnan as an inalienable part of China. Third, by the middle of the fourteenth century mining operations in Yunnan were producing over half of the gold and silver circulating in the Chinese economy, as well as a sizable percentage of the copper and iron used in China, and any plans for the reconstruction of the war-ravaged Chinese economy necessitated Ming control of the mining industry in Yunnan.[16] Finally, the deployment of excess and possibly restless Ming troops to the southwest as soldier-farmers not only could rid China of a troublesome social element but also could increase state revenues as they reclaimed taxable frontier land.

For Hongwu, fighting through Qian to reach Yunnan was to be avoided at all costs, and he accomplished an important diplomatic step in 1372 when Aicui and Song Qin pledged allegiance to the Ming. The Ming emperor knew the prospect of a negotiated settlement with Basalawarmi was slim, yet he ordered the distinguished scholar Wang Wei (1323–74) to lead a delegation to Yunnan in late 1372. When word reached Hongwu in 1374 that Basalawarmi had murdered Wang's delegation, he took the extraordinary step of sending another mission to Yunnan in 1375. This delegation was led by the deputy commissioner of Huguang, Wu Yun (d. 1375), and again the Mongol prince murdered the entire delegation.[17] By 1376, Hongwu had come to the conclusion that nothing short of a full-scale invasion of Yunnan could resolve this strategic dilemma, and in this year he and his advisers began preparing for the invasion of Yunnan. Due to a costly and complex reorganization of China's provincial political institutions, the invasion of Yunnan did not begin until 1381.

In the ninth month of 1381, Hongwu designated Fu Youde (d. 1394) to be his commander in chief of the Yunnan campaign. Fu's orders were deceptively simple: eliminate the Mongol presence in Yunnan and assert Ming control over the main transportation lines linking China proper to this strategically important region.[18] To provide logistical support for the campaign, Hongwu promoted Ma Hua, a longtime military commander who had distinguished himself fighting the Mongols in

Sichuan and Shanxi, to the post of chief military commissioner (*dudu*) of the southwest region, a position he held concurrently with that of Guizhou garrison commander. Ma was instructed to remain in the town of Guizhou to coordinate the mobilization of men and material for the coming campaign. Unfortunately for Ming-Azhe relations, one of Ma's first acts after reaching Guizhou was to dispatch troops into the Bafan region, where he divested the nine military commissioners of their titles and imposed tax and labor levies on the local population. This act challenged Aicui's political sovereignty as the Guizhou pacification commissioner, and relations between the two men deteriorated rapidly.

Ma further irritated Aicui in early 1382, when he ordered the city of Guizhou encircled by a stone wall. Given the enormity of the construction project and the mandatory local investment in human and financial resources, Aicui protested that the city had survived quite well without a stone wall. He also argued that the labor and tax levies needed to build the city wall would fall disproportionately on the shoulders of the local population. Unconvinced, and probably unconcerned with Aicui's protests, Ma publicly posted instructions (in both Chinese and Cuan scripts) on how he wanted the city wall to be constructed. He specified the wall's dimensions, the type of stone to be used in construction, and the speed at which the wall was to be completed. Ma went on to state that even the slightest deviation from these specifications would result in the immediate punishment of the offending laborer. And Ma meant what he said. In the first months of the construction project, the city's southern market had become a macabre execution ground for laborers who had failed to adhere to Ma's rigid construction code.[19] Aicui protested against Ma's actions to the authorities in Sichuan, but to no avail. He then ordered a work slowdown that lasted nearly a month, and when this action failed to modify Ma's stance, Aicui called for a general strike against all construction projects in the city. Within a fortnight Aicui was dead, supposedly poisoned during a meal with Ming officials as they discussed the growing tensions in the city.

With the death of Aicui in 1382, and the emergence of his wife, She Xiang (d. 1396), as regent for the still infant heir to Aicui's title of Guizhou pacification commissioner, Ma embarked on a plan to force the Guizhou Pacification Commission to abandon the town of Guizhou and return to its territory west of the Yachi River, Shuixi.[20] Ma also sought to eliminate the Song patriclan's control of the fertile Shuidong region to the north of Guizhou and to consolidate this territory with the Bafan and Guizhou areas to establish the Ming prefecture system (*junxian*) in central Qian. During an interview conducted several months later Ma claimed he was simply following orders from court officials. Apparently Ma did receive such instructions from officials in Nanjing, but his instructions were not coming from the emperor.

In any case, shortly after Aicui's death Ma accused She Xiang of inciting the local populace to rebel against the Ming state. After tricking her into entering his administrative offices unescorted, he seized her, and whipped her until she was near death. When word of Ma's public humiliation and brutal treatment of She Xiang reached the *zimo* and *mozhuo* leaders in Shuixi and Shuidong, they quickly mobilized a cavalry force estimated at more than 100,000 and started to advance toward Guizhou. Before the large Shuixi force crossed the Yachi River and entered Shuidong, Liu Shuzhen, matriarch of the Song family and herself regent to her infant son and heir to Song Qin's post as vice pacification commissioner, warned the Shuixi commanders that Ma had set a trap and they were marching directly into it.[21]

To diffuse the situation, Liu pledged to personally travel to the Ming capital to inform the emperor of Ma's criminal acts, but the commanders must first call off the attack. Liu promised the Shuixi troops that if her arguments failed to convince the emperor to remove Ma from office, to redress the injustices inflicted upon She Xiang and the people of Guizhou, and to investigate the mysterious circumstances surrounding the death of Aicui, then she would return from the capital and lead the Shuixi and Shuidong forces into battle against Ma and the Ming. Liu's timely intercession convinced the Shuixi force to disperse, and she clandestinely traveled to the Ming capital in what Chinese sources would subsequently describe as a "tribute mission."[22]

Liu, during her imperial audience, reminded Hongwu how Aicui had pledged allegiance to the Ming long before most other Yuan officials in the southwest had, and that he had worked tirelessly on behalf of the Ming emperor to convince other Yuan officials, primarily *tuguan* in Qian and eastern Yunnan, to renounce their ties to the Yuan state. If not for Aicui, Liu argued, the Awangren, Bole, Wusa, Wumeng, Chele, and Mangbu patriclans might still be loyal to the Mongols in Yunnan. Liu also reminded Hongwu that Aicui, She Xiang, and Song Qin had cooperated fully with Ming authorities in preparation of the Yunnan expedition. It was Aicui's cavalry that repeatedly tested Mongol defenses, and She Xiang had agreed to allow a Ming army to travel through the heart of Shuixi so that Ming forces could launch a two-pronged assault against Mongol forces in Yunnan. With She Xiang's loyalty firmly established, Liu presented her indictment against Ma Hua.

Liu charged Ma with gross mistreatment of the laborers working on government projects in Qian, such as the Guizhou city wall, and with intentionally falsifying government documents in order to maneuver She Xiang into visiting his office. Liu vehemently protested Ma's public flogging of She Xiang as an affront to the dignity of the regent (and mother) of a high-ranking official, not to mention the humiliation She Xiang suffered at being tied to a wooden post and whipped. Prior to the appointment of Ma, Liu concluded, the Ming emperor enjoyed the support of the *wuman*, and they were willing to assist the Ming in their fight against the Mongols. Aicui's mysterious death and Ma's cruel treatment of She Xiang had completely altered the situation, and the *wuman* no longer trusted the Ming. Hongwu discussed Liu's accusations with his most trusted confidant, Empress Ma (1332–82), and on the following day announced that the empress had been charged to investigate the events in Qian—this case would be one of Empress Ma's last official acts before her death. A few days later Empress Ma summoned Liu to her personal quarters to explain once again her charges against Ma. At the conclusion of this meeting the empress summoned both Ma and She Xiang to the capital and ordered Liu to remain in the capital to await their arrival.

According to Ming sources the interrogation of Ma, She Xiang, and Liu lasted several days, and on more than a few occasions the emperor himself attended the proceedings. In one of the initial interviews, Hongwu lashed out at Ma for repeatedly stating that his actions in Guizhou were in line with government policy and that his superiors in the capital had been kept abreast of his every move. There had been plenty of opportunity, Ma added, for capital officials to criticize his actions, but they had not. In response, the outraged emperor summoned several high-ranking officials to court to clarify state policy in Qian, and what they said only further infuriated Hongwu, for they confirmed Ma's position. The investigation dominated court life for nearly two weeks, as more and more officials were implicated in what the emperor perceived was an errant and reckless application of government policy. "To control Dian [Yunnan] and bring peace to this part of the realm, we

Fig. 1   She Xiang's tomb, Dafang, Guizhou (photo by the author)

need their [the *wuman's*] support. I have worked hard to gain their trust, and you [officials] have worked hard to undermine this trust. Follow my instructions precisely or else!"[23] Hongwu subsequently ordered the arrest of Ma and several high-ranking capital officials and even threatened several officials with execution, but within a year Ma was pacifying "rebels" in the Songpan region of northern Sichuan, and there are no records of officials having been punished for this incident.

The emperor and empress were evidently impressed by the eloquence and courage of both She Xiang and Liu, and they said as much in 1383 when Hongwu bestowed upon them the titles lady of virtue and obedience (*shunde furen*) and lady of virtue and intelligence (*mingde furen*), respectively.[24] He instructed She Xiang and Liu to continue construction on the city wall since it was nearly completed, but they, not Ming officials, should oversee the wall's construction. Hongwu also recommended a school be built in the city of Guizhou so that their descendants might receive a Chinese education. State funds were allocated to help defray construction costs and to provide a salary for a Han Chinese instructor, but Hongwu was adamant that the school be located in the northern half of the city near the headquarters of the Guizhou Pacification Commission and that Han students not be allowed to enroll in this school. Very few Han Chinese lived in the city of Guizhou at this time, so Hongwu's prohibition against enrolling Han students in this school was probably not a major issue.

At the same time Hongwu and his military advisers confirmed with She Xiang that she would widen and repair the mountain road that ran from Shuidong in the east across the heart of Shuixi to Bijie in the west. Ming commanders wanted the option of deploying troops from the town of Guizhou, on the eastern edge of Shuixi, to Bijie and Wusa, on the western edge of Shuixi, without having to circumvent the entire Shuixi region. Named the Geya Postal Road, the road was considered by Ming commanders to be strategically important during the planning stage of the Yunnan campaign, and Ming troops were deployed to Bijie and Wusa as a diversionary threat to the Mongols. In fact, during the initial stages of the Yunnan campaign, the presence of Ming troops in Bijie drew a sizable Mongol force north away from the advancing Ming army entering Yunnan along the Dian-Qian (Yunnan-Guizhou) highway. Subsequent Ming accounts of the Yunnan campaign highlighted the tactical importance of the Geya Postal Road to the overall success of the campaign. However, after the successful Ming campaign into Yunnan the road apparently did not provide the tactical advantage Ming commanders anticipated, since mention of the Geya Postal Road disappears from Ming Chinese sources altogether for the next 150 years.

Finally, in recognition of the Guizhou Pacification Commission's service to the Ming cause in the southwest, Hongwu bestowed upon Aicui Longdi, Aicui and She Xiang's son and heir to the Guizhou Pacification Commission, the surname "An," which means "peace" in Chinese. From this point forward, Chinese texts referred to those individuals of the Azhe patriclan granted the title of Guizhou pacification commissioner by the surname An. Coincidentally, any mention of the Azhe patriclan as "spirit masters of the Luo kingdom" disappears from most Ming sources following She Xiang's visit to the Ming capital. (See Appendix C.)

Following the verdict against Ma Hua, the Ming state appeared to make an effort to attenuate hostilities between itself and the Azhe patriclan. Ming military units were redeployed away from the Guizhou garrison to areas closer to the Yunnan front. She Xiang was given permission to supervise construction of the city wall around Guizhou, even though the wall's specifications were still determined by Ming officials. Also, She Xiang and Liu Shuzhen were granted the privilege of leading several large "tribute missions" to the Ming capital, which they used to augment their own political and economic status in Guizhou. One myth that purports to explain the unusual frequency of these visits to the capital states that Hongwu had become infatuated with these two women and that he "enjoyed immensely their frequent visits." Whereas there is absolutely no proof to suggest that anything other than a patron-client relationship existed between Hongwu and She Xiang and Liu, it is clear that the Ming emperor and his wife interceded personally to prevent the Ma Hua–She Xiang incident from interfering with the Yunnan campaign, and that Hongwu remained in regular contact with She and Liu following this incident.

## Capturing Qian and Encircling Shuixi

In the autumn months of 1381, as the Ma Hua–She Xiang incident was unfolding, a Ming army of approximately 300,000 troops began making its way south through Hunan, Qian, and Sichuan, toward the Yunnan front.[25] Fu Youde and his two distinguished vice commanders, Lan Yu (d. 1393) and Mu Ying (1345–92), were ordered by Hongwu to lead the main strike force through Hunan and Qian to attack Yunnan.[26] As a diversionary tactic, Hongwu ordered a contingent of troops to separate from the main strike force at Guizhou and march west through Shuixi along the Geya Postal Road (as mentioned above). This strike force was ordered to attack a small Yuan outpost at Wusa (Weining) in the hopes that the Mongols would believe the main Ming army was attacking from Luzhou in southern Sichuan (this was the route Zhuge Liang's army took back in the third century, and one of Qubilai's three Mongol armies also marched south into Yunnan along this road). Hongwu's scheme worked. Mongol commanders deployed nearly 100,000 troops from the Yuezhou (Qujing) garrison to Wusa, which severely weakened their ability to resist the main Ming strike force coming from central Qian, just as Ming commanders anticipated.

On January 14, 1382, Fu trapped the Mongol prince Basalawarmi's force at the Baishi River near Yuezhou and reportedly slaughtered over 100,000 Yuan loyalists in a four-day orgy of violence that sickened even the most battle-hardened Ming soldier. In anticipation of the calamity to take place at the Baishi River, on January 6 Basalawarmi murdered his entire family and committed suicide. The Mongol army, leaderless and with their forces stretched precariously thin, offered little resistance as Ming troops advanced on the lightly defended city of Kunming. By April 9, Lan Yu and Mu Ying entered Dali at the head of a column of Ming soldiers that stretched for over 30 *li*, thus bringing an end to Mongol rule in Yunnan.[27] Hostilities in Yunnan did not end with the defeat of Basalawarmi and the capture of Kunming and Dali, however. Similar to the Mongol conquest of the southwest nearly a century earlier, an additional ten years of vigorous campaigning would be required before Ming officials announced an end to the anti-Ming resistance in Yunnan.[28]

Mongols, Central Eurasians, and indigenes loyal to Mongol rule, as well as locals who simply detested Han Chinese occupation, resisted the Ming with uncanny success. Hongwu was aware that his Yunnan campaign had become bogged down in guerrilla warfare, and he recalled Fu Youde and Lan Yu to the capital on April 1, 1384. Hongwu granted Mu Ying, his adopted son, a fief of 20,000 *mu* of land in Yunnan and ordered him to remain there to "pacify the rebellious barbarians." Fu was not away from Yunnan for long, though. In the early months of 1386, he was ordered back to Yunnan to help Mu suppress an outbreak of anti-Ming violence among the *wuman* in the Yuezhou-Dongchuan region of northeast Yunnan. It took Fu over three years to bring this part of northeast Yunnan under control, but he was unable to forge a lasting peace. Azi, the "barbarian bandit" (*manzei*) Fu supposedly captured then released in 1389, rebelled again in 1391, and then again in 1394, before Mu Ying's son, Mu Chun, captured Azi and had him beheaded.[29]

Mu Ying was also busy trying to contain the ambitions of the Shan leader Si Lunfa (d. 1399), who in the winter of 1385 led an army of over 200,000 soldiers from his base of Luchuan (near modern Tengchong in Yunnan) to attack Ming positions in western Yunnan. Si Lunfa's great-grandfather, Si Ke, had at one point received official recognition as a *tuguan* from the Mongols, but like many others before and after him he used this title to expand his political power at the expense of his less fortunate neighbors. Beginning in 1348, Si Ke's Luchuan forces engaged Mongol-Dali units in western Yunnan on a yearly basis. When Ming armies forced Basalawarmi to concentrate his energies on the advancing Ming armies from the east, Si Lunfa took advantage of the situation to attack Yunnan from the west. When Mu's soldiers occupied Dali in April 1382, Si deftly pledged allegiance to the Ming. He led a tribute mission to Nanjing in 1384, and in return Hongwu bestowed upon Si the title Luchuan pacification commissioner who pacifies Mian (*Luchuan ping Mian xuanwei shi si*). Si's loyalty to the Ming was short lived. In 1385 his Shan troops once again invaded western Yunnan, but this time he attacked Mu's army. This round of violence would last until 1389.[30]

The Yunnan campaign of 1381–82, and the subsequent decade-long anti-Ming violence, resulted in one of the most ambitious frontier conquest and colonization projects in Chinese history. Hongwu, by the time of his death in 1398, had authorized the construction of over forty garrisons (*wei*) in Qian (modern-day Guizhou province) and Yunnan (see Appendixes D and E). The majority of these garrisons were built along two main highways: the Guizhou-Huguang Postal Road (*Xiang-Qian yidao*), which began in the town of Changde in central Huguang and headed west through southwest Huguang and eastern Qian before ending in central Qian at the town of Guizhou. From here the road became known as the Guizhou-Yunnan Postal Road (*Dian-Qian yidao*) and ran west from Guizhou to Kunming and then on toward Dali in western Yunnan. Of the more than forty garrisons established at this time, two garrisons were located in the town of Guizhou, and an astonishing six garrisons were placed in Kunming.

Ming soldiers mobilized for the various military campaigns in Yunnan were furloughed near where they had fought and encouraged to become soldier-farmers. Conservative estimates place the total number of Han Chinese soldiers settled by the Ming state in Qian and Yunnan during the 1380s and 1390s at 250,000. However, because Hongwu wanted to populate the southwest with Han as quickly as possible, he ordered all demobilized soldiers to relocate their families to the southwest within one year of the time their demobilization orders took effect. If the soldier could prove that his father, mother, and siblings were no longer alive, which many soldiers apparently tried to do in order to spare their family an arduous life on a hostile frontier, then he was ordered to marry a local woman and start a family within one year of his demobilization. The unfortunate bachelors who could not find a wife were assigned one from the female criminal population. In all likelihood, during the 1380s and 1390s the Ming state probably relocated nearly one million Han Chinese to the southwest, and this was only the beginning of the Ming colonizing effort.[31]

To the east of Guiyang, along the Guizhou-Huguang Postal Road, the Ming military erected a series of eight garrisons. The four garrisons immediately east of Guiyang, Longli, Xintian, Pingyue, and Xinglong, were combined with two garrisons located along the Guizhou-Guangxi Postal Road (*Qian-Gui yidao*), the Qingping and Duyun garrisons, to form what was called the lower six garrisons (*xialiu wei*) in Qian. The remaining four garrisons along the Guizhou-Huguang route, Pianqiao, Zhenyuan, Pingxi, and Qinglang, were grouped together with two other garrisons, the Wukai and Tonggu, to form the eastern garrisons (*dong wei*). The Wukai and Tonggu garrisons, along with the Tianzhu battalion, oversaw the large and stubbornly independent Miao population of southeast Qian and ensured safe passage along a minor arterial linking western Huguang and eastern Qian with northern Guangxi and southeast China. In total, the Ming military settled approximately 40,000 soldiers and their families along a 300-kilometer stretch of the Guizhou-Huguang route.[32]

To the west of Guiyang the Ming military constructed six garrisons along the 250-kilometer portion of the Guizhou-Yunnan route. These garrisons, Weiqing, Pingba, Puding, Anzhuang, Annan, and Puan, formed what was called the upper six garrisons (*shangliu wei*) in Qian. The upper six garrisons were strategically important for several reasons. First, the westernmost garrison, Puan, was located a few kilometers east of the vital commercial town of Yushi, which was the heart of the Awangren patriclan's Ziqi kingdom during the Song. As the dominant patriclan in Yushi, the Awangren played a crucial role in anti-Ming resistance throughout the 1370s and 1380s, and even though the Ziqi kingdom had been "pacified" by the Ming in 1386, the Ming continued to view the town, its inhabitants, and surrounding population warily. For this reason the Ming stationed ten battalions in Puan, rather than the usual garrison compliment of five battalions. This meant that more than 100,000 Chinese (35,000 troops and their dependents) were settled along this small portion of the postal route by 1390. These Han colonists confiscated land formerly controlled by the Awangren and its vassals, which in turn guaranteed that hostility between the Han and the *na*, *quna*, and subordinate population would continue for years.[33]

The Annan and Anzhuang garrisons were located on either side of the Bei Pan River, the important trade route that had linked Chengdu and Annam ever since the Yelang kingdoms controlled this territory before the second century BCE. With the emergence of Yushi as an important trade center during the Tang dynasty, boats plying the Bei Pan River laden with goods from as far away as Chengdu and Annam were a

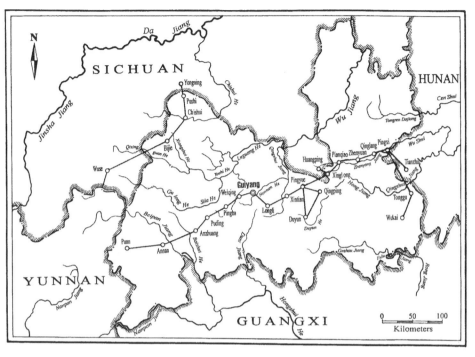

Map 5    The Guizhou garrisons and battalions (*weisuo*), ca. 1400

common sight. An important task assigned to these two garrisons was to supervise the flow of trade along the Bei Pan River. The Puding and Anzhuang garrisons were also responsible for maintaining control over the territory formerly known as the Luodian kingdom. The Bole patri-clan had ruled this area since the third century CE, and, like the Awang-ren, the Bole did not submit easily to Ming suzerainty. Pockets of resis-tance continued to harass Ming patrols well into the fifteenth century.[34] Finally, the presence of such a large concentration of Han troops and civilians along the Guizhou-Yunnan route created the first authentic boundary between Han-controlled territory and the Shuixi region to the north.

By 1391 the Ming military had twenty-five fully operational garri-sons in Qian. The final piece of the occupation plan, however, occurred in September with the creation of an additional garrison, the Guizhou Forward garrison (*Guizhou qianwei*) in the town of Guizhou (modern Guiyang). This second garrison in Guiyang fundamentally altered the

political landscape of the town and heightened tensions once again between the Ming military and the leaders of the Azhe and Song patriclans. Prior to 1391, Guiyang had been partitioned in half. The
Guizhou garrison established in 1371 occupied the southern portion of
the walled town, and the Guizhou Pacification Commission controlled
the northern half. When Ming officials announced the construction of
the forward garrison's headquarters in the western part of the walled
town, She Xiang, still the preeminent political figure within the Azhe
patriclan, returned to Shuixi, leaving a skeletal staff to manage the
pacification commission's affairs in Guiyang. She Xiang died a few years
later, probably disgusted by how she had been manipulated and deceived by the Ming.[35]

The Ming further antagonized the Azhe patriclan by building four
garrisons, Wusa, Bijie, Chishui, and Yongning, along the Sichuan-
Guizhou-Yunnan Postal Road (*Chuan-Qian-Dian yidao*), which was the
new Ming name for the old Qin imperial highway that ran south from
Luzhou into eastern Yunnan. These military installations, known as the
four western garrisons (*sixi wei*), helped to define the northern and
western boundaries of Shuixi, just as the upper six garrisons defined the
southern boundary of Shuixi-Azhe territory, and they completed the
Ming military's encirclement of Shuixi. The battalion strength of these
garrisons was far greater than the norm. For example, the Bijie garrison,
established in 1384, had seven battalions under its control, and the
Chishui garrison, built four years later, had eight battalions assigned to
it. The Pushi battalion was established between the Yongning and
Chishui garrisons solely to assist in ensuring safe transport along this
treacherous stretch of the postal route. The Ming permanently settled
nearly 26,000 soldiers along this stretch of the Sichuan-Guizhou-
Yunnan route. These soldiers and their dependents formed a demographic barrier along Shuixi's western periphery, and they exerted considerable influence over the Wumeng, Chele, and Mangbu patriclans in
the area.[36]

The Ming government linked the various garrisons and battalions
with an elaborate network of smaller postal relay stations (*yizhan*), outposts (*shao*), forts (*bao*), and relay stations (*pu*), so that a string of military units radiated out from each garrison unit. The postal relay stations
were to be constructed along the main arteries and staffed solely by
troops from the nearby guard command. Ideally, each station was no
further than 5 *li* (approximately 2.5 miles) from another station, and

each station cooperated with its surrounding stations to repair roads and ensure safe passage. By way of example, the Wukai garrison built seventy-two fortifications along the roads, trails, rivers, bridges, ferry crossings, mountain passes, and intersections within its area of jurisdiction.[37] These stations were responsible for transmitting documents from one guard command to another so they maintained a stable of horses for couriers and provided food and lodging for government travelers.[38]

This initial phase in the Ming military conquest of the southwest was a political-strategic necessity. Not only did Ming officials see Yunnan as a part of China to be recovered from the Mongols, but a large Mongol presence challenged in real and symbolic ways the political legitimacy of the Ming state. There were also two valid economic arguments motivating Ming expansion. First, Hongwu and his advisers understood that in order for reconstruction of the war-torn country to go forward, control of the rich mineral deposits in Yunnan was essential, and Ming officials moved quickly to seize and exploit the natural resources of the southwest. Second, "the central belief behind [Ming] state economic policy was that moderate taxation combined with vigorous agrarian expansion was the best method to increase revenues; in other words, expanding production rather than raising taxes was considered the best way to increase revenue."[39] This belief in the efficacy and practicality of Chinese classical economics was set during the Hongwu and Yongle reigns, as the Ming state promoted the use of state farms (*tuntian*), both civilian and military, to reclaim land in China proper and to colonize frontier territories like those that existed in the southwest. The southwest was a prime target for economic colonization.

The Yuan precedent was to station a multiethnic army of Mongols, Tibetans, Central Eurasians, Muslims, and Han Chinese in remote parts of the southwest and then to order the local population to provide for the Yuan troops. The early Ming emperors relied instead on Han soldiers and settlers to fill their military garrisons and state farms. By 1398 approximately 134,000 troops had been assigned to garrisons and battalions in Qian alone, and for many of these troops their family members accompanied them to their new posting. Ming soldiers and their relatives generally worked on military farms (*juntian*) adjacent to the battalion post, but the Ming state also encouraged Han settlers to clear and occupy land along the main transportation routes, which linked the separated military garrisons with Han settlements. Incentives such as free seed and tools, as well as tax-exempt status for three years, enticed

Han immigrants to accompany the Ming military into Qian and Yunnan. As a result, at the beginning of the fifteenth century there was nearly 1,000,000 *mu* of registered cultivated acreage listed on Qian military farms, and a little over 1,000,000 *mu* on Yunnan's military farms.[40]

Hongwu was impressed by the amount of cultivated acreage on military farms in Qian and Yunnan. Local officials, however, understood only too well that whereas some garrisons enjoyed near self-sufficiency, such as those established in and around Kunming, most garrisons had difficulty making ends meet. Ming soldiers assigned to the garrisons along the Sichuan-Guizhou-Yunnan route, for example, had trouble acclimating themselves to the harsh climate, and the rocky soil made growing familiar grains nearly impossible. The situation was exacerbated by the fact that prior to the Yunnan campaign of 1381–82, Ming officials were prohibited from taxing the indigenous population out of fear of inciting violence. Consequently, in the early stages of garrison construction, Ming troops and their dependents suffered terribly.[41] Hard-pressed garrison officials refused to abide by the nontaxation policy and turned instead to the local population for help.

For instance, as Ming forces marched south from Luzhou in 1382, Hongwu ordered Fu Youde to establish a garrison in the town of Wusa, named for the dominant Nasu Yi patriclan in the area. By 1384 the Ming increased its presence in the area in dramatic fashion when it posted seven battalions in and around the town of Bijie, which became the Bijie garrison. In a span of two years the Ming military permanently settled approximately 13,000 soldiers and several thousand dependents in an area intractably poor and devoid of cultivated land. The initial deployment of the Wusa and Bijie garrisons was so poorly coordinated that Ming troops repeatedly abandoned their posts due to food shortages and inadequate shelter. At the end of the first year the Bijie garrison commander estimated that he had lost nearly 3,000 troops to starvation, frostbite, and desertion.[42] In response to the deteriorating conditions, in the winter months of 1384 the garrison commanders jointly ordered the four recently recognized native prefectures (*tufu*) of Wusa, Wumeng, Dongchuan, and Mangbu to supply the garrisons with provisions, which they did begrudgingly.[43]

The Wusa patriclan provided the Wusa garrison with an annual "contribution" of 20,000 *shi* of grain and 1,500 fur pelts. The Wumeng, Gukuge, and Mangbu patriclans were each instructed to provide the Bijie garrison with an annual stipend of 8,000 *shi* of grain and 800 fur pelts.[44] Each native prefecture was also given salt, tea, and horse quotas it was obliged to present to the garrison commanders twice a year. On the Yunnan side of the Wumeng Mountains, Ming military commanders had levied on the *wuman* a silver tax known as *chaifa*, and the unfortunate Wumeng and Dongchuan native prefectures were ordered to pay an annual *chaifa* of 2,500 silver taels to the Yunnan authorities at the same time they supplied provisions to the Wusa and Bijie garrisons.[45]

Officials in Sichuan had actually set the precedent of taxing the indigenes two years earlier when, in 1382, they ordered the Bozhou Pacification Commission to provide 2,500 silver taels annually to the financially strapped Guizhou Garrison Command in Guiyang. In 1385, Huguang officials did the same by ordering the Sizhou and Sinan Pacification Commissions to present an annual payment of 2,500 silver taels each to the Guizhou Garrison Command. In 1387, only four years after Hongwu had demonstrated his "magnanimity" to She Xiang and Liu Shuzhen, court officials informed She Xiang during one of her "tribute missions" that the Guizhou Pacification Commission would be assessed an annual tax of 30,000 *shi* of grain, to be presented to the Guizhou garrison commander in monthly installments.[46] Ming colonization of the southwest, it appears, was based in part on a series of economic arguments that made perfect sense to the Ming court; however, instead of the southwest's economy helping China's economy recover from years of decline, it was the colonized who were funding the colonizers.

Another feature of the colonization project was the systematic conscription of indigenous soldiers to fight on behalf of the Ming state. Unlike labor corvée used to build and repair administrative offices, city walls, roads, bridges, and postal stations, military corvée was designed to exploit indigene forces to maintain public order, apprehend bandits and rebels, guard China against foreign invaders, and assist China when it invaded foreign territory.[47] As the previous discussion of Yuan occupation of the southwest pointed out, this type of military corvée was not an innovation particular to the Ming. Chinese states as far back as the Shang dynasty had incorporated indigenes into their armies. In the Yunnan campaigns of the 1380s and 1390s, Ming sources consistently referred to Ming armies operating in the southwest as joint Han-indigene (*Han-tu*) forces. Ming military commanders clearly admired the martial resolve of the indigene soldier, and a close examination of military records reveals Ming commanders often placed indigene troops at the forefront of their armies and utilized them at crucial tactical moments to shift the tide of a battle. The obvious advantage of this practice, at least from the Han perspective, was that the percentage of indigene troops killed in battle tended to be higher than the percentage of Han.

Unfortunately there are no reliable data regarding the number of indigene troops fighting in Yunnan, or what percentage of the Ming armies in Yunnan was composed of indigene soldiers; yet, data for Ming military expeditions in neighboring Guangxi in 1395 and 1406, as well as figures on the ethnic composition of Ming armies operating in southwest China during the fifteenth and sixteenth centuries, suggest that at least 50 percent of an active Ming army in the southwest was probably indigene in composition.[48] The Ming use of indigene troops will play an important role in the Ming invasion of Annam at the beginning of the fifteenth century, as well as in the creation of Guizhou province in 1413.

## Enclosing the Frontier: The Creation of Guizhou Province

The process of gaitu guiliu (replacing tusi with state-appointed officials) has been an integral feature of Chinese history since the formation of the earliest Chinese state in the third century BCE. Whenever the Chinese state annexed frontier territory and imposed its own personnel and governing institutions upon an indigenous frontier population, it was carrying out gaitu guiliu. For its part, the Ming state bestowed tuguan titles and offices on members of the indigenous frontier elite as it sought to win allies in the frontier, but in time as its presence in the frontier became more established the Ming government would replace these indigene-controlled frontier offices with Chinese political units, such as prefectures, departments, and counties. The Ming state's creation of Guizhou province in 1413 was one of the most spectacular examples of the Chinese state carrying out gaitu guiliu.

In 1560 Tian Rucheng (ca. 1500–1563), an official admired for his calligraphy and poetry, published a scathing critique of Ming rule of the southern frontier titled Yanjiao jiwen (A record of the southern frontier). Tucked away in one of the fourteen chapters Tian wrote to describe the "barbarians" (manyi) of the south is an examination of the convoluted history of the Tian family of Sizhou (Tian Rucheng was not related to the Tian of Sizhou).[49] According to the Yanjiao jiwen, the Tian family claimed to have settled in the Sizhou area of northwest

Qian during the Former Han dynasty, although the evidence supporting this claim was highly suspect.[50] It is likely that the Tian, if indeed they were Han Chinese, went to the Sizhou region during the waning years of the Tang, just as had Yang Duan, the patriarch of the Yang patriclan of Bozhou, in response to the Tang emperor's desperate appeal for Chinese assistance to fight the invading Nanzhao forces. In Chinese texts the first mention of the Tian of Sizhou occurs in 1107, when a native chief (*tuqiu*) named Tian Yougong submitted to Song rule; in 1118 he was named head of Sizhou prefecture.[51]

Throughout the Tang and Song dynasties the administrative seat of Sizhou prefecture was located near the present-day city of Wuchuan in northern Guizhou, yet the geopolitical jurisdiction of Sizhou extended far south, to the modern cities of Zhenyuan, Taijiang, and Cengong. To govern such a large territory, branches of the Tian clan were settled in strategic spots throughout the prefecture, in a manner similar to how the Nasu Yi patriclans settled territory. One of these strategic spots was the town of Anyi. Anyi was an important transportation hub for travelers making their way from China proper to the horse markets (Yushi and Bole) in western Qian. When Mongol forces entered Qian from Huguang in 1275, they received the surrender of Tian Jingxian, the political head of Anyi, before the head of the Tian patriclan in Sizhou prefecture capitulated.[52] As a reward for his submission, the Yuan state named Tian head of a newly formed Sizhou Pacification Commission and ordered the commission's headquarters to be built near the present-day city of Cengong. Tian Jingxian's actions naturally antagonized the main branch of the Tian patriclan, located in the old administrative seat of Sizhou, for they now found themselves politically subordinate, at least in the eyes of Yuan officials, to Tian Jingxian's branch.[53] Tian Jingxian took advantage of its initial contact with the advancing Mongol armies to surrender and negotiate with the Mongols for receipt of a political title before the main Tian branch in Sizhou could do so. His rise to political prominence initiated a cycle of violence within the Tian patriclan that would last, some contend, into the 1950s.[54]

The Yuan state, when it established the Sizhou Pacification Commission in 1275, decided to double the size of the former Sizhou prefecture in order to incorporate the many haltered-and bridled prefectures located far to the south of the new Sizhou (Cengong) headquarters. The geopolitical boundaries of the new Sizhou Pacification Commission stretched from the Sichuan-Guizhou border in the north to the

Guizhou-Guangxi boundary in the south, and from the Huguang-Guizhou border in the east to the Bozhou and Shunyuan Pacification Commissions in the west. Creating such an extensive political-military unit gave Tian Jingxian's branch tremendous political clout, which it used to further marginalize the main branch of the Tian patriclan. At the beginning of the fourteenth century the pacification commission was in charge of one prefecture (*fu*), fourteen departments (*zhou*), one county (*xian*), and fifty-two *tuguan* posts. Conversely, members of the main branch of the Tian patriclan now found themselves as mere caretakers of one lone department, the Sizhou department, in a large pacification commission dominated by a branch they considered inferior to their own.

The former main branch of the Tian patriclan, however, took advantage of the lengthy Yuan-Ming transition to try to reclaim its former political stature.[55] Near the end of Toghon Temur's (1320–70, r. 1333–68) long reign as the last Yuan emperor, Tian Maoan, head of the main branch of the Tian patriclan in Sizhou department, broke from the pro-Yuan Tian branch in Cengong and surrendered to Ming Yuzhen (1331–66), the leader of the rebellious Xia state (1357–71) in Sichuan.[56] In a historical pattern strikingly similar to what transpired in 1275, Ming rewarded Tian by creating an entirely new pacification commission, the Sinan Pacification Commission, and by naming Tian as its commissioner. In turn, the pacification commissioner of Sizhou, Tian Sheng, also surrendered to Ming. Since Tian Sheng surrendered after Tian Maoan, Ming determined that the Sinan office would be titled pacification commission (*xuanwei si*), whereas Tian Sheng would be granted the less prestigious title of pacification inspector (*xuanfu shi*). Such a minor distinction proved enormously significant.[57]

Shortly thereafter, Hongwu forced his way into the whirlwind of Sizhou and Sinan affairs. For reasons already discussed, Hongwu did not want to march through hostile Qian territory to reach the Mongols in Yunnan. Instead, he negotiated his way into Qian while skillfully convincing the leaders of Sizhou and Sinan, Tian Renhou and Tian Renzhi, respectively, to cease hostilities and swear allegiance to the Ming in the summer of 1365 (before the Ming dynasty was formally established in 1368). Once Tian Renhou and Tian Renzhi acquiesced, it was only a matter of time before Hongwu moved into central Qian to negotiate with the powerful Aicui.[58] Over the next forty years, relations between Sizhou and Sinan were relatively tranquil, despite the fact that in 1387 the Ming emperor ordered the Sinan Pacification Commission to relocate its administrative offices to the town of Zhenyuan, about 30 kilometers west of Cengong, the seat of the Sizhou Pacification Commission.

Even though a Ming garrison was not formally established in Zhenyuan until 1389, part of the rationale for doing so was to exert closer supervision over the recently relocated Sinan Pacification Commission. The Ming military evidently believed they could manage the Sizhou-Sinan situation by placing Sinan under their direct supervision in Zhenyuan. By 1390, the military occupation and colonization of eastern Qian was nearly complete with the creation of six garrisons: Wukai (1385), Tonggu (1388), Zhenyuan (1389), Pingxi (1390), Qinglang (1390), and Pianqiao (1390). In effect, the Ming military had placed approximately 30,000 Chinese troops in the immediate vicinity of the Sizhou Pacification Commission.

The brief interlude of peace and stability did not last long. The collapse of the Tran dynasty in Annam in 1400, and the emergence of the martial Ming emperor Yongle, intent on annexing Annam and making it a part of China proper, required a massive and sustained show of force. Troops from Sizhou and Sinan were pressed into service in the Annam campaign, as were Ming garrison soldiers from eastern Qian. Yongle's Annam debacle increasingly siphoned Han Chinese soldiers away from their peacekeeping duties in eastern Qian, thus providing Sizhou and Sinan the opportunity to resume hostilities, which they did.[59]

Although the history of the Tran dynasty in Annam is fascinating in its own right, it is far outside the boundaries of our present study. Suffice it to say that, in 1225, at approximately the same time the Mongols were beginning to march west into Central and West Asia, the powerful Tran family consolidated its hegemony over the Red River Valley of northern Vietnam and proclaimed the establishment of the Tran dynasty. The Red River Valley was an exceptionally prosperous region, and the Tran fully understood that the valley's wealth and natural resources cast a hypnotic spell that had lured traders and predatory foreign powers for centuries. For this reason the Tran invested heavily in its military. This investment paid off handsomely in 1257 as Tran troops successfully fended off Uriyangqadai's Mongol force from Yunnan, but this setback did not prevent Mongol armies and Han brigands from raiding Tran territory throughout the thirteenth and fourteenth centuries.[60]

With the founding of the Ming dynasty in 1368, Tran leaders quickly established relations with their invigorated neighbor to the north in hopes it would deal forcefully with the bandit armies that roamed into northern Annam from China. In 1369, Hongwu bestowed upon the Tran ruler the title king of Annam, and the Tran dutifully sent tribute missions to the Ming capital nearly every year. Ming-Tran relations evolved to the point that Hongwu in 1395, just three years before his death, issued an Ancestral Injunction forbidding future Ming emperors from invading Annam. Hongwu's injunction to his descendants was cast aside just eleven years later in 1406, when Ming armies raced into Annam intent on annexing the Red River Valley and making it an integral part of the expanding Ming empire.[61]

The Ming emperor at the time of the Annam invasion was Hongwu's fourth son, Zhu Di. In 1403 Zhu Di proclaimed himself the Yongle (Perpetual Happiness) emperor after having dethroned his nephew, the Jianwen emperor (1377–1402, r. 1399–1402), in a bloody four-year civil war. Yongle also learned in 1403 that a change in the leadership of Annam had occurred. In May of that year envoys from Annam arrived in the Ming capital requesting state recognition for the new king of Annam, Le Han-thu'o'ng (Ho De). Yongle was told that the preceding Tran king failed to produce a male heir, and that Le Han-thu'o'ng was the closest male relative to the deceased king. Yongle and his advisers readily accepted the veracity of the delegation's presentation and extended formal recognition to Le Han-thu'o'ng as the new king of Annam.[62]

Nonetheless, in October 1404 a haggard-looking man claiming to be a prince of the deposed Tran family reached Nanjing with a shocking story that few initially believed. The man, Tran Thien-binh, claimed that in 1400, as civil war raged in China, a ruthless court minister named Le Qui-ly (ca. 1335–1407) had overthrown the Tran king and murdered nearly the entire Tran family in a bloody purge lasting several weeks. Le Qui-ly then proclaimed himself king of Annam, changed his surname to Ho to reflect a new and enlightened beginning, and in 1402 abdicated in favor of his son Le Han-thu'o'ng in order to solidify his family's hold on power. Initially, Ming officials were very skeptical of Tran Thien-binh's tale of court intrigue and regicide, but when a tribute delegation from Annam reached Nanjing in 1405 a lengthy cross-examination of the envoys confirmed Tran's account. Yongle, incensed by what he had heard, ordered an armed escort of 5,000 men to accompany Tran back to Annam, where he was to be installed as the king of Annam. According to Yongle's instructions, Le Han-thu'o'ng, the present king of Annam, was to become a duke, and his father, Le Qui-ly, the cruel minister who had overthrown Tran rule and lied to Yongle, was to be banished from political life. But when the Ming entourage entered Tran territory, it was ambushed by Le's troops and annihilated.[63]

At this point Yongle felt he had no recourse but to disregard his father's Ancestral Injunction and invade Annam. The lies and deceit of Le Qui-ly had tarnished Yongle's stature and prestige as the emperor of Ming China, and the entire episode did nothing to quell lingering suspicions that Yongle was also a usurper, of the Ming throne. On May 11, 1406, Yongle ordered Zhu Neng (d. 1406), the duke of Chengguo, to begin preparations for the invasion of Annam. Yongle justified the invasion on the grounds that repeated forays by Annam forces into southern China threatened the country's security, a situation Hongwu's Ancestral Injunction had not anticipated. The fact that Annam forces were not invading China was unimportant. For Yongle, revenge in Annam was crucial in order to augment support in China. To assist Zhu Neng, Yongle ordered the veteran commander Chang Fu (1375–1449) to mobilize forces in Guangdong, Guangxi, and Huguang to attack Annam from the north. Meanwhile Mu Sheng (1368–1439), the son of Mu Ying and the commander of Ming forces in Yunnan, was ordered to attack Annam from the west. Troops from the Sizhou and Sinan pacification commissions marched into Annam with Chang's army while Aicui Longdi, the Guizhou pacification commissioner (Aicui and She Xiang's son, and also known as Ande), was ordered to contribute troops to Mu's force. Altogether, Yongle mobilized roughly 215,000 troops to invade Annam.[64]

Ming forces began the invasion in late October 1406. Zhu Neng, the commander in chief, died suddenly in November before entering Annam, so Yongle elevated Chang and Mu to joint command of the expedition. Resistance was stiff, as Yongle had expected, and it was almost eight months before Le Qui-ly and his son Le Han-thu'o'ng were captured by Ming troops and sent to Nanjing for execution. At this juncture, Yongle revealed his imperial ambitions. Instead of grooming a member of the Annam elite to rule the country, he decided instead to annex Annam and create a new Ming province, which he called Jiaozhi, after the old Han dynasty name for Annam. Within months of the conclusion of the Annam campaign, a major rebellion broke out among the indigenous populations in western Guangxi. Yongle ordered Chang to lead his battle-weary troops back north into Guangxi to quell the rebellion. Additional reserves from the garrisons and pacification commissions in Qian were also called up to fight in Guangxi, including troops from the Sizhou and Sinan pacification commissions. According to one source, the Ming mobilized nearly 600,000 troops to suppress the Guangxi rebellion.[65]

To make matters worse, in 1408 a former Tran dynasty official named Tran Nguy rebelled against the Ming annexation of Annam and proclaimed the establishment of the Dai Viet kingdom. Ming troops fighting in Guangxi were ordered back to Annam. Mu, having returned to the relative safety of Yunnan following the Annam campaign of 1406–7, was ordered to lead an army of 40,000 troops back to the Red River Valley to suppress Tran's rebellion. On January 9, 1409, Mu's army was ambushed by Tran's Dai Viet army and nearly routed. This forced Mu to return to Yunnan to raise yet another army to fight in Annam. When Yongle learned of Mu's defeat, he ordered Chang, now a much-decorated military commander following his "successes" in the Annam and Guangxi campaigns, to raise an army and return to Annam.[66] The overall effect of the Annam and Guangxi campaigns was to drastically weaken the Ming military presence in eastern Qian, and this in turn allowed Sizhou and Sinan free reign to resume their bloody feud.

Following the death of Sinan Pacification Commissioner Tian Daya in early 1410, the violence between the two branches of the Tian patri-clan began anew. When Tian Daya's son, Tian Zongding, inherited his father's title of pacification commissioner, the Sinan vice commis-sioner, a man named Huang Xi, secretly conspired with the Sizhou paci-fication commissioner, Tian Chen, to attack the Sinan headquarters at Zhenyuan. Tian Chen was aware that a large portion of the Zhenyuan garrison was either in Guangxi or Annam and that the Ming response to his attack on the Sinan headquarters would come at a later date, if at all. When Tian Zongding learned that a large force from Sizhou was ap-proaching the city, he fled north to Sinan, the original administrative seat of the pacification commission, and began to mobilize an army. He also notified the assistant commissioner in chief (*dudu jianshi*) for Gui-zhou, a man named Gu Cheng, who reportedly spent over twenty years in Guizhou "pacifying hundreds of Miao villages," that Tian Chen had attacked not the Sinan headquarters in Zhenyuan, but the Ming garri-son at Zhenyuan.[67] When Gu informed his superiors that the Zhenyuan garrison had been overrun, even though it had not, Yongle ordered Gu to organize a force of 50,000 to bring an end to the violence. The bulk of Ming forces in central Qian were already committed to Annam and

Guangxi, and so Gu was forced to rely almost exclusively on troops from the Guizhou Pacification Commission—the combined forces from the Azhe and Song patriclans.[68]

The campaign to suppress Sizhou and Sinan lasted more than a year, and when it was over much of the leadership in both branches of the Tian family had been killed. Yongle, convinced that his transformation of Annam into Jiaozhi province was nearly complete, decided to do the same in Qian by replacing the Sizhou and Sinan pacification commissions with Ming prefectures. In the second month of 1413, Sizhou and Sinan were each divided into four prefectures. Sizhou, Liping, Xinhua, and Shiqian prefectures were created out of the former Sizhou Pacification Commission, and the Sinan Pacification Commission was divided into Sinan, Tongren, Wuluo, and Zhenyuan prefectures. Ming officials were appointed as magistrates to the eight prefectures, but administrative units below the prefecture, such as departments, counties, and *tuguan* offices, were filled almost entirely by members of the indigenous elite.[69]

The Ming state also tapped the experienced official Jiang Tingzan to be the first Guizhou provincial administration commissioner. Jiang was ordered to set up the commission's headquarters in the newly renamed town of Guiyang (formerly Guizhou), which now became the provincial capital of Guizhou province. A regional military commission was also assigned to Guiyang at this time. The final component to the Ming "three bureaus" (*san si*), the provincial surveillance commission (*tixing ancha si*), was not formally authorized for Guizhou until 1417, but even then the circuits that formed the administrative infrastructure of a surveillance commissioner's responsibilities were not created until 1423.[70]

The creation of Guizhou province in 1413 was a formal announcement by the Ming state that it now claimed territorial sovereignty over all land within the political boundaries of Guizhou, despite the fact that the provincial government administered only eight small prefectures in the eastern third of the province. These eight prefectures, moreover, contained a multitude of differing jurisdictions, counties, departments, military installations, and *tuguan* domains. Ming officials governed these prefectures as best they could, but their real task was to supervise the indigenous elites who staffed the many *tuguan* offices scattered throughout the eight prefectures and to manage the potentially explosive relations between indigenes and Han Chinese settlers.

The other two-thirds of Guizhou province remained beyond the reach of the Ming state. The Azhe patriclan, who did the bulk of the fighting against the Sizhou and Sinan pacification commissions, still governed Shuixi through the traditional granary administration, the Yang family in Bozhou remained independent of government control, and the Song in Shuidong utilized a series of offices forged out of patron-client ties to govern their territory. Moreover, the various Nasu Yi kingdoms in western Guizhou, northeastern Yunnan, and southern Sichuan remained essentially intact, as did the nine kingdoms of the Bafan region in the central portion of southern Guizhou, despite the fact that Ma Hua had carried out *gaitu guiliu* in this region. In short, at the beginning of the fifteenth century Guizhou was a patchwork of different types of political jurisdictions. The Ming state claimed territorial sovereignty over the whole of Guizhou even though it was unable to directly govern much of the province. The indigenous elite recognized the military superiority of Ming China and for this reason accepted *tuguan* titles, if not Ming hegemony. If noticeable cracks in the Ming armor appeared, indigenous elites were quick to throw off the *tuguan* titles and reject Ming hegemony. In 1413, Ming territorial sovereignty over Guizhou was far from certain.

Much of what was discussed in this chapter, the Ming military expansion into the southwest, relations between the Ming throne and the Nasu Yi elite, and creation of Guizhou province, was carried out during the expansionistic pre–Tumu Incident phase in Ming history. Students of Ming history have recognized this period as a time of robust, expansive energy. The Yongle emperor continued his father's ambitious military endeavors by leading several military campaigns into the Central Eurasian steppe. He invaded northern Annam in an attempt to annex the region and create Jiaozhi province, and he used the invasion of Annam as a pretext to eliminate Sizhou and Sinan in Qian and create Guizhou province. Moreover, Yongle had entrusted the court eunuch from Yunnan, Zheng He (1371–1433), with building the largest and most technologically advanced naval fleet the world had ever seen and to sail this fleet to South Asia and Africa. Enthusiasm for such ambitious and costly activities vanished following the events of Tumu, if not before, and strategic concerns toward the Central Eurasian steppe shifted from offensive to defensive planning, as Waldron has demonstrated. In the southwest, however, the Ming government's aggressive colonization program continued unabated.

# 4

## The Periphery Within

Prior to the Yuan dynasty several expansive southwest polities, the Cuan, Nanzhao, Mu'ege, and Dali kingdoms, to name just a few, not only dominated the political landscape of the southwest but at times threatened the integrity of China's southern borders. In an attempt to stave off invasion and gain a measure of influence in the southwest, Chinese states frequently negotiated alliances with the indigenous frontier elite and bestowed upon them titles such as regional inspector, king or prince of a dependent kingdom, and magistrate of a haltered-and-bridled prefecture. Because these titles were either outdated or had little relationship to contemporary bureaucratic offices, China's political elite rarely considered the recipients of such titles to be full-fledged participants in China's bureaucracy. Acceptance of such a title, moreover, did not mean the indigenous elite had submitted to Chinese hegemony or was excessively influenced by Chinese politics. These elites still conducted their affairs much the way they had prior to receipt of Chinese titles, with a high degree of political autonomy. It was, in essence, a negotiated bilateral relationship based on need: the Chinese needed eyes and ears in a strategically important frontier, and the indigenous elite sought Chinese protection from hostile local enemies and access to Chinese goods and services, generally in the form of regular visits to Chinese markets.

Following the Mongol conquest of the southwest, the Yuan government relied extensively on the indigenous elite to rule the area. The Mongols were unfettered by Chinese political culture, institutional

norms, and administrative procedures in how they approached governance. Thus, unlike previous Chinese regimes, the Mongols routinely bestowed upon the indigenous elite contemporary titles, such as pacification commissioner, pacification inspector, military commissioner, and
suppression commissioner, which heretofore were offices granted by the
Song state to Chinese officials. Under Yuan rule the Mongols not only
bestowed contemporary political offices and titles that were equal in stature to what Chinese officials received but also created the Yunnan
Branch Secretariat, which clearly extended China's geopolitical jurisdiction to the heart of the southwest. Equally important, those members of
the indigenous elite who controlled smaller domains and who might
have been magistrates of haltered-and-bridled prefectures during the
Tang and Song periods were designated by the Yuan government as native officials (*tuguan*). The native official designations were seldom found
in China proper, and as such they were unique to China's frontiers.

This chapter will examine how the Ming state, following its initial
conquest and military occupation of the southwest, reversed many of
the trends established during the Yuan and once again differentiated
frontier offices and titles from Chinese offices and titles. The Ming government will link the pacification commissioner, pacification inspector,
military commissioner, and suppression commissioner with the distinc-
tive *tuguan* offices to form a single body of extrabureaucratic frontier offices, and it will situate these offices under a terminological and institutional rubric known as *tusi*.[1] In addition, the Ming government will
continue the trend first noticed in the Yuan and identify a *tusi* office
with a specific territory as part of its attempt to exercise systemic control over the indigenous frontier elite, and this notion of territory will
eventually supplant the earlier, pre-Ming concept of a personal relationship. The Ming will utilize *tusi* offices in its initial annexation and
colonization of the southwest territory and to aid in the subsequent
transition from rule by local collaborator (*tusi*) to rule by state-
appointed official.

In addition to examining *tusi* offices, this chapter will highlight
briefly the ongoing Ming military campaigns in the southwest and the
indigenous response to these campaigns. Instead of looking solely at the
Nasu Yi response to Ming colonialism, which is the subject of Chapter
5, this chapter will show that there was a general level of indigene hostility toward the Ming/Han Chinese presence in Guizhou. Throughout
the fifteenth and sixteenth centuries, Han immigrants settled in Guizhou

in large numbers, seized indigene lands and established settler communities, and compelled the Ming state to extend military protection to their communities. Finally, it is clear that very few mechanisms for incorporating indigenes into Ming society existed. If anything, the available evidence shows the non-Han were deprived of economic resources, as well as social and political status. If the Ming government hoped to "transform" or "turn" the indigenes toward civilization (to become like Han), then their policies had the opposite effect.

## Tusi *Offices: Dual Sovereignty*
## *in the Internal Frontier*

Even before the Ming dynasty was formally established in 1368, Hongwu confronted the thorny issue of how to incorporate into his expanding geopolitical jurisdiction the various Yuan offices used to manage frontier peoples. In 1363, for example, Zhu's army defeated the powerful Greater Han leader Chen Youliang (1320–63) in a decisive battle that brought much of Huguang and Jiangxi under Zhu's control. A sizable portion of Huguang was controlled by frontier leaders who had accepted Yuan suzerainty and had been reconfirmed as such by Chen prior to 1363; therefore, Zhu decided to continue using Yuan offices to govern the predominantly non-Han population of western Huguang. Not until the 1370s did Zhu (now the Hongwu emperor) begin to take a serious interest in the lingering Mongol presence in Yunnan, and one of his first acts was to order a thorough review of how his government might "turn the large number of non-Han officials with Yuan portfolio toward the Ming."[2]

Ming officials adopted the Yuan precedent of using the two-character term *tusi* to indicate those low-level Yuan offices in the southwest staffed primarily by non-Han. The character *tu* has the cognate meanings of indigenous, native, local, and earth, and as such the office prefixed with *tu* was considered a hereditary appointment staffed primarily (but not exclusively) with non-Han Chinese. The character *si* means administrative bureau. But unlike the Yuan, who considered such offices part of their normal bureaucracy, Ming officials quickly fashioned a terminology that labeled *tusi* as distinct from regularly appointed officials: *tusi* offices were located along China's geo-political periphery, *tusi* offices were filled almost exclusively by non-Han who were not trained in the Confucian Classics, nor had they successfully negotiated the laborious examination system, and *tusi* offices were responsible primarily for governing an alien, non-Han population. Furthermore, the Ming prefixed the offices of pacification commissioner, pacification inspector, military commissioner, and suppression commissioner with the character *tu* and, in so doing, relocated these offices outside the normal bureaucracy with the native officials.

When Ming officials reconfirmed a *tusi* to his original Yuan post, they classified the recipient as either a civilian-rank *tusi* or a military-rank *tusi*.[3] Generally speaking, the civilian-rank *tusi*'s domain was located within a recognized provincial boundary. The size of the frontier leader's territory and the number of people living under his/her authority determined whether the *tusi* title was issued as a native prefecture magistrate (*tu zhifu*), native department magistrate (*tu zhizhou*), or native county magistrate (*tu zhixian*), and as the titles suggest these offices mirrored the Ming civilian administration.[4] Civilian-rank *tusi* were usually formed in areas where the economic infrastructure—cultivated land—was productive enough to support a bureaucratic staff, and where Han immigrants had already established a sizable presence. In addition, the civilian-rank *tusi* was obliged to register the population under his/her control and report the total number of households to his/her superiors in the provincial bureaucracy. Census figures were used along with information on the amount of cultivated land and land productivity to determine land and labor taxes owed to the Ming state. Finally, because of the presence of Han Chinese settlers and the inevitable disputes involving land ownership, the civilian-rank *tusi* often adjudicated legal disputes based on Ming law, not solely on the customary practices of the indigene society.[5] The civilian-rank *tusi* offices were truly cross-cultural governing institutions, for they were designed to allow a much greater Chinese presence in the day-to-day supervision of the non-Han population than did the previous haltered-and-bridled prefecture offices.

For example, Ming officials borrowed the Yuan model of using a *darughachi* to share in the management of an administrative unit when they added the office of head constable (*limu*) to the executive staff of each civilian-rank *tusi*. The purpose of the head constable office was to oversee the *tusi*'s political affairs. It was the head constable who introduced Ming law to the non-Han population and adjudicated disputes between non-Han and Han; it was the head constable who registered the population and determined the *tusi*'s tax quotas; and it was the head constable who reported directly to provincial officials, often bypassing the *tusi* office altogether. The head constable post carried considerable influence in areas where the non-Han and Han populations were in continual contact, and in time these posts were highly coveted by local Han Chinese who had passed the lowest rungs of the examination ladder but were unsuccessful in advancing further.[6] The "law of avoidance" did not apply to the head constable office.

Ming bureaucratic oversight of civilian-rank *tusi* is rather difficult to sort out, and responsibility for managing *tusi* changed often. From 1397 to 1530, all civilian-rank *tusi* were subordinate to the regional military commander (*du zhihui si*), which placed them under the authority of the Ministry of War (Bingbu). The ability of the Ministry of War to effectively manage the civilian-rank *tusi* became strained as the Ming annexed new frontier territory and created a number of *tusi* posts; thus, in 1530 jurisdiction over civilian-rank *tusi* was transferred to the provincial administration commissioner (*buzheng si*)—the head civilian authority in the Ming provincial government. From 1530 until the end of the Ming dynasty, in 1644, civilian-rank *tusi* remained under the control of the provincial administration commission, which in turn was directed in its management of *tusi* offices by the Bureau of Honors (Yanfeng si) in the central government's Ministry of Personnel (Libu).[7] Within geopolitically defined China proper, the Ming state relied upon civilian-rank *tusi* offices to govern areas that were settled predominately by non-Han Chinese peoples.

Conversely, military-rank *tusi* enjoyed a higher degree of autonomy from the Ming state than did civilian-rank *tusi*. Indigenous non-Han leaders who were granted this title usually controlled lands that either were outside China's provincial boundaries or were located in remote internal frontiers within a province, such as the Shuixi region of northwest Guizhou, the Bozhou region of northern Guizhou, and the Luoluosi region of northern Yunnan and southern Sichuan. Military-rank *tusi* pledged allegiance to the Ming throne, swore to defend China's borders from hostile foreign powers, and agreed to present tribute to the throne. But because they were located beyond the administrative reach of the Ming state, they were allowed to rule their domains in accordance with their own laws and customs. Military-rank *tusi* were not obligated to conduct a census, nor were they required to pay land and labor taxes to the Ming state at the time of appointment; however, they were required to register their cultivated land and describe briefly the geopolitical boundaries of their territory. The military-rank *tusi* resembled the old haltered-and-bridled prefecture posts of Tang and Song times, since they were theoretically subordinate to the Ming throne but politically and legally independent of the Ming state.[8]

The titles of military-rank *tusi* ranged from the lofty pacification commissioner and pacification inspection commissioner to such mid-level posts as military commissioner and suppression commissioner, to the lowest office of native official (*zhangguan shi*). Initially the office of pacification commissioner was not associated with military affairs, but during the Yuan dynasty the Mongols expanded its scope to include broad civil and military powers. During the Song dynasty the office of pacification inspector was charged with overseeing the military affairs for an area usually no larger than two prefectures in size, but under Mongol rule this post came to possess extensive civil and military authority over large tracts of land. In Tang China the office of military commissioner was first used as a provincial-level military assignment, but it, too, was transformed during the Yuan to include civil authority. The office of suppression commissioner originated during the Song as a high-ranking military office, and under Mongol control it became a relatively minor frontier post subordinate to both the pacification commissioner and pacification inspector.[9] In short, the Ming government transferred these Yuan offices, many of which possessed broad civil and military authority under Yuan rule, into strictly frontier offices under the supervision of the Ministry of War and, in so doing, eliminated an important civil feature of the original Yuan office.

The Ming state, throughout its 276-year history, conferred 1,608 *tusi* titles: 960 were military-rank *tusi* titles and 648 were civilian-rank *tusi* titles. In the three southwest provinces of Yunnan, Guizhou, and Sichuan alone, the state bestowed 1,021 *tusi* titles, or 63 percent of all *tusi* titles issued during the Ming. Of this total, 69 percent were classi-fied as military-rank *tusi*. In Sichuan, 95 percent of the 343 *tusi* titles is-sued by the Ming state were military-rank *tusi*; in Guizhou, 83 percent of the 244 *tusi* titles were military-rank *tusi*; and in Yunnan, 41 percent of the 434 *tusi* titles were military-rank *tusi*. In contrast, of the 337 *tusi* titles issued for Guangxi province during the Ming, 309, or 92 percent, were civilian-rank *tusi*. As mentioned above, the determination whether to issue a civilian or military *tusi* title was based largely on geo-political proximity to China proper, the presence of Han communities, and the potential for economic exploitation of the natural environ-ment. The preponderance of civilian-rank *tusi* in Guangxi and Yunnan, in contrast to Guizhou and Sichuan, reflects the application of this political calculus.[10]

In general there were two ways in which a *tusi* office was established in the Ming. First, during the initial period of military consolidation Ming officials convinced Yuan *tusi* to side with the Ming and in the process reconfirmed *tusi* status. Second, when the Ming government eliminated powerful *tusi* posts, such as the Sizhou and Sinan pacification commissions in 1413, it created several smaller *tusi* offices in its wake, which increased the overall number of *tusi* offices in the area but significantly weakened non-Han resistance to Ming rule—to conquer and divide. This latter policy was particularly effective during the Ming. In fact, by the end of the Ming dynasty, in 1644, the total number of *tusi* posts in the southwest was greater than what Ming officials cataloged at the beginning of the dynasty in 1368, though the total amount of territory under *tusi* control was less in 1644 than in 1368. The Ming state and Han society had continually expanded into the southwest and annexed frontier territory, and in doing so the largest *tusi* domains, the pacification commissions, pacification inspector commissions, and military commissions, were replaced by smaller *tusi* posts, native offices and barbarian native offices.[11]

When the Ming state conferred *tusi* title and office, it authenticated its recognition by issuing a certificate of appointment, a seal, a cap and sash (*guandai*), a tally (*fu*), and a tablet (*pai*). In 1394 it was ordered that high-ranking *tusi* between the ranks of 3b and 5b receive the prestigious *gaoming* imperial patent, whereas lower-ranking *tusi* (between 6a and 9b) received a *chiming* imperial patent (see Appendixes F and G). These patents contained the name of the individual on whom was bestowed this title, the title and rank of the *tusi* post, a brief passage indicating the hereditary nature of the *tusi* title and office, and a brief description of the geopolitical location of the *tusi* domain (the geographic descriptions of *tusi* territory became more precise and elaborate by the middle of the fifteenth century). Most patents contained language indicating the Ming would provide military assistance to the *tusi* if his/her authority were ever challenged. The Ming, so that its support for the *tusi* was clear, required the written script used by the non-Han people in question, if one existed, be engraved next to the Chinese characters on the imperial patent, and that all documents sent to the *tusi* be in duplicate form: one document in Chinese and one in the local script.[12]

The seal was another powerful symbol of imperial recognition, and *tusi* used the imperial seal to authenticate imperial orders, to promulgate law in the name of the Ming throne, and to mobilize men and material for military operations. The seal was particularly important when *tusi* had to conduct business with Ming officials and Han Chinese for it conferred political status that might otherwise not exist. The *tusi's* orders were valid only if stamped with the seal granted him/her by the Ming state, and again the seal was engraved with the local script. Unlike most Ming officials, who received seals made of silver, *tusi* were given bronze seals, though the size and thickness of the seals differed depending on the rank of the *tusi*—larger and thicker seals were given to high-ranking *tusi* such as pacification commissioners and pacification inspectors.[13]

In addition to a cap and sash, which were important status markers for a *tusi*, the *tusi* received a tally and tablet as part of the Ming imperial communication system. The tally would instruct the *tusi* to carry out a specific task, such as patrol a portion of the frontier, guard a major transportation route, and suppress bandits, and the *tusi* could then use the imperial tally to requisition men and material on behalf of the emperor. The tally became a particularly divisive item because Ming officials often found themselves in confrontation with *tusi* who repeatedly used the tally to requisition men and material for operations not specifically identified by the tally.[14]

Unlike regular Ming offices, *tusi* offices were hereditary, and the Ming state drafted rigorous guidelines to ensure a member of the deceased *tusi's* family would inherit the *tusi* office and title. The intent of the inheritance regulations was to guarantee a stable and orderly transition. According to Ming law the deceased *tusi's* eldest son was first in line to inherit the *tusi* post; but, if the deceased *tusi* failed to produce a male heir, then his younger brother was authorized to inherit the post. If there were no surviving sons and brothers, then the deceased *tusi's* uncle or nephew was expected to inherit the post. If all available male heirs were considered unsatisfactory, then the *tusi's* wife, daughter, and daughter-in-law were deemed acceptable, but this option was clearly a last resort.

The Chinese scenario for an orderly succession, however, ran counter to the inheritance customs and practices of many of the non-Han peoples who occupied *tusi* offices, and the ability to enforce these inheritance regulations was dependent in large measure on the proximity of Ming officials to *tusi* and their willingness to get involved in *tusi* affairs. In Guangxi, for example, where a sizable percentage of *tusi* were civilian-rank *tusi*, Ming officials were better able to enforce adherence to its inheritance regulations than, say, in Guizhou and Sichuan, where the majority of *tusi* were military-rank *tusi*. In Guizhou there are examples of virtually every possible relative inheriting the military-rank *tusi* post: son, younger brother, uncle, nephew, cousin, wife, concubine, daughter, and daughter-in-law.[15]

In order to prevent the possibility of someone fraudulently passing him/herself off as the deceased *tusi*'s heir, the Ming state ordered *tusi* to present to provincial authorities a genealogical chart listing his/her entire family. To achieve a sense of thoroughness, this genealogical chart included not just a comprehensive history of the *tusi*'s family, but also the *tusi*'s principal wife, his consorts and concubines, and all his children (male and female) from these relationships. In the management of civilian-rank *tusi*, the Ming government even decided in 1394 that an official from the Ministry of Personnel's Bureau of Honors be dispatched to the *tusi*'s domain to enforce compliance with Ming inheritance procedures. This proved to be an entirely impractical and unenforceable regulation, and rarely were officials from the Bureau of Honors sent to *tusi* domains.[16] Nevertheless, an activist precedent among Ming officials was established by this 1394 decree. It embodied the intent of Hongwu and as such formed the basis for later intrusive measures pertaining to *tusi* inheritance procedures.

For instance, in 1436, local officials—prefecture, department, and county magistrates—were ordered to collect documentation needed to determine the *tusi*'s rightful heir, and to personally interview the *tusi* and his/her designated heir. The documentation most often noted in Ming sources was the *tusi* family's genealogical chart, which not only traced the history of the *tusi* family and its relations with the Ming, but also identified by name the individuals authorized to inherit the *tusi* post. Ming officials were to refer to this genealogical chart when they supervised the inheritance process. A few years later, in 1442, the Ming state required the name of the person designated to inherit the *tusi* post be written down in four separate texts, with one copy each going to the three province-level authorities, the provincial administration commissioner, the provincial surveillance commissioner, and the regional military commander, and the final copy deposited in the archives of the Bureau of Honors. According to this regulation, local officials were to review the inheritance document with the *tusi* every three years.[17]

One additional attempt to extend Ming control over *tusi* inheritance practices occurred in 1459 when it was decided that upon the death of a *tusi* the supervising provincial agency was to appoint an official to determine who should inherit the *tusi* post. This local official was to compile written reports from magistrates located in neighboring prefectures, departments, and counties, who were themselves required to report on their dealings with the deceased *tusi*'s family; he was to examine the *tusi* family's genealogical chart for errors; and finally he was to interview the *tusi*'s surviving family members to guarantee accuracy of the genealogical chart. Provincial officials were allowed no more than six months to complete this review, after which they submitted to provincial officials their recommendation on who should inherit the *tusi* post.[18] With this decree Ming officials exercised more authority over *tusi* affairs than had their Yuan predecessors, and this bureaucratic authority undermined the traditional patron-client features of the *tusi* office.

The stated intent of Ming *tusi* inheritance regulations was to minimize the potential for violence in the naming of a new *tusi*. Understandably, the *tusi*'s family could be quite large, with each uncle, younger brother, son, and daughter the focus of a powerful family/faction, and the death of a *tusi* could easily trigger a struggle among branches of the *tusi*'s family. If the *tusi*'s family negotiated marriage alliances with powerful local families, which they most certainly did, then the death of a *tusi* might lead to open warfare as powerful families and factions used kinship ties to the deceased *tusi* to stake a claim to the *tusi* post. Given the attention Ming officials paid to the *tusi* succession process, one might expect to encounter countless examples of such violence in Ming sources. Surprisingly, this is not the case. Only when officials discussed how best to manage *tusi* did they mention the "inevitability" of violence in the succession process, though concrete examples of such violence are curiously absent from their descriptions. The use of "violence" as a code word to justify juridical and bureaucratic activism can best be seen in a 1540 edict outlining two measures to limit the geographic scope and ethnic features of the violence associated with the *tusi* inheritance process. First, it was stipulated that when a *tusi* married, s/he could only marry another individual living within the boundaries of the *tusi*'s domain, not someone from outside the *tusi*'s jurisdiction;

second, any *tusi* marriage must take place among people of the same ethnic group (*tonglei*).[19]

As Ming forces advanced into the southwest during the last decades of the fourteenth century there was near unanimity between civilian and military officials that military conquest alone would not bring peace and stability to this frontier. History had demonstrated that brute force begets resistance, and the Hongwu emperor said as much in a 1392 edict:

The barbarians [*manlao*] are widely scattered and are unacquainted with propriety [*liyi*]. If we are lenient with them, they will obey us, but if we impose ourselves upon them, they will rebel. Now that we have stationed our soldiers at strategic points, it is just a matter of time before the barbarians become civilized, and we begin to view them as loyal subjects.[20]

Toward this end, when the Ming government decreed all *tusi* to identify potential heirs in 1385, it also stipulated that they receive a Chinese education. The law stated that if the designated individual failed to receive an appropriate Chinese education by a qualified instructor, the Ming state could refuse to recognize that person as the rightful heir. It never stipulated the extent of the Chinese education or qualifying level of education to be attained, nor did it establish a definable benchmark by which to judge the student's capability. Instead, the intent of this decree was to introduce basic spoken Chinese to *tusi* and their immediate male offspring. Ming civilian officials often complained of having to rely on "unsavory Han" to communicate with *tusi*, and Ming military commanders blamed battlefield setbacks on the inability of native troops (*tubing*) to understand their orders accurately. Proposing that the heir to the *tusi* post be introduced to Chinese seemed prudent and practical given the Ming military's presence in the southwest. Expecting *tusi* to receive the type of education that might earn them a job in the Ming bureaucracy was not the intent of the decree (*tusi* and their heirs were prohibited from Ming bureaucratic appointment).

In the same year the Ministry of Rites ordered all children of *tusi* to be granted preferential treatment in entering the country's highest academic institution, the National College (*guozi jian*). This was a significant change from the earlier practice of extending imperial favor (*te'en*) to only the *tusi*'s designated heir to enter the National College. As a result, several hundred students from *tusi* domains did enroll in the National College, but the enormity of covering travel costs, room and board, and educational fees, not to mention the logistics of handling such an ethnically diverse student population, compelled the Ming government to decree in 1396 that Ming officials in Yunnan and Sichuan begin construction of Confucian schools in order to retain *tusi* students in their home provinces. Interestingly, part of the rationale for curtailing *tusi* access to the National College was concern over the demonstrated inability of many non-Han students to master the Chinese language, and the decree specifically mentioned the need "to overcome the language barrier between teacher and student [in these provincial schools] by hiring bilingual teachers" for *tusi* students.[21]

Although Chinese schools had been built in a few of the largest *tusi* domains by 1396, we possess very little reliable information on the construction of schools in the southwest following the edict of 1396.[22] If anything the evidence tells us that Ming officials in Yunnan, Guizhou, and Sichuan were consumed with issues considerably more pressing than building schools, and when they did build schools these were built in urban areas populated by Han Chinese. There were no restrictions preventing *tusi* from sending their children to these schools, and there are ample sources indicating students from *tusi* domains did attend such schools, but their numbers were never very large. Ming officials established schools for Han students, that much is clear, and these schools attracted only a handful of students from *tusi* domains.[23]

Superficial decrees requiring the children of *tusi* to enroll in Chinese schools did not have the desired effect of "transforming the barbarian into Han." By the middle of the fifteenth century Ming officials in Guizhou complained about the unwillingness of *tusi* students to learn Chinese, and they all but confirm the presence of a two-track education system: one for Han students hoping to enter the examination process, and one for the non-Han students from *tusi* domains who "come to school because they are required to."[24] In 1482, Deng Tingzan, magistrate of Chengfan prefecture in Guizhou, acknowledged students from *tusi* domains had attended the prefecture's school ever since its establishment in the Hongwu reign, yet their inability to speak and read Chinese hindered their understanding of the curriculum. He pointed out that because *tusi* students were prohibited from taking the triennial examinations, there was very little incentive for them to study hard and perform well in school. "They [*tusi* students] are not just apathetic about attending school, they are at times hostile."[25] Deng recommended *tusi* students be separated from Han students and placed in remedial language classes with an abridged curriculum. We possess no direct information indicating whether Deng's recommendations were influential during his day, though officials stationed in Guizhou during the middle of the sixteenth century often referred back to Deng's "wise and prudent proposals for educating barbarians."[26]

For example, in 1546 Guizhou Assistant Education Intendant Xu Yueyi relied upon Deng's earlier suggestions to call for an overhaul of Guizhou's education system. Xu proposed a community school (*shexue*) be established in every subcounty unit, such as townships (*xiang*) and communities (*li*), so that the non-Han population could be exposed to a Confucian education without delaying the educational development of the Han students—in fact, it was the educational development of the Han students that most concerned Xu, not the education or cultural transformation of the "barbarians."[27] To make this point, Xu proposed *tusi* be required to fund the construction and maintenance of such schools and to guarantee room, board, and salary for the instructors. Xu argued quite eloquently that his proposal would bring about the rapid "transformation of the barbarian into civilized Han," and it would not cost the state an ounce of silver. Xu's cost-benefit calculus was appealing, though impractical. He knew as well as any Ming official in Guizhou that the vast majority of *tusi* neither possessed the capital needed to build and maintain a school nor had ever exhibited a desire to bring Chinese education to their domains. The intent of Xu's proposal was to restrict non-Han students from attending schools built by Han Chinese for Han Chinese.

Nonetheless, a short time later the Jiajing emperor (r. 1522–66) issued a decree ordering all administrative units in the southwest, including *tusi* domains, to build a community school. As Xu did in his proposal, Jiajing expected each unit to finance the entire cost of the community school. Moreover, Jiajing anticipated that the schools would have a "great transformative impact" in *tusi* domains because all male children residing in *tusi* domains were to attend them. Within seven years of Jiajing's imperial order Guizhou officials boasted that fifty-one community schools were in operation in the province, even though all but two of the schools were established in prefectures, departments, counties, and garrison headquarters populated exclusively by Han Chinese.[28] In fact, all but seven of the fifty-one schools had been built before Jiajing's decree, and these were simply reclassified as community schools in accordance with the emperor's demands. Only one school was built on a *tusi* domain. The emperor's pious decree fell on deaf ears because the state refused to provide its local officials with any tangible financial assistance to build schools, and because it refused to allow barbarians to take the triennial examinations. From the Jiajing reign on, every Ming and Qing emperor issued the same decree commanding schools be built in every local jurisdiction in the southwest (or throughout the country for that matter) in order to "bring a civilizing influence to the common people." That the decree was repeatedly issued indicates, if nothing else, that the spirit and reality of the decree remained unfulfilled.

The financial drain of building and maintaining a school was the most common explanation given for why *tusi* failed to carry out the emperor's directive, but historical records offer two other plausible reasons. First, non-Han societies were by and large hostile toward Chinese institutions on their territory, and the non-Han peoples in the southwest were unconvinced of the efficacy of a Chinese education. Chinese schools were rightly perceived to be a direct assault against indigene traditions, and Ming officials admit as much. Second, Ming officials were generally unwilling to assert the coercive force needed to get *tusi* and indigene society to finance the construction of a Chinese school. Ming officials often faced passive resistance in their dealings with *tusi*, but an intrusive demand like school construction could (and often did) incite a hostile response. The benefit of pushing an indigene society to build a community school was simply not worth the risk.

The Ming state's attempt to incorporate a Confucian curriculum into regulations governing *tusi* offices was symptomatic of a larger intent to extend its political influence into heretofore autonomous and semi-autonomous areas. The Yuan precedent of granting *tusi* titles to members of the non-Han elite provided Ming officials with the blueprint they needed to impose Ming hegemony over the peoples of the southwest frontier. The Ming continued to regard *tusi* offices as a part of the official Ming bureaucracy, but, unlike the Yuan, the Ming state marginalized *tusi* offices into an extrabureaucratic category of exclusively frontier offices. The Ming also expanded the scope of the *tusi* title to include such high-ranking Yuan offices as pacification commissioner, pacification inspector, and military commissioner.

Strict and increasingly detailed inheritance regulations were used to determine *tusi* succession, and enforcement of such regulations mitigated local customary practices and in many cases undermined the integrity of non-Han institutions. The Ming state demanded *tusi* identify their geopolitical jurisdiction, and this in turn facilitated the territorialization of the *tusi* office. The *tusi* office came to be viewed by Ming officials as representative of territory, not of an individual, as it had been during the Yuan dynasty. Finally, the introduction of a culture-based Confucian education system into regulations governing *tusi* inheritance procedures had the effect of easing the psychological distinctions separating Ming (Han Chinese) officials and *tusi* (non-Han elite), even though *tusi* rarely built schools in their domains and non-Han were prohibited from participating in the Ming examination system. The Ming established its hegemony over the southwest by virtue of its military occupation of the region, and it indirectly controlled the non-Han through *tusi* offices. Like the Tang, Song, and Yuan dynasties before it, the Ming negotiated with influential indigenous non-Han leaders to establish *tusi* offices; but unlike these earlier dynasties the Ming asserted greater authority over the *tusi* office and those who filled it. At its core the Ming *tusi* office embodied the notion of dual sovereignty. Ming officials knew this, and the more activist among them strove to end this unique duality in the frontier.

## The Long Fifteenth Century

The Ming occupation of the southwest frontier during the Hongwu reign was the initial salvo, the first in a series of uninterrupted military campaigns that overwhelmed the region during the fifteenth century. When the third Ming emperor, Yongle, eliminated the Sizhou and Sinan pacification commissions and created Guizhou province in 1413, he ushered in a second wave of involuntary troop settlement and dispatched a coterie of civilian officials enthusiastic about making their mark in this remote hinterland. Many believed it was only a matter of time before the internal frontier of Guizhou disappeared, as had countless other frontiers throughout Chinese history. *Tusi* offices represented a transition phase between independence and Ming rule, between military annexation and civilian rule, and the sooner *tusi* offices lost their political value the better it would be for Han and non-Han alike.[29] The cultural divide separating non-Han and Han (the social frontier) could only recede if more Han Chinese settled in the province and "lifted the barbarians toward civilization," and this could happen only when the government replaced *tusi* with state-appointed officials (*gaitu guiliu*).

According to the *New Illustrated Gazetteer of Guizhou Province* (1502), the earliest authoritative Guizhou gazetteer, there were three political divisions in Guizhou at the end of the fifteenth century. First, the provincial administration commission claimed jurisdiction over nine prefectures (*fu*) and four departments (*zhou*). The nine prefectures were located in the eastern half of the province in territory formerly part of the Sizhou and Sinan pacification commissions, and the four departments straddled the main highway between Guiyang and the Guizhou-Yunnan border. Each department was situated next to one of the military garrisons established in western Guizhou in the 1380s.[30] Second, the regional military commander oversaw twenty-four military garrisons, all of which were established during the Hongwu reign. And finally, the gazetteer noted the semi-independent status of the Guizhou and Bozhou pacification commissions, the two largest *tusi* offices in the province, along with approximately 250 smaller *tusi* domains scattered throughout the province.[31]

Wang Zou, the editor of the *New Illustrated Gazetteer*, lamented the fact that during the fifteenth century only one new prefecture had been established in Guizhou, and conversely the number of *tusi* offices had increased threefold. Ming civilian rule had not come to Guizhou after 1413, as Ming officials had promised. Instead, Wang noted, central and western Guizhou were still dominated by the Guizhou and Bozhou pacification commissions, and if not by them then by a host of *tusi* whose allegiance to the Ming throne Wang considered questionable. But, Wang was quick to caution his readers against thinking that not much had happened in Guizhou since 1413. "Blood has been spilt on virtually every inch of Qian [since 1413]. Violence has become a way of life here."[32] It is this violence that jumps out from the pages of the *New Illustrated Gazetteer* and other writings on fifteenth-century Guizhou.

In 1413, the same year Guizhou province was created, Thonganbwa (d. 1445), a charismatic figure who resisted the Ming military presence in western Yunnan, seized control of the state of Luchuan and launched a series of attacks on Ming military installations in western Yunnan. Repeated requests from Ming officials in Yunnan for authorization to challenge Thonganbwa fell on deaf ears at the Ming court. But in 1439, as Luchuan forces threatened the city of Jinchi, the governor of Yunnan, Mu Sheng, finally received permission to mobilize troops from Yunnan, Sichuan, Guizhou, and Huguang to suppress Thonganbwa. Mu's campaign against Thonganbwa proved to be as disastrous as his campaign into the Red River Valley of northern Annam in 1409, and in the following year the Ming court gave Wang Ji (1378–1460) the title "general who pacifies the barbarians" (*pingman jiangjun*) and placed him in charge of the campaign against Thonganbwa.[33]

Wang remained in Yunnan until 1449, first fighting Thonganbwa, and then Thonganbwa's son, Si Jifa. By the time Wang completed his assignment, central Yunnan was fully integrated into the Ming civilian polity, at least on paper and in Ming maps: officials aggressively carried out *gaitu guiliu* and reduced the number of *tusi* offices in the Lake Dian region to just a handful. Though much of the fighting occurred in western Yunnan, Ming forces repeatedly marched through Guizhou to get to the Yunnan front, and soldiers from the garrisons in Guizhou were pressed into military service in Yunnan. By 1446, well before Wang claimed victory over Si, many of the garrisons in Guizhou were without men and material, and "defenses for most garrisons are in the hands of women and children."[34] When it became evident the garrisons in Guizhou had been depleted of men and material, the burden of prosecuting the Luchuan campaign fell disproportionately on Guizhou's *tusi* and their indigene troops.

Powerful *tusi*, such as the Guizhou and Bozhou pacification commissioners, as well as less influential *tusi*, grudgingly assisted the Ming campaign at first, but as soldiers, grain, corvée labor, and horses were siphoned off to the Yunnan front *tusi* and indigene assistance quickly waned. Two powerful *muzhuo* leaders from the Dedu granary—Awei, the *muzhuo* of Yaohu, and Jiana, the *muzhuo* of Adi—joined forces with Qilao leaders in Xibao, a small town located to the south of the Yachi River, between Anshun to the east and Liupanshui to the west, to attack Ming military outposts along the main highway linking Guiyang and Kunming. Each garrison situated along this stretch of the highway, Pingba, Puding, Anzhuang, Annan, and Puan, was attacked by the combined Nasu Yi–Qilao force, and the indigene forces completely destroyed the Puding, Anzhuang, and Annan garrisons.[35]

The assault on Ming garrisons and Chinese settlements along the highway west of Guiyang was repeated to the north of Shuixi as *muzhuo* leaders from the Mukua and Fagua granaries attacked the Chishui and Bijie garrisons. The Bijie garrison was under siege for over three months before reinforcements from Sichuan finally broke through, but by this time all Han settlements in the vicinity of the garrison had been destroyed. The Chishui garrison did not fare much better, but access to the Chishui River and the garrison's proximity to Luzhou allowed it to survive the assault, but just barely.[36]

As Nasu Yi and Qilao forces attacked Ming military installations in western Guizhou in 1447, the Miao rebel Wei Wengtong led a series of assaults on the Xintian, Qingping, and Pingyue garrisons in eastern Guizhou, and by early 1448 those garrisons were in smoldering ruins. Wei's force, estimated to be over 200,000 strong in 1448, fanned out into three directions: one column marched west along the main highway and attacked the provincial capital of Guiyang, although reinforcements from Bozhou quickly forced a retreat; a second column headed north toward Tongren massacring Han along the way; and the third column marched south to attack Han settlements and military installations in Liping prefecture. Wei's motive for attacking Liping prefecture stemmed from a government decision in 1434 to eliminate several Miao *tusi* offices, intimidate the Miao into abandoning their lands, and then settle Han immigrants from Jiangxi on these lands. The *gaitu guiliu* of 1434 nearly doubled the geopolitical size of Liping prefecture, and reportedly the Han Chinese population in Liping quadrupled in two decades. Wei's objective for marching into Liping was simple: "to kill the Han who have stolen our land" and to avenge the injustices of 1434.[37] Nearly every battalion, fort, and outpost linked to the Jingzhou, Wukai, and Tonggu garrisons was destroyed, and innumerable Han villages were completely wiped out.

With the successful conclusion to the Luchuan campaign in 1449, Wang Ji returned to Guizhou with instructions to restore order in Guizhou. Wang did so, but not until after he received an additional 80,000 troops from Beijing, Nanjing, and Jiangxi to augment his Yunnan army. Wang quickly repaired the Puding, Anzhuang, and Annan garrisons in western Guizhou before heading east to confront Wei Wengtong. In due time, Wang cornered Wei and a handful of supporters in the mountains of eastern Liping prefecture in 1451, and, amid much pageantry, he dispatched Wei to Beijing for execution.[38]

With the defeat of Wei's rebellion, a third wave of Ming troops and Han immigrants flooded into Guizhou. Wang set out to reconstruct the garrisons in eastern Guizhou, just as he had in the western half of the province, and staffed the rebuilt garrisons with troops from the Beijing and Nanjing areas. Once again soldiers were ordered either to bring their families with them to settle permanently near the garrisons or to

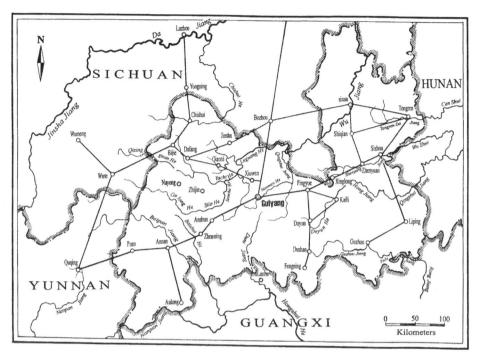

Map 6   Guizhou province, ca. 1550

marry local women and start families. Ming officials also utilized financial incentives to persuade Han from Jiangxi and Hunan to permanently relocate in towns near the Guizhou garrisons. Unlike the previous two state-sponsored relocation programs, this wave of soldiers and
settlers exhibited a greater tendency to occupy land further away from
the Ming garrisons. There are oblique references in the *New Illustrated
Gazetteer* to large swaths of fertile land left unoccupied by indigenes
who feared the advancing Han tide of military colonists following Wei's
capture; yet, sources also indicate *tusi* were recruiting Han farmers to
settle in their domains. One such *tusi* was Yang Wanba of Upper
Fengning in southern Guizhou.[39]

In 1391 Yang Wanba, a native of Jishui county in Jiangxi, as reward
for his exemplary service and demonstrated valor in a military expedition against Miao rebels in the Qingshui River Valley, was given the
*tusi* title of native official (*zhangguang shi*) of Fengning. The entire
Fengning area, in addition to several Miao and Kam villages, became

Yang's personal estate to rule as he saw fit. Before his death Yang took the extraordinary step of dividing his estate between his two sons, which led to the creation of two *tusi* domains, Upper Fengning and Lower Fengning.[40] Upper and Lower Fengning quickly evolved into strikingly different locales. Yang Wanba's descendents in Upper Fengning made it their policy to attract and relocate to Upper Fengning people from the Yang family's native place in Jiangxi, whereas the branch of the Yang family in control of Lower Fengning decided to limit Han settlement in its domain.

To entice Han settlers, in the 1430s the Yangs in Upper Fengning began construction on a large earthen wall around their town for protection. They also enrolled all able-bodied men in a town militia to safeguard the town and surrounding countryside from predators, and they claimed to use Ming law and the customary practices familiar to the people from Jishui to adjudicate matters. As one traveler to Upper Fengning remarked: "Many of the shops, hostels, and restaurants in the town are owned by Han [Chinese] from Jiangxi. When you walk into Upper Fengning, it is as if you have entered Jiangxi. The people here still claim to be from Jiangxi, though their entire families now reside here."[41] Following the defeat of the Wei Wengtong rebellion in 1451, provincial authorities received a request from Upper Fengning that soldiers from the Jishui region of Jiangxi who had participated in Wang's campaign be allowed to settle in Upper Fengning once they were released from military service—a request that was approved.

By the close of the fifteenth century, Ming officials in Duyun prefecture, the closest administrative seat to Upper Fengning, requested that the *tusi* office in Upper Fengning be eliminated and its land incorporated into Duyun prefecture. The main arguments given for this act of *gaitu guiliu* was that a disproportionate percentage of the people living in Fengning were Han, the *tusi* himself was Han, and the "Han living in Fengning deserved the order and stability of Han rule."[42] The Han of Upper Fengning did express some reservations about the loss of *tusi* rule, and for precisely this reason the provincial government exhibited striking administrative flexibility by allowing the Yang family to continue to receive hereditary appointments as the *tusi* of Upper Fengning even after the area became part of Duyun prefecture. In other words, after *gaitu guiliu* Upper Fengning came under the dual administrative control of a state-appointed department magistrate assigned by the Ming court and a *tusi* also anointed by the Ming court.

In contrast, Lower Fengning was a mountainous, poverty-stricken region populated almost exclusively by indigenous non-Han peoples. Chinese, Miao, and Kam bandits roamed the countryside with impunity, and the people residing there "bore the marks of having been robbed repeatedly."[43] For reasons not explained, the Yang family in Lower Fengning prohibited Han from settling in their domain, and in contrast allowed the Miao and Kam who had been dispossessed of their lands in Upper Fengning to relocate there—the Lower Fengning *tusi* still identified himself as of Han descent. Officials in Duyun were aware of the economic plight and demographic composition of Lower Fengning, and possibly for these reasons they never attempted to make Lower Fengning a part of Duyun prefecture. Lower Fengning remained a place known to welcome only "barbarians and savages [*man ye*] and not Han," even after it was incorporated into Duyun prefecture in the eighteenth century.

The growing presence of Han settlers in Guizhou and Wang Ji's brutal suppression of Wei Wengtong's rampage against military installations and Han settlements in eastern Guizhou did not intimidate the local population into submission. On the contrary, a few years later a prominent Miao leader named Huang Long, who lived in a cluster of villages located to the north of Xinglong garrison, transformed his defense militia into what he called "an armor-piercing arrow to strike the Han."[44] According to Huang's confession, the local population suffered untold hardships at the hands of the Han settlers who lived near the garrison. "The Han [settlers] relied on the military to beat, intimidate, and ultimately expel us from our land. They left us no choice but to fight to regain our land."[45] Despite his animosity toward Han settlers, Huang at first directed his militia to attack the Caotang and Huangping military commissions and not Xinglong garrison and Han settlers. Huang and his Miao militia had good reason to take action against the two *tusi* first.

During the Ming campaign against Wei, the cavalry forces of Caotang and Huangping repeatedly burned, pillaged, and murdered their way through the remote mountain villages where Huang and his followers lived, and in the years following the suppression of Wei, these two military commissions continued to plunder the area. To Huang there was very little difference between the Caotang and Huangping *tusi*, Han settlers, and the Ming military: all three had at one time or another preyed upon Huang's people, seized their land, and disrupted

their livelihood. Whole villages were destroyed, young girls were kidnapped, and thousands were killed, all because, as Huang noted in his
confession, Caotang and Huangping could do it and get away with it. In
the ultimate act of desperation, Huang proclaimed himself "great king
who pacifies heaven" (*pingtian dawang*) and marched his ragged force,
the "armor-piercing arrow to strike the Han," down from the mountains
to attack the *tusi* territories of Caotang and Huangping.[46]

Wang, fearful that what he was witnessing was a new round of violence directed against Ming institutions and Chinese settlers, ordered
the Guizhou military superintendent (*tidu junwu*), Jiang Lin, the Xinglong commander in chief (*zongguan dudu*), Fang Ying, and Yang Hui
(1433–83), the influential Bozhou pacification commissioner, to coordinate the campaign to suppress Huang. The Caotang and Huangping
military commissioners were subordinate to Yang's authority, and so it
was only appropriate that Yang be included in the suppression campaign. The one complication to including Yang, though, was that Bozhou was a part of Sichuan province, not Guizhou, and therefore Yang
was obligated to coordinate campaign planning not only with Wang Ji,
Jiang Lin, and Fang Ying (all Guizhou officials), but also with Sichuan
provincial officials. Yang played his hand adroitly when he lobbied Sichuan provincial officials to name him commander of the campaign because, as he told them, "if an official from Guizhou is placed in charge,
then the entire region could possibly fall under Guizhou control at the
end of operations."[47] Sichuan officials won the day, and Yang was allowed to take the lead in the military phase of the operation.

During the initial planning session of the campaign Yang stunned
Jiang and Fang by unrolling a map of the Caotang-Huangping region that
was covered with white circles. When asked what the white circles represented, Yang told his counterparts the white circles indicated Miao villages he intended to exterminate. Jiang and Fang reportedly objected to
Yang's extermination campaign, telling him that such actions would only
drive friendly Miao into Huang's hands and further escalate the violence,
but their pleas evidently had no effect on the headstrong *tusi*.[48] It should
be noted here that Ming and Qing sources on the southwest often portray
Chinese military officials as highly moral men who strove to restrain the
violent behavior of *tusi*, and ameliorate the uncivilized behavior of
the frontier barbarians. In this case, though, we possess evidence to the
contrary: Jiang and Fang were directly implicated in the bloody two-
month campaign in the Caotang-Huangping region that resulted in the

deaths of over 8,000 Miao (their heads were brought to Huangping to be counted!), the complete destruction of 53 Miao villages, and the capture of 1,700 Miao women and children, many of whom were forced to labor in the reconstruction of the Xintian, Qingping, and Pingyue garrisons. As in the case of Wei, Huang was eventually captured by Ming forces, tortured, and sent to Beijing for execution.[49]

As a result of the Wei and Huang uprisings, Ming officials decided against incorporating the devastated Miao mountain villages into the prefectural administration and instead increased its military support to the Bozhou, Caotang, and Huangping *tusi*—bows and arrows, horses, swords, and pikes were made available to these *tusi* on a regular basis. Moreover, officials in Guizhou convinced their Sichuan colleagues to reduce the amount of tribute and tax payments demanded of the Bozhou, Caotang, and Huangping commissioners so that additional resources could be directed toward controlling the rebellious Miao population to the north of the Ming garrisons.[50] In short, by augmenting the military preparedness of the *tusi* in the region, Ming policy exacerbated an already tense situation among the indigenous population, *tusi*, and the Ming state, and Yang relied on Ming assistance to further expand the geopolitical size of his pacification commission. A short time later, Yang was at it again, and this time he was able to deceive the Ming state into creating a new military commission for his favorite son.

As the twenty-fourth hereditary Yang ruler of Bozhou, Yang Hui desperately wanted to name Yang You (1466–1513), a son by a concubine, his successor to the post of Bozhou pacification commissioner. Unfortunately for Yang Hui and Yang You, Yang family regulations strictly prohibited Yang Hui from naming Yang You his heir apparent. According to these regulations, the son borne by Yang Hui's wife was first in line to inherit the *tusi* post. When Yang Hui announced his decision to name Yang You his successor during a celebration attended by the extended Yang patriclan, by his many subordinate vassals, such as the Caotang and Huangping military commissioners, and by Ming officials from Sichuan and Guizhou, members of the Yang patriclan adamantly protested the move. Caught off guard by the intensity of the objections, Yang Hui was compelled to name his son by his wife, Yang Ai (1464–1517), as the heir to the pacification office.[51] Yang Hui's affection toward Yang You did not waver, however.

With the path to *tusi* succession blocked, Yang Hui decided to create a new military commission and secure Ming acceptance of Yang You as its head. Yang Hui and his advisers agreed that territory near the town of Anning, located to the south of the Huangping Military Commission, would be an ideal spot to establish a new military commission. The area was populated by Miao who had been sympathetic to the Wei-Huang uprisings, and thus Yang Hui had a ready-made pretext for sending his military forces into the region: the Miao were rebelling again.[52] Yang Hui ordered his subordinates, the Caotang and Huangping military commissioners, to "pacify" the Miao in Anning. Miao resistance afforded Yang Hui the opportunity to request military assistance from the Ming garrisons, which was forthcoming. As a result, Ming forces participated in the indiscriminate slaughter of the Miao of Anning, and provincial authorities in Sichuan and Guizhou agreed to create a new Anning Military Commission, with Yang You as its commissioner.[53]

With the death of Yang Hui in 1483, a bitter rivalry between the two half-brothers erupted into a struggle for supremacy of the Bozhou and Anning areas, and the ferocity of this struggle ultimately forced the Ming state to intercede militarily. Apparently Yang You authorized three attempts on Yang Ai's life, but when Yang Ai's son was born in 1486, thus ensuring an heir to the Bozhou post, Yang You stopped trying to assassinate Yang Ai. Instead, Yang You decided to draw Yang Ai into a fight by attacking his subordinates in the Huangping and Caoping regions. The violence interrupted traffic along the main highway, which in turn attracted the attention of the Ming authorities. Ming military units from the Pingyue and Xinglong garrisons were ordered to patrol the highway and maintain safe travel, but this simply placed them in the middle of the Yang family feud. On a June day in 1486, a Ming patrol was ambushed by troops loyal to Yang You, and as a result Ming forces throughout central and eastern Guizhou came to the assistance to Yang Ai. Up until this point the Bozhou-Anning feud was seen as little more than one of the many minor irritants Ming officials in this hostile frontier had to deal with, but the ambush of Ming troops by Yang You changed all that: Ming soldiers were participating in a turf war between *tusi*, and Ming soldiers had been killed.[54]

In October 1486, Vice Minister of Justice He Qiaoxin (1427–1503) was ordered to investigate the situation in central Guizhou. By the time He reached central Guizhou, Yang Ai's Bozhou forces had secured Ming assistance and launched an offensive against Anning. Faced with certain defeat, Yang You negotiated surrender terms with the Ming that allowed him and his immediate family to leave Anning and live as exiles in Baoning, Sichuan. For his part, Yang Ai continued as the Bozhou pacification commissioner, although now Bozhou's territory included the Anning area previously granted to Yang You.[55]

Yang Ai's acquisition of Anning did not achieve the overall peace the Ming had hoped for. From his residence in Baoning, Yang You directed supporters in Anning to disrupt Yang Ai's control of the area: minor officials appointed from Bozhou were murdered, crops were burned and villages destroyed, rebellious Miao were incited to attack the Huangping and Caoping commissions, and on several occasions Yang You's followers conducted military raids deep into Bozhou.[56] To end the bloodshed, in 1528 the Ming state agreed to appoint Yang You's eldest son, Yang Zhang, to the post of military commissioner of the Anning area, though Anning was now called Kaili. The Kaili Military Commission was placed under the jurisdiction of provincial authorities in Guizhou, whereas Bozhou continued under the supervision of Sichuan.

The belief that a provincial boundary would somehow prevent the Bozhou-Kaili feud from escalating was conceptually flawed and unrealistic, and pro–*gaitu guiliu* officials would use this case as an example of Ming naïveté in dealing with *tusi*. They argued that the long-term objective of the Ming state should be to replace the indirect method of *tusi* rule with direct civilian rule, not to aid *tusi* in becoming more powerful and acquiring more land.[57] As the Bozhou-Anning episode indicates, however, there was a powerful voice within Ming officialdom promoting the continued use of *tusi* offices in Guizhou:

There is still considerable territory within Guizhou that exists beyond the control of both the provincial apparatus centered in Guiyang and *tusi*, and for this reason it is best to first allow *tusi* to enter these areas and confront the violence of annexation. It is only after the *tusi* is firmly in control should we begin to contemplate *gaitu guiliu* and the prospect of ruling such an area.[58]

Representative of the pro-*tusi* position was Zhou Hongmou's often-cited 1479 memorial written in response to the decade-long raids against Luzhou and Chongqing by the Wumeng and Chele patriclans. At the time Zhou was the junior vice minister of rites, and his opinions carried considerable weight at court:

I am a native of Xuzhou prefecture [Sichuan], and I am familiar with the circumstances of the indigenous population in Xuzhou. . . . During the Hongwu, Yongle, Xuande, and Zhengtong reigns [1368–1449], military commanders were dispatched to this area four times. There have been times when the indigenes submitted to our rule, and times when they did not. By the beginning of the Jing-tai reign [1450], the indigene population in these four counties had grown power-ful. When they captured a Han [Chinese], they would tie him to a tree and shoot arrows at him, saying: "You have been a plague on us for far too long."

During the Tianshu and Chenghua reigns [1457–87], they repeatedly carried out despicable acts against Han. At that time I made the statement that we are incapable of pacifying the indigenous population with force, and powerless to make them obedient through compassion; so, the only way to achieve positive long-term results is to establish *tusi* offices through which we can influence them. . . .

Although it would be impossible to establish a pacification commission in the area, as was done in earlier times, I recommend we create imperial agencies in many different areas that would manage indigenous villages by allowing the indigenes themselves to select a fair-minded and generous-spirited man in each village to be their leader, and this post would be hereditary. If one of these leaders fails to perform adequately, then another should be selected to replace him. In this way the Han will not harass the indigenous population, and the indigenous people will not view the Han with hatred. They will then coexist in peace ever after.[59]

Zhou's memorial was ridiculed by Ming officials as a betrayal of Ming policy and Chinese culture. He proposed establishing imperial agencies in place of the provincial-level civil and military offices to manage *tusi* affairs, and he recommended repeal of the onerous regulations govern-ing *tusi* inheritance procedures; these two proposals most assuredly raised the ire of his fellow bureaucrats. Zhou was sure the violence he witnessed between non-Han and Han was the result of aggressive at-tempts on the part of Ming officials and Han settlers to seize non-Han lands and transform their traditional lifeways. To minimize such vio-lence, Zhou recommended the Ming government take an active role in protecting the non-Han from predatory Han (officials and civilians alike) and allow the non-Han more freedom in governing themselves.

Another powerful voice in support of using *tusi* to govern the non-Han peoples came from the eminent Ming statesman and philosopher-theoretician Wang Shouren (Wang Yangming; 1472–1529). In early 1508 Wang was exiled to the Longchang postal station, located in the Shuidong portion of Guizhou and situated at the easternmost terminus of the Geya Postal Road built and repaired by She Xiang back in the 1380s. During his time in Longchang Wang gained firsthand knowledge of the Song and Azhe patriclans and of the countless Miao and Qilao settlements near Longchang.[60] We know Wang often ventured west into Shuixi, where he met with powerful *zimo* and *muzhou* leaders (*tumu* in Wang's accounts) who were responsible for repairing and policing the road. Wang also traveled south through Shuidong on his many visits to the provincial seat of Guiyang, where he often lectured students and visited with provincial officials.[61]

Wang thought carefully about the nature of *tusi* offices and Ming rule in Guizhou. In an influential memorial he wrote following a military campaign into southeast Guizhou, Wang argued that a lasting peace would come about only if civilian officials and *tusi* were to be appointed side-by-side in areas populated by non-Han and Han: the civilian official would govern the Han population and oversee relations between the indigenous non-Han, the Han, and the Ming state, and the *tusi*, whom Wang assumed would be non-Han, would govern the indigenous non-Han population. The civilian official, Wang maintained, would disseminate information on agricultural techniques, hygiene, and Chinese cultural practices, all with an eye toward the long-term transformation of the "uncivilized into civilized." In those areas populated solely by non-Han peoples, Wang recommended *tusi* be allowed to govern without interference from Ming officials. In such cases, Wang noted in agreement with Zhou, officials should strive to protect *tusi* territory from predatory Han settlers so that the main cause of violence could be minimized.[62]

A perspective very different from the ones presented by Zhou Hongmou and Wang Shouren can be found in Tian Rucheng's richly detailed book, *Yanjiao jiwen*.[63] In 1533 Tian was assigned the post of assistant surveillance commissioner in Guangdong, and while in Guangdong he began to handle a variety of issues concerning *tusi* offices. His opinions toward *tusi* offices are best revealed in his analysis of how the Yang patriclan ruled Bozhou, in particular those passages detailing Yang Hui's manipulation of the establishment of the Anning Military Commission. Tian examined the entire affair and, in the end, leveled a blistering attack at Ming policy toward *tusi*. He chided government officials for their appalling ignorance of circumstances among the barbarians, for their willingness to mobilize government soldiers at the behest of one *tusi* (Yang Hui), and, most important, for failing to understand how the violence between *tusi* (Yang Ai and Yang You) originated in the first place. Ignorance about the southwest was, in Tian's estimation, the Ming state's worst enemy.[64]

According to Tian, the Bozhou-Kaili Rebellion, as the events surrounding Yang You and Yang Ai came to be known at the beginning of the sixteenth century, was nothing more than an attempt by the scheming Yang Hui to prevent his eldest son from inheriting the post of Bozhou pacification commissioner. According to Tian,

One barbarian chief [*yiqiu*] petitioned the government for assistance, and as a result the Ministry of War, unaware of the actual situation, hastily deployed military forces to the region. The emperor was deceived, laws were broken, and the people suffered years of misfortune. As this hardship gripped our border areas, the government's negotiators were concerned with little more than redrawing provincial borders so that they could separate Bozhou and Kaili. These officials never attempted to figure out the origins of the Bozhou-Kaili Rebellion. If we continue to act this way, how will we ever pacify the barbarians?[65]

Like Zhou Hongmou, Tian Rucheng was highly critical of how Ming officials managed *tusi* affairs, but instead of recommending institutional changes that would grant *tusi* greater independence from Ming officials, as Zhou had done a few decades earlier, Tian believed Ming officials had been far too accommodating and passive in their management of *tusi*, and that violence would be an endemic feature of the southwest as long as Ming officials acquiesced to *tusi* demands. China's dynamic political and social institutions would "pacify the barbarians" (*ping yi*), Tian argued, as the empire marched continuously into Guizhou, Yunnan, and Miandian (Burma). "Had not the history of China demonstrated this very fact?" Tian continued:

How do we know that after one hundred generations Yunnan will not have the reputation of a place where Han culture thrives? Look at the changes that have occurred in Min [Fujian] and Guang [Guangdong and Guangxi]. Why should we think the barbarians [*yi*] in Cheli [modern Sipsongpanna] and Miandian would not rejoice the day prefectures and counties are enumerated in their areas and they are finally governed by [Ming] officials?[66]

At the time Tian wrote the *Yanjiao jiwen*, no one disputed the idea that Yunnan and Guizhou were an integral part of the Ming empire. The question officials struggled over centered on how best to extend civilian rule without provoking a violent backlash from the indigenous population. If the timetable for colonization was accelerated, as Tian advocated, the state would need to invest heavily in the military phase of the project, it would need to encourage Han from other parts of China to settle the region, and Ming officials would need to commit themselves to eliminate *tusi* offices.[67] If, however, the timetable was decelerated, as Zhou Hongmou and Wang Shouren proposed, then control costs could be minimized and violence kept at manageable levels, but the implementation of civilian rule would take much longer to complete. This debate continued to dominate policy discussions on the southwest well into the sixteenth century; but by the middle decades of the sixteenth century, a dramatic influx of Han immigrants, the vast majority of whom went to the southwest voluntarily in search of land and money, altered the parameters of the debate in favor of the former.

## The Vanishing Frontier

When Hongwu ordered his conquering army to settle permanently in large garrisons throughout the southwest, it was an involuntary process guided by strategic necessity and the emperor's vision of an empire composed of "self-sufficient rural communities."[68] Each soldier was allocated a tract of land near his military unit, and he was expected to use this land to create a stable life for himself and his family. Ideally, the Ming state hoped to provide each soldier with between 15 and 20 *mu* of land, but in the mountainous landscape of Guizhou where level ground was a rare commodity, each soldier-farmer was fortunate to receive 10 *mu*.[69] Nearly all the land distributed to these soldier-farmers was seized from the local non-Han population, and as a consequence the record of Ming occupation and colonization of Guizhou and Yunnan is rife with conflict. The Ming military consolidated these soldier-farmer lands into state farms, in which ideally 30 percent of the soldier-farmers performed the basic military duties expected of the unit, and the remaining 70 percent farmed the land.[70]

By 1400 it was estimated that Ming soldier-farmers and their dependents had cleared over 1.3 million *mu* of land in Yunnan, and by 1441, they had reclaimed nearly one million *mu* of land in Guizhou.[71] In fact, prior to the sixteenth century the only statistics we have for cultivated acreage in Yunnan and Guizhou are supplied by the Ming military. Figures on cultivated acreage under civilian control for Yunnan first appeared in 1502, and for Guizhou such statistics did not exist until 1542. Even these figures underestimated the total acreage under military and civilian control, since acreage controlled by the non-Han was not registered by Ming authorities. More to the point, prior to 1583 a complete, provincial-wide cadastral survey had never been carried out in Guizhou.[72] The incomplete figures we have concerning cultivated acreage in Guizhou are matched by imprecise population figures.

A cumbersome military presence, a hostile indigene population, and a skeptical settler community exasperated Ming officials. The following short note written by the Guizhou provincial governor in 1555 betrays this frustration: "There is no way I can find out the complete size of the provincial population. Not only do we lack reliable information on the barbarians [*man*], even the army registers for the military households are incomplete. Many of the recent arrivals from Sichuan and Jiangxi do not heed our announcements and refuse to register with local magistrates."[73] The governor's report goes on to mention how census registration was viewed by the population as entailing burdensome fiscal obligations to the state, and the possibility of new and additional taxes more than anything else acted as a powerful disincentive to registering one's household and landholdings with the state.[74] An accurate demographic picture of Guizhou, then, is nothing more than an educated guess based on the figures collected by the officials at the time. If anything, we should assume that the size of Guizhou's population was considerably larger than the figures recorded by Ming officials at the time.

With that said, we know that in 1502 there were 258,693 people (*kou*, or mouths) registered in Guizhou, and forty years later, in 1542, the registered population in Guizhou increased only slightly, to 266,920.[75] However, in 1555 provincial officials concluded what they believed was the first thorough census, and their records show a total population of 512,289—in thirteen years the registered population of Guizhou nearly doubled, with a net gain of 245,369 people. According to the 1555 census, there were 148,957 registered households (*hu*) in Guizhou, with 62,273 households classified as military households (*junhu*), and 56,684 households listed as civilian households (*minhu*). Of the total population, 261,869 people were classified as belonging to military households, and 254,420 people were registered in civilian households. Thus, slightly more than half of the registered population in mid-sixteenth-century Guizhou was associated with the Ming military.[76] (See Appendix H.)

Despite the numerous obstacles confronting Ming officials, a number of sources confirm that in the middle of the sixteenth century large commercial centers were emerging alongside many of the military garrisons established in the 1380s and 1390s, and they rivaled the provincial capital, Guiyang, in geographic size and registered population.[77] For example, the Puan garrison, established in 1382 near the town of Yushi, the seat of the former Nasu kingdom of the same name, had become by the middle of the sixteenth century the centerpiece of the commercially prosperous Puan department.

Puan department, because of its presence as a main transportation hub linking Guizhou, Yunnan, Sichuan, and Guangxi, and the nearby abundance of mineral deposits and forestlands, attracted Han settlers from as far away as Shandong, Shanxi, and Shaanxi. Puan had a registered population of nearly 40,000 in 1555, compared to approximately 30,000 living in Guiyang. The same can be said for the town of Anshun, with 25,000 Han almost entirely from Jiangxi and Huguang residing near the Puding garrison.[78] Finally, the Anzhuang garrison, with a total military contingent of nearly 50,000 soldiers, played an important role in attracting nearly 25,000 Han from Jiangxi, Huguang, and Guangxi to reside in nearby Zhenning department.[79]

Statistics compiled from the government's mid-sixteenth-century census confirm that the civilian population centers in Guizhou were still tied inextricably to the Ming military garrisons established during the Hongwu reign. However, provincial surveys taken in 1597 and in 1602 indicate that a noteworthy demographic shift had occurred during the second half of the sixteenth century. By the end of the century there were far more Han civilians registered in Guizhou than there were in the middle of the century. Moreover, the total number of Han Chinese registered as military personnel had declined almost in exact proportion to the increase in registered Han civilians (an interesting statistical quid pro quo, to say the least).

Based on figures collected in the 1555 census, there were 56,684 civilian households and 62,273 military households in Guizhou. This census registered a civilian population of 254,420 and a military population of 261,869. There were 7,449 more military households than civilian households, and the population figures recorded 5,589 more military personnel than civilians.[80] Yet in 1597 the number of civilian households registered by provincial authorities decreased by 10,118, to 46,566 out of a total of 105,906 households listed for Guizhou. This meant there were 59,566 military households in Guizhou in 1597, down from the 62,273 recorded in 1555. But before we assume that the population for Guizhou in 1597 mirrored the statistical difference in registered households (and this is where working with Ming census figures can get tricky), the 1597 census figures tell us that out of a total population of 509,975, the civilian population amounted to 325,374, whereas the registered military population decreased to 184,601.[81] In other words, from

1555 to 1597 the civilian population in Guizhou increased by 70,954, or 27.8 percent, and the military population in Guizhou decreased by 77,268, or 29.5 percent.

This trend toward a greater civilian presence in Guizhou is confirmed in 1602, when provincial authorities conducted yet another survey of the provincial population and arable land (see Appendix I). According to this investigation, there were 528,781 people living in Guizhou, of which 344,180 were listed as civilians—a net gain in the civilian population of 18,806 since 1597. Interestingly, the 1602 figures indicate no change to the total number of registered military personnel since 1597.[82] In other words, according to government statistics recorded from 1555 to 1602, the registered civilian population in Guizhou increased 35.2 percent. Although it is impossible to determine how many of these new civilians were recent arrivals to Guizhou, we can only infer that the trend we see happening in other parts of China, that is, military personnel abandoning their posts for a more rewarding and lucrative life in the civilian sector, was likely happening in Guizhou as well.

The impressive increase in the registered civilian population in Guizhou could also be the product of several important changes in the Ming tax code implemented during the latter half of the sixteenth century. Prior to the mid-sixteenth century labor service levies and miscellaneous surcharges were assessed based on the registered number of households. Ming officials knew full well that people avoided the burdensome labor tax by refusing to register their households with local officials. Historians have known for some time that a correlation existed between the adoption of the "single whip assessment tax" (*yitiao bianfa*) and the extraordinary increase in China's recorded population during the latter half of the sixteenth century. According to the single whip assessment tax, all tax payments to the state were to be calculated as money payments, including the labor tax. This meant that household registers were no longer a part of the tax calculus, and people were therefore less inclined to avoid registering with local officials.

In addition to the rise of the civilian population, the total amount of registered cultivated acreage in Guizhou increased during the last decades of the sixteenth century. In 1441, just as the Ming military was attempting once again to assert its authority over recalcitrant Miao in eastern Guizhou, the total amount of cultivated acreage was listed as 957,600 *mu*, and the entire amount was classified as military land.[83] Approximately one hundred years later, in 1552, officials in Guizhou registered 908,780 *mu* of cultivated acreage, a slight decrease from what had existed in 1442. Yet, of the total registered acreage, 516,686 *mu* was now listed as civilian acreage, whereas 392,112 *mu* of land remained classified as military acreage. This amounted to a 59 percent reduction in the culti-vated acreage under military control.[84] Approximately thirty years later, in 1580, officials in Guizhou registered 1,540,000 *mu* of cultivated acre-age, with 1,043,509 *mu* under civilian control and 487,624 *mu* under military control.[85] In the twenty-eight years between 1552 and 1580, the amount of registered cultivated acreage under civilian control increased nearly 500 percent. Furthermore, in 1597 the total amount of cultivated acreage in Guizhou amounted to nearly 1,700,000 *mu*.[86]

These increases in Guizhou's registered civilian population and cul-tivated acreage reflect not just quantitative aspects of Ming state/Han society expansion, but underlying qualitative changes as well, changes that had laid the foundation for Han expansion into the southwest out-side of government control. The first qualitative change occurred when Hongwu ordered his commanders to establish military colonies on land that could be easily irrigated, because he believed agricultural yields from irrigated lands far surpassed yields from dry lands, and it was vitally important these newly settled soldier-farmers become self-sufficient as soon as possible. It was for precisely this reason the Ming settled a large contingent of soldier-farmers in the Kunming area, where Sayyid 'Ajall Shams al-Din had constructed drainage and canal networks in the 1270s and 1280s.

As the Mongols demonstrated, the Lake Dian portion of central Yunnan could sustain a large occupation force, yet the mountainous to-pography, fast-flowing rivers, and deep ravines of much of the southwest made it exceedingly difficult to establish an irrigated farming regime outside the Lake Dian region. It was not until the Ming military arrived in the 1380s that irrigated farming was first introduced on a wide scale to Guizhou. And despite the repeated efforts to expand irrigated farm-ing among the soldier-farmers, by 1513 only one-seventh of all military farms in the province claimed irrigation works. Even though the soldier-farmers in Guizhou never achieved self-sufficiency and were dependent upon government-sponsored programs to meet basic sub-sistence needs, the introduction of irrigated farming represented a significant contribution to the agricultural technology of the region.[87]

In addition to irrigated farming, the use of cattle-drawn plows was not widespread in the southwest prior to the fourteenth century; yet the

Ming military farms established by Hongwu changed all that as Han soldier-farmers from all over China brought cattle, plows, and new farming techniques to the southwest. During the five-year period from 1385 to 1390, the Ming state sent over 30,000 head of cattle from Hunan to Guizhou, and throughout the fifteenth century the central government repeatedly sponsored large cattle drives to relocate livestock from Hunan to Guizhou and Yunnan.[88] According to one source, by the end of the fifteenth century farming with cattle-drawn plows was a common fixture in Han communities near Ming garrisons, and reportedly the indigenous non-Han residing in the lowlands of Guizhou had begun to use cattle-drawn plows as well.[89] Chinese farmers also brought to the southwest iron plows, which gradually replaced the traditional wooden hoes used by Han and non-Han farmers. The sturdier iron plow allowed farmers to bring more land under cultivation, and in some instances the cattle-drawn iron plow afforded farmers the option of growing two crops on one field per year because farm labor was now more efficient.

Third, the increase in cultivated acreage occurred both in lowland areas near major urban centers and in mountainous areas far from urban centers. As we have seen, the initial reclamation of agricultural lands was carried out by soldier-farmers assigned to garrisons in the 1380s and 1390s. This trend of reclaiming land near Ming garrisons continued unabated throughout the fifteenth and sixteenth centuries as more and more soldier-farmers were stationed in Guizhou after repeated military campaigns. By the middle of the fifteenth century, Han settlers not associated with the military, as well as indigenous non-Han living near Han settlements, began to bring more and more mountain land under cultivation. Jiang Yingke, a sixteenth-century visitor to Guizhou, noted in a series of poems on Guizhou, "On sheer cliffs, one sees the scars of land burned for planting. When the rains come, the burned scars turn a luxuriant green, and the land gives forth the sweet smell of rice husked by pounding in a mortar."[90]

The opening up of relatively infertile mountain land for agricultural production reflected Han consumption of traditionally non-Han grains, such as buckwheat, oats, rapeseed, and dry-land rice, and non-Han adoption of Han agricultural techniques and practices, especially the use of the iron plow. By the end of the sixteenth century, New World crops such as maize, potatoes, and sweet potatoes were being planted in the mountains of Guizhou and Yunnan. Maize and potatoes required little labor and were surprisingly resistant to disease and inclement weather, and their relatively high yields and good nutritional value provided people a better chance to survive when more conventional foods became scarce.[91]

Finally, the Ming state was thoroughly committed to bringing Guizhou and Yunnan within the fold of China proper. Despite concerns over how best to deal with *tusi*, most Ming officials were convinced Chinese civilization was superior to anything they had encountered in the southwest. Chinese civilization, they believed, possessed the unique capacity to transform "barbarians" into "civilized men," and that the basic transformative properties of Chinese civilization could be attributed to Chinese patterns of land tenure, agricultural techniques, political and legal institutions, and a Confucian education. Ming officials were well versed in Chinese history, especially Song history, and they were familiar with many of the arguments advocating frontier expansion outlined by Wang Anshi, Wang Shao, and other notable Song statesmen.[92] In fact, one important feature of Wang Anshi's frontier policies was the belief that frontier violence would decline in proportion to the rate in which the barbarians adopted Chinese practices. So, when Ming officials used the state apparatus to relocate Han to the southwest, especially during the late fourteenth and fifteenth centuries, they created islands in the southwest frontier that attracted Han immigrants who longed for a new start. Seen from a different perspective, by the end of the fifteenth century there were a number of Chinese communities in Guizhou and Yunnan in which Han Chinese could settle, and they could do so voluntarily with or without government assistance.

It has been mentioned several times now that the early Ming emperors hoped the military occupation of the southwest would eventually become a self-sufficient enterprise, but the settlers never came close to achieving self-sufficiency. At the end of the fourteenth century, Zhang Tan, an official appointed to Yunnan, reported, "the autumn harvest from the state farms provides food for only four months, from the eighth month to the eleventh month. We [Ming officials in Yunnan] must procure food for the next six months, or until the spring wheat is harvested."[93] It is estimated that by the end of the fifteenth century, the Ming state still provided nearly half of the basic provisions for its troops in Yunnan. And even though increases in cultivated land and the development of taxable commercial enterprises added substantially to the provincial coffers, Sichuan, Huguang, and Nan Zhili were still providing annual subsidies to Yunnan in 1626.

Likewise, throughout the Ming period Guizhou remained almost entirely dependent on outside subsidies. When Guizhou was created in 1413, Yongle noted the twenty-odd garrisons could not provide even half of their annual needs. To address this problem, the emperor ordered the use of a system whereby Chinese merchants were awarded contracts to supply grain to the Guizhou military in return for licenses (monopolies) to sell goods produced in the southwest, including salt, horses, tea, lumber, and medicines, on Chinese markets. The Ming first used this license system in northern China in 1371 under the title "Grain-Salt Exchange System" (*kaizhong fa*). The exchange system was first used in the southwest in 1373, but by 1389 military officials in Guizhou were already complaining about the lack of grain for their troops. According to one early Ming source, "the Guizhou military needs 70,000 *shi* [of grain] a year, but it can only produce an annual total of 12,000 *shi*. Therefore, we depend on recruiting merchants to exchange salt for grain to supply the army."[94] The modest gains made by creating a salt-for-grain exchange network for Guizhou collapsed as a result of the prolonged and destabilizing effects of the Hongwu-Jianwen-Yongle transition, but in 1413 Yongle was determined to place the military units in his new province on more secure footing.

In this year the Ming court resurrected the salt-for-grain exchange system and encouraged merchants from Guizhou, Huguang, Sichuan, and Jiangxi to play a more active role in moving grain to the Ming military units in the southwest.[95] The exchange system at its height delivered between 750,000 and 1,000,000 *shi* of grain to the southwest during the Ming—an annual import of approximately 20,000 *shi* of grain. But, even such sizable grain shipments to Guizhou failed to meet the needs of the Ming military. To augment the salt-for-grain exchange system, neighboring provincial governments were ordered to provide direct subsidies to Guizhou in the form of a grant-in-aid (*xieshang*), and by the middle of the fifteenth century Sichuan and Huguang were sending nearly 200,000 *shi* (12,000 metric tons) of grain annually to Guizhou to feed the Ming army. In time, though, it became prohibitively expensive to ship such large amounts of grain from one province to another. For example, in 1497 one official complained that the cost of transporting grain from Huguang to Guizhou was several times the cost of the grain itself. This is why by the beginning of the sixteenth century grain destined for the southwest was being commuted to silver.[96] In 1532, for instance, Guizhou's annual grain subsidy from Sichuan amounted to 109,753 *shi* of grain, which was commuted to 37,475 taels of silver, and its annual subsidy from Huguang was 102,400 *shi* of grain, which was commuted to 30,720 taels of silver.[97]

The Ming government relied heavily on merchants from Huguang, Sichuan, and Jiangxi to manage the Grain-Salt Exchange System and the grant-in-aid program, and as such nearly all of the commercial activity between Guizhou and its surrounding neighbors came under the control of Han merchants. Chinese sources seldom mention a business transaction between Han and non-Han parties, and when non-Han are mentioned at all it is generally in reference to the production process. It was the indigenous non-Han who ventured deep into the mountains to fell timber, who raised horses and sheep for Han consumers, and who dug the salt wells and mine shafts for Han Chinese bosses.

Chinese interest in the mineral resources of the southwest had been long-standing. Ever since the Tang dynasty, Chinese sources have mentioned the abundance of gold, silver, and cinnabar in the southwest, and the inclination of the non-Han to adorn themselves with exquisite jewelry. Following the Mongol conquest, the Yuan state declared the mines in Yunnan and Guizhou state property, and all mining activity was placed under the jurisdiction of the Bureau of Mining. In several noteworthy cases Yuan officials relieved an indigenous non-Han proprietor of his/her ownership rights and turned the mining operation over to trusted Central Asians and Han Chinese. Eventually the mines in Yunnan produced nearly half the gold and silver in circulation in China, and the Yuan government benefited handsomely from the production and distribution of Yunnan's gold and silver, but it did so at the cost of divesting the indigenous elite of its control of the region's mineral resources.[98]

The Hongwu and Yongle emperors understood quite clearly the strategic importance of the southwest's mineral resources to the overall Ming economy, and as a result they continued the Yuan precedent of a state monopoly of the mining and distribution of the region's mineral resources. The importance of Yunnan's silver mines can be gleaned from figures that show between 100,000 and 400,000 ounces of silver were produced annually between 1328 and 1600. Beginning in 1500, however, Ming sources note that as silver production in Yunnan was reaching an all-time high, state silver revenues began to decline precipitously.

Though we may be inclined to assign blame for this decline on the growing influx of silver from overseas, Ming sources tend to be more critical of
the bloated and cumbersome state bureaucracy, corrupt officials, an egregious mismanagement of revenues, and soaring transportation costs as
the primary causes behind the decline in state silver revenues.[99]

When the governor of Yunnan, Xiao Yan, issued his report on the
state of the mining industry in Yunnan in 1584, he presented the extraordinarily high transportation costs as the principal reason why state
revenues from mining had declined. According to Xiao's report:

> The silver mines of Yunnan are a great natural resource, but transportation
> costs are extremely high. Government offices generally receive only about 10
> percent of the revenue generated from silver mines, whereas transport workers
> consume about 90 percent of the revenue. Local officials, mine supervisors, and
> mine administrators also take their share, which leaves very little as tax reve-
> nue. Firms that transport silver from the mines of Yunnan to China proper
> must be reined in. Their greed is staggering.[100]

The thrust of Xiao's ire is directed toward the private transportation
firms that had cornered the market on moving minerals, grains, and consumer goods between China proper and the southwest. The best available
evidence indicates the Ming government began privatizing the mining
industry in the first decades of the sixteenth century in order to decrease
costs and increase revenues. Private firms, it was argued, could mine, refine, and move goods more efficiently and at a cheaper cost than could
state-controlled firms. But as Xiao pointed out, the policy of privatizing
the mining industry had placed the region's natural resources in the
hands of Han entrepreneurs, consigned the indigenous population to a
subordinate role as cheap, expendable labor in the production process,
and removed enormous sums from the state's tax registry.

A distressing example of just how injurious the impact privatization
had on the local population can be seen from a small tract written in
about 1600 by Wang Shixing, an official posted to Yunnan. Wang offers
a succinct description of how a large mine operates, but he concludes
his short essay by lamenting the fact that the indigenous population no
longer controls this valuable natural resource.

> Yunnan enjoys extensive mineral deposits. The indigenes [*tuman*] are given the
> task of digging the mine shaft and extracting the deposits. The pay they receive
> barely supports their daily needs. A mine headman operates the largest mines
> on behalf of the owner. He manages the mine and makes all necessary prepara-

tions for extracting the minerals. He is responsible for recruiting miners and for all initial work expenses.

Once the mine is set up, a furnace is built at the mine to refine the ore, which is carried out under the supervision of state officials. Every day the miners work the mine from dawn to dusk, and the daily haul is divided into four portions. The first portion goes to meet state taxes, and the state supervisor refines this ore and sends it to the provincial governor. The second portion goes to pay common mining expenses. Since the headman is responsible for both government and private expenses, he is in charge of this sum, and it is entered into account books. The third portion goes to the headman as personal expenses. The final portion is divided among the miners. Each group is responsible for refining its own ore. . . .

The indigenes do not realize that their ore is being stolen from them, and their labor aids unwittingly in this theft. They have no idea how to defend their rights to the land and its resources, and no one [of the Han Chinese] is willing to explain to them their rights or help them reclaim their land. Moreover, they have no idea how to establish their own mines. As a consequence, whereas mines are sought-after prizes in other parts [of China], in Yunnan they are unappreciated by the indigenes.[101]

Later, in a poignant part of his essay, Wang notes that during the Yuan and early years of the Ming dynasty the non-Han peoples owned and farmed their own land, controlled market activity in many of the towns and villages, dominated trade networks between towns and villages, and were the principal owners and operators of many of the region's mines. "The minerals extracted from these small-scale mining operations more than satisfied the state's appetite, and for this reason the mines neither scarred the earth nor were dug too deep."[102] By the beginning of the fifteenth century, Wang points out, Chinese (both state and society) demand for gold, silver, and copper became so intense that newer, deeper, and more expensive mines were developed. At the time Wang wrote his tract, there were four kinds of mine shafts in operation in the southwest: shafts excavated downward into the ground were called "wells," shafts cut on a level plane were called "levels," shafts that rose up into the side of a mountain were termed "lights," and shafts that sloped smoothly down were called "oxen sucking up water."[103] The capital required to sink and timber new shafts, pay for the water pumps and drainage equipment, and hire the labor, mules, and support staff to work the mines came exclusively from wealthy Han entrepreneurs, who often demanded the non-Han be dispossessed of their land rights before making the initial investment.

In Guizhou the prized mineral was cinnabar. As the only common source of quicksilver, or mercury, cinnabar had long been an important ingredient in Chinese alchemy and traditional Chinese medicine, and by the sixteenth century cinnabar had become vital to the production of weaponry and consumer items such as mirrors. As did gold, silver, and copper mining, cinnabar production attracted Han speculators in search of fabulous wealth, but it was the physical effects of cinnabar production that attracted the attention of another Ming official, Tian Wen:

Along the banks of Guizhou's many treacherous rivers live men, both old and young, who refuse to leave the banks of the river to reside in town. With pans and pipes, they strain to gather a few fragments from the river. For many, standing in the river has caused their toes to rot and fall off, though the water they stand in is clear; their eyes are red and filled with tears, though their pupils have suffered irreparable damage. Because of the mining, the water appears red, and the clothing worn by the miners is stained red. When a miner obtains even the smallest amount of cinnabar, he proclaims success and becomes quite excited, for he knows he will eat well today.[104]

Tian's investigation into the cinnabar industry in Guizhou led him to conclude that the mining of cinnabar should be permanently prohibited, though he knew the government was helpless to stop the tide of men deluded by dreams of untold profits who arrived in Guizhou daily. Mines were opened and closed with astonishing speed, and it was the social and environmental consequences of cinnabar mining that most concerned Tian. "Cinnabar satisfies neither eyes nor ears with enjoyment," and it has "perverted the spirit of concern for daily necessities." In a final lament Tian asked: "How can this [cinnabar mining] not help but destroy the mountains and valleys of Qian?"[105]

The lure of land and profits was a powerful magnet drawing ablebodied Han from all over China to the southwest. Gone were the days when the Ming state forced its soldiers to eke out a precarious existence on inhospitable state farms. The Han Chinese who came to Guizhou now arrived with money in hand and a strong desire for a better life. Occasionally they received assistance from the state, usually in the form of low-interest loans, tax breaks, and parceled land grants, but in the main it was the security the Ming military presence had painstakingly established since the 1380s that convinced them it was safe to settle in the southwest. By the middle of the sixteenth century Guizhou and the rest of the southwest was beginning to fill up with Han Chinese. Civilian households now outnumbered military households in Guizhou, and the bulk of the cultivated acreage was farmed by people classified as civilians.

Han Chinese confiscated land from the indigenous population, dominated business and trade activities both within Guizhou and between Guizhou and other provinces, and seized (and in some cases purchased) profitable mineral resources from the locals. Ming emperors, Ming officials, and wealthy Han in Guizhou even proposed setting up Confucian schools for the indigenous non-Han so as to begin the process of "turning the barbarian toward civilization," but their proposals usually fell on deaf ears. Nearly all schools built in Guizhou during the Ming were in areas with large concentrations of Han Chinese, and the education offered the non-Han people most assuredly consisted of little more than language instruction sprinkled with moral tomes. In virtually every sphere, political, military, economic, and sociocultural, there existed a clear division between the newly arrived Han Chinese soldier/settler and the non-Han indigene. As we shall see in the next chapter, the growing Han Chinese presence in Guizhou affected the Nasu Yi of Shuixi in ways inconceivable to Ming officials.

5

—

# To Reclaim
# Our Ancestors' Glory

When Ming forces entered the southwest in the 1370s, the head of the Azhe patriclan, Aicui, accepted the hereditary *tusi* title Guizhou pacification commissioner from the Hongwu emperor and agreed to relocate his administrative headquarters to Guiyang. Ming access to the Guizhou Pacification Commission in Guiyang and the formidable geography of Shuixi worked to insulate the Nasu Yi way of life in Shuixi during the initial phase of the Ming military conquest of the southwest. Hongwu nonetheless encircled Shuixi with several military garrisons and demanded the *zimo* in Shuixi provide goods and services to maintain these garrisons; yet, the emperor and his officials were cautious about entering Shuixi and antagonizing the still powerful Guizhou pacification commissioner (Ma Hua sought to drive Aicui and She Xiang out of Guiyang; he did not harbor ambitions to enter Shuixi). According to one Ming account, dated 1420, "The Guizhou pacification commissioner commands an army of over 300,000 strong, and everyone is afraid of the ferocious Luogui cavalry, which reportedly numbers close to 100,000."[1]

During the first half of the fifteenth century the Ming military relied heavily on the Guizhou and Bozhou pacification commissions to assist in the government's Luchuan campaigns in western Yunnan. But as I described in Chapter 4, even before the conclusion of the second Luchuan campaign, in 1449, powerful alliances were being forged among

Nasu Yi, Qilao, and Miao leaders to attack Ming military installations and Han settlements. In 1446, Nasu Yi leaders in Shuixi allied with Qilao leaders in Xibao to attack every Ming garrison and Han Chinese settlement in western Guizhou; in the following year, the Miao leader Wei Wengtong laid waste to Ming garrisons and Han Chinese communities in eastern Guizhou. The unexpected conclusion to the Luchuan campaign allowed the Ming commander Wang Ji to lead his army back into Guizhou to reassert Ming rule, but it would take another ten years of difficult fighting before Ming officials could claim to have restored order in Guizhou.

During the last decades of the fifteenth century and throughout much of the sixteenth century, the Ming government was resolute in its commitment to maintain the presence and effectiveness of its military installations in the southwest, and it did so by continually deploying fresh troops to the region. As we have seen, the overall size of the Han Chinese civilian population in the southwest increased substantially during this time period, as did the total amount of land owned by Han settlers. In addition, Han entrepreneurs came to dominate much of the trade within Guizhou, and between Guizhou and other provinces, and by the middle of the sixteenth century Han control of the region's lucrative natural resources was undeniable. Schools were built, almost exclusively for the Han Chinese population, and the number of official texts (gazetteers) and unofficial writings (travel narratives) on Guizhou and other parts of the southwest offer clear indication that Ming China's elites now considered this region to be an integral part of Ming China.

In this chapter I focus attention on how the Nasu Yi in Shuixi responded to the growing Ming state / Han Chinese presence in Guizhou. Adept leaders of the Azhe patriclan (Guizhou Pacification Commission), such as An Guirong (d. 1513), utilized new methods of agricultural production introduced by Han settlers to increase agricultural output in Shuixi; they hired skilled Han craftsmen to build roads and bridges throughout Shuixi; and they took into service former Ming officials to assist in the management of Shuixi's political and military affairs. Most amazingly, by the end of the sixteenth century Shuixi was viewed by Han and non-Han alike to be the most economically advanced region in Guizhou, and this only whetted the appetite of Ming officials who hoped to secure their place in Ming officialdom by eliminating the Guizhou Pacification Commission and incorporating Shuixi into the provincial bureaucracy. The Ming campaign against Bozhou in the 1590s proved to the leaders in Shuixi that Ming forces would eventually attempt to seize Shuixi; thus, the She-An Rebellion, 1621–29.

## The Ming-An Relationship

According to Ming sources, in the closing decades of the fifteenth century An Guirong and members of the *na* (aristocratic-warrior elite) in Shuixi reversed a recent historical trend in Guizhou and began to seize agricultural land along the Shuixi periphery, much of it owned by Han Chinese. Their intent was not to turn it into pastureland to graze horses and cattle, which was the traditional practice among the Nasu Yi elite, but to keep Han agriculturalists working the land in order to have a steady flow of tax revenue and a guaranteed supply of agricultural products.[2]

In an interview with Ming officials in Guiyang in 1480, An remarked, "The agricultural practices of the Han are superior to our [Nasu Yi] traditional methods, and we want to adopt [these practices] in Shuixi as soon as possible."[3] When a local Ming magistrate requested An's assistance to eliminate a growing slave market at Xibao, An decided instead to seize the town and its surrounding territory, remove the Ming official from office, and divide the land among *zimo* leaders—an example of *gailiu guitu* (replacing appointed [Chinese] officials with *tusi*). As one Ming official commented, "This entire operation [to seize Xibao] was conceived in the [Guizhou] pacification commissioner's office, which is located next to the provincial governor's yamen. Why can't we stop such brazen acts"?[4]

The seizure of Han Chinese lands along the Shuixi periphery and the inability (or unwillingness) of the Ming government to address this problem made the Ming appear impotent to all who knew what was happening. By 1485 An had embarked on a number of ambitious construction projects in both Guiyang and Mugebaizhage (Dafang) that illustrated his growing wealth and prestige. First, he completed construction on a new castle for himself at Mugebaizhage, the traditional seat of the Mu'ege kingdom, in the heart of Shuixi. An's castle sat on an elevated piece of ground overlooking the city, and at its base the castle measured approximately 250 square meters. He built a wall around the entire castle that measured 5 meters in height at its highest—the northern wall. The castle wall had four gates and was built inside a moat measuring 4 meters in width. The southern gate was the largest gate, and it faced the city directly. All non–Nasu Yi traffic was directed through the southern gate, whereas only members of the *na* could use the northern, eastern, and western gates. The cost of building the Mu'ege castle was nearly matched by construction of the Yongxing Temple, a Buddhist establishment commissioned by An's wife, She Mo.[5]

In addition to these construction projects in Mugebaizhage, An began work in the early 1480s on a series of repairs to his administrative headquarters and official residence in Guiyang. According to subsequent Chinese sources, An failed to have the architectural plans reviewed and approved by the provincial governor. When construction of the pacification commission's headquarters neared completion, Ming officials in Guiyang were offended by the grand design that clearly overshadowed the provincial governor's yamen. When An refused to modify his design or remove portions of the building to accommodate the demands of Ming officials, a fire suddenly engulfed the structure and destroyed it. Convinced that Ming officials had set the fire, An decided in 1486 to leave Guiyang and relocate his entire administration to Mugebaizhage. As a consequence, the Ming government formally recognized the head of the Song patriclan of Shuidong as the Guizhou pacification commissioner and conferred upon An the new title of Shuixi pacification commissioner.[6] A series of events in the 1490s only intensified the growing animosity between the two sides.

First, in 1491 Ming troops brutally suppressed a Miao uprising in Shiquan and then transported the remaining 8,500 Miao rebels to Guiyang, where they were publicly executed over a two-week period in the city market. The grisly piles of bodies and heads of the executed remained in the center of the market for several days before local merchants were given permission to dispose of them, but the merchants had difficulty removing the corpses because An paid laborers in Guiyang not to assist them.[7] It is unclear precisely what motivated An to take such an action, but one Ming official noted at the time how "much of the local population has left the city, and those who remain exhibit anger and defiance toward us. It is not safe for Han to venture out [in the city] alone."[8]

Second, in 1494 Ming officials eliminated several large *tusi* offices in southeastern Guizhou and created Duyun prefecture. This territory had formerly been a part of the Mu'ege kingdom, and the divested *tusi* appealed directly to An to intercede on their behalf. The *tusi* hoped to have their titles and offices restored, but when An's delegation arrived in Guiyang to discuss the issue, Ming officials refused to meet with them, claiming the Shuixi pacification commissioner had no authority to discuss the matter. Ming authorities then chastised the *tusi* for appealing to An for assistance and imprisoned those members of the divested *tusi*'s families residing in Guiyang.[9]

In yet another alarming incident, in 1499 the Ming military cooperated with *tusi* forces, minus An and Nasu Yi *zimo* from Shuixi, to suppress a charismatic Nasu Yi leader from Puan named Milu—the bandit princess.[10] Milu was the daughter of the Zhanyi (Yunnan) native prefect, and at a young age she was married to the elderly *tusi* in Puan. When the Puan *tusi* passed away, a struggle over who would inherit his titles ensued between Milu, as regent for her infant son, and the deceased *tusi*'s older sons by his previous wives. The inheritance struggle degenerated into an anti-Ming rebellion when Ming officials contradicted their own inheritance regulations and sided with one of Milu's rivals. By the time Ming forces claimed victory over Milu in 1501, they had captured and publicly executed 5,013 people, attacked over 1,000 villages, destroyed approximately 1,700 dwellings, and confiscated more than 30,000 head of livestock. There is no evidence indicating An directly supported Milu, but Ming officials were displeased that An had turned a deaf ear to their requests that he help mediate the crisis.[11]

Finally, in the early months of 1508, the influential Ming scholar-official Wang Shouren arrived at the Longchan postal station to begin serving time in internal exile for his role in the Liu Jin–Tai Xian Affair.[12] The Longchang station was the easternmost station on the Geya Postal Road established by She Xiang in the 1380s, and it was located in the fertile lands of Shuidong. The territory was until 1486 under An (Azhe) control, but when An Guirong left Guiyang and the Ming government appointed the Song patriclan to the office of Guizhou pacification commissioner, the Song assumed control of Shuidong. It did not take long for Wang to realize that Shuidong was "contested territory between [the Song of] Shuidong and [the An or Azhe of] Shuixi, and it is only a matter of time until the ambitious [An] Guirong marches across the [Yachi] river and seizes Shuidong."[13]

In 1513 An Guirong proved the since-departed Wang Shouren correct as he first sowed dissention among the non-Han peoples in Shuidong and then unleashed his Nasu Yi cavalry to attack the area. In the winter months of 1513, An's cavalry had marched south to Guiyang and was poised outside the city walls demanding Ming officials surrender the city. Before any decisive engagements took place, however, An died suddenly of a mysterious illness—Nasu sources claim he was poisoned by a confidant who had been bribed by Ming officials.[14] An's death abruptly ended the campaign to seize Shuidong and Guiyang, and Nasu Yi forces returned to Shuixi and offered compensation to Ming officials for damage caused by their siege of Guiyang.

Following An's death, the Azhe adopted a less confrontational posture toward the Ming. The new Shuixi pacification commissioner, An Zuo, requested permission to lead a tribute mission to Beijing, and the tribute gifts of timber, horses, and cattle were reportedly well received by provincial officials (of the ninety-three tribute missions the Azhe presented to the Ming throne between 1368 and 1621, most were received by provincial officials in Guiyang). For their part, Ming officials continued to call upon Shuixi leaders to assist in maintaining stability and order throughout Guizhou, Yunnan, and Sichuan, to which the Azhe readily obliged. As the following two examples indicate, however, the Azhe used these instances of cooperation to expand their influence beyond Shuixi and, when possible, to seize land, people, and economic assets.[15]

From 1523 to 1525 the Nasu Yi in Mangbu, the descendents of Tuomangbu, brother of Tuoazhe (founder of the Azhe patriclan), were embroiled in a spiteful inheritance battle. Long Shou, the deceased *tusi's* only son and rightful heir to the *tusi* office, found his path to office obstructed by his uncle, Long Zheng, who claimed the young man was unfit for the position. The crux of the dispute centered on Long Shou's mother, who was An Zuo's niece. Long Zheng rallied supporters to his side by claiming that An and the Azhe in Shuixi exercised far too much influence over the young Long Shou and were conspiring to seize Mangbu territory. Events spiraled out of control in 1524 when Long Zheng sent assassins to kill Long Shou and his mother, then named himself Mangbu *tusi*. This was when Ming officials in Guizhou requested An's assistance.

When word reached Ming officials in Luzhou (Sichuan) the following year that Mangbu and Shuixi were at war, Ming troops from Sichuan were dispatched to investigate. These troops were still north of the Chishui River and had not yet reached the Shuixi-Mangbu area when they learned that An's Shuixi troops had already defeated Mangbu and had handed over Long Zheng to Ming officials in Guizhou for execution. Sichuan officials were even more disturbed to learn that Guizhou's provincial officials had authorized An to bring Mangbu territory under Shuixi control as compensation for his service, which in effect meant Guizhou officials had allowed the Shuixi Pacification Commission to seize territory formerly part of Sichuan province. Officials in Sichuan protested this action, but the Ming court had already backed the decision by Guizhou's officials, thus ending discussion on the issue for the time being.[16]

A few years later, in 1536, Ming officials requested the Shuixi pacification commissioner's assistance in a military campaign to suppress A Xiang, a self-proclaimed king of the Miao in Duyun. In their request for military assistance they made the assertion that because the Duyun region had formerly been part of the Mu'ege (Luodian) kingdom, An Zuo had an obligation to help bring peace and stability to Duyun. Furthermore, the Ming officials argued that part of the problem in Duyun stemmed from the continual demand among the Nasu Yi in Shuixi for slaves to work in their agricultural fields, and that they bore some responsibility for what was taking place there. Ming patrols had recently come to the assistance of several Han Chinese communities who requested protection from marauding Miao bands. According to accounts attributed to Han settlers, the Miao kidnapped Han to sell to the Luogui in Shuixi, and A Xiang was the ringleader of a vast network of gangs that preyed on Han. An eventually sent a small cavalry detachment to Duyun, and Ming officials credit Shuixi troops with capturing A Xiang, but attacks attributed to the Miao on Han Chinese settlers continued and Duyun remained an important hub in the trafficking of humans.[17]

Part of the payoff for helping the Ming military in Mangbu and Duyun was greater access to Chinese markets in Guizhou, Yunnan, and Sichuan, increased contact with Ming officials in Luzhou and Guiyang, and Ming consent to An's acquisition of new lands along the Shuixi periphery. Ever since the Azhe fled Guiyang for Mugebaizhage in 1486, Ming officials had played tough by limiting trade between Chinese and Nasu merchants to the relatively small Bijie market. Following the transfer of Long Zheng to Ming officials, trade between Shuixi and Guiyang resumed, and members of the Nasu Yi elite started to trickle back into the city as part-time residents. The growing presence of Nasu Yi in Guiyang convinced Ming officials in 1544 to side with the Shuixi Pacification Commission's claim that the Bozhou Pacification Commission had failed to negotiate in good faith the transfer of the Shuiyan-Tianwang region to the Shuixi Pacification Commission.

In 1544 Yang Lie (d. 1571) ousted his father, Yang Xiang, and seized the office of Bozhou pacification commissioner. Yang Xiang and his supporters fled to Shuixi, where they received shelter and assistance from the Shuixi pacification commissioner. Following Yang Xiang's death, Yang Lie demanded his father's body be returned to Bozhou for proper burial. An Wanquan, regent to the infant Shuixi pacification commissioner An Wanzhong, agreed to hand over Yang Xiang's body but only on the condition that Yang Lie cede the Shuiyan-Tianwang region to Shuixi control. Initially Yang accepted these terms, but after he received his father's body he refused to comply with the agreement, claiming An Wanquan had blackmailed him. Provincial officials in Sichuan, who did not recognize Yang as the rightful heir to the Bozhou *tusi* office, nonetheless supported Yang's position, thereby precipitating a showdown between Ming officials in Guizhou and those in Sichuan. The stalemate over Shuiyan-Tianwang was broken and violence averted only after officials in Guizhou, under intense pressure from capital officials to end the crisis peacefully, bribed An into accepting a large tract of land south of Xibao as compensation for relinquishing claims to Shuiyan-Tianwang.[18]

In 1561, the Shuixi Pacification Commission acquired yet more territory, this time to the northwest of Shuixi, and gained greater access to markets in Yunnan and Sichuan following its participation in a campaign to suppress violence in Dongchuan—near the ancestral home of the Nasu Yi. According to Nasu documents, several years earlier An Wanquan's sister had married the Dongchuan native prefecture magistrate and bore him his only son, thereby making An the uncle of the infant heir to the native prefecture magistrate post in Dongchuan. In a situation similar to the one in Mangbu described above, the Dongchuan elite grew increasingly alarmed over what it considered Azhe meddling in its political affairs and as a result tried to kidnap the infant heir and place a rival in the prefect post. The kidnap plot failed, and the infant heir and his mother fled to Shuixi, where An immediately offered substantial military assistance.[19]

Before marching into Dongchuan, though, An told provincial authorities in Guiyang about what had transpired in Dongchuan, and that he was prepared to resolve the situation on behalf of the Ming state. Ming officials, possibly unaware of the influence An would exercise in

Dongchuan if he succeeded, were only too willing to accept An's offer to resolve this thorny situation. By the time Shuixi forces left Dongchuan in 1561, the Azhe patriclan and members of the *na* in Shuixi had extended their political jurisdiction over new territories to the north, west, and south of Shuixi. And despite the loss of the Shuiyan-Tianwang territory along Shuixi's eastern boundary with Bozhou, the improvement in relations with the Ming state translated into greater access not only to the markets in Luzhou and Guiyang but also to markets in the various Ming military garrisons surrounding Shuixi.

## Shuixi's Changing Political Economy

Prior to the sixteenth century the most common form of agricultural production in Shuixi was slash-and-burn cultivation. Yaocihai, the Mongol garrison commander in Shuixi, reported to superiors in Chengdu that agricultural production in Shuixi was not just inefficient, but the grains harvested were insufficient to meet the needs of the local population and the occupying Mongol forces. "Our [Yuan] troops in Yixibuxue [Shuixi] will face starvation unless grain shipments from Sichuan arrive soon. The horses are already severely malnourished, and we are unable to respond to even minor disturbances in Yixibuxue."[20] In 1385, the magistrate of Wusa prefecture reported how the "people of Shuixi and Yongning rely exclusively on slash-and-burn techniques to grow grain, and because of this every year they face food shortages. The most important agricultural products are buckwheat, oats, and barley. Wet rice plays only a minor role in the overall agriculture of Shuixi."[21]

A variety of sources indicate that An Guirong's decision to relocate the Azhe administrative headquarters to Mugebaizhage in 1486 had a decisive impact on the future development of the Shuixi political economy. Removed from the glare of Ming officials in Guiyang, An and his successors could demand compensation for Shuixi military assistance, and this is precisely what they did. An negotiated the acquisition of land, people, and access to commercial markets in return for Shuixi military assistance. To the consternation of the tradition-bound *na*, An also encouraged the development of agricultural production in newly acquired areas, rather than the horse, cattle, and sheep herding that had been the main staples of the Shuixi economy. In addition, he championed the use of cattle as farm animals—a method adopted from recent

Han Chinese settlers. Moreover, An was a strong proponent of acquiring Han Chinese laborers to work the newly opened lands. In the words of one Han Chinese adviser to the Adi *muzhuo*, located in the Dedu granary in southern Shuixi, "The leaders of the Luoluo realize they can generate more revenue by farming the land as the Han do than if they continued with traditional methods [slash-and-burn], and they use Han to introduce new farming techniques as well."[22]

By the beginning of the sixteenth century Ming officials were aware of the important changes taking place in Shuixi. Information garnered from Chinese merchants revealed a more open and accessible Shuixi frequented by merchants from Yunnan, Sichuan, and Guizhou. To punctuate this point, in 1546 An Wanquan ordered the Qiansui Road, a secondary name given to that portion of the Geya Postal Road between Mugebaizhage and Bijie, repaired in order to facilitate the easy flow of commerce into the heart of Shuixi. To celebrate the completion of the project, An invited government officials from Yunnan, Sichuan, and Guizhou to witness the opening of the road to commercial traffic. The gathering, according to one eyewitness account, "brought together a strange mixture of people. Officials and Han merchants from Yunnan [Dian], Sichuan [Shu], and Guizhou [Qian] mingled with Luogui officials and Miao and Qilao workers. It was truly a bizarre setting."[23]

About 25 kilometers west of Mugebaizhage a stone stele was recently discovered with Chinese and Nasu texts inscribed on it. The stele was erected to commemorate the completion of repairs made to the Qiansui Road. According to the Chinese text on the stele, the total cost of repairing the road surpassed 300 ounces of gold, but this enormous sum transformed a muddy mountain trail into a wide, paved thoroughfare with stone steps and smooth stones placed along steep mountain grades so merchants could climb the steps on the side of the road and pull their carts up the steep climb.[24] Mountain passes were opened, peaks were leveled off, and cliffs were chiseled away so travel into and out of Shuixi was made easy. Whereas the Chinese text describes the road repairs and the impact they had on travel and commerce, the Nasu text describes the history of the first Nasu Yi leaders to migrate into the Shuixi region from Yunnan, Dumu, Mujiji, and Tuozhe and portrays the Shuixi region as the heart of the Mu'ege kingdom. In an interesting note to the duality of An Wanquan's political authority, the Nasu text lists him as both the king of Mu'ege and the Guizhou (not Shuixi) pacification commissioner.[25]

The expansion of Azhe political authority beyond the geographic boundaries of Shuixi and the introduction of Chinese agricultural techniques into Shuixi had by the 1560s produced a rippling effect that extended far beyond Shuixi. A network of frontier markets quickly sprang up along the Shuixi periphery that integrated more fully the economy of Shuixi with that of the surrounding Han Chinese settlements, military garrisons, and non-Han villages. Shuixi's merchants purchased tea, salt, wine, and manufactured goods from Han merchants in Bijie, Luzhou, Wusa, Qujing, Guiyang, and nearby Ming garrisons while Han merchants purchased horses, timber, sheep, grain, and minerals such as cinnabar, mercury, iron, and lead from Shuixi merchants.[26] In addition, Shuixi craftspeople sold textiles, wood products (the Nasu used wood to make saddles, and their technical ability in this area was greatly admired by Han Chinese), and tiles (the Longjia in Shuixi built their homes with tiles, and their expertise in this area was recognized by all) in Chinese markets located throughout western Guizhou.[27]

In the *Qianji* (A record of Qian), an authoritative text on Guizhou compiled in 1608 by the eminent Ming official Guo Zizhang (1543–1618), it is recorded that "oats grown in Shuixi had become a common fixture in Guiyang's markets, and rice produced in Shuixi was not inferior to the rice grown in China proper."[28] Shuixi's products were sold at a market established by provincial officials just outside Guiyang's west gate specifically for Shuixi's merchants, and the "odd-sounding cacophony coming from this market can be heard from morning to night."[29] In addition to Guiyang, Shuixi merchants sold their wares at a vibrant market in Mangbu, curiously referred to as Rat Street (Shujie), where Han merchants from Guizhou, Sichuan, and Yunnan regularly conducted business.[30] By the early seventeenth century, the economic influence of Shuixi had become such that Liu Xixuan, the Guizhou education intendant (*tixue dao*), reported to his superiors in Beijing that "Shuixi is the agricultural heartland [*fuxin*] of Qian [Guizhou]. Nature has blessed this remote mountain region with fertile soil and moderate rainfall, whereas much of the land owned by Han [Chinese] is unproductive and useless."[31] Liu noted in his report that the most fertile lands and the most advanced economies were to be found in those areas controlled by the Luogui (Nasu)—Shuixi, Yongning, Chishui, Bijie, and Wusa.[32]

The construction of the Dadu River Bridge in 1592 is another example of the growing wealth and prestige of the Nasu Yi in Shuixi. Commissioned in 1590 by the Shuixi pacification commissioner, An Guoheng (d. 1595), the Dadu River Bridge is an impressive display of early modern engineering and skilled craftsmanship. Located some 40 kilometers southeast of Dafang, where the Geya Postal Road crosses the perilous Dadu River, the bridge was built to ease the flow of traffic along the road between Shuidong and Shuixi. Reportedly, travelers heading toward Shuixi from Shuidong congregated at the She Xiang Postal Station for several hours, sometimes even a day or two if the current was high, waiting to cross the river by either ferry or rope bridge. Both were considered quite dangerous, and it was difficult for merchants heading east out of Shuixi toward Shuidong and Guiyang to transport much except for items they carried on their person.[33]

In response to the growing commerce between Shuixi, Shuidong, and Guiyang, An Guoheng ordered the local *zimo*, An Bang, to contribute 1,150 ounces of silver and the labor required to build the bridge. For his part, An Guoheng hired Han Chinese engineers to plan the bridge's design and to oversee the construction phase. The bridge was made entirely of stone, with five large arches, each measuring nearly 14 meters in height, spanning the river at over 70 meters in length. An specified that the bridge be wide enough to permit two-way traffic, so the surface of the bridge was made 7 meters wide.[34] To commemorate the completion of the bridge, An ordered two steles to be placed, one on each side of the bridge. One stele was engraved with Chinese characters, whereas the second stele contained Nasu Yi script. The Chinese stele has seventeen lines of characters (a total of 681 characters) that describe how the bridge was built to aid in the flow of traffic between Shuixi and Shuidong and to incorporate the economy of Shuixi into that of the rest of Guizhou. In contrast, the Nasu Yi stele has twenty-four lines engraved on it (a total of 1,923 characters), and, like the Nasu Yi stele placed along the Qiansui Road, this stele retraces the history of the Nasu Yi people in Guizhou. The ancestors who led the Nasu Yi migration into Shuixi from Yunnan are depicted as heroic figures, and many of the important figures in Nasu Yi history are mentioned. The Nasu Yi stele, however, is not just a short synopsis of Nasu Yi rule of Shuixi; it also describes those periods in history (based on the genealogical records of the Nasu Yi leaders) when the Nasu Yi ruled much of contemporary Guizhou.[35] Whereas the Chinese stele was a rather formulaic presentation of the benefits the bridge would bring in drawing Shuixi, Shuidong, and Guizhou closer economically, the Nasu Yi stele affirmed the unique history of the Nasu Yi people in Shuixi and Guizhou.

Ming officials stationed in Guiyang at the end of the sixteenth century were reporting with surprising regularity how the Shuixi region had become one of the most important agricultural regions in the province, if not *the* most important. Grain harvested from Shuixi was making its way to the Guiyang markets, and if we can trust Guo Zizhang's account, the rice from Shuixi was just as good as any harvested in China proper. Agricultural products were not the only Shuixi commodities sold in Guiyang's markets, though. Chinese had acquired a taste for woolen blankets made by Miao craftsmen in Shuixi. Guizhou's cold, damp winters demanded some sort of protection from the elements, and the skillfully woven patterns and thick mat of the blankets not only secured warmth but also made them a fashionable feature to be displayed in Chinese homes. According to one official who traveled regularly between Huguang, Guizhou, and Yunnan:

The markets in Qian sell products from as far away as Shu [Sichuan] to the north, Dian [Yunnan] to the west, and Guang [Guangdong] to the east, and goods made in Qian can be found in these distant places as well. Plants for medicinal use, horses, jewelry, and Luogui blankets are just a few of the commodities produced in Qian that are for sale in Huguang's markets.[36]

Nasu craftsmen also excelled in woodworking. Sources dating from as far back as the Tang dynasty mention the ease with which one can ride a horse in the Luogui saddle, and Ming commanders made purchases of the saddle a top priority. The traditional Nasu Yi saddle was made from a soft pine that was both sturdy and flexible, and since it forced the rider to sit upright with a straight back, the rider did not fatigue easily. Moreover, the Nasu Yi saddle purportedly distributed the rider's weight more evenly on the horse's back than did Chinese saddles, thus allowing the horse to climb steep hills and negotiate sharp turns with relative ease. That the Ming military consistently requested Luogui saddles to be part of the tribute presented to the Ming throne is sufficient proof that these saddles were highly prized by avid horsemen in Ming China. Ming officials, too, placed orders for the Luogui saddle, which, according to sources, sold briskly on the Guiyang market.[37]

Lacquerware and jewelry made of silver were other Nasu Yi specialties sold in Guizhou's markets. Lacquer jewelry and small curio boxes were produced in large quantities by Longjia and Songjia artisans in Shuixi. Bracelets, necklaces, and waistbands made of reddish-colored lacquer beads were fashionable among the Nasu Yi military aristocracy, and for this reason such items became sought after by those wanting to emulate Nasu Yi dress.[38] Miao artisans reportedly produced much of the silver jewelry sold by Shuixi merchants, but competition from Miao artisans residing outside Shuixi limited demand for Shuixi silver. Instead, it was the style of silver bracelets and necklaces worn by the Nasu Yi elite that captured market share; according to one account, "The visitor intent on purchasing a Luogui bracelet must make sure that the bracelet was in fact produced in Shuixi, and not by Miao in Duyun."[39] In addition to the lacquerware and jewelry, Longjia artisans from Shuixi were renowned for their skills in tile production, and many of the administrative offices and private residences of the wealthy were adorned with tiles produced by these artisans.[40]

Finally, Ming officials also mentioned the existence of mineral deposits in Shuixi and the growing interest on the part of the Nasu Yi elite in exploiting these deposits for profit. Cinnabar, mercury, iron, and lead were frequently mentioned in mid-sixteenth-century Ming texts as minerals mined and/or produced in Shuixi. Cinnabar and mercury were in high demand for their medicinal properties, and it seems clear that these two commodities were shipped to points far beyond Guizhou's borders. Much of the iron produced in Shuixi was sold to Bozhou, where artisans transformed the raw material into swords, knives, and other articles of war.[41] As one late Ming observer noted, "Purchase your horse and saddle from the Luogui, but buy your sword in Bozhou."[42]

Beginning in the latter half of the fifteenth century, then, the Nasu Yi aristocratic-warrior elite in Shuixi began to incorporate into the Shuixi economy agricultural and industrial techniques introduced into Guizhou over the past century by Han Chinese settlers. Under the guidance of several able leaders, such as An Guirong and An Wanquan, the conventional slash-and-burn technique of agricultural production was to a large extent supplanted by more intensive means of production, so by the end of the sixteenth century Shuixi was not only a net exporter of grain to the Guizhou markets, it had acquired a reputation as the most fertile region in the province. New industrial techniques were introduced to exploit the region's natural resources, and traditional handicrafts like saddles, blankets, and jewelry found ready buyers even beyond Guizhou's borders. Moreover, Shuixi's aged transportation system was repaired and expanded in order to facilitate travel between Shuixi and the regional economies beyond its geographic boundaries.

Many within Ming officialdom viewed this expansion of the Shuixi political economy in less than sanguine terms. Ming officials intent on eliminating *tusi* offices and extending Ming institutions of direct rule were concerned about the expanding wealth and power of the Shuixi pacification commissioner. His authority and stature not only rivaled that of the Ming officials stationed throughout western Guizhou, in many instances it eclipsed theirs. Nasu Yi leaders throughout eastern Yunnan, southern Sichuan, and western Guizhou turned increasingly to the Shuixi pacification commissioner for advice and assistance instead of seeking out Ming officials. As one Nasu Yi source put it, "An Guoheng [who ruled Shuixi from 1562 to 1595] speaks with such authority that even the [Ming] officials shudder in fear. Under Guoheng we can reclaim our ancestors' glory."[43] It certainly did not bode well for Ming officials in the southwest that the Shuixi pacification commissioner post was filled by an individual who embodied the glories of Shuixi's Nasu Yi ancestors and the hopes of their descendants. The history of the Nasu Yi in Shuixi during the late sixteenth and early seventeenth centuries is of a regional power beginning to flex its political-economic muscles, much like the Manchus were doing in China's Liaodong frontier.

## Prelude to Rebellion: An Guoheng, An Jiangchen, and the Ming State in Guizhou

In 1562 An Guoheng reached maturity and replaced his influential granduncle, regent An Wanquan, as the political head of the Azhe patriclan and Shuixi pacification commissioner.[44] Ming officials in Guiyang were very familiar with this tall, handsome man. He had received an introduction to Chinese education at the Guiyang prefecture school, and he maintained a residence in the provincial capital where he entertained Guiyang's elite, Han and non-Han alike. He was known to be a serious man with an explosive temper, consumed with contemporary issues but respectful of the unique history of the Nasu Yi people in Guizhou. On more than one occasion he purportedly lectured his Han Chinese guests on the virtues and martial skills of the noble Nasu Yi, even going so far as to demonstrate his skills in archery, fencing, and horseback riding in minor exhibitions.[45] It was because of his youth, political inexperience, and purported acculturation to Chinese ways that proexpansionist Ming officials in Guiyang sought to roll back several of the territorial gains made by the Shuixi Pacification Commission over the last century.

In the autumn of 1570 Ming troops stationed in Anshun department and Puding garrison were ordered to march west toward Xibao, the territory annexed by An Guirong in 1479, and replace the *tusi* in Xibao with Ming officials. Since many of these *tusi* were descendants of Nasu Yi officials who had assisted An Guirong in his campaign into Xibao in 1479, this act of *gaitu guiliu* directly challenged An Guoheng's authority over his own subjects.[46] A month later Ming troops stationed in Guiyang coordinated with the Bozhou Pacification Commission to seize the town of Liuguang (northwest of the Longchan postal station) and surrounding territory adjacent to the Yachi River. Again the objective was to replace the Nasu Yi *tusi* with Ming officials. Unlike Xibao, though, Liuguang was historically part of the Yude granary, one of the main administrative regions under Azhe control, and the town of Liuguang itself was the administrative headquarters for the *muzhuo* in command of the granary. The *muzhuo* in Liuguang was also a *tusi* of the Ming government.[47]

Finally, in the first month of 1571 Ming officials ordered mixed units of Ming and *tusi* troops to attack several Nasu Yi *tusi* located between the Weiqing garrison and the Yachi River. These *tusi* were also *muzhuo* within the Liumu granary, but the duality of their appointments (like those of the Liuguang *muzhuo*) did not seem to concern the Ming officials who drafted this plan.[48] This three-pronged assault against An Guoheng's territory east and south of the Yachi River appeared intent upon not just halting Nasu Yi expansion beyond what was traditionally regarded as Shuixi, but also pushing An and his officials back into Shuixi.

If Ming officials believed An would shy away from a direct confrontation and retreat to the recesses of Shuixi, they grossly miscalculated the young man's resolve. An immediately assembled a huge force estimated at more than 200,000, which one Ming commander reported was "an awesome sight of sounds and colors with the fearsome Luogui cavalry leading a column of war elephants on one side and tigers tethered to chariots on the other side."[49] This force attacked Ming units near Liuguang. An gave instructions to his field commanders that they specifically target Ming forces for attack and refrain from engaging those *tusi* troops allied with the Ming. An decided instead to dispatch envoys to the *tusi* camps in hopes of convincing them to abandon their alliance with the Ming and return home. This tactic proved highly successful. In several critical instances Ming forces found themselves dangerously exposed on the battlefield when *tusi* forces failed to engage in the fight.[50]

At the battle of Muke, for example, Ming forces believed they had cornered a large Nasu Yi cavalry force near the confluence of the Yachi and Miaotiao rivers, but the *tusi* forces who were supposed to block the Nasu Yi retreat by positioning themselves on the opposite side of the Miaotiao River never showed. The Nasu Yi cavalry quickly crossed the Miaotiao River, marched upstream several kilometers, rode back across the Miaotiao, and then attacked the Ming forces from the rear, thus accomplishing precisely what Ming commanders had hoped to do to them. A Ming force of nearly 4,000 soldiers was completely wiped out in one afternoon. After Muke, Ming commanders frowned on coordinating battlefield maneuvers with *tusi* troops, and for this reason the overall number of troops the Ming military could place in the field decreased significantly.[51]

By the summer of 1571 Nasu Yi forces had pushed Ming units out of Xibao, Liuguang, and Liumu and were themselves advancing toward Chinese settlements and Ming garrisons. Desperate to stem An Guoheng's initiative, Ming officials decided to provide financial and military assistance to a disaffected member of the Azhe patriclan, a man named Azhi, who had previously challenged An's claim to political preeminence in Shuixi.[52] Azhi was able to convince the *na* in Shuidong and some disaffected Nasu Yi officials from the Liumu and Yude granaries to turn against An, but he relied upon Ming promises of money, material, and land to gain *tusi* support for his campaign. This time, however, instead of *tusi* forces' abandoning Ming units on the battlefield, failure to prosecute Azhi's campaign against An fell squarely on the shoulders of predatory Ming officials, many of whom refused at the last minute to provide Azhi with the provisions he was promised. With Ming assistance not forthcoming, Azhi quickly abandoned his cause and negotiated his surrender to An. Azhi renounced any political claims to offices and titles within the Nasu Yi polity (though he was returned to Shuidong), and in time he and his supporters were incorporated into An's rapidly expanding geopolitical umbrella.[53]

Azhi's surrender compromised the security of numerous Ming garrisons and Han Chinese communities along the Shuixi periphery. Ming officials had gambled on their ability to keep coalition forces together long enough to peel away *tusi* under Shuixi jurisdiction and, if the opportunity presented itself, to defeat An's forces in battle; however Ming attempts at building and maintaining military coalitions failed miserably. Following Azhi's surrender, An became more confident than ever.

Throughout the 1580s and 1590s An juggled his business interests and the growing economic clout of Shuixi with his desire to challenge the authority of the Ming military installations in western Guizhou. An's forces pushed deep into Shuidong; his cavalry disrupted traffic along the main highway linking Guiyang and Yunnan; and Ming garrisons to the west of Shuixi, in particular the Bijie, Wusa, and Yongning garrisons, were transformed into virtual islands as An's troops closed in from the east and Nasu forces from Yongning marched down from the north.[54] An's ability to project his military power beyond Shuixi and cut off traffic to and from Yunnan led Ming officials to once again affirm the region's strategic importance to Ming control of Yunnan. "If we fail to control the roads through western Qian," one local official argued, "then we will lose control of Yunnan, just as Taizu [Hongwu] predicted."[55]

The ill-planned Ming campaign to seize territory from An had backfired, and officials in Guiyang were growing ever more despondent as events in Guizhou spiraled out of control. At this point the inexplicable happened: An notified officials in Guiyang that he wished to lead a tribute mission to the Ming capital. The officials, probably shocked by this sudden turn of good fortune, accepted An's request, which for all intents and purposes ended the undeclared state of war that existed between Guiyang and the Shuixi pacification commissioner. An and his subordinates would be consumed for months with preparations for the mission, and the mission itself would take two, possibly three, months to complete. The best commanders available to An would be in the capital with him, thus depriving the Shuixi military of any potency.

For his part, An gambled that a tribute mission to the Ming capital not only would afford him the opportunity to judge the state of Ming political-military resolve but also insulate Shuixi from attack from provincial officials. Ming officials in Guizhou, Yunnan, and Sichuan would not dare attack Shuixi while An was presenting tribute to the Ming throne. A tribute mission also would allow him to solidify political ties with subordinates and allies by inviting them to participate. Furthermore, An expected an economic rebound in his favor as the prestige of a tribute mission would grant him the right to negotiate business deals, purchase goods and services from Han Chinese along the tribute route, and lure skilled craftsmen to relocate to Shuixi.

An did indeed lead a large Nasu Yi delegation to Beijing in the winter months of 1590–91. In addition to the tribute gift of 1,000 horses,

300 saddles, and "a plentiful supply of cinnabar," An and his entourage were ordered to provide the imperial court with a large supply of timber to be used to rebuild palaces destroyed by fire.[56] Ever since the Jiajing reign (1522–66), court officials had been routinely dispatched to the southwest with orders to procure timber for imperial palaces. Because the timber was to be used as beams to support the tile roofs of the large palaces and ceremonial halls, it could not be cut into smaller, easily transportable pieces.[57] For this reason, the logistics of felling timber high in the remote mountains of Shuixi and then transporting the logs to Beijing must have required incredible skill and an enormous invest-ment in labor. One account of An's mission to Beijing noted that sev-eral thousand laborers participated in the mission, though precisely what these laborers did, like transporting timber, is left unsaid. An, nevertheless, provided the Ming court with all that was asked of him, and he was rewarded handsomely.

An and his entourage of *na* warriors clearly impressed their Ming hosts. Court records describe this tribute mission as consisting of "im-pressive-looking barbarians [*manyi*] from the south, with exquisitely crafted knee-high leather boots and beautifully colored clothes that af-fect a regal comportment. The men stand tall and stride in an open gait, so they project an air of confidence. Their mannerisms are direct and respectful, and they speak without false flattery."[58] There is no record of the Wanli emperor (Zhu Yizhun; 1563–1620, r. 1573–1620) requesting a demonstration of Nasu Yi folkways, as had been the case in earlier Nasu Yi missions to the Chinese court, but he was deeply impressed by An's retinue, and he bestowed a number of impressive gifts upon those in attendance.[59] One important outcome of An's mission was his agree-ment to assist Ming officials in Sichuan and Guizhou in their dealings with the increasingly recalcitrant Bozhou pacification commissioner, Yang Yinglong (1552–1600).

Yang Yinglong was the twenty-ninth hereditary leader of the Yang family that had settled the Bozhou region of northern Guizhou during the last decades of the Tang dynasty. In 1585, Yang became incensed when the Ming court, in an expression of gratitude to Yang for his assistance in the suppression of troublesome Miao tribesmen in Sichuan, bestowed upon him imperial clothing embroidered with a flying fish. Yang believed his military assistance warranted an imperial garment embroidered with a dragon, similar to the garment given to his grandfather Yang Bin (1486–1518) for comparable military service.[60] A Ming imperial garment embroidered with a flying fish was not as prestigious as one with an embroidered dragon, and Yang believed he deserved such a gift from the Ming emperor to affirm his political authority over the many *tusi* located within the Bozhou Pacification Commission. Nearly all the *tusi* in the Bozhou region came from powerful families who had settled in northern Qian prior to the Ming dynasty, and Yang believed he was owed a tradition-bound loyalty from these families that exceeded anything included in a Ming state–*tusi* relationship.[61]

Yang, ever since his ascension to the post of pacification commissioner in 1571, had encountered difficulty in maintaining the loyalty and obedience of subordinate *tusi* in Bozhou. This tension between the Bozhou lord and his vassals was greatly exacerbated in 1587, when Yang murdered his wife and mother-in-law and then dealt harshly with those subordinates and family members who opposed his actions. By 1591, relations between Yang and several of his more important retainers, specifically the Huangping and Caotang military commissioners, and the Zhenzhou, Bozhou, Yongshan, Zhongan, Baili, and Yuching native officials (*zhangguan shi*), had become so strained that these *tusi*-retainers decided to cast aside loyalty and appeal to the Ming state for help in restraining Yang's eccentric behavior.[62] The *tusi*-retainers claimed in a petition sent to provincial authorities that when they attempted to reason with Yang regarding his treatment of his wife and family members, he responded by chastising them and referring to them as his slaves (*nubei*). When Yang traveled to Chongqing to explain his actions before provincial officials, he was placed under house arrest and forbidden to have any contact with family and subordinates.[63]

At the heart of the problem was the fact that on paper Yang, as the Bozhou pacification commissioner, possessed the political authority to adjudicate all civil problems within Bozhou, oversee the hereditary succession of all *tusi* offices in Bozhou, and create new estates for those loyal to him and withdraw estates from the disloyal. Such political authority granted to the pacification commissioner was a feature of the process of expansion in the late fourteenth century, when the Ming state desperately needed order and stability in a contentious frontier. The early Ming state used *tusi* offices to incorporate the frontier elite within the framework of a centralized Chinese polity without radically altering the traditional patron-client relationships and the frontier elite's traditional methods of rule. *Tusi* offices were an expedient means of extending the Ming polity into frontier areas.

As the Ming state expanded its presence in the southwest frontier during the fifteenth and sixteenth centuries, it asserted political supremacy either by carrying out *gaitu guiliu* or by creating midlevel *tusi* offices that were theoretically subordinate to the pacification commissioner but in reality were indebted to the Ming state—the midlevel *tusi*'s real patron. As a result, by the end of the sixteenth century the actions of a powerful frontier official like Yang were quite limited because his vassals, if they had received appointment as *tusi*, could always appeal to the Ming state to restrain an overbearing lord's behavior. Yang could assert the prerogative that the people residing within his domain were linked to him by traditional of patron-client relationships, but by the end of the sixteenth century the value and legitimacy of such relationships was fraying badly at the edges as the Ming state presented to the midlevel elite an alternative to tradition. This was precisely what was happening in Bozhou, and it was exactly what did not happen in Shuixi. The Ming state was never able to insert itself into Shuixi and co-opt the midlevel elite as it did in Bozhou.

It is entirely possible that An Guoheng, during his tribute visit to the Ming capital, was ordered to assist the Ming military in a campaign against Yang, since there is mention in only one text, dating from early 1592, that An would assist the Ming if he were guaranteed control over the contested Shuiyan-Tianwang region occupied by Bozhou since 1544.[64] In any case, a series of bizarre twists and turns transpired to prevent the immediate outbreak of hostilities between Yang and the Ming state. First, the Ming state was unsure as to how to deal with Yang. Provincial officials in Sichuan were consumed with a large rebellion gripping the Songpan region of northwest Sichuan, and they were more interested in gaining Yang's military assistance to defeat the Songpan rebels than in picking a fight with the powerful Bozhou leader.[65] However, Guizhou officials, such as Governor Ye Mengxiong, were pushing for a quick military resolution to the Bozhou situation because they believed that following the elimination of the Bozhou Pacification Commission most, if not all, of the territory would revert to Guizhou provincial control and thereby bring additional revenue to provincial coffers in desperate need of an infusion of cash.[66]

Second, Yang, in a calculated move designed to gain his release from Chongqing and deflect government pressure away from Bozhou, offered to send a contingent of Bozhou troops to Korea to aid the Ming in its fight against the Japanese hegemon, Toyotomi Hideyoshi. Sichuan au-

thorities were impressed by Yang's offer and released him from house arrest; however, court officials were less enthralled about the possibility of
several thousand heavily armed troops marching along the highways of
China toward Korea.[67] Before long the Ministry of War issued orders to
officials in Chongqing calling for the Bozhou contingent, which had already left Bozhou for Korea, to return to Bozhou.[68] Though court officials declined Yang's offer, his actions nonetheless earned him considerable gratitude, and local officials now proved unwilling to come to the
aid of the many midlevel *tusi* in Bozhou who first complained about
Yang's rule.

On the other hand, Guizhou officials had adopted a sterner approach
toward Yang, but in 1595 An Guoheng died, and Ming officials in
Guizhou were briefly more concerned about an intrapatriclan struggle
for succession in Shuixi than how to handle Yang. An Guoheng was
eventually succeeded by his son, An Jiangchen, who had been intimately involved in his father's political affairs and therefore was aware
of his father's recent policy of cooperation with Ming authorities in
Guizhou. Within months, An dispatched envoys to the Ming capital
bearing "tribute gifts," though the mission was also seen as a confirmation hearing. In any case, An's envoys presented horses and wood to the
Ming throne, and in return they received An's formal investiture as the
Shuixi pacification commissioner, as well as a number of impressive
titles for themselves.[69]

Yang's relations with Ming officials in Sichuan and Guizhou had
never been particularly good, but in the middle of 1596 Yang, following the death of his son in Chongqing and the inexplicable refusal
on the part of Chongqing officials to return the body to Bozhou for burial, adopted an increasingly bellicose tone toward provincial authorities.[70] Initially, his wrath fell upon insubordinate *tusi* in Bozhou, in particular the Huangping and Caotang military commissioners, who Yang
claimed had a hand in his son's death. By the end of 1596, Yang's forces
had marched deep into the southern portion of Bozhou to attack
Huangping and Caotang. The Ming military, not surprisingly, was
quickly drawn into the fight, but its garrisons in eastern Guizhou proved
no match for Yang's army. In 1598, Yang's cavalry had sacked the Xintian and Pianqiao garrisons and had severely compromised Ming control of the main east-west highway in eastern Guizhou.[71] The Guizhou
provincial governor, Jiang Dongzhi, sent a rather small contingent
of three thousand Ming soldiers into southern Bozhou in early 1599,

but after a few initial victories the entire force was annihilated at the Battle of Feilianbao, thus leaving Ming officials in Guiyang vulnerable to attack.[72]

With military resources in Guizhou nearly exhausted, provincial officials turned to An Jiangchen for assistance. To convince An to attack Bozhou, Jiang agreed to hand over the contested Shuiyan-Tianwang region to Shuixi control following the campaign. Ming officials desperately wanted to prevent an alliance between Shuixi and Bozhou, and officials in Guiyang believed that this promise of the Shuiyan-Tianwang territory would be enough to secure the allegiance of An. This pledge of land for military cooperation was, in fact, part of a larger Ming attempt to garner *tusi* assistance against Bozhou, and Jiang's appeal convinced many *tusi* to negotiate terms of cooperation with the Ming. For example, instead of simply accepting the government's position on Shuiyan-Tianwang, An shrewdly traveled to Guiyang to present an alternative proposal: Shuixi forces would assist the Ming military against Yang Yinglong in return for the Shuiyan-Tianwang territory and for a Ming promise to begin replacing Ming posts with *tusi*, especially in the Chengfan area south of Guiyang.[73] In other words, An wanted provincial officials to recall their officials from the recently annexed Chengfan area, which Shuixi troops had helped to pacify, and reappoint members of the indigenous elite to *tusi* posts.

In 1586 Ming officials eliminated the Chengfan Military Commission and established Dingfan department in order to gain control of productive paddy land in Chengfan. At different times throughout history, Chengfan had been under the political control of the Mu'ege kingdom, and the Chengfan leadership, in addition to the Jinzhu Military Commission and sixteen smaller *tusi* located in the greater Chengfan region, still presented token tribute payments to the Azhe in the 1590s. When Ming officials eliminated the Chengfan *tusi* in 1586, they demanded that the local elites in Chengfan end tribute payments to the Azhe, which they did not, and submit all tax payments to Guiyang. What is interesting about An's proposal to Governor Jiang, however, is that he mentions the tribute payments only in passing and instead argues that Ming rule in Chengfan had failed to provide the people with a better standard of living, which was precisely what Ming officials had promised the people of Chengfan at the time of *gaitu guiliu*. An's remarks at the time are unequivocally clear: "The construction of government facilities in Chengfan and in Guiyang has siphoned off the last coppers in the people's pockets. Ming rule has left the people poor and destitute. Those who speak of morality often demonstrate it the least."[74]

By 1599 the Ming state had reached a critical point in its rule of Guizhou: Yang Yinglong's forces had sacked two Ming garrisons along the main east-west highway, terrorized a number of cities in central and eastern Guizhou, and destroyed an entire Ming detachment at the Battle of Feilianbao.[75] Ming troop strength in Guizhou was perilously low (as mentioned in Chapter 4, there was a significant decline in military households during the second half of the sixteenth century), and *tusi* troops had proven themselves to be unreliable in battle. Furthermore, the powerful Shuixi pacification commissioner An Jiangchen publicly challenged the effectiveness of Ming civilian rule by advocating the removal of Ming administrative units in Chengfan and a return of the traditional ruling elite as *tusi*. An's argument was surprisingly similar to what the famous Ming loyalist Gu Yanwu (1613–82) would advocate half a century later: "Because of their long-standing interest in maintaining peace and prosperity in their home districts, the local elite is better prepared to govern their respective areas than is the state bureaucracy."[76]

When court officials received copies of An's recommendations, they immediately replaced the ineffective Jiang Dongzhi with Guo Zizhang, the aggressive, proexpansionist official from Taihe county, Jiangxi.[77] Three weeks later, on April 22, 1599, the Ming court announced the appointment of former vice minister of war Li Hualong (1554–1612), another proexpansionist official with a strong military background, to be the governor of Sichuan, as well as the supreme commander of the Bozhou campaign, with personal charge of all military affairs in Sichuan, Huguang, and Guizhou. Both Guo and Li believed that with the successful conclusion of the Sino-Japanese War in Korea in 1598 the Ming military could now concentrate on delivering a crushing blow to the recalcitrant Yang Yinglong. Neither official mentioned negotiating a resolution with Yang. "Only a demonstrative show of force," Guo would later argue, "can compel those indecisive *tusi* to be in awe (*wei*) of [Ming] rule once again."[78]

Li arrived in Chongqing in July 1599, and he immediately began recruiting his army from soldiers recently demobilized from the Pubei campaign in Ningxia, which ended in 1592, and from the soldiers who had participated in the Sino-Japanese War in Korea. The Ming court assisted Li in this task by promising land, money, and titles to all who participated in the Bozhou campaign, though the Ming court also indicated it had no intention of eliminating the Bozhou Pacification Commission. This apparent contradiction in Ming objectives, to provide land to all who participated in the campaign but not carry out *gaitu guiliu* in Bozhou, was designed to attract as much Han Chinese and *tusi* support as possible without frightening the *tusi* in Sichuan and Guizhou into thinking that the Ming state was preparing to overthrow them as well.[79] The Ming court presented the Bozhou campaign as an action against Yang Yinglong, not the institution of *tusi* offices; however, as preparations for the campaign neared completion, it became increasingly evident that both Li and Guo fully intended to eliminate the Bozhou Pacification Commission and parcel out Bozhou lands to Han Chinese settlers.

By March 1600 an army of over 240,000 troops assembled in five columns positioned at several strategic points to the north and southeast of Bozhou. Despite Li's intent to attract a national army, the force was strikingly regional in composition: 70 percent of the army consisted of *tusi* troops, whereas the remaining 30 percent was made up of Ming regulars.[80] The *tusi* troops came from five neighboring provinces, Guizhou, Sichuan, Yunnan, Huguang, and Guangxi, on the promise that they too would be handsomely rewarded for contributing to this campaign. An Jiangchen's criticism of Ming rule aside, Li and Guo promised to give the Shuiyan-Tianwang territory to An as reward for his cooperation, and thus Ming forces were not deployed to the west of Bozhou. The Huangping and Caotang military commissioners, the two officials whose persistence convinced Guizhou officials to take a more aggressive stance against Yang, were guaranteed large tracts of land registered to Yang, and they contributed heavily to the Ming campaign.

The Ming campaign against Bozhou was a surprisingly short affair. Li launched the attack on March 26, 1600, and by July 15, Yang was dead and Bozhou forces were in complete disarray. In late May, as the campaign reached a decisive stage with Ming forces tightening the circle around Bozhou, the Ming court still maintained that only the land belonging to Yang would be parceled out to participating troops, and that a large-scale program of *gaitu guiliu* was not planned for the Bozhou area. Li, Guo, and many of the local officials assigned to the campaign, however, had a different perspective. By the middle of June both Li and Guo were dropping hints that they were disappointed in how the *tusi* forces had performed, and that the greater Bozhou territory would

experience a more far-reaching program of *gaitu guiliu* and Han settlement than previously disclosed. Whereas the Ming court assured those
*tusi* like the Huangping and Caotang military commissioners that their
domains in Bozhou would remain untouched, Li and Guo were suggesting with a more menacing tone that there would be an across-the-board
*gaitu guiliu* program for Bozhou.[81] By the end of the year Li and Guo had
convinced many in the Ming court to support their program of *gaitu
guiliu.*

The foundation of Li's plan, titled "The Twelve Points for the Reconstruction of Bozhou," called for dividing the former pacification
commission's territory into two large prefectures. The northern half of
Bozhou would form the basis of a new prefecture called Zunyi, with one
department (*zhou*), four counties (*xian*), and one military garrison (*wei*)
placed under its charge; the southern half would become Pingyue prefecture, with one department, three counties, and one garrison. Zunyi
prefecture would be under Sichuan provincial jurisdiction, and Pingyue
prefecture would be a part of Guizhou province. Despite all of the earlier assertions by the Ming court that *tusi* offices in Bozhou would not
be touched, the Ming eliminated all *tusi* posts in the former Bozhou
Pacification Commission, including the Huangping and Caotang military commissions.[82]

The city of Bozhou, where the Yang patriclan had made its headquarters for nearly eight centuries, was renamed Zunyi and made the administrative seat for the new Zunyi prefecture. Ming officials, to make good on
their promise to reward Ming troops with land and money, established a
military garrison in Zunyi with a contingent of 5,000 troops, and each
soldier was ordered to relocate his family to Zunyi or to marry and start a
new household within one year (in announcing this policy Li noted that
he was following Ming precedent first adopted by Hongwu in the 1380s).
Each soldier of the new Weiyuan garrison was allotted 30 *mu* of land to
farm, and additional farmland could be purchased from government
agents at low prices. The same regulations applied to the new Huangping
garrison established in Pingyue prefecture, though due to its close proximity to several of the original Ming garrisons, Guo relocated only 3,000
troops to this garrison.[83]

Based on a land survey completed in early 1601, there was a total of
396,305 *mu* (60,046 acres) of paddy and 885,142 *mu* (134,112 acres) of
land in Zunyi prefecture. Much of this land had been owned directly by
the Yang family, and it was confiscated by Ming authorities at the end

of the campaign to be distributed to garrison soldiers and sold to Han Chinese settlers. Ming military officers were permitted to purchase up to 100 *mu* of land, and Han Chinese civilians, many of whom had gone to Zunyi on the promise of affordable land, were allowed to purchase up to 50 *mu*. Moreover, the non-Han population that resided in Zunyi was prohibited from purchasing any of the land confiscated by the Ming military.[84] It seems clear that the government was intent on creating a large Han Chinese community in Zunyi by allowing only Han Chinese to purchase land and then restricting the size of the land plots for sale so that no one individual or family could dominate an area.

Both Li and Guo sought to make good on their promise to An Jiang-chen and hand over the Shuiyan-Tianwang territory to Shuixi control, but the Ming court refused to permit the transfer of this territory. Court officials argued that An's Shuixi force withdrew from Bozhou on July 8, one week before Yang Yinglong's body was found in the burning rubble of his mountain castle, and that An's forces withdrew even though Ming officials had ordered them to press forward into Bozhou. An eventually withdrew his troops from Shuiyan-Tianwang, and the territory was opened for Han Chinese settlement. As we shall see shortly, the disagreement over Shuiyan-Tianwang and the fact that Ming officials carried out *gaitu guiliu* in Bozhou after they had repeatedly said their objectives were only to get rid of Yang weighed heavily on An and other *tusi* in Guizhou.[85]

Immediately following the Bozhou campaign Guizhou was rife with tension. Many of the *tusi* who had participated in the military campaign had received very little compensation, and their disgust over broken promises translated into a palpable hostility toward the Ming state. The assertive presence of Guo did not ease tensions either. Guo set out to rebuild and staff many of the Ming garrisons that had fallen into disrepair during the sixteenth century. Ming soldiers and their families were recruited to relocate to Guizhou, Han Chinese farmers and merchants were enticed to move to locations near these garrisons through generous loan programs designed to make the purchase of land easier, and *tusi* and non-Han indigenes who resisted Guo's plans for Guizhou were introduced to his brutal efficiency.[86] Under Guo the Ming military became an instrument to intimidate the indigenous population into submission, as was made poignantly clear in 1605, when Ming forces swept through eastern and southeastern Guizhou in order to "pacify the rebellious Miao" who refused to compile land and population registers and to pay taxes. According to Guo's own estimate, over a thousand villages were destroyed, tens of thousands of Miao were killed, and vast tracts of depopulated land were resettled by Han Chinese from Jiangxi and Huguang.[87]

In the years leading up to the Bozhou campaign of 1600, Ming officials in the southwest had grown increasingly assertive about restricting the activities of large *tusi* offices like Shuixi and Bozhou. They knew as well as anyone that the two pacification commissions had taken advantage of the decline in Ming military preparedness over the past century to expand the geopolitical size of their *tusi* domains. The Shuixi Pacification Commission had transformed its backward economy into one of the more advanced economies in the southwest, and it did so primarily at the expense of Ming relations with other *tusi*. Bozhou, however, had repeatedly manipulated its relations with Ming officials in Guizhou and Sichuan to mock the very presence of Ming rule. With the arrival of Guo and other activist officials, the Ming not only became more assertive in its dealings with *tusi*, which the elimination of the Bozhou Pacification Commission exemplifies, but also encouraged Han Chinese from other parts of China to settle permanently in Guizhou. It also appeared to members of the indigenous elite that Ming officials now sought to destabilize *tusi* societies by manipulating the *tusi* inheritance process. With the death of An Yaochen in 1616, the *na* in Shuixi experienced firsthand the Ming government's newfound disregard for Nasu Yi customs, as well as Ming legal precedents, in an attempt to influence the inheritance process of the Shuixi Pacification Commission.[88] This act set in motion a sequence of events that over the next twelve years would culminate in one of the largest rebellions in China's early modern history, a rebellion that nearly succeed in driving the Ming state out of the southwest entirely.

## Origins of the She-An Rebellion, 1621–29

The two characters *she* and *an* are the surnames of the two leaders of the She-An Rebellion: She Chongming, the Yongning pacification inspector, and An Bangyan, the Shuixi vice pacification commissioner and uncle of the pacification commissioner, An Wei. As relatives and members of the aristocratic-warrior elite (the *na*), the An and She patriclans enjoyed extremely close marriage ties, typically by sending daughters to the other patriclan in marriage. It was often the case, for example, that the Shuixi pacification commissioner's sister or daughter would be married to one of the Yongning pacification inspector's sons, and if the son inherited the *tusi* post, then the Shuixi *tusi* became either the uncle or grandfather of the Yongning pacification inspector. The same was true when female members of the She patriclan married into the Azhe patriclan of Shuixi. Such marriage ties extended beyond the two powerful patriclans in Shuixi and Yongning to include the Nasu Yi elite in both Shuixi and Yongning, though the She and Azhe reserved the authority to accept or reject any marriage proposal.

Generally speaking, such marriage ties worked to stabilize political relations between these two powerful neighbors. When, following the conclusion of the Bozhou campaign, proexpansionist Ming officials began to assert their authority over the *tusi* inheritance processes in both Yongning and Shuixi, an act Ming officials steadfastly refrained from in Shuixi and Yongning prior to the seventeenth century, relations between these Nasu Yi polities started to deteriorate. The introduction of a Ming voice into the marriage and inheritance processes worked in two seemingly contradictory ways. First, it exacerbated latent tensions among the various branches of the ruling patriclans so that violent competition replaced traditional mechanisms in the selection of leaders. Second, it created a general recognition in Yongning and Shuixi that the Ming state was becoming more assertive in its dealings with *tusi*, and for this reason the She and Azhe patriclans cooperated more fully to face the intrusive Ming state.

The untimely death of the Yongning pacification inspector She Xiaozhong in 1603 led to a unique circumstance whereby the deceased *tusi*'s concubine, She Shixu, challenged She Xiaozhong's childless wife, She Shitong, over who would hold the pacification inspectorship.[89] She Xiaozhong, prior to his death, had taken up residence in his concubine's dwelling, and as a result much of his administrative staff and authenticating regalia, such as the pacification inspector's seal and charter, was under She Shixu's control at the time of his death. The seal and charter were the most important articles of confirmation for the pacification inspector's post, and She Shixu, despite the fact that she was not the deceased *tusi*'s wife, argued along with her supporters that because She Shitong had not borne She Xiaozhong a child to assume the *tusi* post, they were duty bound to retain possession of the seal and charter and name She Shixu's son the rightful successor to that post.[90]

She Shitong and her supporters were distraught at the possibility of losing their political clout in Yongning, and they took the unprecedented action of appealing to officials in Sichuan for assistance. Because Yongning fell under Sichuan jurisdiction, Ming officials in Chongqing were ordered to resolve the inheritance debate according to precedents set forth in regulations governing *tusi* inheritance procedures. This meant that succession should go through She Xiaozhong's wife and not his concubine, though Ming officials rarely adhered strictly to precedent. Nevertheless, officials were sent to convince She Shixu to return the seal and charter to She Shitong and to renounce any claim to the *tusi* post. For three years officials from Chongqing and Luzhou visited She Shixu in hopes of convincing her to return the charter and seal, but each visit ended in failure. Finally, in 1607 the Sichuan regional military commissioner (*du zhihui shi*), Zhang Shenwu, took advantage of She Shixu's absence from Yongning to order a search of her residence. The residence was destroyed and one hundred guards assigned to protect it were killed, and Ming officials left with the seal and charter.[91]

Zhang's assault on She's residence may have secured Ming control of the seal and charter, but the action galvanized Nasu Yi resentment toward the Ming state. In response, Yongning forces traveled south into Guizhou and destroyed the Moni and Pushe battalions' stations located just north of the Chishui River. The two battalions were relatively easy targets since most of the soldiers posted to them had been killed during the Bozhou campaign. Because the Yongning Pacification Inspector Commission was under Sichuan authority, and the Moni and Pushe battalions were under Guizhou jurisdiction, the Ming court ordered officials from both Sichuan and Guizhou to investigate what had happened at Moni and Pushe.[92]

According to the report drafted by the investigators from Sichuan, despite the minor incongruities surrounding the Yongning inheritance process, which, not surprisingly, were not well explained in the draft report, it was determined that Pushe Battalion Commander Zhang Dace was to blame for the debacle that occurred at Moni and Pushe. Zhang was charged with failure to adequately prepare his troops for battle and with allowing "rebels" to seize his battalion headquarters. The Sichuan report recommended that Zhang be posthumously executed—he was killed in the battle for the Pushe battalion. The Sichuan investigators hoped the trail of blame would end with Zhang, and that officials in Guizhou would bear the Ming court's criticism.[93]

Guizhou investigators, in contrast, assumed a broader perspective of the events that had taken place and asked why the Nasu Yi troops attacked the battalions in the first place. Their investigation revealed that the looting of She Shixu's residence in Yongning had triggered the Nasu Yi troops to attack the two battalions, since they mistakenly believed that the Ming troops who attacked the residence were stationed at the Moni battalion. It was their recommendation, then, that Zhang Shenwu, the Sichuan official who had commanded the raid on She's residence, be questioned. Zhang was never held responsible for what transpired in Yongning; in fact, his supporters in Sichuan rallied to his defense and immediately blamed provincial officials for failing to come to Zhang's assistance even when they knew he followed their orders. The only resolute proposal to emerge from these two investigations was a unanimous call for the elimination of the Yongning *tusi* post, and even this action was averted in 1605 when Ming officials and representatives of the She patriclan met in Chongqing to negotiate an end to the succession crisis. As a result, all parties agreed to accept She Xiaozhong's nephew She Chongming as the next Yongning pacification inspector.[94]

Ming officials in Sichuan and Guizhou felt empowered by the successful arbitration of the Yongning crisis, and this success emboldened Guizhou officials to test Azhe control of Shuixi. In 1616, the Shuixi pacification commissioner, An Yaochen, died following a sudden illness, and his son, An Wei, was immediately named his successor to the *tusi* post.[95] When a delegation of Nasu Yi officials from Shuixi traveled to Guiyang to inform Governor Li Shu that an orderly transition had taken place, they presented the governor with a gold plate engraved with the names of all those members of the Azhe patriclan that had filled the post of pacification commissioner during the Ming. According to custom, the Guizhou governor was to engrave the name of the new pacification commissioner on the plate and then return it to the new pacification commissioner, along with the necessary *tusi* documents verifying the transfer of the inheritance. To the Nasu Yi in Shuixi, the gold plate held particular symbolic importance, because it authenticated Ming acceptance of their inheritance procedures. So, when Li ordered the Nasu Yi delegation to leave Guiyang without the engraved gold plate and authenticating documents, he was challenging the selection of An Wei as the pacification commissioner and, by inference, authorizing others within the Azhe patriclan to claim the title—an interesting means of trying to destabilize the Shuixi polity.[96]

Fortunately for An Wei, his uncle, An Bangyan, had assumed the office of vice pacification commissioner during An Yaochen's tenure, and his presence in Mugebaizhage provided a measure of stability for the young boy. In addition, An Wei's mother was none other than She Xiaozhong's daughter, She Shehui, which meant that any challenger to An Wei's position would need to take into account the combined authority of An Bangyan and She Chongming, She Shehui's cousin. Ming confirmation of An Wei as the Shuixi pacification commissioner remained in limbo until 1621, when officials in Guiyang finally handed the engraved gold plate and authenticating articles to An Bangyan during one of his many visits to the provincial capital. During this five-year period, it appears Li's attempt to undermine An Wei's authority in Shuixi did not influence how the Nasu Yi went about governing themselves, and there is no information indicating an attempt was made by members of the Nasu Yi elite to remove An Wei from power.[97]

In fact, it seems that the central government, in this case the Ministry of War, had forgotten about the Shuixi Pacification Commission. Not until Guizhou Regional Inspector Shi Yongan notified the Ministry of War in the third month of 1621 that An Wei had been waiting for five years to receive his official confirmation did the ministry act. Shi noted in his report to the ministry that during those five years Ming officials had repeatedly attempted to extort money from An Wei in return for assurances that they could complete the confirmation process. The most recent example of attempted extortion occurred just weeks prior to Shi's report, when battalion commander Shao Yingzhen demanded 2,000 ounces of gold from An Wei in return for his assistance in securing An's confirmation papers and engraved gold plate. An's advisers refused to pay any bribes to local officials, according to Shi, and for this reason his confirmation papers had collected dust in Guiyang. Shi's report went even further, though, in condemning the behavior of local officials in Guizhou. Shi's report noted, "Since An Wei's succession [to the pacification commission] in 1616, officials in Guiyang have carried out a number of provocative acts designed to weaken An Wei's authority, and their actions have undermined our relations with this powerful *tusi*."[98]

Li Shu, within a month of his decisive meeting with the Nasu Yi delegation, submitted a request to the Ming court asking that the Wusa, Dongchuan, Mangbu, and Wumeng areas of Yunnan be placed under Guizhou provincial control. Though his request was denied, at the time Li argued, "it will be easier to carry out *gaitu guiliu* in Shuixi if the other

Luogui areas of Yunnan were made a part of Qian."[99] Shortly after Li's request was received at court he was transferred out of Guizhou, and any explanation for how the incorporation of Wusa, Dongchuan, Mangbu, and Wumeng would make the task of *gaitu guiliu* in Shuixi easier went with him. Li's replacement, Yang He, abandoned any notion of annexing these four Nasu Yi areas of northeast Yunnan. Instead, in 1617 Yang informed the vice pacification commissioner, An Bangyan, that Shuixi was forthwith obligated to provide provincial officials with the following information: household and population registers; a complete list of all villages in Shuixi, regardless of size; a list of all political units in Shuixi, their geographic locations, and the names of the Luogui officials governing these units; a registry detailing the yearly taxes and articles of tribute presented to the Luogui by the people of Shuixi; a detailed list of all markets in Shuixi; and the names of Han merchants engaged in commercial transactions with neighboring Miao and Zhongjia villages. These registries and lists were to be presented to provincial officials in Guiyang at the beginning of every year.[100]

Never before had officials in Guiyang demanded such detailed information on Shuixi, and An was not about to undermine his own political authority in Shuixi by ordering Nasu Yi officials there to compile such information for Ming officials in Guiyang. Moreover, it had become inescapably clear to An that Ming officials were intent on challenging Nasu Yi sovereignty over Shuixi, and that eventually a pretext would appear "justifying" the elimination of the Shuixi Pacification Commission. Even more perplexing to An was the total absence of military preparedness on the part of the Ming military in Guizhou. On his routine visits to Guiyang he witnessed the decrepit state of Ming forces there, and Ming forces stationed in the various garrisons surrounding Shuixi were equally unimpressive to him. Yet civilian officials in Guiyang challenged Nasu Yi sovereignty in Shuixi every chance they got; that is, until the ninth month of 1621.[101]

Early in 1621 the Ministry of War ordered officials in Sichuan to send 54,000 troops across the length of China to serve in the Liaodong frontier to assist Ming forces fighting a multiethnic confederation of nomadic, seminomadic, and sedentary peoples who soon would become known as Manchus. The Yongning Pacification Commission was ordered to provide 30,000 *shi* of grain for the war effort, and She Chongming complied with this request. She also seized this opportunity to ingratiate himself to local officials and the Ming court by seeking permission to send 20,000 troops to the Liaodong front.[102] He believed by offering such assistance, especially when the Ming court was desperate for help, he would in time be reimbursed in ways that would prove highly beneficial to himself and to Yongning. *Tusi* knew from historical experience that providing such assistance to the Ming court could be used in the future as a marker to temper the behavior of local officials.

She appointed three powerful Nasu military commanders, Fan Long, Fan Hu, and Zhang Tong, to lead his Yongning "volunteers" to the northeast. A train of family members and servants estimated to total more than 80,000 accompanied the 20,000 troops. When this mass of humanity and livestock reached the outskirts of Chongqing at the end of the eighth month, the Sichuan governor, Xu Keqiu, informed Fan Long that the old and weak, and woman and children—the bulk of the army's train—would not receive provisions from the Ming state.[103] The Ming would not tolerate the Yongning army scavenging for provisions as it made its way north across China, and thus everyone except essential military personnel were ordered to return to Yongning. She's Yongning troops were furious when they received word of Xu's decision, and on the following day, the twenty-third day of the ninth month of 1621, the Yongning force stormed Chongqing, killing Governor Xu, Chongqing Prefect Zhang Wenbing, and more than ten other prominent officials assigned to Chongqing.[104]

When word reached She that his forces had sacked Chongqing, he promptly proclaimed himself the "king of Shu" (*Shu wang*) and ordered his forces to "eliminate the Ming presence" in southern Sichuan.[105] Fan Long was placed in charge of Chongqing, which he occupied for over nine months, and the remaining two commanders, Fan Hu and Zhang Tong, were ordered to attack Luzhou and Zunyi (Bozhou), respectively. He Ruohai, a Han military adviser to She, was placed in command of a force numbering less than 20,000 and ordered to march north to attack Chengdu. When He's army reached the outskirts of Chengdu on the twenty-seventh day of the tenth month, his ranks had swelled to over 100,000. One Ming official lamented the fact that She's army was "swarming like a hive of bees all over the southern half of Sichuan,"[106] whereas another official noted rather dispassionately that "barbarian troops in Shu [Sichuan] have rebelled yet again, but this time traitorous Han [Chinese] are supporting them, so that now they number more than a million strong."[107] By the end of the year, Yongning forces had destroyed more than forty Ming installations, prefectures, departments, counties, garrisons, battalions, and forts throughout southern Sichuan and northern Guizhou, and the siege of Chengdu, though unsuccessful, lasted for 102 days.[108]

As events in southern Sichuan spiraled out of control, An Bangyan traveled to Guiyang to meet with Li Shu, who just had been reappointed to the governor's post, and with the Guizhou regional inspector (*xun'an yushi*) Shen Xun. The purpose of the meeting was to discuss Shuixi's financial contributions to the Sichuan troops destined for the Liaodong front. Shuixi had been ordered to contribute 150,000 ounces of silver to support the Sichuan troops, but An now reasoned that since She's troops were no longer marching to the Liaodong front, he was no longer obligated to make the silver payment. When Shen objected to An's position and demanded the money be paid immediately, An offered a compromise proposal in which he would send 10,000 of his Shuixi troops to the Liaodong front in lieu of the silver payment. Reportedly, Shen responded to An's proposal in the following words: "The character of the barbarians is violent and savage, and we do not know their true intentions, but their soldiers are no better than the soldiers of ancient times, and for these reasons I oppose the use of Luogui troops [in Liaodong]."[109]

Following his meeting with Li and Shen, An informed a few of his most trusted aides of his intention to ignore their demands for money, and that if pushed he, too, would rebel against the Ming. An was evidently pushed sooner than even he expected. As An crossed the Dadu River Bridge and set foot in Shuixi, he turned toward Guiyang and formally declared his intention to destroy the Ming presence in Mu'ege. With a large entourage of advisers and several prominent *zimo* and *mu-zhuo* standing before him, An announced:

To reclaim our ancestors' glory, we have no alternative but to fight. We may not survive the many battles that lie ahead, but our deaths will be noble deaths. From this point forward the Ming designation of Shuixi pacification commissioner shall be replaced by the ancient Mu'ege banner. It is our intent to drive the Han [Chinese] out of [our] kingdom.[110]

An returned to Mugebaizhage and began coordinating with Nasu and non-Nasu allies his plans to attack the Ming administrative and military units scattered throughout western Guizhou, eastern Yunnan, and southern Sichuan.

An Bangyan forged ties with his cousin An Xiaoliang, the Wusa native prefect, and She Chongming in order to attack the Ming garrisons

and battalions to the west of Shuixi. By 1622 years of government neglect had left the Wusa, Bijie, and Chishui garrisons understaffed and in
need of repairs. Ming military patrols had long since relinquished the
policing of the Wumeng Road to the various *tusi* in the vicinity, and so
these garrisons and their satellite battalions were easy prey for the combined Shuixi-Wusa-Yongning forces. The Wusa garrison was quickly
destroyed by An Xiaoliang's forces, after which his Wusa army turned
south with its sights set on eastern Yunnan; several *muzhuo* from the
Mukua granary razed the Bijie garrison before turning north to assist
Yongning forces in their siege of the Chishui garrison.[111] By the end of
the third month of 1622, these three Ming garrisons had been destroyed, and the Han Chinese living along the Wumeng Road were
desperate for protection. This was an area where the kidnapping and
trafficking in Han Chinese had continued unabated since the beginning
of the Ming, and we know that on two separate occasions An Bangyan
and She Chongming had ordered the complete annihilation of Chinese
settlements along the Wumeng Road.[112] (For a fascinating account of a
young Han Chinese boy who was kidnapped and enslaved by indigenes
near Chishui at this time, see Appendix J.)

Along the southern periphery of Shuixi An Bangyan's forces first attacked the Puding garrison before setting their sights on the large Chinese city of Anshun. During An's attack on Anshun, the Ming official
Wen Zhizhang spared the city the misery of a long siege and opened the
city gates to allow An's troops to enter peacefully. In another engagement, Sha Guozhen and Luo Yingkui, two *muzhuo* who were part of the
Ajia granary, joined forces to cross the challenging Pan River and attack the large city of Annan. When the Yunnan regional military
commander (*dusi*) Li Tianchang heard about events taking place in
Guizhou, he mobilized his Yunnan regulars and marched along the
main east-west highway into Guizhou. Luo Yingkui knew of Li's im-
pending arrival and decided to feign surrender by allowing Li's army to
march into the city. After Li and about half of his force had entered the
city, Luo's troops, dressed as civilians, quickly shut the gates, thereby
dividing Li's force in two. Li and the unfortunate Yunnan troops at the
front of the column were slaughtered in the center of the city, and their
heads were thrown over the city wall to scare the remaining half of the
army. This act of brutality worked. The Yunnan army fled home.[113]

An also mobilized support among several non–Nasu Yi leaders.[114]
Wang Longhe and Shi Shengfeng, two disgruntled Han Chinese from

Jiangxi, led a small band of fellow Jiangxi provincials to attack Ming units near the Pianqiao garrison in eastern Guizhou. Wang, during the interrogation following his capture, admitted to coordinating his activities with An through Miao and Han Chinese merchants who traversed the back roads and trails between eastern Guizhou and Guiyang.[115] Song Fanghua, a purported Miao brigand operating in the Longli area, also received instructions from An as to when and where to strike Ming targets. Song noted that despite the isolated location of his base deep in the mountains of Jiugu, he welcomed a steady stream of envoys from An instructing him on how he might assist in the anti-Ming campaign.[116]

Finally, the Miao brigands Tian Bao and A Zhi proclaimed An their leader and harassed Han Chinese settlements near the Xinglong and Qingping garrisons. An sent military officers to help the Miao leaders organize their followers, and Tian used the skills acquired from An to defeat Assistant Regional Commander (*canjiang*) Yang Ming's detachment at Midun Mountain, in what amounted to a very important four-day battle for control of the towns of Maha and Duyun. Tian Bao and A Zhi's younger brother, A Mai, subsequently occupied Maha and Duyun for several months before retreating back into the mountains of Jiugu.[117]

An's desire to coordinate military planning with Nasu and non-Nasu supporters was intended to undermine the Ming military's ability to respond quickly and effectively in defense of Guiyang. This city symbolized Ming colonialism in Guizhou: Guiyang was where the Ming built its dominating political, military, and cultural institutions, and, as such, the destruction of this city would cripple the Ming presence in Guizhou. The city also symbolized the history of the Mu'ege kingdom, for it was from Guiyang, Shiren Mountain (near Guiyang), and Mugebaizhage that the Azhe patriclan had governed its kingdom. When An proclaimed his desire to "reclaim our ancestors' glory," he and every other member of the Nasu Yi elite knew that Azhe glory was inextricably tied to Guiyang. For these reasons, An devoted nearly all of his attention and resources to the Guiyang campaign. When his army emerged from the Shuixi highlands in the second month of 1622, his cavalry of horses and war elephants, reportedly 50,000 strong, led an army of foot soldiers totaling nearly 250,000. As An's army approached Guiyang Li Shu, the provincial governor of Guizhou, ordered the five large gates to the city closed. They would not open again for 296 days.[118]

## The Siege of Guiyang

When Li Shu ordered the gates to Guiyang closed, it was estimated that there were no more than 10,000 households registered in the city, but because people had fled to Guiyang in advance of An Bangyan's army, one official reckoned, "there are nearly 100,000 people milling about in utter desperation. It is impossible to feed such a large population, and sanitation is no longer reliable. Crime has reached epidemic proportions, and even walking the streets in daylight has become dangerous. Even the governor himself was roughed up and insulted by a nervous crowd near the market yesterday."[119] Another official still in Guiyang after the gates closed wrote, "If officials open the five gates to the city and allow those pleading to get in to enter at this time, then the city would be filled with traitors. Today each step you take on the street might be your last."[120]

The anxiety Ming officials must have felt was made even more palpable by the unfortunate fact that Li had just sent the bulk of the troops stationed in Guiyang's two garrisons out of the city to recover the town of Zunyi from She Chongming's forces.[121] Now that An's large Nasu Yi army was positioned between Guiyang and Zunyi, it was impossible for these troops to return to Guiyang. Li's inopportune decision left Guiyang dangerously vulnerable, so much so that when An's advance guard appeared on top of the cliffs overlooking the southwest part of the city on the seventeenth day of the second month of 1622, the city's vulnerability became astonishingly evident as An's troops jokingly tossed rocks down on the helpless gate guards. Ming officials could count on only 5,000 panic-stricken Ming troops to protect the city from the nearly 300,000 Shuixi troops quickly taking up positions around the perimeter of the city. As one official noted after observing the scene unfolding outside the city wall: "I cried from despair at my father's funeral. Today I cried for fear that I will not enjoy a proper funeral."[122]

Before the siege began, Ming officials noted how easy it would be for the attackers to assault all the gates at the same time, thus rendering the defenses on at least three of the five gates useless. However, this never happened. During the first two months of the siege, Shuixi troops concentrated on attacking one gate at a time, and when the defenses proved capable of withstanding the daylong assault, the troops were ordered to withdraw and another gate was attacked by troops stationed

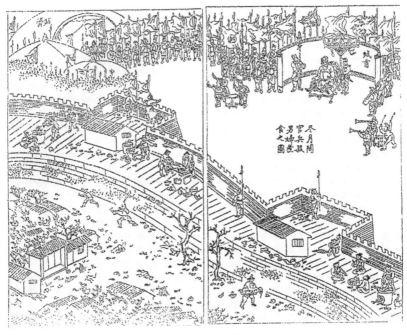

食男官天
之婦兵用
圖煮報間

Fig. 2　The seige of Guiyang

outside it. This tactic not only allowed the defenders to move troops from one gate to another to help fend off the attackers, but it permitted the Ming soldiers to shore up their defenses following an attack. The defenders poured scalding hot water and buckets of human waste on the heads of the attackers as they attempted to scale the city wall, but on most every occasion one or two attackers would succeed in making it over the wall, only to have their quartered bodies thrown back over the wall.[123]

In addition to frontal assaults against the city's wall and gates, An ordered teams of Miao miners to dig tunnels into the city, but here again the defenders anticipated the tactic and either collapsed the tunnels with stones and debris or filled them with the remains of those recently killed in battle. In one instance, two miners broke through into the city and startled a group of disgruntled men, who then dashed into the tunnel in a desperate attempt to make it out of the city. As many as eleven city dwellers may have emerged from the other end of the tunnel before Ming officials discovered the tunnel and destroyed it.[124] The Shuixi force also used large catapults to hurl stones and fireballs into the city, and, in one extraordinary attempt to enter the city, Shuixi engineers constructed a large cart with platforms nearly three stories high in order to drop soldiers down onto the top of the city wall. This tactic, too, failed, and by the fourth month of the siege An reasoned that direct strikes against the formidable wall and gates were useless, so he changed strategy. He decided to starve the city into submission.[125]

Li Shu and the other Ming officials in Guiyang were as adamant about not surrendering as An was about continuing the attack; in fact, Li had issued standing orders to kill anyone seen attempting to escape from the city. Despite these orders, Ming troops frequently accepted bribes from people who then used ropes and cloth to scale down the outside of the city wall. It was reported after the siege that General Huang Yunqing, the Ming commander in charge of securing defenses around the two northern gates, amassed a small fortune by allowing those who could pay his price the opportunity to climb over the wall. At the beginning of the siege Huang charged each person an ounce of gold to scale down the city wall, but as the siege progressed those desperate enough to attempt to escape were required to give all of their worldly possessions to Huang. At the end of the siege Huang reportedly owned nine of every ten buildings in the northwest section of the city.[126]

The trickle of escapees did not change the fact that by the ninth month of the siege the city's food supplies were exhausted. Guiyang had relied on grain from Huguang, Yunnan, and Shuixi to meet the needs of its population, but the siege had ended any hope of importing grain. With the city's granaries empty and people starving, Li made the fateful decision to order the citizens to draw lots to determine who would be killed each day to provide food for the soldiers.[127] During the final weeks of the siege An and his Shuixi troops watched in horror as Ming soldiers stationed in full view on top of the city wall executed, quartered, cooked, and then consumed the inhabitants of Guiyang in a frantic attempt to stay alive.[128] When Wang Sanshan, the newly appointed Guizhou provincial governor, finally lifted the siege on the seventh day of the twelfth month of 1622, Li Shu, Liu Xixuan, and the other Ming officials in Guiyang reported that of the 100,000 people in the city at the beginning of the siege, only 200 people were still alive![129]

By the end of 1622 time had simply run out for An. Ming officials in Guiyang had withstood the siege for 296 days, though the callous and inhuman means used by Ming officials to feed themselves and their troops would forever haunt the careers of those who survived. An, when he began the siege of Guiyang nearly ten months earlier, knew that She Chongming's siege of Chengdu had ended in failure, and that Ming troops from Guiyang had successfully recovered Zunyi from She's Yongning army. Moreover, during the middle of the siege An learned that She's forces in Chongqing had fled the city, and that She's army was disintegrating rapidly as it made its way back to Yongning. He was informed by subordinates that Ming soldiers were rebuilding the burned ruins that were once garrisons and battalions along the Wumeng Road, and An saw clearly that it was only a matter of time before the Ming court organized a large multiprovincial force to reclaim Guiyang. When Wang Sanshan's army reached the outskirts of Guiyang at the beginning of the twelfth month, An decided to abandon the siege and retreat to the security of Shuixi. If he was to fight the Ming, he wanted to do so in Shuixi.[130]

Once the shock of what had taken place in Guiyang subsided, Wang ordered his two most trusted lieutenants, Liu Chao and Zhang Yanfang, to lead 60,000 crack Ming troops into Shuixi. They were ordered to destroy An's army and bring the "rebel leader" back to Guiyang, dead or alive. Wang promised "a reward of 20,000 taels to the man who places the rebel's head on my desk."[131] In the tenth month of 1623, Liu and Zhang crossed the Yachi River at the same spot where just one year earlier An had declared war on the Ming, and they headed straight for Mugebaizhage. To their astonishment, the road to Mugebaizhage was virtually unobstructed, though the dark, rainy skies cast a chord of uneasiness through the ranks of the Ming force. "In the five-day march from the [Yachi] river to Yaozhou," Liu wrote, "we saw the smoke from fires high in the distant mountains, but we did not meet the rebels on the march. They remained beyond our reach."[132] When the Ming force arrived in Mugebaizhage, they promptly destroyed An Guirong's castle, and they scoured the countryside for nearly two months in search of An Bangyan, but to no avail. The lack of supplies and the general hostility of the local population eventually wore on the Ming army, as it had the Mongol army under Yaocihai's command over three hundred years earlier, and in the first month of 1624 Wang ordered Liu and Zhang to withdraw their troops to the Yachi River.

An, upon his return to Shuixi, had ordered his commanders to hide deep in the mountains and await his instructions. Instead of confronting the Ming force in Mugebaizhage, An decided to starve the Ming force out of Shuixi; he was sure the tactic would work here though it had not in Guiyang. When the Ming army began its withdrawal, An ordered his Han Chinese adviser, Chen Qiyu, to shadow the Ming force until it reached the river, then send a message to the Ming commanders requesting a meeting with Wang to negotiate An's surrender. An had no intention of surrendering, and he calculated that his ploy to surrender would coerce Wang to leave the safety of Guiyang for the Yachi River. Chen followed An's instructions precisely and even pretended to defect to the Ming cause, thus gaining the trust of Wang and his advisers. When the opportunity presented itself, Chen and a team of assassins murdered the provincial governor and his entire entourage, and then they quickly escaped back into Shuixi.[133]

Wang's murder dealt a severe blow to the Ming military in Guizhou, but An was unable to build on the momentum the murder had generated. The Shuixi army did cross the Yachi River again to attack Ming positions in Shuidong, and on several occasions Shuixi cavalry units appeared before the gates of Guiyang, each time striking fear and panic in Guiyang's population, but there was never another siege of the city like that of 1622.[134] The Ming military was slowly tightening its noose around Shuixi, and An could do very little about it. In the middle of 1623, Zhu Xieyuan, the supreme commander (*zongdu*) of Ming forces in Sichuan, had nearly completed his work in Yongning: forty-eight villages in Yongning had been destroyed, including She Chongming's home village of Linzhou, and She's father and son had fled to Shuixi for protection. Though She continued to resist the Ming until his eventual capture in 1628, Zhu's relentless campaigning made sure that She no longer possessed a secure base of operations.[135]

Throughout 1624 the Ming military fortified its positions in Chongqing and Zunyi, and by the spring of 1625 Yunnan Governor Min Hongxue had recovered many of the cities previously occupied by Nasu Yi forces in eastern Yunnan.[136] One year later, in the summer of 1626, Zhu's army engaged An's Shuixi force in a series of pivotal encounters north of Guiyang that ultimately broke the spirit of An's Shuixi army. For the next three years, Zhu methodically squeezed An and She until, in the eighth month of 1629, the combined forces of An and She fought the Ming in one last battle near Yongning, which resulted in the battlefield executions of both She and An. Jubilant Ming troops affixed She's and An's heads to the end of long pikes and paraded the heads for nearly a month along the Wumeng Road between Bijie and Luzhou.[137] Following An Bangyan's death, the Shuixi pacification commissioner, An Wei, dispatched Han Chinese envoys to Yunnan, Sichuan, and Guizhou in hopes of negotiating a truce that might keep Ming forces from entering Shuixi, but Zhu had other plans for Shuixi.[138]

## Ode to Shuixi

Zhu Xieyuan began planning for the invasion of Shuixi several weeks before the decisive battle near Yongning. In the sixth month of 1629 he convened a meeting in Chongqing with his commanders to discuss his plans for the "pacification of Shuixi."[139] Zhu's commanders agreed to a strategy that in effect was a scorched-earth campaign. Ming troops were under strict orders not to advance more than 20 *li* without first securing the territory they had just marched through. This entailed building or commandeering structures to be used as blockhouses from which a small unit of troops could control a large area. To secure an area, Ming troops were ordered to fell trees, clear underbrush, and set fire to structures that might give shelter to the enemy. If a cave was found, then the entrance to the cave was to be destroyed so those inside could not escape; mountain streams were to be diverted to deny water to the enemy, farmland destroyed, and harvested grain confiscated.[140] In one of Zhu's many reports to superiors in Beijing, he stated, "in a little more than one hundred days of fighting, [our troops] have obtained over ten thousand [decapitated] heads and several tens of thousands of live captives."[141]

By the middle of 1630, An Wei and his advisers had seen enough. Once again Han Chinese envoys were sent to meet Ming commanders in the field, though their message this time was quite simple: An had ordered his warriors to surrender to the Ming commanders, and on the twenty-third day of the fifth month he would meet with Zhu in Guiyang to surrender his charter and seal as the Shuixi pacification commissioner.[142] As a sign of good faith, An ceded sovereignty of the two granary units in Shuidong to the Ming state. Zhu accepted An's surrender and informed the young man that the Ming forces, too, were tired of war.

The cost of the She-An Rebellion was staggering. During the eight years of warfare, the Ming military had mobilized 560,000 troops to fight in the southwest, and an equal, if not larger number of *tusi* troops participated on behalf of the Ming as well. To move goods and supplies to the troops at the front, the Ming had organized an additional 450,000 people into convoy battalions that stretched from Guiyang and

Bozhou to cities as far away as Nanjing, Yangzhou, and Suzhou. According to figures compiled by the Yunnan intendant censor Wang Zunde, the Ming state's daily expenditures reached over 12,000 taels of silver and over 720,000 *shi* of grain. In all probability the eight-year She-An Rebellion cost the Ming approximately 35,000,000 taels, with an additional 2,000,000,000 *shi* in grain procured for Ming forces.[143]

During the meeting in Guiyang, Zhu presented An with a nine-point plan on how he planned to deal with Shuixi.[144] According to Zhu's plan, he did not intend to establish prefectures, departments, and counties in Shuixi, which would be the normal process of *gaitu guiliu*. Nor would the Ming state impose Han Chinese customs upon the indigenous population. However, the entire indigenous granary system was to be dismantled, and under no circumstances could this indigenous bureaucracy be restored. The An family would continue to occupy the hereditary post of Shuixi pacification commissioner, but the commissioner's entire family, including the heir apparent, would reside permanently in Guiyang as "guests" of the provincial governor.[145] Military garrisons and forts would be constructed at strategic points throughout Shuixi, and Ming troops would be assigned to these units on a permanent basis. Each Ming soldier in Shuixi would be given a set amount of farmland to keep on a hereditary basis, and Han settlers would be encouraged to relocate to Shuixi. Soldiers and settlers would be prohibited from selling their land to indigenes.[146] In short, Zhu proposed a military occupation of Shuixi and the gradual settlement of the region by Han farmers.

Zhu also noted his intent to create several new *tusi* offices in Shuixi. The size of each *tusi* domain would be restricted so as not to allow the *tusi* to gain wealth and power through the acquisition of land. As Zhu explained it to An, "When the land granted [to the *tusi*] is large in size, it provides the *tusi* with resources that can easily lead to recalcitrant behavior."[147] An was led to believe that the majority of the new *tusi* titles would be granted to members of the Nasu Yi elite; yet, records indicate that fifty-three *tusi* titles and domains were bestowed upon Han soldiers who had participated in the Shuixi campaign. Zhu later remarked, "Their [Han Chinese *tusi*] presence among the barbarians will have the necessary civilizing effect so that in the not-so-distant future we will be able to establish the prefecture system in Shuixi."[148] The introduction of the Chinese legal system into the Shuixi region, admittedly haphazard at best, signified Zhu's desire to limit *tusi* autonomy. Once Zhu appointed Han and non-Han as *tusi*, he ordered them to adjudicate criminal cases according to Ming law, with the expectation that Ming law would mold the behavior of the indigenous population so that eventually they could be brought into the fold of Chinese civilization.[149]

The economic potential of Shuixi notwithstanding, Zhu decided on a reconstruction plan very different from the wholesale *gaitu guiliu* carried out in Bozhou thirty years earlier. Because few Han lived in Shuixi prior to 1630, Zhu felt compelled to establish a strong military presence in the region, and this demanded the elimination of the indigenous granary bureaucracy. He created a multitude of hereditary *tusi* posts staffed by members of the Nasu Yi elite and Han who participated in the Ming military campaign in Shuixi. A member of the Azhe patriclan would continue to serve as the Shuixi pacification commissioner, but this allowance was primarily a symbolic gesture designed to placate the still restive indigenous population in western Guizhou, northeast Yunnan, and southern Sichuan. Finally, the voluntary and involuntary relocation of Han to Shuixi was designed to reduce the social-cultural boundaries that differentiated frontier territory from China proper. Zhu argued that once the social-cultural boundaries separating Han and non-Han began to erode and people in Shuixi accepted Han customs and lifeways, Ming prefectures, departments, and counties would replace *tusi* domains as the main political authorities in the region.

This gradualist approach to *gaitu guiliu* and the transformation of the Shuixi internal frontier looked viable to Ming officials in 1630, but fourteen years later the Ming state no longer existed and the entire gradualist plan for Shuixi disintegrated. The Manchu occupation of Beijing in 1644 and the subsequent forty years of anti-Qing resistance turned the southwest into the final battleground between pro-Qing and anti-Qing forces, during which the Nasu Yi of Shuixi would attempt once again to assert their authority as rulers of an independent Mu'ege kingdom.

# 6

———

# *Trampled Earth*

For over half a century, from roughly 1620 to 1680, the southwest frontier was in turmoil, much like the rest of China, and despite Zhu Xieyuan's best-laid plans for Shuixi the Ming state was incapable of restoring political authority over Guizhou and Yunnan following the She-An Rebellion. Subprefecture, prefecture, and even several provincial offices remained unstaffed during the 1630s and 1640s, and with the demise of the Ming in 1644, so, too, went the notion of civilian rule. "The Ming civilian bureaucracy," as Lynn Struve noted, "was eclipsed by military organizations which originally had developed outside Ming control."[1] As one might suspect, many of these military organizations harbored anti-Ming sentiments. Gao Yingxiang (d. 1636), the godfather of several of China's most notorious anti-Ming rebels, was able to channel popular antipathy due to years of economic decline, bureaucratic ineptitude, and bone-jarring famine toward establishing a sprawling base of anti-Ming resistance in North China. Gao's uncanny ability to consistently outwit his Ming adversaries distinguished him from many of the other small, regional warlords roaming the North China countryside, and his "national" stature attracted both the capable and desperate who hoped to capitalize on Gao's potential. Two of Gao's most notable lieutenants were Li Zicheng (1605?–45) and Zhang Xianzhong (1605–47).

As a postal courier in Shaanxi, Li had proven himself to be a skilled horseman, expert marksman, and leader of men by the time the great famine of 1628 engulfed Shaanxi and forced him to abandon his government job. To survive, Li led a small band of followers into the neighboring hills, and from there they attacked merchant caravans, government officials, and people of wealth. Government soldiers and local militias quickly responded to Li's growing menace, so in 1631 Li decided to increase his power by joining forces with the renowned "dashing king" (*chuang wang*), Gao Yingxiang. Cultivated for years by Gao, Li became part of Gao's loosely coordinated military organization that stretched over much of North China. According to most contemporary accounts, this organization consisted of thirteen leaders commanding seventy-two smaller units, and it purportedly comprised over half a million men.

The leaders met in 1635 at a meeting presided over by Gao in Rongyang, Henan, after which each leader was granted an exclusive sphere of operation. Li, who now styled himself the "dashing general" (*chuang jiang*), was given control over his home turf in Shaanxi. Following Gao's capture and execution in 1636, the remaining leaders selected Li to assume the title of dashing king, but it was not until early 1641, when Li ordered the execution of the prince of Fu (Zhu Changxun; 1586–1641), burned his palaces, and redistributed over 2,000,000 *mu* of his land to the poor and hungry, that Li began to attract the following necessary to ascend the national stage.[2] In the spring of 1644, Li announced the founding of the Da Shun kingdom, and by April 1644 his army entered Beijing and forced the Ming emperor Chongzhen (r. 1628–44) to commit suicide.[3]

As the drama of Li's campaign against the Ming unfolded in North China, Zhang Xianzhong, a participant at Gao's conference in Rongyang in 1635, had appointed himself in 1643 king of the Great Western (Daxi) kingdom, and in the spring of 1644 Zhang was leading his followers west from Huguang into the fertile Sichuan basin. From Chengdu Zhang sought to utilize the region's economic wealth to extend his political-military reach beyond the basin, hoping some day to unify China under his rule. But, Zhang's ambitions were never realized. First, many of the major cities in Yunnan, northern Guizhou, and eastern Sichuan were still under the authority of Ming loyalists who steadfastly resisted Zhang's overtures, and, despite the collapse of Ming rule in Beijing, Ming forces surrounding the Sichuan basin were stubbornly opposed to Zhang's imperial pretensions. Second, the rapid and unanticipated defeat of Li's army in Beijing brought the Shun-Qing battle to the Sichuan basin's northern edge, as fleeing Shun troops filtered back into Shaanxi and Sichuan in a desperate attempt to escape pursuing Qing forces.

Finally, because of the constant warfare that had engulfed Sichuan during the 1630s and 1640s, a large portion of the population fled to more stable areas, such as Yunnan and Guizhou, thus leaving vast stretches of the Sichuan countryside completely depopulated.[4] The southwest became the terminus for anyone fleeing the Manchu advance, not just those people from Sichuan. Ming imperial family members, Ming scholar-officials, and ordinary Han Chinese escaped to the southwest in search of security and hope, but it was a futile search. The Ming sympathizers who fled to the southwest were pursued relentlessly by Qing forces, and in short order the southwest, too, became contested terrain.

This chapter will examine the impact of the Ming-Qing transition in the southwest, and in particular how the change affected the Nasu Yi in Shuixi. The Ming-Qing transition in the southwest was a great deal more violent than was the Yuan-Ming transition, as Qing forces under Wu Sangui (1612–78) destroyed the Ming resistance and then attempted to transform the southwest into a base from which to launch an assault against the Qing dynasty itself. An important component of Wu's overall strategy in the southwest was to utilize the economic wealth of Shuixi to challenge Qing hegemony, and his military-political occupation of this region was critical to ending Azhe rule in Shuixi. When the Qing Kangxi emperor announced at the close of the seventeenth century that Qing rule of the southwest was not only more inclusive (more civilian officials, fewer military officials) than Ming rule but also more effective in penetrating "barbarian" society and "turning them toward civilization," he was speaking specifically of the Nasu Yi in Shuixi.

## The Ming-Qing Transition in the Southwest

In the final months of 1646, Zhang Xianzhong, after exhausting the economic resources of the Sichuan basin and slaughtering much of Chengdu's population, led his army north to engage a formidable Qing force. Before his death at the hands of an elite Manchu reconnaissance unit on January 2, 1647, Zhang summoned his four most trusted generals, Ai Nengqi, Li Dingguo (d. 1662), Liu Wenxiu, and Sun Kewang (d. 1660), and admonished them to cooperate to resist the entreaties of Ming loyalists, and to expel the Manchus from China.[5] Following Zhang's death these four generals, of whom Li and Sun were the most influential, marched the remnants of Zhang's Great Western Army into southern Sichuan, taking the city of Chongqing late in 1646. By the third month of 1647, Great Western forces had pushed further south, into Guizhou, seizing Zunyi (formerly Bozhou) and Guiyang from Ming loyalists. Ironically, by the beginning of summer Li and Sun ordered their forces west into Yunnan on the pretext of assisting the Ming over-lord of Yunnan, Mu Tianbo. Mu Tianbo was a descendant of the Hongwu emperor's adopted son, Mu Ying, who, it will be recalled, was enfeoffed in Yunnan following the campaigns of the 1380s and 1390s. Successive members of the Mu family had extended the family's land-holdings and commercial interests both in Yunnan and in China proper, making it one of the wealthiest families in all of China.[6] In January 1646, a disgruntled pacification commissioner, Sha Dingzhou, drove Mu from the Kunming region, and it was to assist Mu that Sun and Li entered Yunnan. Within a year, Great Western forces had de-feated Sha, rescued Mu, and controlled much of southern Sichuan, Guizhou, and Yunnan.

Qing forces inexplicably refrained from pushing deeper into Sichuan, Guizhou, and Yunnan following their defeat of Zhang in 1647. Wu San-gui, the principal Qing commander in this theater, was ordered to posi-tion his forces along the Sichuan-Shaanxi border in order to secure Shaanxi from further incursions from the south. This defensive posture allowed Sun, Li, and a whole host of minor warlords free rein through-out southern China. In 1652, for example, Li launched several highly successful guerrilla strikes into southern Huguang and Guangxi that undermined the Qing presence in these areas. In early August, a small contingent of Li's troops carried out a surprise attack on the city of Gui-lin. The Qing commander in Guilin, Kong Youde, became so distraught over the ease with which Li's troops stormed the city that he committed suicide, thus depriving the Qing of one its best field commanders in South China. Shortly thereafter, Li's troops in Hengzhou (present-day Hengyang) ambushed and killed the Manchu prince, Nikan, who had been commissioned by the Manchu court to retake southern Huguang.[7] As a result of Li's daring campaigns of 1652, only Wuzhou, the east-ernmost city in Guangxi, remained under Qing control. Many of the lo-calities in Guangxi that had recently pledged allegiance to the Qing now swore fealty to the Southern Ming court of Yongli, to whom Li now pledged allegiance.[8]

Li's successes on the battlefield in 1652 marked the beginning of the end of anti-Qing resistance in South China. Li's battlefield victories, the fall of Guilin and the loss of two prominent Qing military commanders, mass defections in Guangxi and parts of southern Huguang to the Ming cause, and the belief that Yunnan, Guizhou, and southern Sichuan were solidly in the Southern Ming camp convinced the Qing court that a more aggressive stance toward the Ming loyalists in southern China was needed. Moreover, when Sun escorted Yongli and the Southern Ming court from Guangxi to Anlong, a remote border town in southwestern Guizhou, it must have seemed to Beijing that the various warlords, misfit rebels, and sincere Ming loyalists were beginning to coalesce around the Southern Ming court. Sun, from his headquarters in Guiyang, was also hard at work creating an alternative capital in southern China: he established a crude facsimile of Ming China's capital bureaucracy, complete with government ministries and support staff; he appointed officials to fill the numerous political offices in the south (many of these were simply paper appointments, and political posts throughout the south often remained empty); and he carried out civil service examinations based on his interpretation of the classics. Sun was attempting to attract the educated Han elite to his cause, and from Beijing's perspective he was having some success.[9]

Manchu officials in Beijing had no idea that Sun had, for all intents and purposes, kidnapped the Yongli emperor and was keeping him hostage in Anlong (Yongli remained in Anlong under Sun's close guard for four years). Nor could they have known that Sun and Li had been at odds for several years, ever since Sun decided unilaterally to intervene in Yunnan in 1647. Sun's desire late in 1648 to acquire the title "prince of Qin" (*Qin wang*) from the Yongli court would have officially confirmed Sun's preeminence over Li, something the able military commander and his subordinates resisted. Furthermore, Sun's removal of the Yongli emperor to Anlong, and his unwillingness to provide Li with timely assistance during the latter's military strikes into Huguang and Guangxi, had strained their relationship.[10] In response to the ominous events taking place in South China in 1652, the Shunzhi emperor (1638–61, r. 1644–61) appointed the distinguished, though near blind, Chinese commander Hong Chengchou (1593–1665) governor-general of Huguang, Liang-Guang, Yunnan, and Guizhou, with instructions to eliminate the Ming loyalist movement and anti-Qing resistance in South China. In spite of Beijing's newfound commitment to pacify South China, Hong made little headway against Sun and Li until 1657, when, as a result of the escalating rivalry between Sun and Li, the two unleashed their forces on each other and effectively decimated the anti-Qing camp.[11]

The Qing campaign against the Southern Ming took a decided turn for the better in December 1657 when a distraught Sun, betrayed and humiliated by his closest advisers and soundly defeated by Li's troops, surrendered to Hong in Hunan.[12] Within a month of Sun's surrender, the Qing court issued orders calling for the invasion of Guizhou and Yunnan and for the capture of the Southern Ming emperor Yongli. Wu Sangui was given the title "generalissimo who pacifies the west" (*pingxi da jiangjun*) and ordered to lead his army from his Sichuan-Shaanxi camp into Guizhou, where he would join up with several forces entering Guizhou from the east. Hong was instructed to lead his beleaguered Chinese army west along the Hankou Route toward Guiyang. Alongside Hong was Lodo (1616–65), the grandson of Šurgaci (1564–1611) and recently named commander in chief of Manchu forces in the campaign. From Guangxi Jobtei, another esteemed Manchu military commander, was assigned the task of marching a large Chinese army, accompanied by Manchu and Mongol cavalry units, into southeastern Guizhou and then on to Guiyang. The invasion of Guizhou began in the spring of 1658, and by the end of the year Li's army, or what was left of it after the confrontation with Sun a year earlier, had been pushed out of Guizhou toward Yunnan. Li had evacuated the Southern Ming court to Kunming in 1656, so Yongli was safe for the moment.[13]

In the last weeks of 1658, after the fall of Guiyang, Qing forces began the assault against Yunnan. In January 1659, as Qing troops breached Li's defenses along the Yunnan-Guizhou border, the Yongli court was escorted out of Kunming by Li and Mu Tianbo, heading west toward Dali and the China-Burma border. In the last days of March, the Yongli court sought refuge in Burma. At this point, Hong's old age, poor health, and blindness had gotten the better of him, and his request to return to Beijing was granted. Shortly thereafter, Shunzhi entrusted Wu with the task of capturing Yongli and eliminating Ming resistance in Yunnan. To carry out this assignment, Wu was given civil and military control of Yunnan province. The emperor also granted Shang Kexi (d. 1676) the title "prince who pacifies the south" (*pingnan wang*), with civil and military control over Guangdong, and named Geng Jimao (d. 1671) the "prince who tranquilizes the south" (*jingnan wang*), with similar authority over Sichuan, although in the following year Geng was reassigned to Guangxi.[14] Hong, upon his return to Beijing, recommended that a Yunnan-Guizhou governor-generalship be established, and that Wu fill the post so that Wu could oversee the eventual pacification and consolidation of the entire southwest. Hong argued that due to the unsettled climate in Guizhou and Yunnan, the governor-general should spend half of the year working in Anshun, Guizhou, and the other half in Qujing, Yunnan. That these two cities were situated so close to each other, Anshun in western Guizhou and Qujing in eastern Yunnan, indicates just how critical Hong felt control of this area was to the overall pacification of the southwest.[15]

## Building a Fiefdom: Wu Sangui in Yunnan and Guizhou

Wu, by the time of his appointment as governor-general in 1660, was receiving nearly 9,000,000 taels annually in financial support from the Qing government—an astounding sum considering China's land tax, the main component of state revenue at this time, generated no more than 30,000,000 taels annually.[16] In the following year the Ministry of Revenue, concerned over the enormous financial drain the campaign was having on state coffers, recommended to the Qing court that it begin to cut expenditures for the southwest campaign. The ministry reported that the Southern Ming court was now in Burma, where the Yongli emperor lived as a pauper hostage of the Burmese, and that Ming loyalist forces either had surrendered to the advancing Qing forces or lay strewn on the battlefields throughout the southwest. Furthermore, the assistance Qing forces received from tusi in prosecuting the campaign led the ministry to conclude that there would be very little local resistance to the new Qing presence in the southwest. Tusi, the ministry argued, could be used to govern the non-Han population in the southwest, as they had during the Yuan and Ming dynasties, thereby negating the need for a large occupation force. For these reasons, the ministry proposed that the size of the Qing armies in the southwest be reduced, and that Qing soldiers either be resettled in the southwest or allowed to return to their homes in China proper.[17]

Wu countered the ministry's arguments by pointing out that large portions of the southwest remained beyond Qing control, and most but certainly not all of the indigenous non-Han peoples welcomed the advancing Qing armies. Southern Ming and anti-Qing resistance west of Kunming was still widespread, Wu maintained, and as long as the Yongli emperor was alive and beyond the grasp of the Qing there was the possibility he could be used as a potential rallying cry for Ming loyalists. Fortuitously for Wu, a court decision regarding a reduction in state subsidies and the demobilization of Qing forces was not immediately forthcoming. Even after Wu captured and executed the Yongli emperor in 1661, the Qing court refused to curtail subsidies to its forces in the southwest, but not because Wu's arguments proved particularly persuasive and insightful.

Instead, the delay in a court decision on this matter was more a result of the political climate surrounding the transition from the Shunzhi emperor, whose final years were marred by controversy and political neglect, to the youthful Kangxi. The initial years of the Kangxi reign were managed by four regents, of whom Oboi (d. 1669) emerged as the most influential. Oboi and his fellow regents were concerned with settling old scores within the Manchu warrior aristocracy, extending Qing control over all of China proper, especially the Jiangnan region, and confronting the growing menace of Zheng Chenggong (1624–62), the Ming loyalist whose naval fleet wreaked havoc along the China coast. Wu and the other two princes in South China, Shang Kexi in Guangdong and Geng Jimao in Guangxi, were providing valuable service to the Qing cause, and their actions were much appreciated at court. Nonetheless, the Ministry of Revenue's recommendation to reduce state subsidies to Wu's forces undoubtedly convinced the Qing commander that he needed to acquire a more stable revenue base as quickly as possible, and he set out to do just that.[18]

Wu launched one of the most ambitious land confiscation and reclamation programs in the southwest since the Hongwu emperor sent his Ming armies into the frontier in the last decades of the fourteenth century. Wu confiscated the Mu family's numerous estates in Yunnan. It was estimated the extended Mu family possessed nearly 2,000,000 *mu* of prime agricultural land in Yunnan, they owned and operated a number of highly lucrative mining enterprises in both Yunnan and Guizhou, and they coordinated through agents the sale of commercial goods from China in the southwest. Between 1660 and 1665, Wu reportedly seized much of this property and parceled it out to soldiers in units of 5 *mu*. Each soldier was expected to cultivate the 5 *mu* of land himself, and to marry and begin a family within one year of receiving the grant. Borrowing a page from Hongwu's occupation policies of the 1380s, Wu ordered soldiers with families in China proper to relocate to the southwest. Mu Tianpo's personal landholdings, estimated to include over 10,000 *mu* of land, became Wu's personal property, and by 1665 it was estimated that Wu's personal landholdings amounted to almost 70,000 *mu*.

In 1665 Yunnan Governor Yuan Maogong reported that approximately 25,000 *mu* of wasteland had been brought under cultivation.[19] In the same year Guizhou Governor Luo Huijin reported that over 12,900 *mu* of wasteland in Guizhou had also been reclaimed for cultivation.[20] Land reclamation was the cornerstone of Ming economic policy in the southwest, and Wu aggressively promoted this policy during his tenure in the southwest, not just to increase his own personal wealth, which he most certainly did, but to reward those soldiers who had fought on behalf of the Qing.

Wu, even before he was named governor-general of Yunnan and Guizhou, had initiated plans detailing the placement of Qing military installations in Yunnan and Guizhou and the settlement of troops and their families near these installations. Wu established four distinct types of military units in the southwest. First, he settled many of the Qing troops that formed the Huguang and Guangxi armies into the Four Aid and Extermination Defense Commands in Yunnan (*Yunnan yuanjiao sizhen*). Wu situated these defense commands not in Kunming, which was what the Ming military had done late in the fourteenth century, but in medium-sized towns located along the main roads leading into Kunming. These four defense commands operated as a first line of defense to protect Kunming and the Lake Dian region, and they were positioned in an arc extending to the north of Kunming, as if the anticipated threat to Kunming would come from China proper, not from south of Kunming. Wu did not establish a defense command south of the Lake Dian region.[21]

The Right Defense Command (*youzhen*) was established in Qujing, the same town Hong Chengchou recommended to share the governor-general's office with Anshun. Qujing was strategically situated along the main route linking Guiyang and Kunming, and it was where the Wumeng Road intersected with the Hankou Route. With two of the three main routes linking China proper and Yunnan connecting in Qujing, it made sense to place a large concentration of troops here. The Left Defense Command (*zuozhen*) was located in the town of Wuding, to the northwest of Kunming and near the main route linking Chengdu and Kunming, the Chengdu Route. The Forward Defense Command (*qianzhen*) was located directly east of Kunming in the town of Chusong, along the road connecting Kunming and Dali. This garrison was also near the Chengdu Route, so it, too, could provide assistance to the Left (Wuding) Defense Command in case this route became obstructed.

Finally, the Rear Defense Command (*houzhen*), located due east of Dali along the road linking Dali and Kunming, was more or less a first line of defense against hostile elements in western Yunnan. Wuding, Chusong, and Erhai had hosted Ming troops as garrison towns, and Uriyangqadai, the Mongol commander who oversaw the Yuan military occupation of the Dali kingdom, had established military detachments in each of these towns.[22] The people residing near each defense command, many of whom were the descendants of Ming soldiers involuntarily settled here in the fourteenth and fifteenth centuries, were now forcibly removed from their homes, and their lands were divided among the conquering Qing troops.

Each defense command was placed under the charge of a regional commander (*zongbing guan*), who was to receive 50 *mu* of land. Subordinate to the regional commander were three brigade commanders (*youji*) and three assistant brigade commanders (*shoubei*), each receiving 25 *mu* of land, and six company commanders (*qianzong*) and twelve squad leaders (*bazong*), who were granted 10 *mu* each. The company commanders and squad leaders were usually stationed in small forts and outposts some distance from the main defense command, near mountain passes, river crossings, and important intersections along roads and trails. On paper, each defense command had at its disposal 900 guards (*shoubing*) to man the forts and outposts of the defense command, but sources indicate that company commanders and squad leaders rotated the guard assignments so these 900 guards were not permanently stationed in the forts and outposts. In addition to the 900 guards, each defense command had a cavalry force of approximately 600, but the size of the cavalry fluctuated yearly depending on the military situation at hand. Each defense command had a force of 1,500 soldiers permanently stationed on or near the defense command site. The total number of troops in each defense command, then, was approximately 3,000. Altogether there were about 12,000 soldiers in the Four Aid and Extermination Defense Commands in Yunnan created by Wu, and each soldier was given 5 *mu* of land.[23]

The four defense commands were part of a larger districting process that resulted in the creation of six military circuits, each headed by a circuit commander. These circuit commanders had a support staff to assist in the management of each circuit, including coordinating military activities with the defense commands. Although previous scholarship has led to the belief that the military apparatus Wu put in place at this time was staffed by men personally loyal to him, an examination of the individuals who filled regional commander posts in the defense commands and the circuit commander posts in the military circuits shows this certainly was not the case. For example, of the ten commanders appointed to these offices at this time, five were previously associated with Hong Chengchou and the Huguang army, and two were linked to Jobtei and the Guangxi army. Moreover, many of the subordinate officials assigned to defense commands were also from the Huguang and Guangxi armies. It is true Wu recommended many of these officers be appointed to their posts, and Beijing agreed with Wu's requests, but this should not be construed to mean that they were Wu's men. Wu rewarded his own men differently. He settled his troops in the richest agricultural region in the southwest, in and around Lake Dian, and he made his headquarters in Kunming.[24]

By 1661 the troops that formed Wu's army were already distinct from the Qing soldiers stationed in the defense commands. Known as the "Army Under the Feudatory's Direct Control" (*fanxia*), this force of nearly 11,000 seasoned, well-armed troops was now beyond the reach of the Ministry of War. This was Wu's Praetorian Guard. The ranks of the command structure were staffed with relatives and other men who had been at Wu's side since 1644. For example, the highest-ranking officer next to Wu was the lieutenant (*dutong*), who was assisted by the vice lieutenant, and the offices of the right and left lieutenants. Wu Yingqi, Wu Sangui's nephew, filled the lieutenant post for several years; Wu's son-in-law, Xia Guoxiang, was both a vice lieutenant and a right lieutenant; and Wu's trusted comrade, Yang Shen, whom Wu had known since childhood, acted as lieutenant, vice lieutenant, and regional commander of the Menghua-Jingdong-Chusong-Yaoan Military Circuit. The longer Wu remained in the southwest, the more he relied upon commanders in this force. Ma Ning and Shen Yingshi, assistant lieutenants in Wu's army, were later given concurrent appointments as regional commanders of defense commands. The same was true for some of the fifty-three commanders (*zouling*) who supervised the day-to-day activities and training of this force. The subordinate commanders and regular troops in Wu's army received considerably more *mu* of land per soldier than did troops in the defense commands, and this was some of the best land in the southwest.[25]

Wu also confronted the task of resolving the plight of the Ming loyalists defeated in battle by establishing two large brigades, the Brigade of Loyal Braves (*zhongyong ying*) and the Brigade of Righteous Braves (*yiyong ying*). The two brigades consisted of over 12,000 troops, and each soldier in them was allotted 5 *mu* of land. Many of the officers in Yongli's Southern Ming court were a part of these two brigades. Ma Bao, one of Sun Kewang's most trusted lieutenants, was appointed commanding officer of the Brigade of Loyal Braves. For reasons never made clear, Ma betrayed Sun and joined forces with Li Dingguo and the Yongli emperor in 1657. As a reward to Ma for his service to the Southern Ming court (Ma reportedly rescued the emperor from Sun's guards in Guiyang and delivered him to Li's camp), the Yongli emperor granted Ma the title duke and recommended to Li that Ma be placed in command of Southern Ming forces along the Yunnan-Guizhou border. (Sun often referred to Ma's betrayal as the most humiliating event in his life, and he used his desire to avenge this humiliation to seek a commission in the Qing military, a commission he never received.) When the Yongli court slipped into Burma, Ma's force, decimated by death, disease, and desertions, made a frantic last stand along the banks of the Lancang River (one of the main tributaries of the Mekong River), after which Ma surrendered to Wu. Ma Weixing, Wang Hui, Gao Qilong, and Li Rubi shared similar experiences with Ma Bao, and all became high-ranking commanders in these two brigades.[26]

In addition to the Qing military occupation of the southwest, Wu was concerned with revitalizing civilian rule, but because of the chaotic circumstances and lack of financial resources he made little headway in this regard. Wu appeared intent on constructing political offices in Yunnan and Guizhou that were similar to what the Qing government was establishing in China proper, and several offices did appear on paper; however, few civilian posts were ever filled by officials—one source lists only nine civilian offices in Yunnan staffed by Wu's appointees.[27] Most appointments Wu made were to provincial-level offices, and only a handful of prefecture and subprefecture posts were ever staffed. Much ink has been spilled regarding the extent to which the Qing government acquiesced to Wu's political-military appointments, known as "selections by the [generalissimo who pacifies the] west" (*xixuan*), and the Ministry of War and the Ministry of Personnel did object to what they perceived to be Wu's heavy-handed tactics in getting "his men" appointed to office both in the southwest and in China proper, but as I mentioned earlier the Qing court was consumed with equally pressing matters. In fact, Wu himself was not terribly concerned with establishing civil institutions to rule the southwest.[28]

## *Prince Wu in Shuixi*

Hong Chengchou, prior to his departure to Beijing, reportedly warned Wu Sangui that officials posted to frontiers were susceptible to criticism from many different quarters, and that he needed to be very careful in how he managed the occupation of the southwest. History has shown, Hong noted, that the court dispatches its most trusted officials to the frontier, because the task of maintaining peace in a violence-prone region often overwhelms less skilled men. China's new overlords, the Manchus, understood the importance of posting dependable and talented officials in the frontier only too well. Their unique background as frontier warriors who overcame enormous odds to conquer China made them extremely sensitive to frontier affairs, and Wu benefited from Manchu support as he built a Qing presence in the southwest. But capital officials have their eyes on money, Hong cautioned, and a persistent drain on state coffers could easily undermine court support and end one's career prematurely.

By the time of Hong's departure in 1659, the pro-Ming/anti-Qing resistance in the southwest was beginning to show signs of collapse, and both Hong and Wu had high praise for the many *tusi* who had "turned toward civilization" and submitted to Qing rule. When Qing armies converged at Guiyang, they had already relied quite extensively on *tusi* for assistance, and Qing commanders knew the assault on Yunnan would require additional *tusi* help. In 1661, for instance, Wu requested from the Ministry of War that *tusi* charters (*haozhi*) be bestowed upon fifty-six *tuguan* (civilian officials) and sixteen *tusi* (military officials) throughout Guizhou and eastern Yunnan.[29] One of these *tusi* charters was meant for a man named An Kun, the Shuixi pacification commissioner.

Elements of Wu's army marched south from Luzhou along the Wumeng Road toward the town of Bijie, located along the western edge of Shuixi, and it was in Bijie that An allegedly surrendered to Wu's field commanders. Though the historical record is rather murky on this account, it seems the Shuixi pacification commissioner was able to reassert his authority over the Shuixi region and the Han Chinese population that had settled there following the end of the She-An Rebellion in 1629, and that the traditional Nasu Yi granary units were intact and operational.[30] Nevertheless, the Wumeng Road was one of the main routes into Yunnan, and Wu believed this stretch of the Wumeng Road would be heavily defended by Li Dingguo and Southern Ming forces.[31] An provided provisions to Wu's force, mostly horses and cattle, and from Bijie An's cavalry took the lead in the Qing army's march toward Qujing. An personally negotiated the Qing army's safe passage through Wusa, and a large contingent of Shuixi cavalry were reported to have led the Qing column as it entered Yunnan. Nearly a year later, elements of An's cavalry were seen fighting against the Southern Ming near Dali, thus providing valuable assistance to the Qing cause.[32]

Ironically, as An's troops were fighting on behalf of the Qing, Wu was describing in a series of memorials how An and members of the Nasu Yi elite were secretly plotting with remnants of the pro-Ming resistance to attack Qing forces in Guizhou. In one of his memorials to the Qing throne, Wu wrote, "The Shuixi pacification commissioner was openly supporting [the Qing] but secretly rebelling [against the Qing] [*yangshun yinni*]."[33] In another memorial, Wu noted that "An Kun is a clever man whose attempts at genuine sincerity always seem to fall short of the mark. He has been of assistance in the past, but he never inspired trust. Now we learn that he is listening to [pro-Ming] rebels and providing them a safe haven. This must be stopped."[34] Wu's description of An as a deceitful and calculating anti-Qing rebel, however, concealed another compelling reason for why the equally cunning Wu wanted to eliminate An's control of Shuixi: Wu saw Shuixi as an untapped region of enormous wealth and potential, and he wanted to use this wealth for his own purposes.

Despite the nearly 9,000,000 taels in provisions Beijing was providing its forces in South China, in 1659 Wu and Hong Chengchou were scrambling to alleviate signs of mass starvation among their troops (the diary of Dzengšeo, a Manchu bannerman fighting in the southwest, offers a gripping account of how he and his fellow bannermen, some of the best-supplied troops in China at the time, endured severe privations during the campaign).[35] When they levied a grain tax on the major population centers in Guizhou and Yunnan in order to feed their soldiers, "the towns emptied overnight, the harvested grain disappeared, and angry soldiers roamed the roads and mountain trails looking for food."[36] In several instances, Wu alludes to his displeasure with An and other *tusi* in Guizhou for failing to assist Qing troops stationed in

Guizhou, even remarking at one point, "Shuixi is the wealthiest region in Guizhou. This I have seen with my own eyes. Yet grain from here rarely makes it to our troops. Merchants from Shuixi have gotten fat off our need for grain."[37] Nevertheless, it was Wu's account of An's fomenting an anti-Qing rebellion that became the mainstay in Chinese historical texts. Nasu records, however, deny that An harbored any anti-Qing sentiments but point instead to Wu's desire to seize Shuixi land as the chief motive behind his Shuixi campaign.[38]

According to Wu's version of events, in the early months of 1662 two Southern Ming loyalists, Pi Xiong and Chang Jinyin, entered Shuixi to enlist the support of An. They claimed to be followers of the "prince who brings peace" (*kaiping wang*), and that they traveled from Guangxi to Shuixi to meet with the Shuixi pacification commissioner because they had heard of his loyalty to the Ming cause. An was careful not to arouse suspicion at this time, and he refrained from taking any action that might reveal his true intentions. He did offer shelter to Pi and Chang, though he did not notify Qing authorities in Guiyang of their visit. In time, additional Ming sympathizers began to congregate in Shuixi, most notably Liu Yongning, Ding Diaodian, Li Hualong, and Ni Shenglong, all of whom claimed to be former officials in the Yongli court. This cabal of Ming loyalists, according to Wu, held several meetings at a place called "Adu Corral" (*Adu niuchang*), where they spread the word of rebellion among the local population. They described how Li Dingguo continued to resist Qing forces in Yunnan, and they talked of a new prince established on the sea with a dynastic name of "Pingshun" (probably a reference to Zheng Chenggong). An apparently fell under the sway of these charismatic men and secretly plotted to attack Qing troops in Guizhou and Yunnan.[39]

As part of the preparatory work for the rebellion, An supposedly dispatched several trusted confidants to various parts of the southwest to enlist popular support for the rebellion. One individual in particular, Chen Jincai, was sent to Sichuan to recruit followers in his native province, but in the border town of Luzhou Chen drew attention to himself by proclaiming in a drunken stupor that he was part of a large network of anti-Qing rebels. The local brigade commander, Shen Yinshi, apprehended Chen without incident and extracted a confession that implicated the An in Shuixi. Shen immediately notified Wu, who was still campaigning in Yunnan, and the comical account of a drunken rebel might have ended there if it had not been for several similar stories of apprehended "messengers" spreading the word of rebellion in the streets of Guiyang, Anshun, Zunyi, and Chongqing. Alarmed by the potential for rebellion in Shuixi, Wu notified Beijing of the situation and was granted permission in the second month of 1664 (it was the Deliberative Council that signed off on the campaign) to march into Shuixi and eliminate the Shuixi Pacification Commission.[40]

Wu did not approach this campaign lightly. He planned to surround Shuixi with forces from Yunnan, Guizhou, Huguang, and Sichuan, just as the Mongols had in 1283. He ordered his commanders to study the history of the Mongol invasion of Shuixi, and he ordered a thorough review of the Ming campaign into Shuixi during the She-An Rebellion. Wu's strategy was to divide his Yunnan force into two attack columns, one moving north from Qujing toward Bijie, and the other, which he personally commanded, entering Shuixi from the south using Anshun and Puding as staging areas to attack present-day Zhijin. A sizable portion of Wu's personal force, the Army Under the Feudatory's Direct Control, accompanied him to Anshun, whereas the bulk of the force that marched toward Bijie consisted of recently defeated Southern Ming troops and Qing soldiers from the Huguang and Guangxi armies. Wu believed the Bijie force, in addition to the Sichuan, Huguang, and Guizhou forces, would act to hold An and his army in Shuixi. Wu planned for most of the glory and spoils of war to go to his personal army. He was supremely confident in the ability of his army to defeat An's forces and occupy Shuixi. However, Wu made one error that nearly cost him his life and quite possibly could have altered the history of Qing China.[41]

In preparation for the assault, Wu ordered Guizhou Provincial Military Commander (*tidu*) Li Benshen to assemble provisions from Sichuan and Guizhou near the front so that he could more effectively provide Wu's army with supplies as it marched toward Mugebaizhage. Wu also anticipated that Li's presence (Li commanded a force of 20,000 troops) would force An to divert valuable resources away from Wu's main battle formation, thereby diminishing even further An's capability. But in the written orders Wu sent to Li, he miswrote the characters for the place where he wanted Li to station his troops. Wu wanted Li's force to assemble near the Liugui River, but in his correspondence to Li he inadvertently wrote "Luguang River." The only explanation given for this near-catastrophic miscommunication relates that Wu wrote the character "liu," which means "six," in the formal style, which is pronounced "lu," and Li assumed, without waiting for an explanation concerning the differences between "gui" and "guang," that Wu intended for his force to take up its position near the Luguang River. As a result, Li marched his army and provisions far to the north (a distance of three days by horse) of where Wu had intended them to be. Unaware of this grave error, Wu commenced his campaign to eliminate the Shuixi Pacification Commission.[42]

According to Nasu sources, it was only at this time, with Qing forces surrounding Shuixi and preparing to attack, that An realized he was in serious danger. These sources do not mention Southern Ming rebels' establishing a base of operations in Shuixi, nor do they indicate that An failed to provide financial assistance to Qing forces in Guizhou. Instead, the sources portray An as at pains to understand why Wu was turning on him when elements of his Nasu Yi cavalry were assisting the Qing in Yunnan. In any case, as Wu's force entered Shuixi from Anshun, An quickly forged an alliance with the Wusa native prefect An Chongji and with the Lu patriclan in Wumeng in order to secure his flank from Qing troops approaching from Yunnan and Sichuan, and then he mobilized his sizable army, estimated to be over 100,000 strong, to confront Wu. The two armies met at Guoyongdi (present-day Guoyong village, in Zhijin county).

An's tactical knowledge of the terrain and superior cavalry quickly surrounded Wu's overmatched foot soldiers and forced Wu's soldiers to retreat to the small walled town of Guoyongdi. Wu's troops lacked the military power to fight their way out of An's siege, and after a couple of weeks it was clear to Wu and his commanders that the presence of Li's army was having little effect on how An conducted operations. The specter of the siege of Guiyang during the She-An Rebellion certainly plagued the thoughts of Wu and his commanders, and in a fit of desperation Wu ordered the Yongshun brigade commander, Liu Anbang, to fight his way out of Guoyongdi to seek help. Sadly, Liu and his entire squad were captured, tortured, and executed long before they got beyond eyesight of the town wall. The sight of Liu's men as dismembered corpses tied to wooden stakes outside Guoyongdi's walls caused morale within the walls to plummet, and on at least one occasion there was an attempt on Wu's life. Wu's force remained under siege in Guoyongdi for over two months.[43]

How was it that An's numerically superior force, which had surrounded Wu's army in Guoyongdi for over two months, proved unable to bring the attack to a successful conclusion? Wu, in his reminiscences about this campaign, reveals that he had an accomplice in An's command staff, and that his own survival was undoubtedly due to the accomplice's timely actions. Prior to the start of the campaign, Wu contacted a close relative of An's named Cha Jiana. Wu and Cha had known each other since 1658, when An allowed Wu and his personal entourage to pass through Shuixi on their way to Guiyang. Cha and Wu worked closely together during the latter's Yunnan campaign. Wu, prior to his campaign into Shuixi, approached Cha with an offer of title, rank, and land if he helped Wu in his campaign against An. According to Wu, he learned after the campaign that Cha had advised An not to attack Guoyongdi during the siege for fear that Wu had set a trap. An apparently listened to Cha's advice and did not push to eliminate Wu, which even Wu admitted An could have easily accomplished.[44] An lost an opportunity to defeat Wu at Guoyongdi, and Wu never rewarded Cha for saving his life.

The siege of Guoyongdi was eventually lifted, but only after a stroke of luck. During the siege An Kun's uncle, An Rudian, sent out reconnaissance teams to scout for Qing forces. One such team inadvertently stumbled upon Li Benshen's encampment at the Liuguang River, and after a brief skirmish the reconnaissance team was taken captive. During the interrogation of the team, Li learned of Wu's plight at Guoyongdi and immediately mobilized all available Qing forces to lift the siege. Instead of pressing forward with the siege, or even confronting Li's army, An broke camp and returned to Mugebaizhage. He disbanded his army and ordered them to return to their homes, "so they could contest every foot [*chi*] of ground in Shuixi."[45] Following the siege at Guoyongdi, An and the Nasu Yi elite fought a guerrilla style of warfare reminiscent of how the She-An Rebellion ended for the Ming military, and it took Wu nearly three years to pacify Shuixi—the campaign began in the second month of 1664 and did not end until the twelfth month of 1666.

Near the end of the campaign Wu described in detail how he intended to establish Qing control over Shuixi.[46] Civilian institutions staffed with Qing officials would replace the Shuixi Pacification Commission and the numerous *tusi* scattered throughout the region, Han would be resettled in Shuixi and encouraged to exploit the region's natural resources, and Chinese schools would be built in order to "turn barbarians into Han." Wu, like Ming officials before him, believed that

Shuixi was the economic core of Guizhou, and that Qing control over Shuixi would assist in filling provincial coffers. According to Wu:

Today there are only about ten prefectures in Guizhou, and a few more than that in Yunnan. These prefectures lie in a straight line that runs through the center of Yunnan and Guizhou. The territory that lies beyond this line of prefectures is dominated by *sheng* [unfriendly] Miao tribes. It is for this reason that annual tax revenue in each province is insufficient. Because the tax revenue generated in Shuixi alone equals 60 percent of Guizhou's total annual tax revenue, I recommend the revenue from Shuixi be used to fund basic administrative needs in Guizhou. To accomplish this I propose Shuixi be divided into prefectures, and that we encourage Han [Chinese] to farm land. The additional revenue can be used to provision the military and assist the government in special circumstances. Such development will attract more people to Guizhou, and more land will be reclaimed. What were once considered Guizhou's weaknesses, a small population and limited arable land, have become its strong points today. This plan is based on a thorough examination of the situation.

Based on our investigation of the Shuixi region, we know that the Luogui divided the territory into eleven granary units, and following the She-An Rebellion Ming officials simply granted the title *tusi* to the head of each granary unit. In view of the vast expanse of land, Shuixi could easily be divided into four prefectures [*fu*]. But I am afraid that as a result of the campaign there has been a great loss of life in Shuixi, and since the beginning of the campaign many people have fled their homes, so any estimate on the size of the population in Shuixi can only be a guess.

How would it be, then, if we established three prefectures? We recommend the four granary units of Longkua, Dedu, Duoni, and Ajia be formed into one prefecture, with its headquarters at Bila [Bijie]; the four granary units of Fagua, Shuizhu, Mukua, and Jiale form another prefecture, this one headquartered at Dafang [formerly Mugebaizhage]; and the three granary units of Yizhu, Zewo, and Xiongsuo make up the final prefecture, with its administrative seat at Shuixi [Qianxi]. A prefecture magistrate should be assigned to each prefecture, and each magistrate should be subordinate to the Guizhou provincial administration commissioner. If, in the future, the amount of land under each prefecture's control expands, and the names on the population registers increase, then it will be difficult to govern this region with only three prefectures, and we will need to add to the number of officials posted to this region. This is my plan for establishing civilian rule [in Shuixi].[47]

Wu's memorial is part history lesson, part bold plan for the political incorporation of Shuixi. He reminds the Qing court of the difficulty Ming officials encountered during the 1620s with the She-An Rebellion. The Ming state expended tremendous manpower, material, and finances in its attempt to assert control over the region, but after twenty years the project had failed. Wu, by contrast, possessed the correct policy. His lengthy military campaign had broken the resistance and intimidated the survivors, and the granary units, which apparently still existed in Shuixi despite Zhu Xieyuan's stated objective to eliminate this institution, would be used to create Qing prefectures. Finally, and not inconsequentially to the overall aim of the campaign, Wu portrayed Shuixi as an exceptionally wealthy region capable not only of sustaining three newly created prefectures, but also of providing valuable financial assistance to the Guizhou provincial treasury. In short, the incorporation of Shuixi (and other *sheng* Miao areas beyond Qing control) into the Guizhou political economy would eradicate political and military resistance to the Qing presence and help alleviate the financial burden of providing enormous state subsidies to officials in the southwest.

Not long after the Qing court received Wu's memorial, Guizhou Governor-General Yang Maoxun offered his perspective on how best to handle Shuixi. Yang's memorial proved to be a stern rebuke of Wu's plans for Shuixi, and he claimed to have the support of many of the officials appointed by the Qing court (this was Yang's way of saying he and those who supported his plan were not Wu's men). Unlike Wu, whose memorial shied away from any detailed discussion of the indigenous population, Yang based his concerns about using Han Chinese civilian institutions to govern the people of Shuixi squarely on what he saw as the "interminably violent nature of the barbarians." According to Yang's observations:

Killing is common among the barbarians [*miao-man*], and for this reason the methods used to control them need to be different from those used in China proper. Most of the barbarians live in remote, inaccessible locations high up in the mountains, and it is exceedingly difficult to send troops to these areas. Much of the violence in Shuixi revolves around property disputes and personal animosities, and these circumstances need not to be handled by [our] troops. [Our] troops should be used only in cases when a large concentration of barbarians has amassed to carry out revenge-driven wars, or when they attack Han [Chinese] settlements.

Therefore, it is best to rely on old precedents [*tusi* offices] to govern Shuixi. We must communicate with the barbarian chiefs our expectations and clearly announce rules of right and wrong so that individuals involved in wrongdoing will know the punishment. They will either pay with their lives, or pay in livestock. Reports of such transgressions must also be filed with superiors, something that was not done in the past. Because these barbarians value property more than life itself, adjudicating cases according to principle is enough to serve as punishment. After a certain amount of time has past, the barbarians will come to understand proper rules of behavior and realize their previous mistakes. They will be reborn civilized, and they will no longer fight and kill. This is the principle of attaining peace in the frontier by a judicious use of military force. Otherwise, we will be forced to exterminate them all.[48]

What is most interesting about Yang's memorial is that he does not mention An Kun and the anti-Qing conspiracy, nor does he depict the Shuixi economy as potentially beneficial to the Qing state. Instead, Yang describes the inhabitants of Shuixi as unsophisticated savages who value property more than life itself, and he writes that because they live in such a remote area, it is best to leave them to their own devices. These omissions challenge Wu's two basic tenets: the Qing government should eliminate the Shuixi Pacification Commission because An, influenced by members of the Southern Ming resistance, rebelled against Qing rule; and the Qing government should incorporate Shuixi because the region's economy not only can support his *gaitu guiliu* policy, but its surplus revenue could fill the Guizhou provincial treasury with much-needed cash.

Shuixi is neither a hotbed of anti-Qing conspirators, according to Yang, nor a gold mine waiting to be exploited. Yang does recommend anointing indigenous leaders with *tusi* titles, as the Yuan and Ming governments had done, but he proposes increased government supervision of *tusi*. "The loose rein used previously to restrain the behavior of *tusi* must be tightened like a noose around the throat of each *tusi*, so that they understand clearly what we [our officials] expect of them."[49] Yang's memorial certainly angered Wu, and Wu would exact revenge on Yang and those who supported Yang in short order; nonetheless, the Qing court supported Wu's plan and approved the elimination of the Shuixi Pacification Commission and the creation of three prefectures, Bila, Dafang, and Qianxi. A few months later, the court formally approved the following names for the three prefectures: Bila became Pingyuan prefecture, Dafang became Dading prefecture, and Qianxi remained Qianxi prefecture.[50]

But, the fighting in Shuixi was not over. An Kun and his wife, née Lu, fled first to Wusa with An Chongji, then to Wumeng where the wife's father was the Wumeng native prefect. Because Wusa Native

Prefect An Chongji sided with An Kun at this time, Wu eliminated the Wusa native prefecture and created in its place Weining prefecture (Weining prefecture was now made a part of Guizhou).[51] In Wumeng, An's wife gave birth to his only son, An Shengzu. An Kun, An Chongji, and others associated with the "rebellion" were subsequently captured and executed by Wu's forces, though An Shengzu, because of his infancy, was allowed to remain with his mother's family in Wumeng. According to Wu, nearly all of the Southern Ming rebels who had convinced An to join their anti-Qing cause committed suicide rather than face capture. Not one Southern Ming rebel from Shuixi was ever interrogated, publicly executed, or sent to the Qing capital. Furthermore, Wu's troops were still in the midst of conducting a gruesome occupation campaign. Chinese accounts estimate that no less than 100,000 noncombatants—men, women, and children—were killed between the second month of 1664, when the campaign began, and the twelfth month of 1666, when Wu declared the campaign over.[52] Nasu accounts do not offer a quantitative figure on the number of noncombatants killed by Qing forces, but it is clear that numerous villages in Shuixi, Wusa, and Anshun prefecture were completely depopulated as a result of Wu's campaign.[53]

Wu's forces were not engaged only in Shuixi. Several *tusi* in central and eastern Yunnan took advantage of Wu's embroilment in Shuixi to attack Qing installations and Chinese settlements in Yunnan. Wang Yaozu, the *tusi* of Xingxing, Guizhou, organized a large confederation of culturally diverse *tusi* to attack Kunming. Wang's attempt to seize the Yunnan capital failed, but not before he laid waste to a number of Han Chinese villages near Kunming. What brought these *tusi* together, it appears, was Wu's confiscation of *tusi* lands on which to settle his troops.[54] The *tusi* confederation established an imperial reign title for Wang Yaozu, Daqing (Grand Clarity), and divided its forces into five large columns, but Yunnan Governor-General Bian Sanyuan quickly mobilized all available resources to counterattack the *tusi* confederation. Concerned over events in Yunnan, Wu left the Shuixi front and returned to Kunming to oversee the campaign there. Wei Yuan, the nineteenth-century historian and political activist, credits Wu's return to Kunming as an important turning point in the war against the *tusi* confederation: "If Wu had not returned to Kunming when he did," Wei maintains, "Qing forces in Yunnan might have collapsed under the weight of fighting on three fronts: in Shuixi against An Kun, in central and eastern Yunnan against the *tusi* confederation, and in western Yunnan where Mongol forces had seized the Zhongdian area of Lijiang native prefecture and threatened Dali."⁵⁵

Following the defeat of the *tusi* confederation, Wu established Kaihua prefecture and Yongding department on land previously controlled by rebel *tusi*, and he settled a large contingent of Qing troops in Kaihua and Yongding as an occupation force. Wu also made preparations for the military occupation of Shuixi, and in a memorial to the Qing throne Wu requested financial assistance for his troops garrisoned in Shuixi, Kaihua, and Yongding. To buttress his argument, Wu proposed an ambitious plan to attract Han Chinese from China to settle in Kaihua, Yongding, and Shuixi, and he wanted the Qing court to extend grants so that soldiers and settlers could purchase cattle, seed, tools, and basic necessities to establish themselves permanently in these areas.⁵⁶ One can sense from the Qing court's response to Wu's request for additional funds that officials there were skeptical of Wu's motives. A directive was issued authorizing military grants totaling no more than 30,000 taels and a one-time shipment of 15,000 *shi* of grain to be divided among the troops stationed in the four newly created Pingyuan, Dading, Qianxi, and Weining prefectures.⁵⁷

This is certainly much less than what Wu expected, and it is unclear whether the grain shipment and military grant ever made it to the troops in Shuixi, because in the third month of 1666 Qing troops (these were formerly Southern Ming troops) stationed in Pingyuan (Bijie) rose in revolt against their commanding officers and began pillaging Qing administrative units, Han settlements, and indigenous communities along the Wumeng Road. They raided granaries in Luzhou and Weining and briefly joined ranks with soldiers stationed in Dading to attack, once again, hapless Nasu and non-Nasu indigenes living in central Shuixi. Several of the perpetrators interrogated following the suppression of this incident claimed that they had gone six months without receiving grain provisions, and that they were starving to death in Pingyuan. "We acted out of desperation," one soldier remarked during his interrogation.⁵⁸

The Pingyuan Mutiny, as the event came to be known in Chinese sources, struck the Qing court as an intriguingly odd incident given Wu's glowing description of Shuixi's economic potential. We can be reasonably certain that more than one official in Beijing inquired, probably in a rhetorical voice, how it was that the economic wealth of

Shuixi, anticipated to fund not only civilian rule in Shuixi but much of the provincial treasury, could not feed a handful of Qing soldiers in Pingyuan. The Oboi regency, which was still in charge of the day-to-day operation of government affairs, decided to look into the incident more closely and sent its own team of investigators to Pingyuan. This was an extraordinary move on the part of the regency, for it directly challenged, quite possibly for the first time, Wu's authority over all matters in the southwest. This investigation team was made up of officials from the Ministry of Revenue, several investigating censors from the Censorate, and two local officials the Qing court trusted, Bian Sanyuan, the governor-general of Yunnan, and Luo Huijin, the governor of Guizhou. According to a summary account of the investigation team's preliminary work, the annual military grant allocated for troops in Guizhou came to approximately 720,156 taels. This stipend came from three sources.[59]

First, revenue from the Guizhou land tax was to contribute approximately 58,000 taels annually to its soldiers, but the investigators learned that the provincial treasury could only contribute two-thirds of this amount. Shanxi province had been ordered to contribute 20,000 taels to cover this discrepancy, but funds from Shanxi, the investigators learned, never reached Guizhou. It was also discovered that Shuixi had been unable to contribute to provincial coffers because the level of economic activity following the protracted campaign could barely sustain the subsistence needs of its population—a not-so-subtle jab at Wu.[60] Second, in 1664 officials in Guizhou were ordered to withhold nearly 150,000 taels from taxes levied on the province's silver mines. The investigators learned that not a single tael of the silver tax was ever delivered to Guiyang, and they could not determine where the money had gone. To resolve this dilemma, the investigators ordered Shandong province to transfer the equivalent of 100,000 taels of rice to Guizhou; however, only 80 percent of this shipment made it to Guizhou, because officials in Jiangxi had secretly diverted the equivalent of 20,000 taels of the rice shipment to augment their provincial treasury.

Finally, Shandong had been ordered in 1663 to provide Guizhou's military with 518,227 taels, most of it coming from Shandong's land tax. It just so happened that two of the investigating censors were from Shandong, and they informed the team that due to several years of drought and famine in Shandong, the central government had relieved

Shandong of its financial obligations to other provinces in 1664, and this included the stipend meant for Guizhou.[61] The Qing court did attempt to remedy the situation by ordering Zhejiang, Shanxi, and Wuhu (a county in Anhui) to deliver 320,000 taels to Guizhou immediately, and for Huguang to skim an additional 100,000 taels from its salt tax revenue for Guizhou's military. But officials in Huguang responded to this order by providing only 50,000 taels, because they, too, claimed not to have money to spare.[62]

Money and rice did begin to enter Guizhou, but the amount was still insufficient to support the troops stationed there, that is, according to the original benchmark of 720,156 taels. There were officials in Beijing, it should be noted, who believed the Pingyuan Mutiny was a hoax designed to force the government to provide additional support to Wu's forces in the southwest. Nevertheless, prior to the outbreak of the mutiny, the total amount of provisions Guizhou received from the above provinces came to 483,690 taels, well short of the expected 720,156 taels.

Throughout the three winter months of 1665 and the first three months of 1666 (a total of six months), the province received not a single tael as stipend for its military.[63] Wu Sangui's report on the Pingyuan Mutiny was a scathing rebuke of the Ministry of Revenue mismanagement of not just Guizhou's financial house, but the entire country. Wu told how he repeatedly donated funds from his personal savings to help Qing soldiers in Guizhou make ends meet, and that he had levied a tax on the merchant community in Yunnan specifically to meet the needs of Qing soldiers in Guizhou. However, Wu had other reasons for damning the Ministry of Revenue. This was the one ministry in the capital that had consistently criticized Wu's costly military campaigns and occupation schemes in the southwest, and the Ministry of Revenue was often able to prevent Wu from influencing its personnel decisions in the southwest. In a sense, then, the investigation team sent by Beijing criticized the ministry for its incompetence in managing the country's financial affairs, thus giving ammunition to Wu to attack his most vocal critic, but it also exposed the enormity of the state subsidies the Qing government was providing Wu.[64]

The investigation team concluded that the Qing military in Guizhou was confronting a crisis situation, and it recommended 614,297 taels in provisions be sent to Guizhou immediately. For his part, Wu was authorized to take possession of the Ming garrisons in Guizhou and

Yunnan and to seize all land and commercial operations owned by people associated with the garrisons. This "enclosure" (*quandi*) program was similar in many ways to the encirclement and exclusion program carried out by the Manchus in and around Beijing during the 1640s and 1650s, and the individuals who drafted orders to Wu made note of the successes of the Manchu program in Beijing. The intent of this program was to settle Qing forces in these garrisons throughout Guizhou and Yunnan, because, it was argued, the Chinese residing near the garrisons had created "exceptionally productive islands amid a desolate landscape."[65] The original inhabitants of these garrison communities were relocated to peripheral areas in the southwest where they were expected to reclaim land and quickly transform it into "new islands of wealth," but they were given only one month to leave the garrisons, and the process was marred with violence.

In Shuixi Wu used the encirclement and exclusion program to relocate the Qing occupation forces to the Ming garrisons that surrounded Shuixi, and he ordered the original inhabitants of these garrisons to settle in Shuixi to reclaim land and promote commerce. Wu complained that a substantial number of the former garrison residents refused to leave the garrisons and settle in Shuixi. Many simply vanished, never to be heard from again, and he blamed lax officials for not vigorously enforcing the policy. However, several Qing officials, Yunnan Governor Yuan Maogong among them, lamented the misery this encirclement and exclusion program was causing the people, and they noted rather sarcastically that the program did not seem to be resolving the financial strain afflicting the southwest. They pointed out that instead this draconian policy made the financial situation in the southwest worse. As one official noted, "We removed peasants from the land and asked soldiers to plant grain. Soldiers lack the skills and disposition to work the land. Naturally our tax revenue has declined, and now people barely have enough to eat."[66]

In addition to the ill-conceived encirclement and exclusion policy, Wu was granted control over the extremely lucrative mining (gold, silver, copper, iron, and lead) and salt well industries in the southwest; he was allowed to monopolize the tea and horse trade between China and such foreign entities as Burma, Tibet, and Annam; and he levied a tax called the "provisions to assist" (*zhuxiang*) tax upon the remaining *tusi*, who heretofore had never paid taxes directly to the Chinese state.[67] In each instance Wu increased the base tax rate from what had existed during the Ming.

Take the salt industry, for example—during the last decades of the sixteenth century Ming reports indicate that the salt tax in Yunnan generated nearly 45,000 taels; yet, during Wu's brief tenure he was able to extract an annual salt levy of just over 100,000 taels. Wu's tax rate on 1 *jin* (0.6 kilogram) of salt varied between 6 and 8 *li* (a *li* equals a thousandth of a tael), which was an enormously high rate of tax when compared with tax rates in Zhejiang, where 1 *jin* of salt was taxed just less than 2 *li*, and in Sichuan, where the tax rate on 1 *jin* of salt was less than 1 *li*. Wu's control over the tea and horse trade not only allowed for fabulous profits, especially when dealing with the Tibetans, who had an insatiable appetite for Chinese tea, but also provided Wu with valuable contacts that would come into play during his rebellion against the Qing beginning in 1673.[68]

Needless to say, the elimination of the Shuixi Pacification Commission and the Qing occupation of Shuixi did not produce the economic dividends Wu had promised. Instead, the military campaign into Shuixi and the occupation of this region proved to be an enormous financial drain on the Qing government. There were times when the Qing court seemed cautiously hopeful that Wu's Shuixi campaign would rebound in Guizhou's financial favor, but the Pingyuan Mutiny and the subsequent investigations exposed for all to see how enormous the financial burden of the Qing military occupation of the southwest had become. The Shuixi campaign, the mutiny, and the subsequent investigations also cast doubt on the veracity of Wu's reports to the throne. The Qing court's immediate response to the Shuixi quagmire was to authorize Wu to raise revenue in order to offset state subsidies to the southwest, but now Wu's actions were monitored more closely by officials sent to the southwest by Beijing. Chinese history overflows with examples of trusted regional commanders who were able to manipulate relations with imperial courts to build independent satrapies, and to many in Beijing at this time what Wu was doing in Guizhou and Yunnan seemed strikingly similar to the centrifugal forces unleashed by the security commissioners (*jiedu shi*) of the Tang dynasty. History had taught the officials in Beijing that they would need to remove Wu from his position of authority in the southwest, and the sooner the better.[69]

## The Rebellion of the Three Feudatories

Wu Sangui knew his actions in the southwest were attracting the wrong kind of attention in Beijing. Confidants in the Qing capital reported that gossip on the streets was of the lavish wealth Wu had accumulated, the fabulous palaces he had built for himself and his family, and his growing political influence within Qing officialdom. There was idle talk of his friendly relations with Tibet and Burma, and men of talent were beginning to flock to the southwest in hopes of finding employment. Wu knew the Manchu throne had become irritated by this disconcerting cacophony, and it was probably for this reason that Wu, in 1667, submitted to the Qing throne his resignation from public office.[70] Wu claimed old age, failing eyesight, and an inhospitable climate had taken a toll on his ability to serve the Qing emperor, but those who had recently visited with the prince described him as robust, full of vigor, and looking exceptionally young for his age. Instead of a sincere request to retire, Wu's attempt to resign was little more than a nervous official's hope to deflect public criticism and demonstrate loyalty, and in the end Wu expected his request to be denied.[71]

On this occasion the Qing court, still under the control of the Oboi regency, called Wu's bluff and accepted his resignation. As word of Wu's resignation circulated among Qing officials, an avalanche of memorials poured into Beijing beseeching the emperor to keep Wu in office. The Oboi regency, which continued to exercise executive authority for the youthful Kangxi emperor until 1669, grudgingly relented to the show of support for Wu and reversed its decision, thus denying Wu's request to resign.[72] Nonetheless, concern over Wu's actions in the southwest and the support he garnered from officials continued to fester at the Qing court. When the Oboi regency was abolished in 1669, Kangxi noted that military commanders must not be allowed to remain in one post for too long, nor should they be excused from presenting themselves to the throne, a clear reference to the three feudal princes Wu Sangui, Shang Kexi, and Geng Jimao. When Kangxi learned in 1673 that the Qing government had provided nearly 20,000,000 taels to Wu, Sheng, and Geng, the political and fiscal dangers inherent in this situation demanded that he act decisively to end the three feudatories. Kangxi ordered the feudatories abolished, government financial support withdrawn, and the three princes to return to the northeast.[73] To no one's surprise, Wu refused to relinquish his post, and on December 28, 1673, he declared his intent to remove the Manchus from Chinese soil.[74]

To this end, Wu announced his intent to resurrect the political and cultural institutions of the Ming dynasty, but, because of his defection to the Qing cause in 1644, his relentless pursuit of Li Zicheng and the Southern Ming court, and his personal supervision of the Yongli emperor's execution in 1662, Wu could not restore the Ming dynasty in name. Instead, he proclaimed the creation of the Zhou dynasty, and he named himself the "generalissimo of the expedition army of all under heaven" (*tianxia du zhaotao bingma da yuanshuai*). Although it is beyond the scope of this study to examine the subsequent eight years of turbulent civil war, known popularly as the Rebellion of the Three Feudatories, I will mention that by the summer of 1676 Wu's armies were clearly on the defensive.[75] Wang Fuchen, the former provincial military commander of Shaanxi and Wu Sangui's godson, surrendered to Qing forces in Shaanxi on July 11, 1676. Wang's capitulation allowed Manchu armies to control the Gansu corridor to the west, and challenge Wu's armies in Sichuan to the south.[76] Shortly thereafter, on November 9, Geng Jingzhong, who joined Wu's rebellion on April 21, 1674, succumbed to relentless Qing assaults into Fujian, but not before he martyred the Qing official Fan Chengmo.[77] In the summer of 1677 Shang Zhixin, Shang Kexi's son and the real leader of rebel forces in Guangdong, also recognized the futility of continuing the rebellion and surrendered to the Qing. As Qing forces advanced toward the southwest only Guangxi, the western half of Hunan, and the three southwest provinces of Yunnan, Guizhou, and Sichuan remained under Wu's command, but his control over the southwest was already on the wane.

In a desperate attempt to stem the advancing Qing tide, Wu, on March 23, 1678, proclaimed himself the Zhaowu emperor of the Zhou dynasty. Wu's self-coronation did not solidify Han Chinese support for his anti-Qing cause as he had anticipated it would; instead, his claim to imperial title only alienated once and for all the Ming loyalists and staunch anti-Qing intellectuals who, despite Wu's previous transgressions against the Ming throne, had invested emotional and political capital in his rebellion. Shortly after the announcement Wu relocated his forces to Hengzhou, Huguang, where he began preparations for what he believed would be the decisive battle for China. But on October 2, 1678, a delirious and incapacitated Zhou monarch succumbed to an acute case of dysentery, and with Wu's unexpected death the war's momentum swung decisively in Kangxi's favor.[78]

Wu Sangui's grandson, Wu Shifan, quickly assumed control of rebel forces and was introduced as the Honghua emperor of the Zhou dynasty, yet his term in Hengzhou was short lived. On March 24, 1679, Qing armies, having already shattered Zhou defenses in northern Huguang, captured Hengzhou and forced Wu Shifan to retreat to Yunnan, leaving a blood-stained wake through Guizhou in his path. In November Kangxi ordered his highly decorated Manchu commander Tuhai (d. 1682) to lead a massive assault into Sichuan. By February 1680 Tuhai's army had reclaimed Chengdu, and in March Kangxi rejoiced at news of Chongqing's capture. As Qing forces descended on Chongqing Kangxi bestowed upon the current governor-general of Sichuan and Huguang Cai Yurong (1633–99) the title "general pacifying the remoteness" (*suiyuan jiangjun*), with orders to assist the Manchu prince Jangtai (1636–90), the "general tranquilizing remoteness" (*dingyuan da jiangjun*). It was Jangtai and Cai who led the Qing campaign against Zhou forces in the southwest.[79]

Before Jangtai and Cai launched their attack on Guizhou in May 1680, Kangxi announced that all land in Yunnan and Guizhou confiscated by Wu Sangui and his subordinates would be returned to its rightful owners once hostilities ended. The intent of the imperial edict was to incite support for the Qing cause in Wu's base, the southwest. The Qing emperor calculated that the non-Han, who had suffered the most under Wu's occupation, would immediately side with the Qing and attack the Han Chinese soldiers and farmers who not only benefited the most from Wu's land-confiscation policies, but were Wu's base of support.[80]

In Shuixi An Shengzu, An Kun's son, who was born in Wumeng not long after Wu Sangui occupied Shuixi, drew support from Wumeng and Shuixi to attack Wu's forces in western Guizhou and eastern Yunnan. Wu's troops in Guiyang were repeatedly harassed by An's agents, especially after the rebellion had started and Wu had moved his forward camp to Huguang. When Wu Shifan retreated through Guizhou, the Zhou army was decimated along the roads of western Guizhou as Nasu and non-Nasu troops lined the roads, trails, and waterways waiting to avenge earlier injustices. When Jangtai's advance column reached the city of Guiyang, its troops were warmly received by Nasu Yi forces that had been in possession of the city for several weeks.[81]

Qing commanders realized rather early on that An Shengzu's control over the Nasu Yi in Shuixi had declined significantly following Wu Sangui's occupation of Shuixi. During An's absence in Wumeng, other members of the Nasu Yi elite had emerged as important military-political figures, and they proved instrumental in organizing Nasu Yi forces in support of the Qing cause. For this reason, Qing officials recommended to Kangxi that he make a symbolic gesture by appointing An Shengzu to the post of Shuixi pacification commissioner, but the pacification commissioner office they envisioned no longer exercised political control over Shuixi. Instead, local officials proposed rewarding those members of the Nasu Yi elite "who performed loyal and valiant service in the suppression of rebel forces" with *tusi* posts in Shuixi (just as Zhu Xieyuan and Wu Sangui had done earlier). They identified forty-eight individual Nasu Yi leaders to be appointed to *tusi* offices in Shuixi, a figure strikingly similar to the overall number of *muzhuo* in the traditional Nasu Yi granary system.

Kangxi's edict on the reconstruction of Shuixi accepted many of the recommendations put forth by local officials. The four prefectures established by Wu Sangui, Pingyue, Qianxi, Weining, and Dading, would remain as the definitive political units in Shuixi, though each prefecture would now receive a full complement of degree-holding Qing officials and support staff.[82] Kangxi authorized the creation of forty-eight *tusi* offices in Shuixi, and he appointed to the posts those members of the Nasu Yi elite recommended by local officials. As Kangxi remarked, "*Tusi* offices in the four prefectures of Pingyue, Qianxi, Weining, and Dading were originally headed by Miao barbarians, and they govern a population different from the common people [Han Chinese]. It is best to continue to rely on *tusi* to rule these places [where non-Han Chinese live]."[83] Moreover, these *tusi* offices were made directly subordinate to the Qing officials in Guiyang, not to the Shuixi pacification commissioner as they had been in the past. As the Shuixi pacification commissioner, An Shengzu was ordered to live in Guiyang. He was permitted to travel to Shuixi only to pay his respects to deceased ancestors in Dafang and to participate in important Nasu Yi festivals. An was not under house arrest, for he moved about the city unrestricted and often socialized with local officials, but he certainly could not leave the city without the approval of the provincial governor, and such approval was seldom granted.

Kangxi explained the interesting political mixture of state-appointed Qing officials and hereditary *tusi* in Shuixi by pointing out that this was a qualitatively new and unique form of governance that could only apply to specific frontier settings:

Since the closing years of the Ming, armies have repeatedly *trampled the earth* [in Shuixi], so that now it is a very different place from before. The Miao have turned toward civilization, and we must assist them in their desire for a better life. The time has come [for us] to play an active role in the day-to-day affairs of Shuixi. Our officials will carry out this task. But, they will need the help of the local elite [*tusi*] in the short term. Eventually the *tusi* offices will disappear, and Shuixi will be indistinguishable from China proper.[84]

## The End of the Shuixi Pacification Commission

An Shengzu remained in Guiyang until his death in 1697, and local officials were mindful of his commanding presence in the city's multi-ethnic community. An and his immediate family lived in a large compound in the northwestern portion of the city, a section dominated by the Nasu Yi elite and long populated by non-Han Chinese. Local officials recorded with some consternation how An's administrative offices were frequently inundated with visitors, both Han and non-Han, who sought his assistance. As one official noted, "Travelers from Shuixi come to pay their respects, others seek guidance in matters concerning the barbarians, whereas others simply line up outside his headquarters hoping to receive a token of appreciation [money]. The pacification commissioner's office is a beehive of activity."[85] An was certainly a respected member of the Guiyang community, and, if Nasu Yi sources are taken uncritically, his stature irritated jealous Qing officials.

According to both Chinese and Nasu Yi sources, An produced no surviving male heir, though he reportedly fathered four daughters. When An's death came in 1697, his family presented Qing officials with a list of possible successors (this list should have been presented to officials prior to An's death), but these officials immediately notified Beijing that the Shuixi pacification commissioner died without a male heir. Since this *tusi* office was viewed as a purely symbolic post, the officials cited recent reforms to *tusi* regulations to recommend the elimination of this hereditary post.

The reforms stipulated that candidates for *tusi* offices be direct male heirs of the previous *tusi*. In addition, direct male heirs were required to demonstrate attendance at a school that imparted a Confucian curriculum and under examination to prove they had successfully acquired a modest understanding of Chinese culture. If neither of these critical standards could be met, Qing officials were authorized to deny government appointment. The increased contact between Qing local officials and *tusi*, which I have discussed elsewhere, was itself a noteworthy bureaucratic innovation over what had existed during the Ming.[86] The officials who proposed these reforms reasoned that if a *tusi* outlived his usefulness as a political intermediary between the government and the indigenous frontier population, his hereditary claim to the office could be revoked and granted to another individual, or the office could be eliminated altogether. Qing officials need only declare the *tusi* had not produced a male heir, or the male heir had failed to acquire the necessary Chinese educational qualifications needed to inherit the office. Following An Shengzu's death in 1697, officials in Guiyang discussed abolishing the Shuixi Pacification Commission with officials in Beijing, and they even interviewed a number of An's closest relatives to gauge their reaction to the possible elimination of the office. After three long years, the Qing government determined a suitable male heir was unavailable to inherit the office and recommended the Shuixi Pacification Commission be abolished.

Kangxi issued an imperial decree in 1701 formally abolishing the Shuixi Pacification Commission. In his decree he mentioned the long history of the An family in the region, beginning with Tuoazhe and the valuable assistance he provided the famous Shu Han general Zhuge Liang. Kangxi also mentioned Aicui and She Xiang's contributions to the founding Ming emperor's military campaigns into the southwest, and the Ming government's enfeoffment of the An family at the beginning of the Ming. Finally, he noted with admiration how An Shengzu had sided with the Qing at a critical moment during the Rebellion of the Three Feudatories. The emperor's edict concluded with the following lines: "I hereby abolish the Shuixi Pacification Commission. The office has outlasted its usefulness. The people [of Shuixi] have lived under civilian rule for several years now, and they have prospered under our magnanimity and guidance. Barbarians can become civilized, and Shuixi is proof of this."[87] For the Qing officials in Guizhou, Kangxi's words must have wrung hollow. They knew the "barbarians" (Nasu Yi) had not become civilized like Han Chinese, nor had they been denied the ability to preserve their own identity. What had changed was their ability to militarily resist the Chinese (Qing) state.

# Conclusion

In *China's March Toward the Tropics*, Herold Wiens sifted through an enormous amount of fragmented and incomplete documentation to present an extraordinarily rich outline of China's southern expansion. Successive waves of Han immigrants fleeing political instability, economic destitution, and natural disasters in North China and the attraction of fertile, sparsely inhabited, and unexploited lands in the south both pushed and pulled Han Chinese toward the tropics. This surge southward, Wiens argued, was carried out almost exclusively by private individuals, and the Chinese state became part of China's march southward only after it felt pressured to protect Han settlers from hostile indigenes. Over time the sheer weight of Han settlers in the southern frontiers swamped the indigenous population, of whom we know very little. There is a benign quality to Wiens's portrait of Chinese expansion into the southern frontiers, and this study takes issue with this historical explanation.

First, I have shown that prior to the Yuan and Ming dynasties the southwest was settled territory. There were many peoples and kingdoms in the southwest, and the Nasu Yi discussed in this book represented just one among many. From the third century CE on there were at least four distinct Nasu Yi kingdoms governing present-day eastern Yunnan and the whole of Guizhou province, and they remained in control of this enormous tract of land until the Mongols invaded the southwest in 1253. Mongol forces eventually defeated the Mu'ege kingdom in 1283 after several years of bitter fighting, but the Yuan state proved unable and unwilling to consolidate control over Mu'ege territory. Eventually, the Nasu Yi elite of Mu'ege reemerged as rulers of their territory during the 1290s, though now they were Yuan officials with *tusi* designation.

The Ming emperor Hongwu was determined to assert Ming control over the southwest. He could not tolerate a large Mongol presence in Yunnan, nor could he hope to rebuild the war-ravaged Chinese economy without Yunnan's natural resources. Hongwu assembled one of the largest armies in Chinese history and dispatched it to the southwest to defeat the Mongols and permanently settle the area. The Ming military colonization of the southwest in the 1380s and 1390s has few rivals in Chinese history, and this colonization did not end with the death of Hongwu in 1398 or with the creation of Guizhou province in 1413. It had just begun. In contrast to the situation along Ming China's northern frontier, where military and civilian officials adopted a decidedly defensive strategy to protect the country from marauding Mongols (the construction of the Great Wall), in the southwest the Ming maintained an aggressive posture even after the Tumu Incident of 1449.

Throughout the fifteenth and sixteenth centuries the Ming state continually dispatched soldiers and civilians to the southwest to replenish the military garrisons. During the fifteenth century Ming soldiers were in a perpetual state of conflict as they sought to secure the boundaries of Yunnan and Guizhou from external enemies and to pacify hostile indigenes within the two provinces. Troop strength declined in relation to the brutality of the campaign, thereby necessitating that the government redeploy troops to the garrisons in order to maintain an adequate presence. By the later decades of the sixteenth century the level and intensity of military campaigns had declined somewhat, though not entirely, and Ming soldiers increasingly abandoned military life in the garrisons to take up civilian life in the towns nearby.

As the Ming consolidated control over China proper it relied extensively on the Yuan model of using *tusi* offices to establish relations with indigenous frontier peoples. During the Yuan dynasty *tusi* offices were primarily jurisdictional in nature, inasmuch as the *tusi* was bound to the Mongol qan in a personal relationship based on reciprocity. There existed an agreed-upon set of conditions governing this relationship, and each party was duty bound to fulfill specified obligations. As the Ming pressed into the southwest it recalibrated *tusi* offices as extrabureaucratic posts marginally linked to the regular Chinese bureaucracy, and in so doing *tusi* offices became increasingly associated with territory, not the emperor. In short, the Ming state transformed the Yuan model of the *tusi* office from a personal to an impersonal relationship and replaced the conditional framework of obligations with an unconditional set of state-sponsored regulations.

Ming success in colonizing the southwest can be measured in part by how it was able to redefine the state's relationship with *tusi* offices and by the elimination of powerful *tusi* offices like the Bozhou and Guizhou pacification commissions. The Rebellion of the Three Feudatories completed the task of eradicating potent indigenous resistance to Chinese colonization of the southwest, and the abolition of the Shuixi Pacification Commission in 1701 was more an afterthought on the part of Qing officials than any serious attempt to acquire territory. Early Qing policies toward the southwest, especially the Kangxi-era reforms to *tusi* offices and Yongzheng's program to eliminate *tusi* offices in Guizhou and Yunnan, should be seen as the culmination in a long process of colonial expansion into the southwest, and not the beginning salvo as it has been often depicted by students of Qing history.

Finally, this study has shown that during the Yuan and Ming dynasties officials did not actively promote a Confucian civilizing mission among the indigenous non-Han peoples. From when the first Mongol army entered the southwest in 1253 to the end of the Rebellion of the Three Feudatories in 1681, Chinese officials were concerned almost exclusively with extending military and civilian control over the region and tethering it to China proper. The Ming institutionalization of *tusi* offices segregated the indigenous population within the larger Ming state umbrella, and the indigenous non-Han peoples were kept separate and unequal from Han Chinese in virtually every sphere of life. The Ming throne certainly proposed extending the Chinese education system to the non-Han peoples, but Ming officials rarely built schools beyond Han Chinese enclaves.

The non-Han peoples were prohibited from taking the Ming examinations, which were probably the one tool at the state's disposal that could potentially "transform barbarian into civilized Han." Officials certainly justified the use of military force against the indigenous non-Han by arguing their intent to "civilize the barbarian," but when it came time to establish schools and encourage indigenes to assimilate into Chinese society, their pronouncements rang hollow. Not until the Kangxi and Yongzheng reigns of the Qing dynasty were there concerted efforts on the part of both the central government and local officials to extend the Chinese education system to the non-Han peoples in the southwest, but by this time the southwest and its peoples had been subjected to nearly 500 years of Chinese colonization. Civilizing the barbarians through education was the last phase in the colonization process. The moral tone of bringing civilization to the barbaric southwest frontier masked the brutality of Ming colonization of this region.

## Reassessing the Role of the State

The general parameters of the march thesis and the minor role accorded the state in China's southern expansion came under critical scrutiny in 1987 with the publication of Richard von Glahn's influential study, *The Country of Streams and Grottoes: Expansion, Settlement, and the Civilizing of the Sichuan Frontier in Song Times*. First, von Glahn illustrated the importance the Song state attached to developing the economic resources of Southern Lu, especially the region's salt mines, following a discernible increase in military activity along China's northern and northwestern borders. Song officials were desperate for revenue to augment Song military preparedness in the north, and the potential profits from the Southern Lu salt mines convinced officials to exploit this natural resource. Initially, state investment in the salt mine industry reaped handsome rewards, but a century of unrestrained exploitation left the salt mines in Southern Lu exhausted, and the state, recognizing the prohibitive costs of maintaining a presence in this otherwise resource-poor region, began to withdraw from Southern Lu. According to von Glahn, the state's departure from Southern Lu precipitated a decline in the number of Han settlers entering the Southern Lu frontier, and within a few years indigenes reclaimed land vacated by Han Chinese.

Second, von Glahn described the tensions that existed between Han Chinese settlers and the Song state. The earliest Han immigrants to Southern Lu went there in search of land and economic opportunities, and they quickly determined that the best land was under indigene control. They tried to compensate the indigenes for their land, either through purchase, barter, or trade, but when these attempts failed the settlers forcibly seized indigene lands. Predictably, the indigenes responded to violence with violence, and this spawned a cycle of revenge-driven hostility that compelled the Song state to intervene, but, as von Glahn points out, on more than a few occasions the state acted against the interests of Han Chinese settlers and on behalf of the indigenes.

Third, von Glahn sets the stage for his examination of Song expansion into southern Sichuan by providing descriptions of the three largest indigenous societies in the area. The Buek, who were said to closely resemble Han Chinese in "standards of behavior," were in fact a diverse group of regional cultures whose civilization began to decline following Han military incursions into the Lake Dian region of central Yunnan near the end of the second century BCE. The Klao lived primarily in lineage-based villages without a unifying political authority. By the Song dynasty Klao settlements dotted the entire southwest landscape from present-day Hunan in the east to modern Yunnan in the west. The Yi, who are discussed extensively in this book, were the third indigenous society described by von Glahn.

Von Glahn's description of these three indigenous societies serves two purposes. First, it shows the extent to which the southwest was settled territory, and that these three peoples (and many others not discussed) had resided there for centuries. Second, he uses the indigenes' original society as a benchmark to measure Han Chinese success in acculturating the Klao and Yi peoples they encountered. According to von Glahn, the zone of contact between the intrusive settlers and the indigenes was truly "uncommon ground," and the process of sinicization that others saw operating during China's migration southward (a reference to Wiens's work) simply was not evident during Song China's expansion into Southern Lu. The boundaries separating Han and non-Han ebbed and flowed during this wave of Song Chinese expansion into the southwest frontier, and once the Song state withdrew from the region the long-standing boundaries that divided Han from non-Han returned.

These three features of von Glahn's study—an analysis of the fiscal concerns of the Chinese state, a critical assessment of relations between the Chinese state and Han settlers, and an examination of the indigenous frontier population—in 1993 became the focus of yet another study, John R. Shepherd's *Statecraft and Political Economy on the Taiwan Frontier, 1600–1800*. Shepherd places particular emphasis on the critical role of the state in Qing China's colonization of Taiwan, and as such his study offers a qualitatively new paradigm to analyze state/society expansion into its surrounding frontier territories. Shepherd argues that Qing expansion into Taiwan was determined by a cost-benefit analysis that calculated Taiwan's strategic importance to the Qing state, the revenue potential of Taiwan's economy, and the estimated cost of first pacifying and then governing Taiwan. "More than any other factor," Shepherd tells us, "the fiscal limitations of the late imperial state restricted its incorporation of frontier territories and determined the allocation of land rights in the territories it did incorporate."[1] Shepherd describes how due to such fiscal constraints Qing officials in Taiwan developed a large repertoire of policies designed to open the Taiwan frontier to Qing exploitation.

In a narrative impressive for its complexity and readability, Shepherd describes how in 1683 Qing officials decided to quarantine Taiwan from Han Chinese immigration. These officials understood, as did Song officials working in the Southern Lu frontier six centuries earlier, that unrestricted Han migration into an area and the ensuing encroachment on indigene lands would spawn a cycle of revenge-driven violence, thereby forcing the state to intervene militarily. Such frontier operations were prohibitively expensive, and Taiwan's economic infrastructure was deemed incapable of providing the revenue necessary to sustain even a modest police action. Moreover, these Qing officials were convinced that an aggressive and persistent campaign to settle the island with Chinese would not appreciably change the revenue potential of the Taiwan economy. Simply put, the costs of establishing Qing civilian and military institutions in Taiwan far exceeded the fiscal capability of the Taiwan economy.[2]

However, by the Yongzheng reign Qing officials were obliged to admit in public what they had long suspected in private: the quarantine policy implemented in the 1680s to stem the flow of Han settlers to Taiwan had failed. In a dramatic reversal of policy, officials were encouraged by the activist emperor to replace earlier quarantine measures with pro-immigration and colonization policies. It was now argued that an increase in the size of the Han population in Taiwan would provide a revenue base sufficient to finance civil and military institutions. Before long this brash optimism regarding the colonization of Taiwan disappeared as the wisdom and foresight of the quarantine policy drafted in the 1680s shone through. Not only was Taiwan's revenue base pitifully small and undeveloped, but the costs of controlling the Han and indigene populations far exceeded the financial benefits of extending civilian rule to Taiwan. As a result, during the middle decades of the eighteenth century Qing officials once again imposed restrictions on Han immigration to Taiwan as a way to minimize the state's fiscal burden.

Within this larger discussion of how Qing policy vacillated between quarantine and colonization, Shepherd focuses on the long-term continuity of such cost-effective measures as the allocation of land rights, the recruitment of local militias, and the promotion of educational opportunities for both Han and non-Han in order to elucidate how the cumulative presence of the Qing state affected the indigene population in Taiwan. For example, the allocation of land rights was a tactical policy designed to minimize as much as possible the hostility surrounding Han encroachment on indigene lands. Any decrease in frontier violence was a net financial gain for the state. Moreover, state support of indigene land-ownership claims guaranteed that indigenes would continue to own fertile land in Taiwan's coastal plain for the foreseeable future; this is an important point because one of Shepherd's goals in writing his study was to show how the displacement scenario, the belief that Han immigration either destroyed Taiwan's indigenous populations or forced its survivors to flee to the remote mountains of eastern Taiwan, was not entirely accurate. It was the state's allocation of land rights that guaranteed indigene landownership and provided indigenes with a measure of economic security during uncertain times.

An insufficient revenue base was not the only obstacle Qing officials faced in Taiwan. Cultural differences between Qing officials (elite culture), Han Chinese settlers (non-elite culture), and indigenes also required careful attention if the Qing state was to incorporate Taiwan into the Qing empire. Here, though, the rationale of cost-benefit analysis, which might tame even the most passionate advocate of expansion, was largely offset by Confucian political theory. In an ideal Confucian world, the measure of good government was the ability to rule by moral persuasion. The emperor, who enjoyed the Mandate of Heaven (*tianming*), relied upon his officials, who supposedly personified Confucian morality as a result of their rigorous academic training, to impart wisdom and civility to the general population so that they, too, could become moral subjects of a universal civilized order. The moral transformation of the general population, Han and non-Han alike, was to be carried out not through stern measures, harsh laws, and intimidation, but through education. Thus, it was often written that Han Chinese officials were charged "to govern by refinement and to transform through education" (*wenzhi jiaohua*).[3]

However, in frontier areas like Taiwan, Han Chinese officials seldom overstated the ease in which Confucian morality and Han values could transform and guide the non-Han population. During the early years of the Yongzheng reign, when aggressive immigration policies toward Taiwan dominated court policy, Qing officials occasionally concentrated their limited resources to inculcate the indigenous elite with Confucian moral values and Chinese social customs in hopes of creating a loyal elite, part indigene and part Han. Only the most optimistic of Taiwan's local officials believed such values and customs could filter down into indigene society and transform immoral into moral, uncivilized into civilized, and non-Han into Han. Wang Gungwu said it best when he suggested that the Chinese urge to civilize was rather weak; nonetheless, the ideological rationale for domination, which Stevan Harrell has so astutely termed the "Confucian civilizing mission," was intended for a Chinese audience because the long-term moral objectives of the civilizing mission justified the immediate violence of the mission.[4] In other words, the reality of implementing the Confucian civilizing mission encountered obstacles the concept never imagined, and historians, infatuated by the altruism of the concept, continually turned a blind eye to the historical record of naked aggression.

Several of the issues von Glahn and Shepherd addressed found expression in yet another study, James A. Millward's *Beyond the Pass: Economy, Ethnicity, and Empire in Qing Central Asia, 1759–1864*, published in 1998. As the title indicates, Millward examined the fiscal and ethnic policies that formed the broader framework of Qing colonization of the Central Eurasian region that now forms China's Xinjiang province. The Manchu overlords of China, according to Millward, extended Qing control over this remote portion of Central Eurasia not for economic reasons, nor because Han settlers had moved into this region and formed a natural bridge linking China proper and Central Eurasia. Instead, the Manchus were concerned about the strategic impact an aggressive Inner Asian Zunghar empire might have on Qing relations with various Mongol allies in Central Eurasia and with the dGelugs-pa religious establishment (the Yellow Hat sect) in Tibet (Peter Perdue expands upon Millward's arguments in his 2005 publication, *China Marches West*). Any erosion of Manchu preeminence in its relations with Mongols and Tibetans in Central Eurasia would seriously undermine the vitality of the Manchu empire and possibly threaten Manchu control of China.

After Manchu forces defeated the Zunghars and secured for themselves the role of patron in the priest-patron relationship with Tibet, they encountered the same economic trap Shepherd described for Taiwan. The strategic importance of Central Eurasia made it imperative that Qing military garrisons be established throughout the region; yet, the Xinjiang economy was incapable of generating sufficient revenue to provide Qing forces with even the most basic necessities, and as a result during the second half of the eighteenth century Qing control of Central Eurasia was sustained by generous subsidies sent annually from China proper to Xinjiang (not unlike the situation in Guizhou province during the fifteenth and sixteenth centuries). Criticism of these subsidies compelled the Qing court to alter its policies slightly by encouraging Han and Central Eurasian entrepreneurs to develop the region's economic resources. Local officials in Xinjiang were also granted considerable leeway in devising economic strategies that might make the military occupation of Central Eurasia less dependent on Chinese finances. But Qing officials in Xinjiang, like their counterparts in Taiwan, feared an outbreak of violence once Han Chinese merchants entered Xinjiang, and they, too, sought to protect the economic rights of the indigenous Uyghur population.

In the 1820s, following a series of predatory raids into Xinjiang by nomadic forces located in western Turkestan, the Qing state abandoned its policy of accommodation toward the indigenous Uyghur population and adopted aggressive procolonization measures designed to relocate Han merchants and peasants in Xinjiang. The Qing state was now less willing to protect the economic and religious rights of the Uyghurs. According to Millward's summary of the words of the influential statecraft thinker Gong Zizhen (1792–1841), "Once the land was reclaimed, populated with private Chinese farmers, and put under Chinese style provincial administration, the expanded agricultural base could be properly taxed. Thus, he [Gong] promised, would 'the center give up people to benefit the west, and the west give up people to benefit the center.'"[5] Ironically, when the Manchu court began to colonize this portion of Central Eurasia with Han merchants and peasants, the Qing empire in Central Asia became "domesticated," as Millward eloquently put it. The adoption of procolonization policies had the psychological effect of altering how China's elites viewed Central Eurasia, for Xinjiang was no longer seen as a distant frontier, but as an integral part of China.

Three recent publications, Emma Teng's *Taiwan's Imagined Geography*, Peter Perdue's *China Marches West*, and C. Patterson Giersch's *Asian Borderlands*, build upon this earlier research to provide a comprehensive portrait of China's frontiers, especially Qing China's frontiers. Each work offers a detailed description of the indigenous non-Han peoples under examination; each discusses the frontier economy and its revenue potential in support of Qing colonization efforts; each analyzes tensions between the Qing central government and local society, and the extent to which China's elites came to accept the frontier in question as an integral part of China; and each work illustrates the speciousness of ascribing simple notions of civilization and barbarity to the frontier setting. Taken together, these studies show conclusively how Qing frontier policy differed over time and space; most important, though, they place the Qing state squarely in the center of their examination of Qing expansion. In particular, Perdue's work makes note of the striking similarities between the rise of the early modern European nation-state, as described by Charles Tilly and others, and Qing China's confrontation with the emerging Zunghar and Russian states in Central Eurasia.

This book places the state at the center of an analysis of China's expansion into the southwest frontier during the Yuan and Ming dynasties. The political autonomy of Mu'ege, Dali, and several other smaller kingdoms in the southwest came to an abrupt end in 1253 when Mongol forces, desperate to open a second front against Song China, attacked the Dali kingdom. It would take another twenty years of difficult fighting in the southwest before the Mongols secured control over Yunnan and modern-day Guizhou, but by then Song resistance had weakened considerably and the southwestern front no longer seemed vital to the Mongol conquest of Song China.

The Yuan government decided to govern the southwest with the same political institution it used to govern Chinese territory when it established the Yunnan Branch Secretariat in 1274, and as a result the southwest became part of the mainstream political apparatus of the Yuan state. In much the same way the Xinjiang frontier was domesticated during the Qing, as described by Millward, the presence of the Yunnan Branch Secretariat persuaded the political elite in Yuan China to view Yunnan and the southwest as a part of China, albeit an exotic part of China. This is not to suggest that the Yuan state's creation of the Yunnan Branch Secretariat was part of a broad-based procolonization program to incorporate the region culturally into China proper. The Mongols were not interested in swamping the southwest with Han Chinese settlers, whom they distrusted, nor were they fascinated by the prospect of transforming the indigenous population into Han, or even

Mongols for that matter. They saw the southwest as part of a larger multicultural Mongol empire, and this is best seen in how they controlled the region.

The Mongols relied extensively on the indigenous elite to govern territory and people—informal empire. In return for absolute fealty to the Mongol qan, indigenous elites received *tusi* titles (the Mongols also conferred *tusi* titles upon Han Chinese in China). This *tusi* title embodied a personal relationship in the mold of patron-client. The Yuan state refrained from imposing cultural policies that might erode indigene institutions and *tusi* authority, it assured *tusi* they could continue to adjudicate matters according to their own traditions, and it gave *tusi* assurances that internal and external challengers to their personal rule would be dealt with harshly by their patron, the Mongol qan. Although subject to the qan, indigenous elites as *tusi* continued to govern their territory and peoples as they had before the Mongols arrived.

Despite its lack of direct political control over much of the southwest, the Yuan state was successful in integrating the political economy of Yunnan with China proper. By 1350 the overwhelming percentage of China's silver, copper, and cinnabar were excavated from mines in Yunnan, and timber from the forests of Guizhou and Yunnan was used widely in the construction of palaces and government offices throughout China. The importance of the southwest to China's political economy, and the strategic implications of a large Mongol presence in Yunnan after the collapse of the Yuan state in 1368, required action by the founding Ming emperor, Hongwu. The Ming state's political legitimacy as inheritor of all that had been governed by the Yuan state, its financial dependence on precious metals mined in the southwest, and its military security in the face of persistently hostile Mongol forces in Yunnan demanded Ming action.

Hongwu, when his armies entered the southwest in the 1380s, was obliged to bind the region more firmly to Ming China than had the Mongols, and the brutal military occupation of the southwest in the last decades of the fourteenth century testify to this change in policy. The initial wave of Chinese troops sent to the southwest in the 1380s constructed close to fifty large military garrisons along the main transportation routes in what would become Yunnan and Guizhou provinces, and Han Chiense troops were stationed permanently in these garrisons. Each soldier was ordered to start a family once he had been assigned to a garrison, or, if he had a spouse and children back in China, he was expected to relocate his family to the garrison. As Timothy Brook has shown, Hongwu believed that vigorous agrarian expansion combined with moderate taxation was the best means to increase state revenues.[6] In less than twenty years the Ming state had settled nearly one million Han Chinese in the southwest, and by the middle of the fifteenth century the soldier-farmers assigned to the military garrisons and Han immigrants residing near these garrisons owned and cultivated over 2,000,000 *mu* of land, which represented virtually all the registered land in the southwest at the time.

The previous discussion of the fiscal limitations of the premodern Chinese state and the inability of frontier territory to generate revenue sufficient to sustain state control costs should inform us that early Ming procolonization policies in the southwest were plagued by financial uncertainty. This was certainly the case in the Southeast. Similar to the early phase of Qing occupation of Central Eurasia, according to Millward's description, the Ming colonization of the southwest was subsidized with revenue from China proper. Additional expenses for roads, city and garrison walls, forts and mountain outposts, postal relay stations, dikes, dams, and bridges further increased state expenditures and placed an extraordinary burden on court and local officials to find new revenue sources. The only plentiful revenue source in the southwest during the Ming period was land, and much of it was under *tusi* control and occupied by non-Han peoples.

To limit control costs, the Ming state proposed a dual-track approach of increasing its control over the semiautonomous *tusi* it inherited from the Yuan and confiscating *tusi* territory in order to settle Ming troops and Han immigrants in the southwest (a procolonization scheme similar to what Yongzheng proposed for Taiwan in the early decades of the eighteenth century). Under the Yuan dynasty, *tusi* enjoyed a high degree of independence from the Yuan state, and, as long as *tusi* remained loyal to the Mongol qan and supplied troops and material aid when asked, the Yuan state for the most part left *tusi* alone. Following the Yuan-Ming transition, Hongwu sought to lure prominent *tusi* in the southwest away from their allegiance to the Mongols by making the office of *tusi* appear to be an "official" position in the Ming bureaucracy.

The attraction of becoming a Ming official under the supervision of the Ministry of War was augmented by handsome bribes, unfettered access to Chinese markets and goods, and numerous opportunities to visit the Ming capital as a leader of tribute missions. The downside for the *tusi*, though this was probably not apparent to him/her at the time, was that Chinese elites now saw *tusi* and their heretofore independent domains as an integral part of the Ming realm. For Ming China's elites, the territory of the *tusi* domain replaced the personal relationship that had bound *tusi* to China's Mongol rulers during the Yuan. Put another way, the domestication of the southwest, which was based in large measure on a personal type of relationship during the Yuan dynasty, was now grounded in territory.

The Ming government also went far beyond the Yuan in managing the affairs of *tusi*. Officials in the Ministry of War were charged with the delicate task of ensuring that *tusi* remained loyal to the Ming state while at the same time reducing *tusi* autonomy and undermining indigene leadership. For instance, *tusi* were ordered to designate a male heir as successor, following a principle of succession not all indigene societies in the southwest adhered to, and this male heir was required to attend a Chinese school to receive a Chinese education, although prior to the sixteenth century such schools were rare in the southwest. As we have seen, this stipulation was designed primarily to assuage the cultural sensibilities of Ming China's elites, and it provided them with a powerful moral façade for the violence Ming China inflicted upon the indigenous peoples of the southwest. Furthermore, prior to the eighteenth century nearly all of the Confucian schools built in Yunnan and Guizhou were situated in Han Chinese population centers, not among the indigenous peoples, and non-Han students were prohibited from participating in the triennial examinations.

The second track, the confiscation of *tusi* lands, is most commonly represented by the succinct Chinese phrase *gaitu guiliu*. There were a few noteworthy instances during the Yuan when state officials carried out *gaitu guiliu* in the southwest, primarily in Yunnan; however, it was during the Ming dynasty that state confiscation of *tusi* and indigene lands became widespread. The fifty-odd Ming military garrisons established during Hongwu's reign were built on lands confiscated from the indigenous population, and these garrisons and their adjoining civilian populations seized even more land during the fifteenth and sixteenth centuries as Ming military campaigns continued to buffet the region.

As the principal instrument of Ming colonization, the military garrisons crushed indigene resistance, promoted the settlement of Han immigrants in the southwest, and prepared the region for the eventual transition to civilian rule—*gaitu guiliu*. Throughout the fifteenth century the garrison forces in Guizhou and Yunnan were used repeatedly to "punish," "pacify," and "tame" recalcitrant indigenes and disobedient *tusi* within provincial borders. These garrison forces participated in Ming China's long and costly war against the Luchuan kingdom in northern Burma (an area that now corresponds roughly to the Dehong autonomous *zhou* in southwest Yunnan), and in the 1465–66 pacification campaign against the Yao at Dateng Xia (Big Rattan Gorge) in Guangxi. Even though the state's role in the colonization of the southwest decreased slightly in the sixteenth century, private entrepreneurs and Han immigrants began to settle in the southwest in greater numbers, and it was during the last century of Ming rule that the combination of public and private investment in the southwest led to the region's becoming more fully tied to the political economy of China.

The Ming state's sustained use of procolonization policies in the southwest had the psychological effect of transforming how China's political-cultural elite viewed the southwest frontier. By the beginning of the seventeenth century, the exoticism and strangeness that typified Chinese accounts of the southwest during the first two centuries of Ming rule began to give way to official and unofficial descriptions of Han Chinese communities in the southwest. For instance, Xu Xiake's richly textured narrative of his journey through the southwest in 1637 and 1638 is replete with short descriptions of the Han travelers and Han communities he encountered. Only when Xu is not talking about his own emotional state or the exquisite scenery does he attempt to describe the non-Han barbarians he encounters.[7] China's elites were beginning to view the southwest not as a distant frontier populated exclusively by non-Han, but as an integral part of China where Han Chinese resided in large numbers.

This transformation was affirmed during the middle decades of the seventeenth century, first as the southwest became the final battleground between Ming loyalists and Qing forces, and then when it became the site where the tumultuous Rebellion of the Three Feudatories was fought. Three hundred years of Ming colonization of the southwest had, by the end of the seventeenth century, resulted in the region's incorporation into the political economy of China. From this perspective, then, the procolonization measures implemented by Yongzheng and Ortai in the 1720s and 1730s should be viewed more as the culminating sweep designed to clean up lose ends and less as the starting point for China's incorporation of the southwest.

*Appendixes*

—

# Appendixes

## Appendix A
### *Granary (Zexi) Units and Muzhuo Offices in the Shuixi-Shuidong Region*

Granaries (present-day location) *muzhuo* offices: present-day location

1. Mukua granary (northwest Dafang county): Dafang city
   a. Awu *muzhuo*: Dongguan
   b. Ahu *muzhuo*: Maoli
   c. Huasha *muzhuo*: Xiangshui
   d. Guizong *muzhuo*: Bazi
   e. Caigela *muzhuo*: Jule
   f. Wuguadi *muzhuo*: Changshi
   g. Shaozou *muzhuo*: Songhe
2. Fagua granary (eastern Dafang county): Dafang city
   a. Bulu *muzhuo*: Yangchang
   b. Yini *muzhuo*: Machang
   c. Zongji *muzhuo*: Fengshan
   d. Yizhi *muzhuo*: Xingsu
   e. Yili *muzhuo*: Zhujia
   f. Dechu *muzhuo*: Huangni
3. Shuizhu granary (Nayong county): Nayong city
   a. Heigong *muzhuo*: Weixin
   b. Yige *muzhuo*: Zhailuo
   c. Xiongkua *muzhuo*: Mucheng
   d. Desu *muzhuo*: Tianba

4. Jiale granary (northwest of Liupanshui city): Liupanshui city
   a. Agua *muzhuo*: Meihua [Weining county]
   b. Heikua *muzhuo*: Muguo
   c. Zuerjia *muzhuo*: Nankai
5. Ajia granary (southeast of Liupanshui city): E'jiao
   a. Longkua *muzhuo*: E'jiao
   b. Yima *muzhuo*: Yangmei
   c. Ashiwo *muzhuo*: Bide
6. Dedu granary (between the cities of Liupanshui and Liuzhi): Suojia
   a. Binglie *muzhuo*: Deke [southeast Nayong county]
   b. Yaohu *muzhuo*: Luobang
   c. Adi *muzhuo*: Liuzhi
7. Longkua granary (eastern Zhijin county): Guahua
   a. Nuoni *muzhuo*: Longchang
   b. Mishou *muzhuo*: Machang
   c. Zhedai *muzhuo*: Shangpingzhai
8. Duoni granary (western Zhijin county): Zhijin city
   a. Langbai *muzhuo*: Zhongzhai
   b. Bajia *muzhuo*: Chadian
   c. Awumi *muzhuo*: Bainitang
9. Zewo granary (northern Qianxi county): Dingxin
   a. Age *muzhuo*: Shipan
   b. Bawa *muzhuo*: Huaxi
   c. Atan *muzhuo*: Longtan
10. Yizhu granary (eastern Qianxi county): Qianxi city
    a. Badi *muzhuo*: Shajing
    b. Zheshe *muzhuo*: Guijing
    c. Kuopo *muzhuo*: Shazhai
11. Xiongsuo granary (Jinsha county): Jinsha city
    a. Na'e *muzhuo*: Guihua
    b. Guiji *muzhuo*: Taizhong
    c. Neilu *muzhuo*: Xinhua
12. Yude granary (east of the Yachi River in western Xiuwen county): Muke
    a. Age *muzhuo*: Xiaojing
    b. Longer *muzhuo*: Huishui
    c. Longye *muzhuo*: Jiuping

13. Liumu granary (east of the Yachi River in northwest Qingzhen county): Yachi
    a. Difei *muzhuo*: Wangzhuang
    b. Huana *muzhuo*: Liuchang
    c. Zhele *muzhuo*: Maixi

---

SOURCES: Ma and Luo, *Cuanwen congke*, 115–41, 184; Hu, *Ming Qing Yizu shehui*, 31–36; *Dading fuzhi*, 11/1b–14a.

## Appendix B
## *The Personal Adviser (Jiuzong) and Household Staff (Jiuche) Offices in the Shuixi-Shuidong Granary Administration*

1. The *Zimo*'s Personal Advisers
    a. *Gengju*—political-religious adviser
    b. *Mokui*—political-religious adviser
    c. *Zhuokui*—political-religious adviser
    d. *Bumu*—civilian-economic adviser
    e. *Qimo*—civilian-economic adviser
    f. *Beisuo*—civilian-economic adviser
    g. *Maxie*—military adviser
    h. *Xiba*—military adviser
    i. *Heizha*—military adviser
2. The *Zimo*'s Household Staff
    a. *Amuche*—secretary
    b. *Butu* and *zhuoyi*—etiquette and protocol
    c. *Baixiang* and *baisu*—transportation and communication
    d. *Chemo*—in charge of rituals in sacrifices to gods and ancestors
    e. *Xiangmu*—prepared utensils, vessels, and buildings used in sacrifices
    f. *Yuanyue*—bodyguards
    g. *Suwen*—instructor in arts of war
    h. *Mushi*—announced decrees and proclamations
    i. *Chengmu*—recorder

---

SOURCES: Ma and Luo, *Cuanwen congke*, 115–41, 184; Hu, *Ming Qing Yizu shehui*, 31–36; *Dading fuzhi*, 11/1b–14a.

# Appendix C
## Guizhou Pacification Commissioners
### During the Ming Dynasty

Name; Chinese name (year inherited commissioner's title)

1. Longzan Aicui; None (1372)
2. Aicui Longdi; An De (1391)
3. Longdi Puzhi; An Bupa (1398)
4. Puzhi Nakao; An Zhong (1423)
5. Nakao Benzhe; An Ju (1436)
6. Benzhe Longzhi; An Longfu (1443)
7. Longzhi Longpu; An Guan (1461)
8. Longpu Bujiu; An Guirong (1475)
9. Bujiu Zhiba; An Zuo (ca. 1493)
10. Zhiba Anzong; An Wanzhong (1512)
11. Anzong Zhie; An Wanyi (1522)
12. Zhie Longze; An Wanquan (1528)
13. Longze Baoxi; An Ren (1539)
14. Baoxi Fenlao; An Guoheng (1555)
15. Fenlao Longgu; An Jiangchen (1597)
16. Longgu Longde; An Yaochen (1608)
17. Longde Longdie; An Wei (1621)
18. Longdie Efen; An Kun (ca. 1640)

SOURCES: Ma and Luo, *Cuanwen congke*, 152–58; Yu, "Mingdai Guizhou" 1: 5–7.

# Appendix D
## Garrisons and Battalions (Weisuo) *Established in Yunnan*
### During the Hongwu Reign (1368–98)

Name (date est.); present-day location; number of battalions (*qianhu suo*)

1. Chuxiong garrison (1382); Chuxiong; 5 battalions
2. Dali garrison (1382); Dali; 8 battalions
3. Linan garrison (1382); Jianshui; 5 battalions
4. Qujing garrison (1382); Qujing; 5 battalions
5. Tonghai garrison (1382); Tonghai; 5 battalions
6. Yongchang garrison (1382); Baoshan; 5 battalions

7. Yunnan Forward garrison (1382); Kunming; 5 battalions
8. Yunnan Left garrison (1382); Kunming; 5 battalions
9. Yunnan Rear garrison (1382); Kunming; 5 battalions
10. Yunnan Right garrison (1382); Kunming; 5 battalions
11. Erhai garrison (1387); Xiangyun; 7 battalions
12. Pingyi garrison (1388); Fuyuan; 6 battalions
13. Yaoan battalion (1388); Yaoan
14. Jingdong garrison (1390); Jingdong; 5 battalions
15. Malong battalion (1390); Malong
16. Menghua garrison (1390); Menghua; 5 battalions
17. Mumi battalion (1390); Xundian
18. Anning battalion (1391); Anning
19. Dingyuan battalion (1391); Mouding
20. Liuliang garrison (1391); Liuliang; 5 battalions
21. Yiliang battalion (1391); Yiliang
22. Yimen battalion (1391); Yimen
23. Yuezhou garrison (1391); Yuezhou; 5 battalions
24. Yanglin battalion (1392); Songming
25. Yunnan Central garrison (1393); Kunming; 5 battalions
26. Yunnan garrison (1395); Kunming; 5 battalions
27. Zhongtun battalion (1395); Dayao
28. Lancang garrison (1396); Yongsheng; 5 battalions

SOURCE: *Yunnan tongzhi* (1736), 12/2a–33a.

## Appendix E
### *Garrisons and Battalions* (Weisuo) *Established in Guizhou During the Hongwu Reign (1368–98)*

Name (date est.); present-day location; number of battalions (*qianhu suo*)

1. Tianzhu battalion (1370); Tianzhu; subordinate to Jingzhou garrison, Hunan
2. Guizhou garrison (1371); Guiyang; 5 battalions
3. Yongning garrison (1371); Xuyong county; 5 battalions
4. Huangping battalion (1378); Huangping; subordinate to Guizhou Regional Military Commandery
5. Annan garrison (1382); Jinglong; 5 battalions
6. Pingyue garrison (1382); Fuquan; 5 battalions

7. Puan garrison (1382); Panxian; 10 battalions
8. Puding garrison (1382); Anshun; 5 battalions
9. Wusa garrison (1382); Weining; 5 battalions
10. Bijie garrison (1384); Bijie; 7 battalions
11. Wukai garrison (1385); Liping; 5 battalions
12. Cengtai garrison (1387, abolished in 1394); Bijie
13. Chishui garrison (1388); Chishui River; 8 battalions
14. Tonggu garrison (1388); Jinbing; 5 battalions
15. Anzhuang garrison (1389); Zhenning; 5 battalions
16. Xinglong garrison (1389); Huangping; 5 battalions
17. Zhenyuan garrison (1389); Zhenyuan; 5 battalions
18. Duyun garrison (1390); Duyun; 5 battalions
19. Longli garrison (1390); Longli; 5 battalions
20. Pianqiao garrison (1390); Shibing; 5 battalions
21. Pingba garrison (1390); Pingba; 5 battalions
22. Pingxi garrison (1390); Yubing; 5 battalions
23. Pushi battalion (1390); Pushi; subordinate to Guizhou Regional
    Military Commandery (*du zhihui si*)
24. Qinglang garrison (1390); Qingxi; 5 battalions
25. Qingping garrison (1390); Kaili-Qingping; 6 battalions
26. Weiqing garrison (1390); Qingzhen county; 5 battalions
27. Xintian garrison (1390); Guiding; 5 battalions
28. Guizhou Forward garrison (1391); Guiyang; 5 battalions

SOURCES: *Guizhou tongzhi* (1555), 3/1b–11a; *Guizhou tongzhi* (1597), 5/1b–19b; *Guizhou tongzhi* (1692), 6/4b–15a; *Guizhou tongzhi* (1741), 12/4b–27a; Guo, *Qianji*, 5/2a–18a.

# Appendix F
## *Military-Rank* Tusi *(Native Officials) and Executive Staff*

1. Pacification commissioner (*xuanwei shi*): 3b
   a. Vice commissioner (*tongzhi*): 4a
   b. Assistant commissioner (*fushi*): 4b
   c. Assistant commissioner (*qianshi*): 5a
   d. Registry (*jingli si*): 7b
   e. Comptroller (*dushi*): 8a
   f. Jailor (*siyu*): 9b

2. Pacification inspector (*xuanfu shi*): 4b
    a. Vice inspector (*tongzhi*): 5a
    b. Assistant inspector (*fushi*): 5b
    c. Assistant inspector (*qianshi*): 6a
    d. Registry (*jingli si*): 8b
    e. Administrative assistant (*zhishi*): 9a
    f. Records (*zhaomo*): 9b
3. Military commissioner (*anfu shi*): 5b
    a. Vice military commissioner (*tongzhi*): 6a
    b. Assistant commissioner (*fushi*): 6b
    c. Registry (*qianshi*): 7a
4. Suppression commissioner (*zhaotao shi*): 5b
    a. Assistant commissioner (*fu zhaotao*): 6a
    b. Head constable (*limu*): 9b
5. Native official (*zhangguan shi*): 6a
    a. Assistant native official (*fu zhangguan*): 7b
6. Barbarian native official (*manyi zhangguan shi*): 6a
    a. Assistant barbarian native official (*fu zhangguan*): 7b

SOURCES: She, *Zhongguo tusi zhidu*, 20–32, 38–43; Huang, "Mingdai tusi zhidu," 27–217; Wu, *Zhongguo tusi zhidu yuanyuan*, 157–78, 209–38; Gong, *Zhongguo tusi zhidu*, 53–152; *Da Ming huidian*, 118/23a–30a; *Ming shi*, 75/1849–50, 76/1875–76.

# Appendix G
## Civilian-Rank Tusi (Tuguan) *and Executive Staff*

1. Native prefecture magistrate (*tu zhifu*): 4a
    a. Vice magistrate (*tongzhi*): 5a
    b. Assistant magistrate (*tongpan*): 6a
    c. Assistant magistrate (*tuiguan*): 7a
    d. Registry (*jingli si*): 8a
    e. Comptroller (*zhishi*): 9a
    f. Records (*zhaomo*): 9b
    g. Head constable (*limu*): 9b
2. Native department magistrate (*tu zhizhou*): 5b
    a. Vice magistrate (*tongzhi*): 6b
    b. Administrative assistant (*panguan*): 7b
    c. Head constable (*limu*): 9b

3. Native county magistrate (*tu zhixian*): 7a
   a. Vice magistrate (*xiancheng*): 8a
   b. Assistant magistrate (*zhubu*): 9a
   c. Head constable (*limu*): 9b
   d. Clerk (*dianshi*): NR

---

SOURCES: She, *Zhongguo tusi zhidu*, 20–32, 38–43; Huang, "Mingdai tusi zhidu," 27–217; Wu, *Zhongguo tusi zhidu yuanyuan*, 157–78, 209–38; Gong, *Zhongguo tusi zhidu*, 53–152; *Da Ming huidian*, 118/23a–30a; *Ming shi*, 75/1849–50, 76/1875–76.

# Appendix H
## *The Population of Guizhou, 1555*

Administrative unit: household (*hu*) figure; population (*dingkou*) figure

1. Guizhou prefecture: 5,948; 30,744
2. Sizhou prefecture: 757; 9,110
3. Sinan prefecture: 2,637; 23,666
4. Zhenyuan prefecture: 872; 8,657
5. Shibing prefecture: 817; 7,411
6. Tongren prefecture: 939; 4,153
7. Duyun prefecture: 9,219; 24,618
8. Liping prefecture: 3,665; 24,514
9. Yongning department: 2,369; 10,096
10. Zhenning department: 15,210; 25,578
11. Anshun department: 8,270; 25,227
12. Puan department: 3,141; 39,525
13. Guizhou garrison: 2,316; 5,397
14. Guizhou Forward garrison: 2,964; 6,237
15. Longli garrison: 1,182; 6,710
16. Xintian garrison: 2,357; 21,977
17. Pingyue garrison: 3,150; 21,979
18. Qingping garrison: 897; 2,184
19. Xinglong garrison: 1,094; 3,915
20. Duyun garrison: 1,312; 21,113
21. Weiqing garrison: 6,035; 13,758
22. Pingba garrison: 1,617; 6,066
23. Puding garrison: 6,565; 24,470
24. Anzhuang garrison: 2,486; 48,857
25. Annan garrison: 2,486; 6,892

26. Puan garrison: 2,656; 6,998
27. Bijie garrison: 2,885; 6,641
28. Wusa garrison: 3,551; 8,355
29. Chishui garrison: 5,615; 33,682
30. Yongning garrison: 6,789; 15,247
31. Huangping battalion: 547; 1,467
32. Pushi battalion: 493; 1,389
33. Kaili Pacification Commission: 646; 2,841
34. Guizhou Pacification Commission: 2,145; 12,924

SOURCE: *Guizhou tongzhi* (1555), 3/47a–55b.

# Appendix I
## *The Population of Guizhou, 1602*

Administrative unit: household (*hu*) figure; population (*dingkou*) figure

1. Guiyang prefecture: 6,695; 42,768
2. Guizhou garrison: 2,316; 5,397
3. Guizhou Forward garrison: 2,988; 8,477
4. Weiqing garrison: 6,035; 13,758
5. Pingba garrison: unknown; 8,994
6. Anshun prefecture: 2,998; 18,829
7. Puding garrison: 1,025; 2,837
8. Zhenning department: 2,621; 15,872
9. Anzhuang garrison: 7,873; 48,857
10. Yongning department: 3,041; 12,830
11. Annan garrison: 3,486; 7,896
12. Puan department: 3,249; 46,816
13. Bijie garrison: 2,437; 4,132
14. Chishui garrison: 1,971; 3,940
15. Yongning garrison: 2,177; 6,065
16. Pushi battalion: 65; 182
17. Longli garrison: 1,116; 5,245
18. Xintian garrison: 1,435; 9,494
19. Pingyue prefecture: 1,702; 8,087
20. Pingyue garrison: 2,905; 21,227
21. Duyun prefecture: 13,774; 43,747
22. Duyun garrison: 1,328; 21,138
23. Qingping garrison: 756; 2,370

24. Xinglong garrison: 1,056; 1,820
25. Huangping battalion: 305; 530
26. Zhenyuan prefecture: 893; 8,151
27. Sizhou prefecture: 806; 9,198
28. Sinan prefecture: 2,183; 28,327
29. Shibing prefecture: 825; 8,357
30. Tongren prefecture: 943; 12,400
31. Liping prefecture: 3,773; 42,293
32. Guizhou Pacification Commission: 3,714; 33,183

SOURCES: Guo, *Qianji*, 3/2a–11b; *Guizhou tongzhi* (1741), 6/13a–17a.

# Appendix J

*The following passage is an account of a young boy named Zhang Changqing who, as the narrative informs us, was kidnapped in 1622 from his home in Chishui, near where the Chele (Nasu Yi) patriclan resided.*

In the second month of Tianqi 2 [1622] She Chongming [the Yongning pacification commissioner] and his son [She] Yan led more than one hundred troops from their barracks [*ying*] to attack the town of Chishui. . . . After a four-day siege, She's troops captured Chishui. . . . Zhang Dazhuang [the Chishui guard commander (*wei zhihui shi*)] was captured following the siege, and because of his hatred toward She Chongming he was executed. Zhang Dazhuang's mother, née Liu, and her two grandsons were also captured and taken away. The reason [Zhang] Dazhuang's mother and two sons were not killed along with Dazhuang was because the Zhang family was well known in Chishui, and it was believed that the remaining family members in Chishui would pay a handsome sum to gain their release. . . . On the following day She ordered née Liu and the two young boys to be sent to different camps [where they spent the evening]. As he left camp as ordered the next morning, Zhang Changchun [Dazhuang's younger son] saw his grandmother dead in a field. . . . At this time Zhang Changqing [Dazhuang's elder son] was thirteen years old and Zhang Changchun was eleven, and they lived with the barbarians [*man*] for more than a month before they broke camp. The boys were then taken to Heisong Village [*zhai*]. Zhang Jingsheng [Zhang Dazhuang's nephew] found out where Changqing and Changchun were located, and he paid a ransom for their return. The boys were eventually returned to their families in Chishui.

In the eleventh month the barbarians returned to Chishui and kidnapped the two boys again. . . . When the boys were handed over to She Yan, Zhang Changqing was sold as a slave to the local chief [*toumu*] named Guishi, and Zhang Changchun was sold as a slave to a local chief named Aqi. In the spring of 1623, the barbarian chief [She Chongming] ordered the two kids to learn the barbarian language and to dress like the barbarians. He also ordered them to live like barbarian children, to learn to ride a horse, and to learn the skills of a warrior. While learning to ride, Changchun fell off his horse and died.

In the fourth month the imperial [Ming] court ordered its soldiers to fight the barbarians She Chongming and his son Yan. In response, She Chongming first led his troops to the town of Zhenyi, and then [they] traveled several hundred *li* (1 *li* = 0.36 miles or 0.576 kilometers) to a dangerous place called Moxiang Barracks [*ying*]. After about a month in Moxiang, Changqing was sold to the Red Barbarians [*hong man*], but because Changqing tried to escape from the Red Barbarians he was sold again to the Silver River Barbarians [*yinhe man*]. The Silver River Barbarians practice very strange customs, and their customs are very different from the Red Barbarians'. Among the Silver River Barbarians both horses and dogs are good at running, and only the local barbarians can control them.

At this time Changqing thought, "instead of waiting to die it would be better to try to escape." One evening he stole one of the best horses and rode east as fast as he could for about 30 to 40 *li*. At nightfall he came upon a river. The river was wide but shallow. There was no one around but debris filled the river. Because the situation was dangerous he decided to abandon the horse and cross the river. Just then he heard his pursuers coming so he hid in the river next to a large rock. The barbarians set their dogs loose, because their dogs can detect human scent. As the dogs approached the rock his pursuers, with torches in hand, came ever closer to the rock where Changqing was hiding. He was nearly captured. But suddenly a mountain tiger roared in the woods behind the pursuers and the dogs immediately stopped barking. Frightened by the tiger, his pursuers fled as quickly as they could. Changqing then decided to sleep during the daytime and travel at night. He traveled like this for three days and nights until he reached Moxiang.

When he entered Moxiang, it was midnight so he went to the military camp. Several of the Lin [Yongning] barbarians asked him questions and he answered them in the Lin language. At this time he noticed an old man to the side looking suspiciously his way. The old man was aware that Changqing spoke the Lin language with a Han [Chinese] accent, so he spoke to Changqing in the Han language. The old man took Changqing to a private room and asked him where he was from, and Changqing answered his questions. The old man said that he had been a slave in Moxiang since the town of Xichuan was destroyed several years earlier. As the old man recalled this, he burst into tears. The old man then led Changqing to where five or six Han women were staying, and when they met they all cried like they were long-lost relatives. After a short time the women gave Changqing food and drink, they changed his clothes, and they let him stay in their dwelling and work in the fields.

Fanlong, the local chief of Moxiang, and his brothers began to behave irrationally and they rebelled. Changqing knew he needed to escape and return [to Chishui]. At this point the old man heard that the Silver River Barbarians were planning to come to Moxiang to apprehend Changqing, and if that happened Changqing would probably die, so he planned to send Changqing away. There was a government military official named Ding San located in the town of Jianwu, near Moxiang, and Ding San often had communication with the barbarians in Moxiang. The old man thought it a good idea if he could get Changqing to go with Ding San, which he was able to do in the second month of 1624.

SOURCES: *Bijie xianzhi*, 8/4a–b; Qu, *Wanli wugong lu*, 23/18b–22b; Hu, *Ming Qing Yizu shehui*, 27.

*Reference Matter*

---

# Notes

## Introduction

1. I use the word "China" to describe a geopolitical entity, not an ethno-cultural unit. For example, the Yuan and Qing dynasties were not "Chinese" dynasties in the ethno-cultural sense. The Yuan state was created by Mongols in order to govern China following the Mongol conquest of China, and many of the features inherent in the Yuan bureaucracy were markedly different from those of its Chinese predecessor, the Song dynasty (960–1279). From the Mongol perspective, the Yuan state was part of a much larger Mongol geopolitical unit, the grand qan's qanate. The Qing state was created in 1636 by a multi-cultural confederation of peoples generally referred to as Manchus. When the Manchus began their conquest of China in 1644, they incorporated China into their fledgling empire. Thus, Yuan China was part of a larger Mongol empire, and Qing China became the cornerstone of an equally expansive Manchu empire. Interspersed between the Yuan and the Qing was the Han-dominated Ming dynasty.

2. According to China's 1990 census, there are 6,572,173 Yi living in China. Of this total, 4,060,327 Yi reside in Yunnan; 1,798,037 in Sichuan; 707,275 in Guizhou; 6,074 Yi in Guangxi; and the remaining number of Yi are scattered throughout southern China. The Yi are one of the fifty-six nationalities (*minzu*) of China.

3. The Nuosu in southern Sichuan have also utilized a written script for centuries, and historians are only just beginning to exploit this rich reservoir of information. See Bradley, "Language Policy for the Yi," 202; Nishida, *A Study of the Lolo-Chinese Vocabulary*.

4. As Stevan Harrell has shown in his extensive body of work on the Yi, but most eloquently in his article titled "The History of the History of the Yi," the

term "Yi" is particularly troublesome. It is an artificial term that has very little (if any) relationship to the people it purports to identify.

5. Wiens, *China's March Toward the Tropics*, xi–xii.

6. Ibid., 130–86.

7. Wiens cited Wolfram Eberhard's "Kultur und Siedlung der Randvolkers China," *T'oung Pao*, supplement to vol. 36 (1942). For a representative example of Eberhard's work in English, see Eberhard, *China's Minorities: Yesterday and Today* and *Local Cultures of South and East China*.

8. As far as I can tell, Mark Elliott was the first person to use the phrase "hegemonizing history" to describe the sinicization thesis and its impact on Manchu history (*The Manchu Way*, 32).

9. Morgan, *Ancient Society*. See also Harrell, "The History of the History of the Yi," 3–36; and idem, "Introduction: Civilizing Projects and the Reaction to Them," 63–91.

10. Harrell, "Introduction: Civilizing Projects and the Reaction to Them," 63–91; idem, *Perspectives on the Yi*, 1–17.

11. According to Wu Gu, "in the early 1980s, during the process of excavating the remains of Kunming Man, archaeologists uncovered three pottery shards with symbols that had characteristics of writing—show a connection with Yi writing. In the process of excavating remains from the Chunqiu [Spring and Autumn] (771–481 BCE) and Zhanguo [Warring States] (480–221 BCE) periods at Caohai in Weining (Guizhou), another group of pottery pieces with incised symbols was found, and people have also matched these up with traditional Yi writing" ("Reconstructing Yi History from Yi Records," 21–34).

12. Keightley, *The Origins of Chinese Civilization*; Chang, *Early Chinese Civilization*; Shaughnessy, *Sources of Western Zhou History*; Dull, "The Evolution of Government in China," 55–85; Gernet, *A History of Chinese Civilization*, 51–82.

13. According to Nasu Yi tradition (a tradition followed to this day), when two strangers meet they are culturally obligated to identify clan membership by reciting their genealogical record. Failure to do so accurately casts suspicion upon the offending individual and could lead to violence (Hill and Diehl, "A Comparative Approach to Lineages Among Xiao Liangshan Nuosu [Yi] and Han," 51–67).

14. Hill, "Captives, Kin, and Slaves in Xiao Liangshan," 1035–36. In constructing her argument, Hill relied on Moses Finley's seminal work, *Ancient Slavery and Modern Ideology*, and Ira Berlin's fascinating study of early nineteenth-century New England society, *Many Thousand Gone*.

15. Isaac, *The Limits of Empire*, 372–415.

16. Perdue, *China Marches West*, 60.

17. Waldron, *The Great Wall of China*, 72–164; Perdue, *China Marches West*, 61.

18. Waldron, *The Great Wall of China*, 108–64; Perdue, *China Marches West*, 61–63.

19. Hsiao, *Qingdai tongshi*, 786.

20. Doyle, *Empires*, 38. For additional information, see Eisenstadt, *The Political Systems of Empires*; Fieldhouse, *The Colonial Empires*; Furnivall, *Colonial Policy and Practice*; and Chase-Dunn and Hall, *Rise and Demise*.

21. Sahlins, *Boundaries*, 7–8.

22. Lee, "Food Supply and Population Growth in Southwest China, 1250–1850," 711–46; Hostetler, *Qing Colonial Enterprise*; Huang, *Autocracy at Work*.

23. Miyazaki, "The Confucianization of South China," 21.

24. Hechter, *Internal Colonialism*, 38–41.

25. Crossley, "Thinking About Ethnicity in Early Modern China," 1–35; Keyes, "Toward a New Formulation of the Concept of Ethnic Group," 203–13; Honig, *Creating Chinese Ethnicity*; Bentley, "Ethnicity and Practice," 24–55; Elliott, *The Manchu Way*, 1–37.

26. Leong, *Migration and Ethnicity in Chinese History*, 14.

27. Smith, *The Ethnic Origins of Nations*, 34–57.

28. *Gaozong Chun huangdi shilu*, 33/15a.

## Chapter 1

1. *Hou Hanshu*, 87/2887–97; Chen, "Lun Yizu gudai fenqi," 107–19; Li, "Guanyu Qiangzu gudaishi," 165–82; Hu, "Lun Han Jin de Di Qiang," 153–70; Yü, "Han Foreign Relations," 422–35; Fang, *Yizu shigao*, 14–18; Hou, Shi, and Weng, *Guizhou gudai minzu*, 111; Beckwith, *The Tibetan Empire*; Scott, "A Study of the Ch'iang"; Harrell, "The History of the History of the Yi," 63–91.

2. In Yi-language texts published in Guizhou, the migrations were the result of a large tribal division that occurred in a place in northeastern Yunnan called Lonibo.

3. Zhang, *Yizu gudai wenhua shi*, 3–11; Long, *Zhongguo Yizu tongshi gangyao*, 1–7; Wu, "Reconstructing Yi History," 21–34; Wu, "Nzymo as Seen in Some Yi Classical Books," 35–48.

4. Wu, "Reconstructing Yi History," 22–23.

5. *Xi'nan Yizhi*, juan 7–8, 253–64; juan 5–6, 115–301; xuan, 165–306; Ma and Luo, *Cuanwen congke*, 67–87, 152–58; Fang, *Yizu shigao*, 148–50, 172–77; Zhang, *Yizu gudai wenhua shi*, 61–63; Long, *Zhongguo Yizu tongshi gangyao*, 17–19; Wu, "Reconstructing Yi History," 28–30. Dumu was the thirty-first-generation descendant of Ximuzhe. Ximuzhe purportedly lived near the Jinsha River in southern Sichuan during the fifth century BCE, and his descendants slowly migrated south into northeastern Yunnan by the end of the third century BCE (Zhang, *Yizu gudai wenhua shi*, 56–61).

6. *Xi'nan Yizhi*, juan 6, 13; xuan, 110–28; Ma and Luo, *Cuanwen congke*, 87–99; Zhang, *Yizu gudai wenhua shi*, 56–65; Jjissyt, *Hnewo teyy*, 7–16; Feng, *Le'e*

*teyi*, 1–27; Hou, Shi, and Weng, *Guizhou gudai minzu*, 111; Hu, *Ming Qing Yizu shehui*, 5–25; Harrell, "The History of the History of the Yi," 63–91; *Xi'nan Yizhi, juan* 6, 13–14, 46; *juan* 7–8, 253–64.

7. The Bijie District of northwest Guizhou is 26,846 square kilometers in size and encompasses nearly three-quarters of the Shuixi region. The remaining one-quarter is now the northern portion of the Liupanshui Municipality, or the area north of the Bei Pan River. Shuixi is roughly equal in size to Massachusetts, Rhode Island, and Connecticut combined (37,589 square kilometers) (*Guizhou shengzhi*, 238).

8. Lombard-Salmon, *Un exemple d'acculturation chinoise*, 67–109. The highest peak in the Leigong Mountain range is Leigong Mountain, which reaches a height of 2,179 meters. The highest mountain in the Fouding Mountain range is Fouding Mountain, which reaches 1,835 meters.

9. "Shuixi" literally means "water-west," or "west of the water." In this case the Yachi River was considered the "water" (*shui*), thus the area west of the Yachi River was known as the Shuixi region.

10. Guizhou's rugged terrain posed a particularly vexing challenge for China's traditional cartographers. The compilers of the 1850 edition of the *Guiyang Prefecture Gazetteer* admitted as much in their introduction to the gazetteer: "Making maps is quite difficult, but creating an accurate map of Guizhou is nearly impossible. Familiarity with Pei Xiu's [a third-century CE cartographer] six canons of cartography is of little use in mapping Guizhou. There are numerous deep gorges in southern Guizhou that twist and turn in such contorted ways that it is impossible to put to paper what you do not understand with the eyes. Moreover, southern Guizhou is crawling with underground streams that appear for all to see, and then suddenly disappear never to be seen again" (*Guiyang fuzhou*, 1/3a).

11. *Guizhou shengzhi*, 237–52.

12. For additional information on these fertile limestone depressions in southwest China, see von Glahn, *The Country of Streams and Grottoes*, 29–30.

13. Hou, Shi, and Weng, *Guizhou gudai minzu*, 24–25.

14. Until the middle of the eighteenth century Zhaotong was identified on Chinese maps and in Chinese sources as Wumeng. See *Xi'nan Yizhi, juan* 6, 13; *xuan*, 110–28; Ma and Luo, *Cuanwen congke*, 87–99; Jjissyt, *Hnewo teyy*, 7–16; Feng, *Le'e teyi*, 1–27; Hou, Shi, and Weng, *Guizhou gudai minzu*, 111; Hu, *Ming Qing Yizu shehui*, 5–25; Fang, *Yizu shigao*, 148–50, 172–77; Harrell, "The History of the History of the Yi," 63–91; Wu, "Reconstructing Yi History," 21–34; Wu, "Nzymo as Seen in Some Yi Classical Books," 35–48.

15. *Sanguo zhi*, 35/921–22; *Huayang guozhi*, 4/357; Hou, Shi, and Weng, *Guizhou gudai minzu*, 106–8, 112–13. Interestingly, contemporary Chinese sources saw this territory as part of the former Yelang kingdom, and at roughly the same time Yi sources described the Bole migration into the Anshun region

of western Guizhou, Chinese sources depicted a mass exodus of Yelang residents, estimated at more than 100,000 households, making their way north to Ba and Shu (southern Sichuan).

16. *Sanguo zhi,* 35/921–22; *Huayang guozhi,* 4/357; Hou, Shi, and Weng, *Guizhou gudai minzu,* 106–8, 112–13.

17. Ma and Luo, *Cuanwen congke,* 110–13; *Xi'nan Yizhi,* juan 7–8, 284–312. The Awangren were also referred to in both Chinese and Nasu texts as the Deshi. See Ma, "Names and Genealogies," 91–93; Jjissyt, *Hnewo teyy,* 18; Feng, *Le'e teyi,* 29; Long, *Zhongguo Yizu tongshi gangyao,* 27.

18. *Xi'nan Yizhi,* juan 6, 13–14, 46; juan 7–8, 253–64. For additional information on the Nasu conquest of the Pu agriculturalists in Shuixi, see *Xi'nan Yizhi xuan,* 165–306; Ma and Luo, *Cuanwen congke,* 67–87, 152–58; Jjissyt, *Hnewo teyy,* 27–29, 65–69; Feng, *Le'e teyi,* 59–63; Zhang, *Yizu gudai wenhua shi,* 70–78; Fang, *Yizu shigao,* 148–50, 172–77; Hu, *Ming Qing Yizu shehui,* 5–25; Hou, Shi, and Weng, *Guizhou gudai minzu,* 181–82, 194–95. "Luodian" in Chinese is rendered "Mu'ege" in Nasu. Mugebaizhage is the present-day city of Dafang. After Mowang established his capital at Mugebaizhage, he had Tuoazhe's cremated remains transported from Luogen to Mugebaizhage. Tuoazhe's tomb was relocated to Huoyan Shan (Flame mountain), also known as Jihuo Feng (Jihuo peak), near present-day Dafang. At this time, Guiyang was a small village known to Chinese as Gunuo, and the present-day city of Duyun was called Zuyidai. Both Gunuo and Zuyidai were under Mu'ege control.

19. Von Glahn, *The Country of Streams and Grottoes,* 39–67, 126–41. Wuman was a generic term used by Chinese authors to describe the "barbarians" in this part of Nanzhong under Cuan hegemony, but "Black Luoluo" is a descriptive term that came to be applied specifically to the Nasu Yi aristocracy at a later date.

20. Beckwith, *The Tibetan Empire,* 14–36.

21. For the most extensive historical account of the Nanzhao kingdom, see Fang, *Zhongguo xi'nan lishi dili kaoshi,* 409–607. See also Hou, Shi, and Weng, *Guizhou gudai minzu,* 136–37; Backus, *The Nan-chao Kingdom,* 61–85. The Nanzhao kingdom was a confederation of six Tibeto-Burman tribes who, in the mid-seventh century, gradually consolidated their control over the Lake Erhai region of northwest Yunnan. The six tribes of Erhai were the Mengshe, Mengjuan, Yuexi, Langqiong, Shilang, and Dengchuan.

22. Backus, *The Nan-chao Kingdom,* 84–90; Hou, Shi, and Weng, *Guizhou gudai minzu,* 137. Pilege's tribe, the Mengshe, was also known as the Nanzhao because they lived south of the other five tribes, and thus the Nanzhao name came to represent the confederation. Legend has it that Pilege (also written as Pi Luoge in Chinese) invited the leaders of the other five kingdoms to a banquet at his residence in Weishan. Apparently Pilege constructed a special dining hall built of wood. After his guests had had their fill of food and wine,

Pilege ordered the doors to the dining hall closed, and the building set aflame, killing the leaders of the five kingdoms. This is the origin of the torch festival, which is still commemorated throughout much of Yunnan today.

23. Backus, *The Nan-chao Kingdom*, 84–95.

24. Fang, *Zhongguo xi'nan lishi dili kaoshi*, 409–607; Backus, *The Nan-chao Kingdom*, 105–7.

25. *Xi'nan Yizhi*, juan 7–8, 296–302; Ma and Luo, *Cuanwen congke*, 85, 156; Fang, *Yizu shigao*, 173–90; Chen, "Guanyu 'Liuzu,' 'Luodian guo,'" 175–80; Hou, Shi, and Weng, *Guizhou gudai minzu*, 180–90.

26. The ten commanderies in the Qianzhong Circuit were Qianzhou, Sizhou, Jinzhou, Xuzhou, Jiangzhou, Feizhou, Yizhou, Bozhou, Zhenzhou, and Nanzhou. Protectorates were usually established along the commandery's frontier, whereas area commands were located at strategic points throughout the commandery. See *Zizhi tongjian*, 11/145–46; *Jiu Tang shu*, 97/3298–3303; Fang, *Zhongguo xi'nan lishi dili kaoshi*, 320–27; *Guizhou shengzhi*, 10–11; Hou, Shi, and Weng, *Guizhou gudai minzu*, 138.

27. *Zizhi tongjian*, 11/145–46; *Jiu Tang shu*, 97/3298–3303; Fang, *Zhongguo xi'nan lishi dili kaoshi*, 320–27; *Guizhou shengzhi*, 10–11; Hou, Shi, and Weng, *Guizhou gudai minzu*, 165–70. In Chinese the character *ji* represents a bridle or indicates the act of restraining a horse, whereas the character *mi* means to control an animal with a rope, like a halter.

28. Of the three circuits located in the southwest, Jiannan, Qianzhong, and Lingnan, there were 404 haltered-and-bridled prefectures, or nearly half the total haltered-and-bridled prefectures that existed in Tang frontiers (Fang, *Zhongguo xi'nan lishi dili kaoshi*, 320–27; *Guizhou shengzhi*, 10–11; Hou, Shi, and Weng, *Guizhou gudai minzu*, 165). In 698, in response to Tang military advances throughout the southwest, the Qianzhou Area Command was relocated to Zhuangzhou, in central Guizhou near present-day Guiyang. Following a series of military defeats, the Zhuangzhou Area Command was moved north above the Wujiang River to Bozhou, thereby creating the Bozhou Area Command. In 712, the area command was returned to Qianzhou. Chinese sources describe the creation of haltered-and-bridled prefectures as an "attraction" (*zhao*), "agreement" (*fu*), "surrender" (*xiang*), "opening" (*kai*), or "division" (*xi*).

29. Fang, *Zhongguo xi'nan lishi dili kaoshi*, 320–27; Wu, *Zhongguo tusi zhidu yuanyuan*, 80–89; Gong, *Zhongguo tusi zhidu*, 16–22. Xiangzhou was to the north of the present-day city of Weng'an; Manzhou, the present-day city of Kaiyang; Juzhou, present-day Guiyang; Zhuangzhou, near present-day Huaxi; and Yingzhou was located along the southern shore of Hongfeng Lake. See *Jiu Tang shu*, 97/3301–3; Hou, Shi, and Weng, *Guizhou gudai minzu*, 138–39.

30. *Jiu Tang shu*, 97/3302–3; Hou, Shi, and Weng, *Guizhou gudai minzu*, 138–40.

31. *Jiu Tang shu*, 97/3302–3; Wu, *Zhongguo tusi zhidu yuanyuan*, 90–91; Hou, Shi, and Weng, *Guizhou gudai minzu*, 140.

32. *Jiu Tang shu*, 97/3302–3; Wu, *Zhongguo tusi zhidu yuanyuan*, 90–91; Hou, Shi, and Weng, *Guizhou gudai minzu*, 140.

33. Hou, Shi, and Weng, *Guizhou gudai minzu*, 140. One interesting tidbit of historical information noted that the Xie clan strictly prohibited raising girls born into their family, thus girls born to the Xie were sent away (married out) at an early age. However, the Xie refused to marry their newborn daughters to the prominent families in the mountains, i.e., the *wuman*.

34. *Jiu Tang shu*, 97/3304–6; Hou, Shi, and Weng, *Guizhou gudai minzu*, 140.

35. Hou, Shi, and Weng, *Guizhou gudai minzu*, 140.

36. Ibid., 182. According to Ma Yao, the primary reason behind Nanzhao's attack on southern Sichuan and Chengdu was to replenish the kingdom's work-force of skilled slaves. In the Azhe patriclan's genealogy, Agengawei was listed as the forty-seventh-generation descendant of Mujiji. See Ma and Luo, *Cuan-wen congke*, 67–87, 152–58; Fang, *Yizu shigao*, 148–50, 172–77. The *New History of the Tang* notes that Agengawei ruled a large territory known to Chinese at the time as the Zangge kingdom, and it was called this because much of the territory under Agengawei's control lay within the geopolitical scope of the Han dynasty's Zangge Commandery. Moreover, "Agengawei's Zangge kingdom is located some 900 *li* [1 *li* = 0.36 miles or 0.576 kilometers] east of Kunzhou [Kunming] and it covers a vast expanse of land" (*Xin Tang shu*, 222/6314).

37. *Xin Tang shu*, 222/6314–16; Chen, "Guanyu 'Liuzu,' 'Luodian guo,'" 175–80; Li, "Guizhou Yizu tusi yan'ge kao," 35–36; Hou, Shi, and Weng, *Guizhou gudai minzu*, 182.

38. *Xin Tang shu*, 222/6315; Hou, Shi, and Weng, *Guizhou gudai minzu*, 182–88; *Guizhou shengzhi*, 14. The Yushi kingdom controlled the Puan, Panxian, Xingren, and Xingyi areas of present-day southwest Guizhou. There were five powerful *wuman* patriclans located in the Zhenxiong region of northeast Yun-nan, the Wusa, Atou, Yiniang, Wumeng, and Bipan; and the Wusa patriclan controlled the present-day cities of Weining, Hezhang, and Zhaotong. To the east and west of Zhenxiong were the Bumangbu and the Acheng patriclans, re-spectively. In Nasu script, the character *dian* can mean either a flat plain or an administrative unit.

39. Fan, *Manshu jiaozhu*, 1/31–35; Ling, "Tangdai Yunnan de Wuman," 57–86; Hu, "Songdai Yizu," 58–67; von Glahn, *The Country of Streams and Grot-toes*, 24–38.

40. Fan, *Manshu jiaozhu*, 1/31–35; Chen, "Guanyu 'Liuzu,' 'Luodian guo,'" 176–77. The Tang used the term *buluo*, which is regularly translated into En-glish as "tribe," to describe the *wuman* patriclans. According to Chen, the Chi-nese characters *guizhu* adopted by Tang officials to describe the political leaders

of the *wuman* was a mistranslation of the Cuan characters *zimo*. A literal translation of the Nasu characters would be "lord of the forest," or *linjun* in Chinese.

41. *Xin Tang shu*, 222/6315.

42. Fan, *Manshu jiaozhu*, 1/31–35.

43. Backus, *The Nan-chao Kingdom*, 218–20.

44. Ibid., 220–21. Apparently Shilong became irate when the Chinese envoys informed him that he would need to change the first character of his name, *shi*, because it was against Tang dynastic law to use characters that were part of the personal names of Tang emperors. In this case, the character *shi* in Shilong's name was written the same as the *shi* of the Tang dynasty's second and most celebrated emperor, Li Shimin (Song Taizong; 599–649, r. 626–49).

45. *Xin Tang shu*, 222/6282; *Zizhi tongjian*, 250/8092, 8094–95; Fan, *Manshu jiaozhu*, 4/92–108, 10/238; Backus, *The Nan-chao Kingdom*, 220–26. Even though Bozhou was well outside Li Hui's jurisdiction, and Tang officials in Chang'an had not authorized him to leave his post in Jiaozhi, Li risked punishment to relieve Bozhou.

46. *Xin Tang shu*, 222/6282; *Zizhi tongjin*, 250/8092, 8094–95; Fan, *Manshu jiaozhu*, 4/92–108, 10/238; Backus, *The Nan-chao Kingdom*, 220–26.

47. *Zizhi tongjian*, 250/8095.

48. Song, *Yangshi jiazhuan*, 10/30–35.

49. Fang, *Zhongguo xi'nan lishi dili kaoshi*, 635–44; Backus, *The Nan-chao Kingdom*, 197–240.

50. *Song shi*, 4/27a–29a; Hou, Shi, and Weng, *Guizhou gudai minzu*, 147–48.

51. Tian, *Qian shu*, 3/76.

52. *Song shi*, 4/27a–29a; Hou, Shi, and Weng, *Guizhou gudai minzu*, 147.

53. Interestingly, Zhao Kuangyin used the old Tang dynasty designation for the Azhe patriclan's kingdom, Zangge, in his communiqué to Pugui. Evidently this was the last time the Song state identified the Azhe patriclan's kingdom as the Zangge kingdom. Pugui was the thirty-third-generation descendant of Wuana.

54. Hou, Shi, and Weng, *Guizhou gudai minzu*, 182–83.

55. Shuidong literally means "east of the water," and the water referred to is the Yachi River.

56. Hou, Shi, and Weng, *Guizhou gudai minzu*, 149; *Guizhou tongzhi* (1555), 13/9b.

57. Fan, *Manshu jiaozhu*, 1/31a; Ling, "Tangdai Yunnan de Wuman," 57–86; Hu, "Songdai Yizu," 58–67; von Glahn, *The Country of Streams and Grottoes*, 23–38; Fang, *Yizu shigao*, 433–34, 459–62.

58. Hou, Shi, and Weng, *Guizhou gudai minzu*, 182–83; *Song shi*, 4/28b–34a; Chen, "Guanyu 'Liuzu,' 'Luodian guo,'" 176–77. Yaozhou prefecture was established during the Tang dynasty.

59. Fan, *Manshu jiaozhu*, 2/4a–11b; Ling, "Tangdai Yunnan de Wuman," 57–86; Hu, "Songdai Yizu," 58–67; von Glahn, *The Country of Streams and Grottoes*, 24–38; Hou, Shi, and Weng, *Guizhou gudai minzu*, 154.

60. Hou, Shi, and Weng, *Guizhou gudai minzu*, 153–54. According to one firsthand account, "Each year after the winter season had subsided, the barbarians [*man*] and their horses would come to Luzhou; officials would be dispatched to inspect them closely. From Jiangmen Village they would float the horses on rafts to Luzhou. A total of ninety-three people, a mixture of barbarian officials and [Chinese] people, tended to the horses on the rafts. In all, several thousand people make the trip to market [every year]. They remain at Luzhou for three days, selling their horses and buying goods they need like tea, hemp, rice, wine, deer, cloth, leopard skin, and salt" (Fang, *Yizu shigao*, 462–72).

61. Fang, *Yizu shigao*, 460–62; Hou, Shi, and Weng, *Guizhou gudai minzu*, 182–83; *Song shi*, 5/3b–4a.

62. Regarding the Luoshigui and Luodian kingdoms, see Chen, "Guanyu 'Liuzu,' 'Luodian guo,'" 176–77. Both the Luodian and the Luoshigui kingdoms were area polities established in present-day Guizhou by the Mo patriclan descendant Wuana; only the time frame and geographic scope were different, and the name of the kingdom was different. See *Xin Tangshu* 222/6317–18; *Song shi* 496/14231; Hu, "Songdai Yizu," 60–61.

63. Though the Awangren had, by this time, already accepted the bureau (*bu*) appointment from the Dali state, they willingly accepted the conferred Song titles as a way to counter the influence of the Dali state.

## Chapter 2

1. Allsen, *Mongol Imperialism*, 24–27; idem, "The Rise of the Mongolian Empire," 321–413; Rossabi, *Khubilai Khan*, 19–20; idem, "The Reign of Khubilai Khan," 414–89; *Yuan shi*, 3/15. Möngke was the eldest son of Tolui and Sorqaghtani Beki, and a grandson of Chinggis Qan.

2. Allsen, *Mongol Imperialism*, 21–23; idem, "The Rise of the Mongolian Empire," 392; Rossabi, *Khubilai Khan*, 19; idem, "The Reign of Khubilai Khan," 414–17. Jochi was the eldest son of Chinggis Qan.

3. Allsen, *Mongol Imperialism*, 1; idem, "The Rise of the Mongolian Empire," 392–93; Skelton, *The Vinland Map*, 90.

4. Allsen, *Mongol Imperialism*, 21–33; idem, "The Rise of the Mongolian Empire," 392–96; Rossabi, *Khubilai Khan*, 17–19; idem, "The Reign of Khubilai Khan," 414–17. Whereas the regional qans were able to wrestle a degree of independence from the two qans, Ögödei and Güyüg, it was during the tenure of two regents, Ögödei's wife Toregene, who served as regent from 1241 to 1246, and Güyüg's wife Oghul Qaimish, who served from 1248 to 1251, that the regional qans demanded greater autonomy. In fact, the naming of Möngke as

grand qan in 1251 was the final assault of political independence against the Ögödei lineage and represented the ascendancy of the Tolui lineage.

5. Allsen, *Mongol Imperialism*, 45–79; idem, "The Rise of the Mongolian Empire," 392–96; Rossabi, *Khubilai Khan*, 20. Allsen, in his chapter titled "Politics of Centralization," argues that these two campaigns were designed to centralize political power around the grand qan and to confront rebellious regional qans, in particular the Chaghadai.

6. Boyle, "Dynastic and Political History of the Il-khans," 340–51; Humphreys, *From Saladin to the Mongols*, 333–55; Allsen, *Mongol Imperialism*, 1–3, 47–48. Hülegü's advance force led by Ked Buqa continued south until September 1260, when it was crushed by the Egyptian Mamluks at the battle of Ain Jalut. For Ked Buqa's defeat at Ain Jalut, see Smith, "Ain Jalut: Mamluk Success or Mongol Failure?" 307–45.

7. Allsen, *Mongol Imperialism*, 48; "The Rise of the Mongolian Empire," 403–5; Rossabi, *Khubilai Khan*, 19.

8. Allsen, *Mongol Imperialism*, 4; idem, "The Rise of the Mongolian Empire," 407–13; Rossabi, *Khubilai Khan*, 19; idem, "The Reign of Khubilai Khan," 418–22.

9. Allsen, "The Rise of the Mongolian Empire," 405–6; *Yuan shi*, 121/2979–81.

10. Allsen, *Mongol Imperialism*, 24. The *Yuan shi* informs us that a Han Chinese official from Shaanxi named Guo Baoyu was the main architect of the Dali campaign. During an audience with Chinggis Qan, Guo was asked to explain how he might attack Song China. Guo responded by stating, "The strength of the heartland should not be underestimated. It is for this reason that the bravery and fierceness of the tribes of the southwest should be put to use by first conquering them, and then using them to encircle Jin territory, thereby achieving your objective" (*Yuan shi* 149/3521). See also Armijo-Hussein, "Sayyid 'Ayall Shams al-Din," 152–54.

11. *Yuan shi*, 121/1310–15; Fang, *Yizu shigao*, 243–44; Rossabi, *Khubilai Khan*, 25–26; Armijo-Hussein, "Sayyid 'Ayall Shams al-Din," 154–57.

12. Allsen, "The Rise of the Mongolian Empire," 405–7.

13. Cleaves, "The Biography of Bayan," 185–303. The Mongol campaign against Dali came at a great price. Reportedly, Qubulai began his campaign with approximately 100,000 men, but by the time his armies marched into Dali only 20,000 could be counted.

14. Fang, *Yizu shigao*, 243–44, 277–80; Armijo-Hussein, "Sayyid 'Ayall Shams al-Din," 156–57.

15. *Yuan shi*, 121/1310–13, 166/1784; Fang, *Yizu shigao*, 243. According to the biography of Xin Juri (Duan Xingzhi's younger brother) in the *Yuan shi*, "Duan Xingzhi was presented a map of the region [Yunnan] and formally asked to pacify the area and establish a taxation system. Möngke was very pleased

[with Duan's demeanor] and bestowed on Xingzhi the title of maharaja and made him leader of all the barbarians. Möngke then named Xin Jufu [Duan Xingzhi's uncle] leader of the army. Xingzhi then put his younger brother Xin Juri [also known as Duan Shi] in charge of administering the realm and, together with Xin Jufu, led Bo and Cuan armies to join Uriyangqadai in his campaign against Jiaozhi" (166/3910).

16. Allsen, *Mongol Imperialism*, 24; Uriyangqadai's biography in the *Yuan shi* is the best account we have of the Mongol campaign in the southwest (121/2979–81).

17. According to Charles Hucker, the brigade consisted of 10,000 soldiers divided into ten battalions of 1,000 soldiers each. In Yuan China, the brigade commander was regularly seen as the military authority at the route (*lu*) level of territorial administration (*A Dictionary of Official Titles*, 562).

18. *Yuan shi*, 121/2980; Fang, *Zhongguo xi'nan lishi dili kaoshi*, 790.

19. Hou, Shi, and Weng, *Guizhou gudai minzu*, 183–84. In Song sources, the Azhe patriclan are the leaders of the "Spirit Kingdom of the Luo Clan" (*Song shi*, 73/53–55; von Glahn, *The Country of Streams and Grottoes*, 24–37).

20. As a further check on their behavior, *darughachi* (political residents) were posted to the courts of the tributaries. Although the sources note only the presence of a pacification inspector (*xuanfu shi*) at the Nanzhao court, there undoubtedly was a *darughachi* on the scene as well; for, as Hsia Kuang-nan points out in *Yuandai Yunnan shide zongkao* (Taipei: 1968), 65, every office of pacification inspector had attached to it both an inspector and a *darughachi*. These officials, usually Mongols or Central Asian Turks, had the general responsibility of ensuring that the orders and policies of the grand qan actually were carried out on the local level. In many cases the *darughachi* had a body of troops under his command to enforce his authority (Cleaves, "Daruya and Gerege," 237–59).

21. Rossabi, "The Reign of Khubilai Khan," 431; idem, *Khubilai Khan*, 82–85.

22. Rossabi, "The Reign of Khubilai Khan," 433–34; idem, Rossabi, *Khubilai Khan*, 82–85; Cleaves, "The Biography of Bayan," 185–303; Franke, *Sung Biographies*, 749–51.

23. Virtually everything we know about Sayyid 'Ajall Shams al-Din (Ch. Saidianchi Shan Siding) comes from his biography in the *Yuan shi*. When he was just a young boy, in 1220, his father, a prominent local figure in the Central Asian city of Bukhara (in present-day Uzbekistan), surrendered to Chinggis Qan his mounted cavalry of one thousand troops and offered his young son as hostage. Along with his father, Sayyid 'Ajall was made a member of Chinggis's personal bodyguard (*kesig*) (*Yuan shi*, 125/3063–70). See also Armijo-Hussein, "Sayyid 'Ayall Shams al-Din," 168–73.

24. *Yuan shi*, 125/3063–70; Rossabi, *Khubilai Khan*, 201–3; Armijo-Hussein, "Sayyid 'Ayall Shams al-Din," 1–15; Fang, "Guanyu Saidianchi," 47–50. Sayyid 'Ajall, following his stint as part of Chinggis Qan's personal bodyguard, was appointed by Ögödei to be *darughachi* of two districts, Taiyuan and Pingyang (both in modern Shanxi), and he was subsequently named judge of Yanjing (Beijing). Under Möngke, Sayyid 'Ajall was acting director of the six ministries before being named general administrator of Yanjing District. Because of Sayyid 'Ajall's impressive record, Qubulai named him pacification commissioner of Yanjing District. In 1261 Sayyid 'Ajall was named director of political affairs of the Secretarial Council; in 1264 he was appointed acting chief of the secretarial council of the five districts (Shanxi and eastern Sichuan). Sayyid 'Ajall was also intimately involved in military affairs, especially in eastern Sichuan. As Rossabi points out, Yunnan was the only region in China to be ruled by Muslims. He speculates that Qubilai appointed Muslims to Yunnan for two reasons: first, the business acumen of Central Asian Muslims was well known to all, and second, Yunnan controlled vital commercial routes between China and Southeast Asia. Sayyid 'Ajall died in 1279, and in 1297 he was posthumously awarded the title of prince of Xianyang. Two of his sons, Nasir al-Din and Masud, succeeded him as governors of Yunnan, and they continued their father's policies.

25. Fang, *Yizu shigao*, 248; Armijo-Hussein, "Sayyid 'Ayall Shams al-Din," 183–88.

26. Fang, *Yizu shigao*, 248–52; Armijo-Hussein, "Sayyid 'Ayall Shams al-Din," 168–73.

27. Endicott-West, "The Yuan Government and Society," 593. Sayyid 'Ajall is also credited with relocating the administrative seat of political control from Dali to Shanchan (Kunming), where it has remained ever since.

28. *Yuan shi*, 166/53; Gong, *Zhongguo tusi zhidu*, 24. The office of pacification commissioner originated during the Tang dynasty as a position responsible for leading military campaigns and important diplomatic missions. Only the most able and influential were assigned to this prestigious position. However, by the end of the eighth century the office became increasingly identified with bandit suppression and pacification duties in frontier areas, and as a result it lost some of its appeal to nonmilitary personnel hoping to advance their political careers. By the end of the Tang dynasty, the office was further distanced from the civilian realm when it became a permanent hereditary frontier post. In other words, an official assigned to the pacification commission could no longer expect his appointment to be a brief tour of duty. He and his family might never be allowed to leave the frontier. The Song pacification commission was similar to its Tang predecessor, and so when Sayyid 'Ajall reached Yunnan in 1274, he had a blueprint of a hereditary frontier office that combined the functions of both civilian and military rule. See *Yuan shi*, 91/41;

Gong, *Zhongguo tusi zhidu*, 23–28; Wu, *Zhongguo tusi zhidu yuanyuan*, 129–33; She, *Zhongguo tusi zhidu*, 4–13; Hucker, *A Dictionary of Official Titles*, 104, 250–51; and Allsen, *Mongol Imperialism*, 51. The basic demands that the Mongols imposed on all of their sedentary subjects are clearly summarized in Qubilai's order in 1267 to the ruler of Annam: (1) the ruler must come personally to court, (2) sons and younger brothers are to be offered as hostages, (3) the population must be registered, (4) militia units are to be raised, (5) taxes are to be sent in, and (6) a *darughachi* is to take charge of all affairs (*Yuan shi*, 209/2196).

29. Endicott-West, "The Yuan Government and Society," 594. According to Hucker, "The circuit as a territorial unit of government was also part of the Censorate's field of operations. Surveillance Bureaus (*suzheng lianfang si*) of the Censorate were established in the circuit." The Censorate was responsible for interrogations and audits relating to government operations at all levels, from pacification commissions and route commands down to districts, and for submitting reports and impeachments to the metropolitan Censorate (*yushi tai*) (*A Dictionary of Official Titles*, 461).

30. "*Darughachi* is a Mongol word; regarding the appointment of officials to prefectures (*fu, zhou, jun*) and districts (*xian*), each had a Mongol or Central Asian assigned as the Overseer (*darughachi*). They were appointed alongside the regular heads of many agencies in both central and territorial administrations as mandatory co-signers of all documents issuing from these agencies; commonly hereditary posts for Mongols with status in the Mongol military hierarchy" (Hucker, *A Dictionary of Official Titles*, 468). According to Endicott-West, "a similar feature existed at all levels below the Branch Secretariat. For each, a *darughachi* was appointed at the same rank and with the same salary and amount of office land as the other principal official. For example, the head official of a county, the magistrate (hsien-yin), was allotted the same salary and amount of office land as was the county *darughachi*, and the two officials were equal in rank. . . . Khubulai's imperial decrees reserving the office of *darughachi* for Mongols (or Western and Central Asians if there were no Mongols) proved difficult to enforce, and the Mongolian office of *darughachi* was sometimes filled by Chinese" (Endicott-West, "The Yuan Government and Society," 595–96).

31. Endicott-West, "The Yuan Government and Society," 595.

32. Fang, *Zhongguo xi'nan lishi dili kaoshi*, 1095–117; idem, *Yizu shigao*, 245–49, 281–84; *Yuan shi*, 122/2998–3003.

33. *Yuan shi*, 166/53–54; Gong, *Zhongguo tusi zhidu*, 53–152; She, *Zhongguo tusi zhidu*, 20–32, 38–43; Wu, *Zhongguo tusi zhidu yuanyuan*, 157–78, 209–38; Armijo-Hussein, "Sayyid 'Ayall Shams al-Din," 189–96. According to a 1319 text, following the death of a *tusi*, his son, nephew, or brother was to inherit the office. If none of these individuals existed, then the deceased *tusi*'s wife could inherit the office. Based on Gong's assessment of the evidence, the Yuan

inheritance regulations were far less strict than what would be enforced during the Ming and Qing dynasties.

34. Fang, *Yizu shigao*, 253–58; Gong, *Zhongguo tusi zhidu*, 2–22; Wu, *Zhongguo tusi zhidu yuanyuan*, 80–127.

35. Fang, *Yizu shigao*, 253–58; Gong, *Zhongguo tusi zhidu*, 2–22; Wu, *Zhongguo tusi zhidu yuanyuan*, 80–127.

36. Fang, *Yizu shigao*, 253–58; Gong, *Zhongguo tusi zhidu*, 2–22; Wu, *Zhongguo tusi zhidu yuanyuan*, 80–127; Armijo-Hussein, "Sayyid ʿAyall Shams al-Din," 189–96.

37. Bai, *Huizu renwu zhi: Yuandai, Saidianchi Shans al-Din*, 19–20. This was also translated in Armijo-Hussein, "Sayyid ʿAyall Shams al-Din," 180–81. Though wet-rice cultivation had existed in Yunnan since the Han dynasty, it was not until after Sayyid ʿAjall implemented these economic reforms that this type of cultivation came to dominate the agricultural landscape of central Yunnan.

38. Armijo-Hussein, "Sayyid ʿAyall Shams al-Din," 206.

39. *Yuan shi*, 8/2032. According to the *Yuan shi*, the Mongols had already adopted a policy of promoting education. During Ögödei's reign, there was a policy designed to recruit Chinese scholars and build schools throughout North China. In his second year of rule, Qubilai decreed that schools be built in every district (in North China). Based on this information, Rossabi has argued that Sayyid ʿAjall introduced Chinese customs, not Muslim, Central Asian, or Mongol customs, to the southwest. This claim by Rossabi, if correct, is certainly intriguing and requires further study. There is no question that Qubilai and Sayyid ʿAjall sought to establish schools in Yunnan based on a Chinese "Confucian" curriculum, but before we get carried away thinking that this is proof of the sinicization process in action, bear in mind that many of the schools remained, for the most part, in the planning stage and were never built. Also keep in mind the messengers: a Central Asian Muslim and the Mongol qan. The "simultaneity thesis" that has become popular recently seems particularly informative here. As ruler of a numerically inferior conqueror elite, Qubilai (and his officials) employed a multiplicity of policies that allowed them to govern a potentially hostile multiethnic population. To govern China, for instance, Qubilai erected discriminatory policies that prevented members of the Chinese elite from ever participating in the highest echelons of government, but when it came to ruling the Chinese masses, the Yuan state was not averse to using Chinese cultural institutions to soothe and control the people. The emperor or qan and his officials had not been sinicized, but they were employing institutions that embodied Chinese cultural properties in order to control a population. If that population became "sinicized" in the process, then those proponents of the sinicization thesis might be better served to separate mechanisms of political control from cultural institutions. See Rossabi, *Khubilai Khan*, 214.

40. Fang, *Yizu shigao*, 467–72.

41. *Xichang xianzhi*, 14/5a–b; Fang, *Yizu shigao*, 467–70; Gong, *Zhongguo tusi zhidu*, 336–37.

42. Fang, *Zhongguo xi'nan lishi dili kaoshi*, 800–801, 925–39; idem, *Yizu shigao*, 468.

43. Wusa is the present-day city of Weining, located in northwest Guizhou. Caoni is the present-day city of Bijie, also in northwest Guizhou.

44. Fang, *Zhongguo xi'nan lishi dili kaoshi*, 825–31; idem, *Yizu shigao*, 470–72, 500–506; *Yuan shi*, 122/ 3113–14; von Glahn, *The Country of Streams and Grottoes*, 90–141.

45. Fang, *Yizu shigao*, 435–39, 463–65. The eight Nasu patriclans in the Wusa-Wumeng area were the Wusa, Atou, Yixi, Yiniang, Wumeng, Bipan, Mang, and Acheng.

46. Fang, *Yizu shigao*, 470–72. The military households of the Wusa state farm totaled 110. There were 86 civilian households. In 1290, there were 114 Cuan and Bo military households on state farms in Wusa. The Wusa Pacification Commission supervised 49 postal stations (45 horse and 4 water stations); the Wumeng Pacification Commission supervised 9 stations (5 horse and 4 water).

47. The Mongols referred here to the area of western Guizhou inhabited by the Azhe, Bole, Awangren, and Wumeng patriclans.

48. *Yuan shi*, 63/15; Fang, *Yizu shigao*, 508; Gong, *Zhongguo tusi zhidu*, 27. The city of Shanhua is near the present-day city of Changsha, in Hunan.

49. Fang, *Zhongguo xi'nan lishi dili kaoshi*, 942. Xintian is the present-day city of Guiding in Guizhou.

50. There were nine small kingdoms in the Bafan area: the Chengfan, Fengfan, Fangfan, Hongfan, Da Longfan, Xiao Longfan, Jinshifan, Luofan, and Lufan. See Gong, *Zhongguo tusi zhidu*, 766–78; *Guizhou shengzhi*, 19–21; Fang, *Zhongguo xi'nan lishi dili kaoshi*, 943–44.

51. According to these registers, there were 1,186 villages and 89,400 households among the nine tribes of Bafan (Fang, *Yizu shigao*, 508). In addition to the nine military commissions, Liu established three barbarian native offices (*manyi zhangguan si*) in the Bafan area. For a list of these tribal commands, see *Guizhou shengzhi*, 21. The office of military commissioner originated during the Tang dynasty as a quasi-military post authorized by the central government to handle trouble spots throughout the realm. Initially, officials appointed to this post were assigned such tasks as managing famine relief programs; overseeing dike, road, and canal repair projects; and leading police actions and military campaigns to quell violence. Unlike the office of pacification commissioner discussed above, the military commissioner was closely associated with military affairs, and for this reason appointment to the post of military commissioner did not carry with it the honor and prestige of the office of pacification commissioner. For instance, toward the end of the Tang, the office of military commissioner was often assigned concurrent with the title of security commissioner

(*jiedu shi*), with responsibility for suppressing frontier violence. A predominantly frontier office during the Song, the office of military commissioner acquired broad military and civil powers, similar to the pacification commissioner and pacification inspector; however, the military commissioner was clearly subordinate to the above two offices. As Mongol armies entered the southwest during the middle of the thirteenth century this office became yet another piece in the Mongol repertoire of extrabureaucratic offices to be established in the southwest. See *Yuan shi*, 91/41; Gong, *Zhongguo tusi zhidu*, 23–28; Wu, *Zhongguo tusi zhidu yuanyuan*, 129–33; She, *Zhongguo tusi zhidu*, 4–13; Hucker, *A Dictionary of Official Titles*, 104, 250–51.

52. *Yuan shi*, 91/41; Gong, *Zhongguo tusi zhidu*, 23–28; Wu, *Zhongguo tusi zhidu yuanyuan*, 129–33; She, *Zhongguo tusi zhidu*, 4–13; Hucker, *A Dictionary of Official Titles*, 104, 250–51.

53. Fang, *Yizu shigao*, 508; idem, *Zhongguo xi'nan lishi dili kaoshi*, 942–52; *Guizhou shengzhi*, 19–21.

54. Fang, *Zhongguo xi'nan lishi dili kaoshi*, 942–44, 971–74; idem, *Yizu shigao*, 472–73, 506–14. The area of Shuidong includes present-day Guiyang, Xiuwen, and Qingzhen.

55. Fang, *Zhongguo xi'nan lishi dili kaoshi*, 971–74; idem, *Yizu shigao*, 472–73, 506–14. According to several sources, the Chinese characters for "Yixibuxue" represent a transliteration of the Mongol script used to render "Shuixi" into Mongolian; in addition, the Mongolian script was apparently a transliteration of the indigenous Nasu (Cuan or Yi) characters for "Shuixi."

56. Fang, *Yizu shigao*, 472–73; idem, *Zhongguo xi'nan lishi dili kaoshi*, 508–11, 983–89; *Yuan shi*, 122/3113–14; 123/3129–31.

57. Fang, *Yizu shigao*, 508–15; idem, *Zhongguo xinan lishi dili kaoshi*, 971–74, 983–89; *Yuan shi*, 122/3113–14.

58. Fang, *Zhongguo xi'nan lishi dili kaoshi*, 984; *Yuan shi*, 123/3129–31.

59. *Guizhou tongzhi* (1555), 9/2b; *Yuan shi*, 11/226.

60. *Yuan shi*, 123/3129–31; Fang, *Yizu shigao*, 508–15; idem, *Zhongguo xi'nan lishi dili kaoshi*, 971–74, 983–89.

61. *Yuan shi*, 11/227–28; 123/3129–31, 3134–36; Fang, *Yizu shigao*, 508–15; idem, *Zhongguo xi'nan lishi dili kaoshi*, 971–74, 983–89.

62. *Yuan shi*, 11/230; Fang, *Yizu shigao*, 508–15; idem, *Zhongguo xi'nan lishi dili kaoshi*, 971–74, 983–89.

63. *Yuan shi*, 12/240, 242; Fang, *Yizu shigao*, 508–15; idem, *Zhongguo xi'nan lishi dili kaoshi*, 971–74, 983–89.

64. Caoni is the present-day city of Bijie, Yixibuxue is present-day Dafang, Pingchiande is present-day Qianxi, Daguzhai is present-day Jinsha, and Mopoleipo is present-day Zhijin.

65. *Yuan shi*, 12/244; Fang, *Yizu shigao*, 508–15; idem, *Zhongguo xi'nan lishi dili kaoshi*, 971–74, 983–89. Bozhou is present-day Zunyi, Wusa is present-day

Weining, Ayong Man is present-day Xuyong, in Sichuan province, and Luodian is present-day Anshun.

66. Fang, *Zhongguo xi'nan lishi dili kaoshi*, 971–74; idem, *Yizu shigao*, 472–73, 506–14.

67. *Yuan shi*, 12/247, 255. Shang Shexiong, the former rebel leader, was named the military commissioner of the various grottoes of Youba.

68. *Yuan shi*, 12/248, 254. When, in 1282, the Yunnan Branch Secretariat ordered Amou, the patriarch of the Wusa patriclan and head of the Wusa Tribal Command since 1278, to send Wusa reinforcements to the Miandian front, he rebelled. Soldiers from Sichuan heading for Miandian instead found themselves fighting in Wusa throughout much of 1282 and 1283. Eventually, the central government decided to maintain uncontested Yuan control of the Wumeng road, so in 1284 it established the Wusa-Wumeng Pacification Commission and staffed it with Mongol and Central Asian administrators (Fang, *Zhongguo xi'nan lishi dili kaoshi*, 470–71).

69. *Yuan shi*, 12/253; *Guizhou shengzhi*, 18–35; Fang, *Yizu shigao*, 508–15; idem, *Zhongguo xi'nan lishi dili kaoshi*, 952–53, 971–74, 983–89.

70. *Yuan shi*, 12/255–56; Fang, *Yizu shigao*, 508–15; idem, *Zhongguo xi'nan lishi dili kaoshi*, 952–53, 971–74, 983–89. Yaocihai was quite familiar with Ali, for he had named Ali battalion commander of Yixibuxue soon after the Mongol forces pacified the town of Yixibuxue. Prior to this appointment, Song Tianfu had been a tribal commander stationed in the Shuidong portion of the Shunyuan Route; but, with this new appointment and the near total withdrawal of Yuan officials from the region, Song became the sole Yuan authority in Shuidong.

71. Polo, *The Travels of Marco Polo*, 177–78.

72. *Yuan shi*, 14/48. The Mongol occupation continued to reverberate throughout the Shunyuan-Bafan region; for example, in 1290 an estimated three thousand Miao braves attacked the city of Shunyuan.

73. *Yuan shi*, 14/48–49.

74. Fang, *Zhongguo xi'nan lishi dili kaoshi*, 953. The official title of the Shunyuan-Bafan pacification commissioner was *Shunyuan-Bafan dengchu xuanwei si du yuanshuai lu zongguan fu*, or the pacification commissioner of Shunyuan, Bafan, and adjoining territories, concurrent with chief military commander and Shunyuan route commander.

75. *Guizhou shengzhi*, 18–35; Fang, *Yizu shigao*, 508–15; idem, *Zhongguo xi'nan lishi dili kaoshi*, 952–53, 971–74, 983–89. The Shunyuan-Bafan Pacification Commission covered a vast geographic expanse: it included the present-day cities of Guiyang, Longli, Kaiyang, Xiuwen, Xifeng, Qingzhen, Changshun, Huishui, Pingtang, Luodian, Duyun, and Dushan.

76. *Guizhou shengzhi*, 18–35; Fang, *Yizu shigao*, 508–15; idem, *Zhongguo xi'nan lishi dili kaoshi*, 952–53, 971–74, 983–89. The nine military commissions

of Bafan were Chengfan, Fangfan, Hongfan, Wo Longfan, Da Longfan, Xiao Longfan, Jinshifan, Luofan, and Lufan.

77. *Guizhou shengzhi*, 18–35; Fang, *Yizu shigao*, 508–15; idem, *Zhongguo xi'nan lishi dili kaoshi*, 952–53, 971–74, 983–89. I do not mean to be overly specific about the institutional arrangements made by the Yuan state, but I do want to point out that in the third month of 1295, the Yixibuxue Pacification Commission was detached from the Bafan-Shunyuan Pacification Commission and placed under the control of the Yunnan Branch Secretariat, and from this point on Yixibuxue remained under Yunnan control.

78. Fang, *Yizu shigao*, 474; Hou, Shi, and Weng, *Guizhou gudai minzu*, 267–68.

79. The Lanna kingdom had its capital in the present-day city of Chiang Mai, in northern Thailand. A succinct summary of the Mongol-Lanna war can be found in Wyatt, *Thailand: A Short History*.

80. Fang, *Yizu shigao*, 474–76, 516–21; Hou, Shi, and Weng, *Guizhou gudai minzu*, 267–68.

81. Fang, *Yizu shigao*, 474–76, 516–21; Hou, Shi, and Weng, *Guizhou gudai minzu*, 267–68.

82. Armijo-Hussein, "Sayyid 'Ayall Shams al-Din," 128–29; Wang, *Dali xingji jiaozhu Yunnan*, 66.

83. Armijo-Hussein, "Sayyid 'Ayall Shams al-Din," 136–39; Wang, *Dali xingji jiaozhu Yunnan*, 72–73.

84. Fang, *Yizu shigao*, 474–76, 516–21; Hou, Shi, and Weng, *Guizhou gudai minzu*, 269–70.

85. Fang, *Yizu shigao*, 474–76, 516–21; Hou, Shi, and Weng, *Guizhou gudai minzu*, 269–70. During Ahua's visit to the Yuan capital in 1334, Grand Qan Toghon Temur (1320–70, r. 1333–68) bestowed upon Ahua three additional titles, the dragon and tiger general (*longhu da jiangjun*), the marquis of the Luodian kingdom and the Shunyuan Commandery (*Shunyuan jun Luodian guo*), and the duke of the Ji kingdom (*Jiguo gong*).

86. Millward, *Beyond the Pass*, 232–52.

## Chapter 3

1. *Guizhou tongzhi* (1987), 8–9; *Taizu Hongwu shilu*, 71/4–5. Wang Zou offered this brief historical sketch of Aicui in the *Guizhou tujing xinzhi*: "Aicui was a descendant of Huoji. During the Shu Han period, Huoji assisted Prime Minister Liang [Zhuge Liang] in capturing Meng Huo and was invested as king of Luodian. Throughout history Huoji's descendants, such as Apei in the Tang, Pugui in the Song, and Ahua in the Yuan, all have been recognized by the Chinese government, so that today Huoji's descendants reside in Shuixi and go by the title *da guizhu*" (*Guizhou tujing xinzhi*, 3/1a–b).

2. *Guizhou tongzhi* (1987), 8–9; Fang, *Yizu shigao*, 474–76, 516–21. The Guizhou Garrison was established on January 23, 1372 (or the seventeenth day of the twelfth month of Hongwu 4). During the latter part of the Yuan dynasty there were many *tuguan* domains in the area, but at the beginning of the Ming dynasty many of these small *tuguan* were consolidated under the authority of four large pacification commissions: Guizhou, Sizhou, Sinan, and Bozhou.

3. Hou, Shi, and Weng, *Guizhou gudai minzu*, 180–98; *Guizhou tongzhi* (1987), 9–11; Fan, *Manshu jiaozhu*, 4/92–108; Ling, "Tangdai Yunnan de Wuman," 57–86; Hu, "Songdai Yizu," 58–67; von Glahn, *The Country of Streams and Grottoes*, 24–38; Hu, *Ming Qing Yizu shehui*, 5–7. Yao prefecture was located in present-day Dafang, Hao in present-day Zhijin, Lu in Bijie, Tangwang near Liupanshui, Jian to the northeast of Dafang, Gong in Qianxi, Yi to the northeast of Qianxi, and Hui in Zhijin. In the territory east of the Yachi River, Juzhou prefecture was located in present-day Guiyang, and Qingzhu in Qingzhen. Ten years later, in 1381, Hongwu ordered officials to register the entire Chinese population. Ming officials recorded the name, age, and birthplace of the head of household, his occupation, the size of his house, and the amount of land and number of animals he owned. The information was kept in a document called the Yellow Register (*huangce*).

4. Ma and Luo, *Cuanwen congke*, 115–41, 184; Hu, *Ming Qing Yizu shehui*, 31–33; *Dading fuzhi*, 11/3a.

5. Ma and Luo, *Cuanwen congke*, 115–41, 184; Meng, "Liangshan Yizu," 277–309; Hu, *Ming Qing Yizu shehui*, 31–36; Wu, "Nzymo as Seen in Some Yi Classical Books," 35–48. The Chinese term for the *muzhuo* office is *tumu*.

6. Ma and Luo, *Cuanwen congke*, 115–41, 184; Meng, "Liangshan Yizu," 277–309; Hu, *Ming Qing Yizu shehui*, 31–36; *Dading fuzhi*, 11/1b–14a; Wu, "Nzymo as Seen in Some Yi Classical Books," 30–33. According to Chinese ethnohistorians, the Ming term for the indigenous Pu people was "Qilao."

7. Ma and Luo, *Cuanwen congke*, 115–41, 184; Meng, "Liangshan Yizu," 277–309; *Dading fuzhi*, 11/1b–14a; Hu, *Ming Qing Yizu shehui*, 31–33; Li, "Guizhou Yizu tusi yan'ge kao," 35–36.

8. *Xi'nan Yizhi*, 6/175–267, 8/284–312; Wang and Wang, *Yizu yuanliu*, 132–40; Ma and Luo, *Cuanwen congke*, 115–41, 152–58, 160–203; Meng, "Liangshan Yizu," 277–309; Wang and Chen, "Yizu liuzu yuanliu," 162–74; Fang, *Zhongguo xi'nan lishi dili kaoshi*, 715–21; idem, *Yizu shigao*, 145–50; Hou, Shi, and Weng, *Guizhou gudai minzu*, 180–98; Hu, *Ming Qing Yizu shehui*, 31–33; Li, "Guizhou Yizu tusi yan'ge kao," 35–36.

9. *Xi'nan Yizhi*, 6/175–267, 8/284–312; Wang and Wang, *Yizu yuanliu*, 132–40; Ma and Luo, *Cuanwen congke*, 115–41, 152–58, 160–203; Meng, "Liangshan Yizu," 277–309; Wang and Chen, "Yizu liuzu yuanliu," 162–74; Fang, *Zhongguo xi'nan lishi dili kaoshi*, 715–21; Fang, *Yizu shigao*, 145–50; Hou, Shi, and Weng, *Guizhou gudai minzu*, 180–98; Hu, *Ming Qing Yizu shehui*, 31–33; Li,

"Guizhou Yizu tusi yan'ge kao," 35–36. See also *Dading fuzhi*, 11/3a; *Guizhou tongzhi* (1692), 32/14b–17a; *Guizhou tongzhi* (1741), 25/14b–15b.

10. *Dading xianzhi*, 21/7b. The *sujie* and *zesu* could be bought and sold, acquired as booty in revenge wars, presented as gifts, and even killed if the *na* so desired. For example, in 1576 Guizhou Pacification Commissioner An Guoheng presented as a gift to one of his *muzhuo* in Shuidong a man named An Zhi. An Zhi could read and write Chinese, and therefore he possessed a valuable technical skill. In addition to An Zhi, An Guoheng gave the *muzhuo* the wealthy Mao family village (*Maojia zhai*) along with twenty-four hamlets surrounding the village.

11. *Xi'nan Yizhi* (1991), vol. 6. 175–267; *Xi'nan Yizhi* (1994), vol. 8, 284–312; Wang and Wang, *Yizu yuanliu*, 132–40; Ma and Luo, *Cuanwen congke*, 115–41, 152–203; Meng, "Liangshan Yizu," 277–309; Fang, *Zhongguo xi'nan lishi dili kaoshi*, 715–21; idem, *Yizu shigao*, 145–50; Hou, Shi, and Weng, *Guizhou gudai minzu*, 180–98; Hu, *Ming Qing Yizu shehui*, 31–33; Li, "Guizhou Yizu tusi," 35–36; *Guizhou tongzhi* (1692), 32/14b–17a; *Guizhou tongzhi* (1741), 37/2a–57b. According to sources, there existed another caste within Nasu Yi society, one called *kehu* (guest house). The people given this designation were, for the most part, Han Chinese who had fled to the southwest frontier and were able to obtain this special status because of a particular skill or knowledge deemed valuable by the officials in Shuixi. These *kehu* acquired the protection of a powerful *na* and were supposedly able to pass their nonslave status on to their descendants, usually signified by the wearing of a special article of clothing and by providing gifts annually to their lord (Hu, *Ming Qing Yizu shehui*, 28–30).

12. *Yuan shi*, 23/3129–36; *Guizhou tongzhi* (1555), 23/24b–25a; *Guizhou tongzhi* (1692), 32/10b–11a; Guo, *Qianji*, 3/2a–3a.

13. *Guizhou tongzhi* (1987), 8–9; Fang, *Yizu shigao*, 474–76, 516–21. By the end of the Yuan dynasty, Chinese merchants were bypassing Yushi and Bole for the markets in Shunyuan, where Ahua had established his administrative headquarters.

14. Fang, *Yizu shigao*, 145–50; Hou, Shi, and Weng, *Guizhou gudai minzu*, 180–98; Hu, *Ming Qing Yizu shehui*, 31–33.

15. *Ming shi*, 311/8006–8; *Taizu Hongwu shilu*, 146/5b–6a.

16. Langlois, "The Hung-wu Reign, 1368–1398," 143–46; Lee, "Food Supply and Population Growth," 711–46.

17. *Ming shi*, 124/12a–13a; Langlois, "The Hung-wu Reign, 1368–1398," 143–45.

18. *Taizu Hongwu shilu*, 139/1, 140/7a–10a, 142/2a–5b, 143/4a–b; *Ming shi*, 311/8002–3, 314/8091–92; *Guizhou tongzhi* (1987), 23; Goodrich and Fang, *Dictionary of Ming Biography*, 466–71.

19. *Taizu Hongwu shilu*, 144/7, 151/1, 155/1, 156/5, 159/7; *Guizhou tongzhi* (1987), 32–40; *Ming shi*, 316/8169; Tian, *Yanjiao jiwen*, 4/50b–51b; Mao, *Mansi hezhi*, 2/4b–5b.

20. *Taizu Hongwu shilu*, 144/7, 151/1, 155/1, 156/5, 159/7; *Guizhou tongzhi* (1987), 32–40; *Ming shi*, 316/8169; Tian, *Yanjiao jiwen*, 4/50b–51b; Mao, *Mansi hezhi*, 2/4b–5b.

21. *Taizu Hongwu shilu*, 144/7, 151/1, 155/1, 156/5, 159/7; *Guizhou tongzhi* (1987), 32–40; *Ming shi*, 316/8169; Tian, *Yanjiao jiwen*, 4/50b–51b; Mao, *Mansi hezhi*, 2/4b–5b. Since the death of her husband, Song Qin, a few years earlier, Liu Shuzhen not only had assumed control of the Guizhou vice pacification commissioner post (*xuanwei shi tongzhi*) in charge of Shuidong but also had acquired the reputation of being a wise and fair administrator.

22. *Taizu Hongwu shilu*, 144/7, 151/1, 155/1, 156/5, 159/7; *Guizhou tongzhi* (1987), 32–40; *Ming shi*, 316/8169; Tian, *Yanjiao jiwen*, 4/50b–51b; Mao, *Mansi hezhi*, 2/4b–5b. See also *Xi'nan Yizhi*, 316–20; Tian, *Qian shu*, 3/63–65.

23. *Guizhou tongzhi* (1987), 127.

24. *Taizu Hongwu shilu*, 159/7; Tian, *Yanjiao jiwen*, 4/51b–52a; *Guizhou tongzhi* (1987), 37–38. According to all the biographical information we have on Empress Ma, she was indeed an influential actor. She was one of only a handful of people Hongwu trusted, and he constantly looked to her for advice on affairs of state. For more information, see Goodrich and Fang, *Dictionary of Ming Biography*, 1023–26.

25. *Taizu Hongwu shilu*, 139/1, 140/7–10, 141/3–6, 142/2–5; *Guizhou tongzhi* (1987), 24–29.

26. *Taizu Hongwu shilu*, 139/1, 140/7–10, 141/3–6, 142/2–5; *Guizhou tongzhi* (1987), 24–29. Lan Yu was also known as the marquis of Yongchang, whereas Mu Ying, Hongwu's adopted son, had been named the marquis of Xiping.

27. For the attack on Basalawarmi, see *Ming shi*, 2/36, 3/39–40, 124/3719–20, 129/3799–803; *Taizu Hongwu shilu*, 139/1, 140/1, 140/5–8; Goodrich and Fang, *Dictionary of Ming Biography*, 466–71. For the attack on Dali, see *Ming shi*, 3/45–56, 126/3756–66; *Taizu Hongwu shilu*, 141/2, 141/3–4, 142/1–2, 142/3–5, 143/2–3, 143/2–3, 143/8–9, 144/2, 146/6, 153/1; Goodrich and Fang, *Dictionary of Ming Biography*, 1079–83.

28. In a manner similar to what von Glahn described in the southern Sichuan frontier during the Song dynasty, Ming officials were highly critical of field commanders who repeatedly claimed to have inflicted a crushing defeat upon the enemy. Far too often these "victories" occurred not on the battlefield but at the negotiating table, and when one party felt the terms of the agreement had been breached, violence would ensue. Ming officials frequently saw their "stolen peace" returned. Von Glahn, *The Country of Streams and Grottoes*, 89.

29. *Ming shi*, 3/45–56, 126/3756–66; *Taizu Hongwu shilu*, 193/7, 195/3, 214/4–5, 235/4, 236/2–3.

30. Goodrich and Fang, *Dictionary of Ming Biography*, 1208–14. According to John Langlois, Jr., "In early 1388 the border war against the Shan nation took a turn for the worse at Lu-ch'uan in Yunnan. Ssu Lun-fa attacked in February, but was turned back by forces of Mu Ying. He attacked again in April with an estimated 300,000 troops and 100 war elephants. The Shan rebels were repulsed after a big battle in May. Ssu Lun-fa lost over 40,000 men and 37 elephants, but the Shan leader himself was not captured. Towards the end of July, Fu Yu-te led an army against the Lolo rebels of T'ung-ch'uan. In October, Mu Ying joined forces with Fu Yu-te to fight A-tzu, the son of a recently deceased native chieftain of Yueh-chou. In January 1389, A-tzu took Pu-an, but eventually surrendered Yueh-chou the following month. Mu Ying petitioned to have a garrison (*wei*) established at Yueh-chou to serve as a Ming defense bastion for that part of Yunnan. The Shan chieftain Ssu Lun-fa surrendered in early December, 1389, and Lu-ch'uan was pacified" ("The Hung-wu Reign, 1368–1398," 160).

31. *Taizu Hongwu shilu*, 143/10; *Da Ming huidian*, 1/551; Lombard-Salmon, *Un exemple d'acculturation chinoise*, 166–71; *Guizhou tongzhi* (1555), 7/12.

32. *Guizhou shengzhi*, 33–58; *Guizhou tongzhi* (1987), 50; *Guizhou tongzhi* (1555), 5/1–18.

33. *Guizhou shengzhi*, 33–58; *Guizhou tongzhi* (1987), 50; *Guizhou tongzhi* (1555), 5/1–18.

34. Guo, *Qianji*, 4/15.

35. *Guizhou tongzhi* (1987), 43. In 1387 She Xiang reported during a tribute visit to Nanjing that her son, the Guizhou pacification commissioner, was residing in Shuixi, though she was living in Guiyang.

36. *Taizu Hongwu shilu*, 140/8–10, 141/4–6, 142/2–3, 147/16–17, 159/7, 194/4; *Guizhou tongzhi* (1987), 28–29, 47–50.

37. *Guizhou tongzhi* (1741), 5/21b.

38. *Taizu Hongwu shilu*, 140/8–10, 141/4–6, 142/1–3, 143/10, 144/5, 147/16–17, 155/3, 157/1, 159/7, 194/4; *Guizhou tongzhi* (1987), 28–29, 47–50.

39. As James Lee points out, "Within the first 16 years of Ming rule, that is from 1368 to 1385, over 180 million *mu* of 'newly cultivated land' (*kentian*) were registered by the central government. Although the total registered cultivated acreage continued to increase from 350 million *mu* in 1381 to over 850 million *mu* in 1393, several recent studies have suggested that these increases reflect changes in the land registration system rather than changes in the extent of cultivated land" ("The Political Economy of a Frontier," 43; see also Liang, *Zhongguo lidai hukou, tiandi, tianfu tongji*, 331).

40. Theoretically there were 134,000 troops posted to Qian's garrisons and battalions, whereas Yunnan's contained approximately 110,000 troops. There were no civilian farms in Qian, but there were 933,929 *mu* of military farms; in Yunnan there were 20,500 *mu* of state farms and 1,087,743 *mu* of military

farms. In southwest China alone there were over 2,000,000 *mu* of military land that represented nearly all of the registered land in the middle of the fifteenth century, and one-quarter of all registered land in the early seventeenth century.

41. *Taizu Hongwu shilu*, 119/8, 139/1, 141/4–6, 143/10, 146/1, 146/7, 147/13, 150/4; *Guizhou tongzhi* (1987), 23–30.

42. *Taizu Hongwu shilu*, 149/4–6, 152/3, 154/1; *Guizhou tongzhi* (1987), 33–34.

43. Wusa is the present-day city of Weining; Wumeng is present-day Zhaotong; Dongchuan is present-day Huize; and Mangbu is present-day Zhenxiong.

44. *Taizu Hongwu shilu*, 150/8–9; *Guizhou tongzhi* (1987), 33–34; *Ming shi*, 27/8169.

45. *Taizu Hongwu shilu*, 162/3–4.

46. *Da Ming huidian*, 2/694.

47. She, *Zhongguo tusi zhidu*, 3–45; Wu, *Zhongguo tusi zhidu yuanyuan*, 129–207; Gong, *Zhongguo tusi zhidu*, 23–109.

48. She, *Zhongguo tusi zhidu*, 3–45; Wu, *Zhongguo tusi zhidu yuanyuan*, 129–207; Gong, *Zhongguo tusi zhidu*, 23–109.

49. Tian, *Yanjiao jiwen*, 59/1a–27b. Much of Tian's ire was directed against the policies advocated by Wang Shouren (Wang Yangming).

50. Ibid., 59/7a.

51. Ibid., 59/7a.

52. Ibid., 59/7b; Wu, *Zhongguo tusi zhidu yuanyuan*, 107–8. Anyi means "Pacify the Barbarians" and is the present-day city of Zhenyuan.

53. Ibid., 59/7b; Wu, *Zhongguo tusi zhidu yuanyuan*, 107–8. This created some confusion between the two towns named Sizhou; the former Sizhou was located to the north, near present-day Wuchuan, and the newly named Sizhou was situated to the south, near Cengong.

54. Tian, *Yanjiao jiwen*, 59/7b; *Yuan shi*, 6/7b–9a; Wu, *Zhongguo tusi zhidu yuanyuan*, 132–33.

55. Tian, *Yanjiao jiwen*, 59/7b–8a; *Yuan shi*, 6/8b–10a; Wu, *Zhongguo tusi zhidu yuanyuan*, 132–55.

56. Tian, *Yanjiao jiwen*, 59/7b–8a; *Yuan shi*, 6/8b–10a; Wu, *Zhongguo tusi zhidu yuanyuan*, 132–55.

57. Tian, *Yanjiao jiwen*, 59/7b–8a; *Yuan shi*, 6/8b–10a; Wu, *Zhongguo tusi zhidu yuanyuan*, 132–55.

58. *Taizu Hongwu shilu*, 15/9, 15/14, 16/7, 40/2, 42/1–2, 70/9.

59. Chan, "The Chien-wen, Yung-lo, Hung-hsi," 229–31.

60. Ibid.

61. Ibid.; Dreyer, *Early Ming China*, 206–10.

62. Chan, "The Chien-wen, Yung-lo, Hung-hsi," 229–31; Dreyer, *Early Ming China*, 206–10. Given Yongle's egregious disregard of his father's decrees on imperial succession, it is not surprising that the emperor and his advisers

refrained from investigating with any degree of thoroughness the validity of the Tran genealogy.

63. Chan, "The Chien-wen, Yung-lo, Hung-hsi," 229–31; Dreyer, *Early Ming China*, 206–10.

64. Chan, "The Chien-wen, Yung-lo, Hung-hsi," 229–31; Dreyer, *Early Ming China*, 206–10.

65. *Taizong Yongle shilu*, 42/6, 50/9–10, 50/11; *Guizhou tongzhi* (1987), 64–65.

66. Chan, "The Chien-wen, Yung-lo, Hung-hsi," 229–31; Dreyer, *Early Ming China*, 206–10.

67. *Taizong Yongle shilu*, 70/9, 73/2; *Guizhou tongzhi* (1987), 59–60, 61, 65–66.

68. *Guizhou tongzhi* (1987), 67.

69. *Taizong Yongle shilu*, 87/5–7; *Guizhou tongzhi* (1987), 66–76. The three new Ming departments were Anshun, Zhenning, and Yongning.

70. *Taizong Yongle shilu*, 105/5, 26/4. In the ninth month of 1423, four circuits were established in Guizhou: Guining, Anping, Xinzhen, and Siren. The Guining circuit included the Guizhou Pacification Commission and the following garrisons: Guizhou, Guizhou Forward, Qian, Wusa, Bijie, Chishui, and Yongning. The Anping circuit included the Weiqing, Pingba, Anzhuan, Annan, Puding, and Puan garrisons, as well as the departments of Anshun, Zhenning, Yongning, and Puan. The Xinzhen circuit was composed of the Xinglong, Qingping, Pingyue, Xintian, Longli, and Duyun garrisons, in addition to the Huangping Battalion and the prefectures of Zhenyuan, Liping, and Xinhua. The Siren circuit was made up of Sinan, Tongren, Wuluo, Shiqian, and Sizhou prefectures.

## Chapter 4

1. She, *Zhongguo tusi zhidu*, 20–32, 38–43; Huang, "Mingdai tusi zhidu," 27–217; Wu, *Zhongguo tusi zhidu yuanyuan*, 157–78, 209–38; Gong, *Zhongguo tusi zhidu*, 53–152; Jiang, *Mingdai Yunnan jingnei de tuguan yu tusi*, 12–87.

2. *Ming shi*, 300/7982; Mao, *Mansi hezhi*, 1/1a–b; Wu, *Zhongguo tusi zhidu yuanyuan*, 157–58; Gong, *Zhongguo tusi zhidu*, 53.

3. The term *tusi* originated in Ming times. Moreover, of the twenty-five Standard Histories, the *Ming shi* is the first to contain biographies of *tusi*.

4. *Ming shi*, 75/1849–50, 76/1875–76; Wu, *Zhongguo tusi zhidu yuanyuan*, 157–58; Gong, *Zhongguo tusi zhidu*, 53; She, *Zhongguo tusi zhidu*, 21–23; Huang, "Mingdai tusi zhidu," 27–217. For a discussion on civilian-rank *tusi* in Guangxi, see Cushman, "Rebel Haunts and Lotus Huts." These civilian *tusi* offices were also identified by the former Yuan term, *tuguan*, but they were now considered civil officials (*wenzhi*).

5. *Ming shi*, 75/1849–50, 76/1875–76; Wu, *Zhongguo tusi zhidu yuanyuan*, 159–64, 167–68, 178–91; Gong, *Zhongguo tusi zhidu*, 66–71; She, *Zhongguo tusi*

*zhidu*, 21–23; Huang, "Mingdai tusi zhidu," 27–217; Cushman, "Rebel Haunts and Lots Huts," 181–84.

6. *Ming shi*, 75/1849–50, 76/1875–76; Wu, *Zhongguo tusi zhidu yuanyuan*, 159–64, 167–68, 178–91; Gong, *Zhongguo tusi zhidu*, 66–71; She, *Zhongguo tusi zhidu*, 21–23; Huang, "Mingdai tusi zhidu," 27–217; Cushman, "Rebel Haunts and Lots Huts," 195–96. The head constable office was more fully utilized by the Qing state.

7. *Da Ming huidian*, 6/132a–b, 118/77b–78a; Mao, *Mansi hezhi*, preface, 1b–2b; Gong, *Zhongguo tusi zhidu*, 67–68; She, *Zhongguo tusi zhidu*, 21–22; Wu, *Zhongguo tusi zhidu yuanyuan*, 162–63.

8. *Ming shi*, 76/1873–76; Wu, *Zhongguo tusi zhidu yuanyuan*, 159–64, 167–68, 178–91; Gong, *Zhongguo tusi zhidu*, 66–71; She, *Zhongguo tusi zhidu*, 21–23; Huang, "Mingdai tusi zhidu," 27–217.

9. In 1428, though, the Ming government decreed that in an area with more than four hundred households, a native official would be established, and in areas with fewer than four hundred households, a barbarian native official would be established. See *Ming shi*, 76/1873–76; Wu, *Zhongguo tusi zhidu yuanyuan*, 159–64, 167–68, 178–91; Gong, *Zhongguo tusi zhidu*, 66–71; She, *Zhongguo tusi zhidu*, 21–23; Huang, "Mingdai tusi zhidu," 27–217. The native office (*zhangguan si*) and barbarian native office (*manyi zhangguan si*) titles were first used in the Yuan at the subdepartment level. During the Ming dynasty, the *zhangguan si* office was known by many different titles, including *manyi guan*, *Miaomin guan*, *Qianfu zhang*, and *fu Qianfu zhang*.

10. Gong, *Zhongguo tusi zhidu*, 57–63; Li, "The Control of the Szechwan-Kweichow Frontier Regions," 40; Lee, "The Political Economy of a Frontier," 82–164; Goodrich and Fang, *Dictionary of Ming Biography*, 1080–81. According to She Yize, the general pattern was for the Ming state to grant high-ranking military titles of the Yuan dynasty to *tusi*, but very few military titles were bestowed on officials in Guangxi, with one major exception. In 1369, the Ming reappointed Mo Tianhu as military commissioner, but in the following year he rebelled, thus ending the use of such high-ranking *tusi* titles in Guangxi. See She, *Zhongguo tusi zhidu*, 18–19; *Ming shi*, 317/12a–12b. In addition, the *Ming shi* (76/22a) lists the lowest military-rank *tusi* offices as *wei zhihuishi* and *qianhu suo*; at the very lowest level were the *baihu suo* and *toumu*.

11. Gong, *Zhongguo tusi zhidu*, 71–110; Wu, *Zhongguo tusi zhidu yuanyuan*, 203–7; She, *Zhongguo tusi zhidu*, 30–37; Huang, "Mingdai tusi zhidu," 27–217.

12. *Da Ming huidian*, 6/128; *Ming shi*, 315/8156, 320/8039; Mao, *Mansi hezhi*, 8/2a; Wu, *Zhongguo tusi zhidu yuanyuan*, 162–64; Gong, *Zhongguo tusi zhidu*, 68–71; She, *Zhongguo tusi zhidu*, 21–23.

13. *Ming shi*, 72/1746–48, 316/8176; Wu, *Zhongguo tusi zhidu yuanyuan*, 162–64; Gong, *Zhongguo tusi zhidu*, 68–71; She, *Zhongguo tusi zhidu*, 21–23.

14. *Da Ming huidian*, 108/1621; *Ming shi*, 315/8161, 314/ 8105, 315/8158–59, 314/8209.

15. Gong, *Zhongguo tusi zhidu*, 74–80; Wu, *Zhongguo tusi zhidu yuanyuan*, 168–78; She, *Zhongguo tusi zhidu*, 22–25; *Ming shi*, 72/1752, 310/7982, 313/ 8085, 316/8169; *Da Ming huidian*, 6/123, 42/771, 121/1743–44; *Tuguan dibu*, shang/34 (599/349), shang/35 (599/349), shang/42 (599/353), shang/52–53 (599/358), shang/76–77 (599/370), xia/40 (599/398), xia/57–58 (599/406–7), xia/61–62 (599/408–9), xia/66 (599/411).

16. Gong, *Zhongguo tusi zhidu*, 78–79; Wu, *Zhongguo tusi zhidu yuanyuan*, 175–76; *Da Ming huidian*, 6/123–24; *Tuguan dibu*, shang/24 (599/344), xia/40 (599/398).

17. Gong, *Zhongguo tusi zhidu*, 74–80; Wu, *Zhongguo tusi zhidu yuanyuan*, 168–78; She, *Zhongguo tusi zhidu*, 22–25; *Ming shi*, 313/8085, 316/8169; *Da Ming huidian*, 6/123–24, 121/1743–44; *Tuguan dibu*, shang/34 (599/349), shang/ 52–53 (599/358), shang/76–77 (599/370), xia/57–58 (599/406–7), xia/61–62 (599/408–9).

18. Gong, *Zhongguo tusi zhidu*, 74–80; Wu, *Zhongguo tusi zhidu yuanyuan*, 168–78; She, *Zhongguo tusi zhidu*, 22–25; *Ming shi*, 313/8085, 316/8169; *Da Ming huidian*, 6/123–24, 121/1743–44; *Tuguan dibu*, shang/34 (599/349), shang/ 52–53 (599/358), shang/76–77 (599/370), xia/57–58 (599/406–7), xia/61–62 (599/408–9).

19. *Da Ming huidian*, 121/1744.

20. *Ming shi*, 317/5a.

21. *Taizu Hongwu shilu*, 162/2517, 202/4a–5a, 239/1b; *Da Ming huidian*, 77/ 1221–24; *Ming shi*, 316/8186; *Guizhou tongzhi* (1555), 23/2b. In 1444 an imperial edict announced that all heirs of *tusi* and *tuguan* posts must attend school. In 1492 an edict even ordered new *tusi* to study Chinese rules of conduct and Chinese laws before taking charge of *tusi* affairs. In order to encourage the *tusi*'s children to accept Chinese lifeways, in 1499 the court ordered that only an heir who had studied at a local Confucian school since the age of ten could succeed to office without the approval of provincial authorities. He required only a testimonial from the director of education of the school he attended. Finally, in 1503 the court agreed with the Ministry of War and the Censorate that an heir would not be permitted to succeed to the hereditary *tusi* post if he had not received a Confucian (Chinese) education.

22. *Taizu Hongwu shilu*, 239/1b. In 1380 both the Guizhou and Bozhou pacification commissions had constructed schools in their domain headquarters that purportedly made use of a Confucian curriculum, and in the early 1390s the Sinan and Sizhou pacification commissions had both built "Chinese" schools.

23. *Ming shi*, 6/1851–52. Contrary to the information presented above, the *Ming shi* states that Confucian schools were built in most of the *tusi* areas.

24. Mao, *Mansi hezhi*, 2/9.

25. Ibid. In 1409 the governor of Yunnan, Chen Min, dispatched a memorial to the capital in which he stated that since the middle of the Hongwu reign (1368–98) Yunnan had been actively building schools, and now that Yunnan's student population had grown he requested the triennial examinations be held in Yunnan. From this time onward, Yunnan held the provincial examinations (*xiang shi*) (Gong, *Zhongguo tusi zhidu*, 103). In 1425 the Ming state authorized students from Guizhou to take the provincial examination in Huguang, but in the following year Yunnan and Guizhou combined their triennial examinations. Not until 1536 did Guizhou hold its own triennial examinations. Regarding the number of provincial-level students allowed to pass and go on to the metropolitan examination, according to information presented in 1536, the Yunnan quota was forty, and the quota for Guizhou was set at twenty-five. In 1547 the number of students in Guizhou allowed to pass the provincial-level examination was increased by five, thus bringing the quota total to thirty.

26. *Guizhou tongzhi* (1987), 437–99; *Guizhou tongzhi* (1555), 23/12b.

27. *Guizhou tongzhi* (1555), 23/2b–3b; *Da Ming huidian*, 77/1221–24.

28. *Guizhou tongzhi* (1555), 23/4a–b.

29. A number of factors were considered in the Ming decision: the region's strategic importance to the Ming state's control of Yunnan; the extent to which the area's economic infrastructure could support Ming political and military institutions; the overall size of the Chinese population, especially in the eastern half of Guizhou; and the topography of the region and its impact on the ability of the Ming military to project its authority throughout the region.

30. *Guizhou tujing xinzhi*, 2/1a–3b.

31. Ibid., 3/1a–3b, 4/1a–1b, 2a–b, 6/1a–2a, 7/1b, preface, 2b. In addition to the Azhe and Yang patriclans, the text describes the Song family in Shuidong, the Jin family in Jinzhu, the Yu family of Kangzou, as well as the Awangren and Bole patriclans in western Guizhou. For additional information on these families, see Gong, *Zhongguo tusi zhidu*, 752–53, 766–68, 839–40; and *Ming shi*, 316/8168–76, 8185–88.

32. *Guizhou tujing xinzhi*, preface, 1a–b.

33. Twitchett and Grimm, "The Cheng-t'ung, Ching-t'ai, and T'ien-shun Reigns, 1436–1464," 314–15. Thonganbwa is often represented in Chinese texts as Si Renfa. Luchuan was situated in present-day western Yunnan, roughly near the modern cities of Ruili and Longchuan. According to the *Guizhou tongzhi* (1987), in the third month of 1439, Mu Sheng requested 31,500 troops from Huguang, 10,000 troops from Guizhou, and 8,500 troops from Sichuan to assist in the campaign (105).

34. In addition to the troops stationed at Guizhou's *weisuo* units, indigenous troops mobilized by *tusi* were ordered to the Luchuan front. *Guizhou tongzhi*

(1987), 106–9; *Yingzong Zhengtong shilu*, 101/9, 104/6–7, 113/11, 116/1, 117/2, 131/4–5, 146/1, 147/5.

35. *Yingzong Zhengtong shilu*, 187/17, 187/21, 188/6, 188/18, 191/21; *Guizhou tongzhi* (1987), 110–18.

36. *Yingzong shilu*, 188/20, 189/19, 191/6, 191/15, 192/3, 192/23; Twitchett and Grimm, "The Cheng-t'ung, Ching-t'ai, and T'ien-shun Reigns, 1436–1464," 314–16.

37. *Yingzong shilu*, 176/4, 176/10, 177/2–6, 178/2, 179/6, 181/25, 183/31–32; *Guizhou tongzhi* (1987), 110–25. In several instances the Ming state adopted the name of the formal *tusi* administration for its new administrative unit following *gaitu guiliu*. For example, the Shibing *zhangguan si* became Shibing county, Maha *zhangguan si* became Maha department, and Qingping *zhangguan si* became Qingping county.

38. *Yingzong shilu*, 203/8–9, 206/8, 207/15–16; *Guizhou tongzhi* (1987), 110–25.

39. *Yingzong shilu*, 210/4–5, 212/2, 214/1, 216/20–21; *Guizhou tongzhi* (1987), 123–49.

40. Gong, *Zhongguo tusi zhidu*, 900–902.

41. Xu, *Xu Xiake youji*, 47.

42. Guo, *Qianji*, 17/3b.

43. Xu, *Xu Xiake youji*, 48.

44. *Yingzong shilu*, 223/15, 225/5, 226/1, 240/3–4, 243/4; *Guizhou tongzhi* (1987), 155–58.

45. *Guizhou tongzhi* (1987), 157.

46. In 1384, the Hongwu emperor bestowed the title of Caotang military commissioner upon Song Bangzou, a descendent of Chinese mercenaries who had answered the Tang emperor's call to fight the invading Nanzhao forces, just as the Yang patriclan in Bozhou had done. Hongwu ordered the Caotang military commission to be politically subordinate to the powerful Bozhou pacification commission, and this administrative hierarchy remained in place even after the creation of Guizhou province in 1413. Song was authorized to grant minor titles to worthy recipients in the Caotang region, such as the Lu, Cai, Luo, and Jiang families, and each family maintained an armed militia to protect its area. As one Ming official noted when looking over the landscape of Caotang, "the *tusi*," in this case referring to Chinese families that had been assigned *tusi* posts by the Caotang authorities, "were like islands in a sea of Miao" (Guo, *Qianji*, 13/17a–20a).

47. *Guizhou tongzhi* (1987), 155.

48. *Yingzong shilu*, 240/3–4; *Guizhou tongzhi* (1987), 156.

49. *Yingzong shilu*, 240/3–4, 243/4; *Guizhou tongzhi* (1987), 157–58. Following the suppression of Huang Long, the Ming military withdrew from the Caotang-Huangping area and hurriedly rebuilt its ailing military infrastructure

in Guizhou. The devastated Caotang-Huangping area was technically within the jurisdiction of the Bozhou pacification commission, and for this reason Yang Hui acted as if the territory and its inhabitants were his property. Nevertheless, when the Ming state conferred the title of military commissioner upon Song Chaomei of Caotang in 1384, this act of imperial recognition emboldened Song and his descendants to act as if they were obligated to two lords, the Yang patriclan in Bozhou and the Ming state. The newfound imperial recognition allowed Song to use the Ming state to stymie the authority of the Bozhou. The same could be said for the Wen patriclan of Huangping, who were also granted the title of military commissioner in 1384 by Hongwu. According to several Ming accounts, Yang Hui used the campaign against Huang Long as a pretext to punish the Caotang and Huangping military commissions by ordering their forces into battle first, thus reserving his Bozhou forces for less dangerous mop-up operations. Ming field commander Jiang Lin noted caustically the tense situation when he said, "[Yang] Hui relies on others to win his battles, but he quickly claims all the glory" (*Guizhou tongzhi* [1987], 158).

50. *Yingzong shilu,* 240/3–4, 243/4; *Guizhou tongzhi* (1987), 157–58.

51. Mao, *Mansi hezhi,* 4/12b–14a; Tian, *Yanjiao jiwen,* 4/59a–b; Li, "The Control of the Szechwan-Kweichow Frontier Regions," 67–68, 184–89.

52. *Xianzong Chenghua shilu,* 140/1–2, 151/3, 160/14, 162/6, 169/2, 180/3–4, 194/1–2, 197/3–4; *Guizhou tongzhi* (1987), 181–86, 190–92.

53. *Xianzong Chenghua shilu,* 194/1–2, 197/3–4; *Guizhou tongzhi* (1987), 185–86, 190–92.

54. *Xianzong Chenghua shilu,* 194/1–2, 197/3–4; *Guizhou tongzhi* (1987), 185–86, 190–92.

55. *Xiaozong Hongzhi shilu,* 282/17; *Guizhou tongzhi* (1987), 195–98.

56. Tian, *Yanjiao jiwen,* 4/59b–60a.

57. Ibid., 4/60a.

58. *Guizhou tongzhi* (1987), 234.

59. *Xianzong Chenghua shilu,* 198/1–3.

60. *Ming shi,* 5159–69; *Guizhou tongzhi* (1987), 234–39; Goodrich and Fang, *Dictionary of Ming Biography,* 1408–16. Longchang is the present-day city of Xiuwen. It was also during a three-year stint at Longzhang that Wang experienced an intellectual awakening (the foundation for Ming Neo-Confucianism) that was to have a profound impact on the intellectual history of China, Japan, and Korea.

61. *Guizhou tongzhi* (1987), 235–37.

62. Ibid.

63. Tian Rucheng was a native of Hangzhou. He received his *jinshi* degree in 1526 and immediately embarked on a controversial political career. There are two editions to the *Yanjiao jiwen:* the first published under this title in 1560 with preface by Tian Rucheng; the second, titled *Xingbian jiwen,* was published

in 1557 with preface by Gu Mingru. See *Ming shi*, 7372; Goodrich and Fang, *Dictionary of Ming Biography*, 1286–87.

64. Tian, *Yanjiao jiwen*, 4/59a–60a.

65. Ibid., 4/61a–b.

66. Ibid., 4/52b. Tian's position with respect to *tusi* and Ming policy toward the southwest frontier was the antithesis of what had been advocated by Wang Shouren and his supporters, and Tian littered his text with unflattering comments about the failures of Wang's policies in the southwest.

67. *Xiaozong Hongzhi shilu*, 184/1–2, 189/4–5; *Guizhou tongzhi* (1987), 225–30.

68. Brook, *The Confusions of Pleasure*, 87.

69. *Guizhou tongzhi* (1555), 3/35a–46b; *Guizhou tongzhi* (1987), 284; Wang, *Mingdai de juntun*, 27–64; Jiang, *Mingdai Yunnan jingnei de tuguan yu tusi*, 5–79.

70. *Guizhou tongzhi* (1555), 3/41b–42a.

71. Liang, *Zhongguo lidai hukou, tiandi, tianfu tongji*, 325; *Yunnan tongzhi* (1553), 1/37a–b; *Yingzong Zhengtong shilu*, 80/9.

72. *Guizhou tongzhi* (1597), 19/9b.

73. *Guizhou tongzhi* (1555), 3/47a; *Guizhou tongzhi* (1597), 7/12a. In 2001, 75.4 percent of the registered population in Guizhou was classified as Han Chinese.

74. Brook, *The Confusions of Pleasure*, 26–27.

75. *Guizhou tongzhi* (1987), 232.

76. *Guizhou tongzhi* (1555), 3/47a. If one adds military and civilian households, the total (118,957) is 30,000 less than the total figure given in the text. Likewise, if one adds the figures given for military and civilian "mouths," the total (516,289) is 4,000 greater than what was given in the text. Information like this makes determining the size of Guizhou's population very difficult.

77. *Guizhou tongzhi* (1555), 3/47a–55b. As was made clear in the previous chapter, the Ming garrisons in Guizhou were built in towns that were originally established by the local population.

78. Ibid., 3/52a.

79. Ibid., 3/51b.

80. Ibid., 3/22a–b.

81. *Guizhou tongzhi* (1597), 3/23b–24b.

82. According to Guo Zizhang, of the total number of registered households (111,552) in Guizhou in 1602, 51,212 were listed as civilian households and 60,340 were classified as military households. The registered military population in 1602 remained unchanged from its 1597 figure of 184,601. According to the *Ming shi*, in Hongzhi 4 (1491) there were 43,367 households in Guizhou, whereas in Wanli 6 (1578) there were 43,450 households. The figures in this text were compiled in Wanli 25 (1597) and in Wanli 30 (1602). According to figures compiled in the previous Guizhou gazetteer (1597), there were 148,957 households and 512,289 people (*dingkou*) in mid-sixteenth-century Guizhou.

Military households accounted for 72,273 (this figure is different by 10,000 from what is recorded above), whereas the military population (*dingkou*) was 261,869. The civilian households totaled 66,684 (this figure is also different from the previous figure by 10,000), whereas the population was estimated at 250,420. According to the figures compiled in Wanli 25, there were 105,906 households, and a population of 509,975. There were 59,340 military households, with a total military population of 184,601. There were 46,566 civilian households, with a total population of 325,374. In Wanli 30, based on the Yellow Register, there were 48,746 households, with a total population of 324,989 (Guo, *Qianji*, 3/2a–3a).

83. *Yingzong Zhengtong shilu*, 80/9.

84. *Guizhou tongzhi* (1555), 3/35a–b.

85. *Guizhou tongzhi* (1597), 19/9b–12b.

86. Ibid.; Guo, *Qianji*, 19/2a–3a.

87. *Guizhou tongzhi* (1597), 19/11b–12a; Guo, *Qianji*, 19/3a. In 1513, there were about 700 military farm complexes in Guizhou, but only 93 included irrigation works.

88. Guo, *Qianji*, 19/7a; *Yunnan tongzhi* (1736), 27/32a–b; *Dianhai yuhengzhi*, 7/4b–5a.

89. Guo, *Qianji*, 19/5b.

90. *Guizhou tongzhi* (1741), 45/38a–b.

91. As early as 1576, the local history of Yunnan recorded, "In Jingdong Prefecture the non-Han [Chinese] used to plant oats as their staple, but now plant rice and corn" (*Yunnan tongzhi* [1574], 4/11a). By the early seventeenth century maize had become an important crop among the Nasu of the Ailao Mountains, but, according to Guo Zizhang, buckwheat remained the staple crop in both Yunnan and Guizhou (*Qianji*, 4/3b–7a).

92. *Guizhou tongzhi* (1987), 370; von Glahn, *The Country of Streams and Grottoes*, 205–20.

93. *Yunnan tongzhi* (1736), 33/12b.

94. *Taizu Hongwu shilu*, 79/4.

95. *Taizong Yongle shilu*, 88/3.

96. *Guizhou tongzhi* (1555), 4/2a–b; *Guizhou tongzhi* (1597), 18/13a–16b, 19/6b–7b; Guo, *Qianji*, 19/1b, 19/17a; Li, "The Control of the Szechwan-Kweichow Frontier Regions," 63–65.

97. *Guizhou tongzhi* (1555), 4/2a–b; *Guizhou tongzhi* (1597), 18/13a–16b; Guo, *Qianji*, 19/17a.

98. Fan, *Manshu jiaozhu*, 1/31–35; *Yuan shi*, 94/2382–84.

99. *Guizhou tongzhi* (1597), 4/10b–23b; Guo, *Qianji*, 5/1b–14a.

100. *Guizhou tongzhi* (1597), 4/10b–23b; *Yunnan tongzhi* (1736), 6/6b–12a; Guo, *Qianji*, 5/1b–14a.

101. Wang, *Qian zhi*, 3/2b–3b; Wolf, *Sons of the Shaking Earth*.

102. Wang, *Qian zhi*, 3/3b.
103. Tian, *Qian shu*, 4/79–80.
104. Ibid., 4/80.
105. Ibid.

## Chapter 5

1. Shuixi forces were composed of Miao, Pu (Qilao), Zhong (Buyi), and Han Chinese marching in front of the Nasu cavalry. Thus, the entire male population of the Shuixi region was eligible to be mobilized for war (Hu, *Ming Qing Yizu shehui*, 36–37). At the beginning of the sixteenth century, the Guizhou pacification commissioner boasted he had 480,000 troops under his command. And during the Jiajing reign (1522–66), Ming officials estimated that the Guizhou pacification commissioner could bring nearly 500,000 troops to the battlefield.

2. *Xianzong Chenghua shilu*, 198/1b–3b.

3. *Dading fuzhi*, 8/11b.

4. *Guizhou tongzhi* (1987), 532.

5. In 1981 a large bronze bell, the Chenghua Bell (*chenghua zhong*), was discovered in an elementary school in Dafang. The bell had both Chinese and Nasu characters written on its side. It was cast in 1485 (the twenty-first year of the Chenghua reign) and placed in the recently constructed Yongxing Temple. The contents of the Chinese and Nasu inscriptions are different, but both indicate the arrival of Buddhism in Shuixi and its patronage by the Azhe (An) patriclan. See Ma and Luo, *Cuanwen congke*, 211–14; and Wu and Long, "Guizhou Dafang xian Yizu lishi," 183–84, 190–91.

6. *Xianzong Chenghua shilu*, 278/6b–7a; *Guizhou tongzhi* (1987), 195–98. Chinese sources throughout the sixteenth century vacillate on how they refer to An Guirong's descendants: either they are identified as the Guizhou pacification commissioners or they are depicted as the Shuixi pacification commissioners.

7. *Guizhou tongzhi* (1987), 198–99.

8. Ibid., 201.

9. Ibid., 204–5.

10. *Xiaozong Hongzhi shilu*, 38/11a–b, 86/1a, 87/6b, 88/8a–b; *Guizhou tongzhi* (1987), 182–83, 208. For information on Milu, see *Xiaozong Hongzhi shilu*, 151/9b–11b, 154/13a–15b, 176/10b–11b; *Guizhou tongzhi* (1987), 215–19.

11. *Xiaozong Hongzhi shilu*, 189/4a–5a; *Guizhou tongzhi* (1987), 221–32.

12. *Guizhou tongzhi* (1987), 234; *Ming shi*, 195/5159–68; Goodrich and Fang, *Dictionary of Ming Biography*, 1408–10.

13. *Guizhou tongzhi* (1987), 235–37.

14. Ibid., 240; *Wuzong Zhengde shilu*, 101/3a–4a.

15. *Guizhou tongzhi* (1987), 243–45; *Wuzong Zhengde shilu*, 126/1a–b, 126/10a–b.

16. *Shizong Jiajing shilu*, 24/13a–b, 40/4b, 43/4a–b, 44/6a–b, 48/7a, 53/1a–b, 53/4a; *Guizhou tongzhi* (1987), 247–48.

17. *Shizong Jiajing shilu*, 187/7b–8b, 201/6b, 204/7a–8a; *Guizhou tongzhi* (1987), 248–49.

18. *Shizong Jiajing shilu*, 284/1a, 286/5a–7b; *Guizhou tongzhi* (1987), 264.

19. *Shizong Jiajing shilu*, 290/3a; *Guizhou tongzhi* (1987), 295–96.

20. *Yuan shi*, 12/256.

21. *Dading fuzhi*, 4/14a; *Ming shi*, 311/23b.

22. Qu, *Wanli wugong lu*, 23/15b; *Guizhou tongzhi* (1987), 303–4, 305–8, 308–15, 324–25, 333–34; *Dading xianzhi*, 18/7b.

23. *Guizhou tongzhi* (1741), 13/27b; Ma and Luo, *Cuanwen congke*, 204–10.

24. *Dading fuzhi*, 2/4a–b; Wu and Long, "Guizhou Dafang xian Yizu lishi," 191–92. The stele, titled *Xinxiu Qiansui qu beiji*, is dated 1592.

25. *Dading fuzhi*, 2/4a–b; Wu and Long, "Guizhou Dafang xian Yizu lishi," 191–92.

26. Liu, *Qiannan shiji*, *Weicheng rilu*, 2/13b–14b; *Guizhou tongzhi* (1987), 347–48, 370. To the southeast of Shuixi, in an area where Nasu, non-Nasu, and Han Chinese lived, there were several markets established by Chinese merchants who supposedly named their markets after the twelve heavenly stems and earthly branches. In 1638 Xu Xiake traveled along the southern portion of the Shuixi region between Qingya and Shuicheba, and he noticed many Sichuan merchants engaged in commerce there.

27. Liu, *Qiannan shiji*, *Weicheng rilu*, 2/13b–21a; *Guizhou tongzhi* (1987), 303–4, 513–24, 536.

28. Guo, *Qianji*, 2/4b.

29. *Guizhou tongzhi* (1987), 383–84.

30. Hu, *Ming Qing Yizu shehui*, 12.

31. Liu, *Qiannan shiji*, *Weicheng rilu*, 2/13b–14b. In 1607 the Ming court asked local officials to prepare 12,298 of Shuixi's "finest" trees to be cut and shipped to Beijing.

32. Liu, *Qiannan shiji*, *Weicheng rilu*, 2/19a–20a.

33. Ma and Luo, *Cuanwen congke*, 161–203; Wu and Long, "Guizhou Dafang xian Yizu lishi," 186–90.

34. *Dading fuzhi*, 2/4a–b; Wu and Long, "Guizhou Dafang xian Yizu lishi," 187–88.

35. Wu and Long, "Guizhou Dafang xian Yizu lishi," 188–89.

36. *Guizhou tongzhi* (1741), 13/29a–b; *Guiyang fuzhou*, 40/17a; Bao, *Nanzhong jiwen*, 94/48.

37. Bao, *Nanzhong jiwen*, 94/48–49; Wang, *Qian zhi*, 3/5a–b; *Dading fuzhi*, 5/5a–b; Hu, *Ming Qing Yizu shehui*, 11.

38. Bao, *Nanzhong jiwen*, 94/48; Wang, *Qian zhi*, 3/7b–9a; *Dading fuzhi*, 5/5b; Hu, *Ming Qing Yizu shehui*, 11.

39. Wang, *Qian zhi*, 3/8a; *Guiyang fuzhou*, 40/11b; Bao, *Nanzhong jiwen*, 94/48–53; Hu, *Ming Qing Yizu shehui*, 11.

40. *Guiyang fuzhou*, 40/8b–9b; Bao, *Nanzhong jiwen*, 94/48–53; Hu, *Ming Qing Yizu shehui*, 11.

41. *Dading fuzhi*, 5/7b–9a; *Guiyang fuzhou*, 40/8b–9b; Bao, *Nanzhong jiwen*, 94/50; Wang, *Qian zhi*, 3/9a–b.

42. *Guizhou tongzhi* (1741), 48/16a.

43. Qu, *Wanli wugong lu*, 23/15a.

44. *Guizhou tongzhi* (1987), 300–301; *Shizong Jiajing shilu*, 425/1; Qu, *Wanli wugong lu*, 23/1–17b.

45. Qu, *Wanli wugong lu*, 1a–27a; *Guizhou tongzhi* (1987), 308–14. Prior to 1570 An Guoheng had made a number of tribute missions to the Ming capital, and each time he was listed as a "tribal leader" (*tushe*), not the pacification commissioner. In the fifth month of 1570, Ming authorities were informed that An Guoheng had killed his uncle An Wanquan and usurped the post of pacification commissioner (*Muzong Longqing shilu*, 44/9b–10b).

46. *Guizhou tongzhi* (1987), 303–4; *Muzong Longqing shilu*, 44/9b–10b.

47. *Guizhou tongzhi* (1987), 303–5; *Muzong Longqing shilu*, 44/9b–10b.

48. *Guizhou tongzhi* (1987), 305–6.

49. Qu, *Wanli wugong lu*, 4b–6a; *Guizhou tongzhi* (1987), 306.

50. Qu, *Wanli wugong lu*, 5b–6a; *Guizhou tongzhi* (1987), 312–14; *Muzong Longqing shilu*, 55/36a–b.

51. Qu, *Wanli wugong lu*, 6b–8a; *Guizhou tongzhi* (1987), 313–14.

52. *Shenzong Wanli shilu*, 77/11a–b, 79/6a.

53. Qu, *Wanli wugong lu*, 15a–19b; *Guizhou tongzhi* (1987), 305–15; *Muzong Longqing shilu*, 62/3a–b.

54. Qu, *Wanli wugong lu*, 16a–24b; *Guizhou tongzhi* (1987), 330–34; *Shenzong Wanli shilu*, 175/1b–2b, 190/8a–b, 194/6b, 200/11a–b, 202/6a–b, 230/8b–9a, 307/9b. Ming officials grew increasingly concerned about reports describing how Han Chinese settlements were under assault, and how those captured were sold to Nasu merchants for transport to Shuixi, Yongning, Wumang, and Dongchuan (*Guizhou tongzhi* [1987], 324–25).

55. Qu, *Wanli wugong lu*, 16a–24b; *Guizhou tongzhi* (1741), 52/8a–14b.

56. Qu, *Wanli wugong lu*, 16a–24b; *Guizhou tongzhi* (1741), 52/13b–15b.

57. Qu, *Wanli wugong lu*, 20b–24b; *Mingshi gao*, 1/33, 2/298; *Ming shi*, 1/83, 7/1995; Li, "The Control of the Szechwan-Kweichow Frontier Regions," 82.

58. Qu, *Wanli wugong lu*, 22a–24b; *Guizhou tongzhi* (1987), 347–48.

59. Qu, *Wanli wugong lu*, 22a–24b; *Guizhou tongzhi* (1987), 347–48.

60. *Shenzong Wanli shilu*, 8/17a, 57/13a–b, 101/3a, 169/3a, 170/12a–13b, 185/4a–b, 190/7a; Li, "The Control of the Szechwan-Kweichow Frontier Regions," 84–85.

61. *Shenzong Wanli shilu*, 185/4a–b, 232/3a; Li, "The Control of the Szechwan-Kweichow Frontier Regions," 84.

62. *Shenzong Wanli shilu*, 230/6a–b, 289/11a–b; Li, "The Control of the Szechwan-Kweichow Frontier Regions," 86–87; *Guizhou tongzhi* (1987), 345–50.

63. *Guizhou tongzhi* (1987), 349–52.

64. *Shenzong Wanli shilu*, 375/1b–2a, 378/2a–4a; *Guizhou tongzhi* (1987), 555–57.

65. *Shenzong Wanli shilu*, 235/2b; Li, "The Control of the Szechwan-Kweichow Frontier Regions," 88.

66. *Shenzong Wanli shilu*, 247/8a, 235/2b; *Guizhou tongzhi* (1987), 361–62; Li, "The Control of the Szechwan-Kweichow Frontier Regions," 88–89.

67. *Shenzong Wanli shilu*, 266/4a–b, 266/5b–6b, 271/5b–6a, 278/3a–4b.

68. Li, "The Control of the Szechwan-Kweichow Frontier Regions," 89–91.

69. *Guizhou tongzhi* (1987), 357–59, 370; *Shenzong Wanli shilu*, 284/7a–b, 324/3b–4b.

70. Li, "The Control of the Szechwan-Kweichow Frontier Regions," 90–94; *Guizhou tongzhi* (1987), 369–72.

71. *Guizhou tongzhi* (1987), 370–73, 393.

72. Ibid., 370–73; *Shenzong Wanli shilu*, 333/7a–b.

73. *Guizhou tongzhi* (1987), 383–90; *Shenzong Wanli shilu*, 320/4a–5a.

74. *Guizhou tongzhi* (1987), 385.

75. *Shenzong Wanli shilu*, 329/2a–b, 332/4a–b; *Guizhou tongzhi* (1987), 383–90, 404–5, 422–23, 513–24. Though my focus is on Yang Yinglong's activities in Guizhou, I must point out that Yang's forces were threatening much of southern Sichuan, especially the major city of Chongqing.

76. Gu, *Rizhi lu jishi*, 9/35b.

77. *Shenzong Wanli shilu*, 332/5b. For additional information on Guo Zizhang, see Goodrich and Fang, *Dictionary of Ming Biography*, 775–77.

78. *Shenzong Wanli shilu*, 332/9b; *Guizhou tongzhi* (1987), 383–90, 404–5, 422–23, 513–24, 524–26, 530–32. For additional information on Li Hualong, see *Ming shi*, 228/5982–85; Goodrich and Fang, *Dictionary of Ming Biography*, 822–26.

79. *Shenzong Wanli shilu*, 338/2a–3b, 339/2a–b, 339/13b–14b, 344/4a–5b.

80. Ibid., 343/5a–6b, 343/8b–9b; *Guizhou tongzhi* (1987), 411; Li, "The Control of the Szechwan-Kweichow Frontier Regions," 124–25. By relying heavily on *tusi* troops, the government was able to negotiate around the fact that it had very little money to contribute to the campaign. The Ming state spent over 1,878,000 taels of silver on the Pubei campaign in 1592, and over 7,822,000 taels of silver in fighting the Japanese in Korea from 1592 to 1598. To help pay

for the campaign, the financially strapped state announced on November 27, 1599, an additional grain surtax to be levied in Huguang and Sichuan. Every *shi* of grain was to be taxed an additional 0.12 taels of silver. As a result, Sichuan was able to raise 123,425 taels, and Huguang raised 260,223 taels. Private donations contributed 1,616,722 taels.

81. *Guizhou tongzhi* (1987), 414–15; Li, "The Control of the Szechwan-Kweichow Frontier Regions," 150–51.

82. *Guizhou tongzhi* (1987), 513–24, 524–25; Li, "The Control of the Szechwan-Kweichow Frontier Regions," 152; *Shenzong Wanli shilu*, 357/8a–b, 358/6b.

83. *Shenzong Wanli shilu*, 358/13a–14; *Guizhou tongzhi* (1987), 349–52, 370–73; Guo, *Qianji*, 5/2a–b; Li, "The Control of the Szechwan-Kweichow Frontier Regions," 78–118.

84. *Guizhou tongzhi* (1987), 524–25, 530–32; *Guizhou tongzhi* (1597), 4/8b–9a.

85. *Guizhou tongzhi* (1987), 383–90, 513–24, 525–26, 530–32, 536, 546–49; Qu, *An Guoheng zhuanlie*, 23/19a–b.

86. *Shenzong Wanli shilu*, 374/3a–b, 383/13a–b, 430/5b–6b; *Guizhou tongzhi* (1987), 513–24, 524–26, 530–32, 536, 557–63, 586–89.

87. *Shenzong Wanli shilu*, 414/5b–6b, 420/2a–4b, 422/6a–b.

88. *Guizhou tongzhi* (1987), 570–73.

89. She Shixu was An Wanquan's daughter and niece of the current Shuixi pacification commissioner, An Jiangchen. She was renowned for her beauty and intelligence, and she reportedly spoke and read Chinese, which she learned while growing up in Guiyang. *Shenzong Wanli shilu*, 130/6a–b, 132/11a–b, 135/8a–b; Xu, "Lun She An shijian," 19–20; Hu, "Yetan She An qiyi de xingzhi," 26–27; Hu, *Ming Qing Yizu shehui*, 93–101; *Xi'nan Yizhi*, 328–32.

90. *Shenzong Wanli shilu*, 386/10a–11b, 387/11a–b, 418/20a–21b; *Guizhou tongzhi* (1987), 564–66.

91. *Shenzong Wanli shilu*, 432/9a–10b; *Guizhou tongzhi* (1987), 564–66.

92. *Shenzong Wanli shilu*, 432/9a–10b, 434/14b–15b, 438/3a–5b.

93. *Shenzong Wanli shilu*, 474/3b–4b, 498/15a–16b; *Guizhou tongzhi* (1987), 565–66.

94. *Shenzong Wanli shilu*, 474/3b–4b, 498/15a–16b; *Guizhou tongzhi* (1987), 566.

95. *Shenzong Wanli shilu*, 543/8b; *Guizhou tongzhi* (1987), 565–66. An Yaochen was An Jiangchen's younger brother. The succession, therefore, bypassed An Jiangchen's children in favor of An Yaochen and his children.

96. *Guizhou tongzhi* (1987), 577–79, 598–99.

97. *Shenzong Wanli shilu*, 570/13a–b; *Guizhou tongzhi* (1987), 598–601.

98. *Guizhou tongzhi* (1987), 566, 570–73, 598–99; *Xizong Tianqi shilu*, 11/13b–14b, 12/28a.

99. *Guizhou tongzhi* (1987), 618–19; *Ming shi*, 249/6450–51.

100. *Guizhou tongzhi* (1987), 595.

101. Ibid., 598–99, 635; *Shenzong Wanli shilu*, 596/12b–13b.

102. *Guizhou tongzhi* (1987), 630–32; *Xizong Tianqi shilu*, 4/14b.

103. *Guizhou tongzhi* (1987), 630–32; *Xizong Tianqi shilu*, 9/14a–b; Xu, "Lun She An shijian," 20–23; Hu, "Yetan She An qiyi de xingzhi," 26–27; Hu, *Ming Qing Yizu shehui*, 93–101; *Xi'nan Yizhi*, 328–32.

104. *Guizhou tongzhi* (1987), 630–32; *Xizong Tianqi shilu*, 9/14a–b; Zha, *Zuiwei lu*, 34/2802; Xu, "Lun She An shijian," 20–23; Hu, "Yetan She An qiyi de xingzhi," 26–27; Hu, *Ming Qing Yizu shehui*, 93–101; *Xi'nan Yizhi*, 328–32.

105. She Chongming remained the "king of Shu" until 1628, when he changed his title to "king of Greater Liang" (*Da Liang wang*).

106. *Guizhou tongzhi* (1987), 630–31; Xu, "Lun She An shijian," 20–23; "Yetan She An qiyi de xingzhi," 26–27; Hu, *Ming Qing Yizu shehui*, 93–101; *Xi'nan Yizhi*, 328–32.

107. *Guizhou tongzhi* (1987), 630–31.

108. Ibid.

109. Ibid., 635; *Xizong Tianqi shilu*, 11/13b–14b; Xu, "Lun She An shijian," 20–23; Hu, "Yetan She An qiyi de xingzhi," 26–27; Hu, *Ming Qing Yizu shehui*, 93–101; *Xi'nan Yizhi*, 328–32.

110. *Guizhou tongzhi* (1987), 635; Xu, "Lun She An shijian," 20–23; Hu, "Yetan She An qiyi de xingzhi," 26–27; Hu, *Ming Qing Yizu shehui*, 93–101; *Xi'nan Yizhi*, 328–32.

111. *Guizhou tongzhi* (1987), 636, 637–39; Xu, "Lun She An shijian," 20–23; Hu, "Yetan She An qiyi de xingzhi," 26–27; Hu, *Ming Qing Yizu shehui*, 93–101; *Xi'nan Yizhi*, 328–32.

112. *Guizhou tongzhi* (1987), 637; Xu, "Lun She An shijian," 20–23; Hu, "Yetan She An qiyi de xingzhi," 26–27; Hu, *Ming Qing Yizu shehui*, 93–101; *Xi'nan Yizhi*, 328–32.

113. *Guizhou tongzhi* (1987), 638–39, 640–42; Xu, "Lun She An shijian," 20–23; Hu, "Yetan She An qiyi de xingzhi," 26–27; Hu, *Ming Qing Yizu shehui*, 93–101; *Xi'nan Yizhi*, 328–32.

114. *Guizhou tongzhi* (1987), 638–39, 640–42; Xu, "Lun She An shijian," 20–23; Hu, "Yetan She An qiyi de xingzhi," 26–27.

115. *Guizhou tongzhi* (1987), 637–40; Xu, "Lun She An shijian," 20–23; Hu, "Yetan She An qiyi de xingzhi," 26–27; Hu, *Ming Qing Yizu shehui*, 93–101; *Xi'nan Yizhi*, 328–32.

116. *Guizhou tongzhi* (1987), 637–40; Xu, "Lun She An shijian," 20–23; Hu, "Yetan She An qiyi de xingzhi," 26–27; Hu, *Ming Qing Yizu shehui*, 93–101; *Xi'nan Yizhi*, 328–32.

117. Ibid.

118. Each foot soldier in the Shuixi army brought with him two horses for mount, and every five soldiers had a servant. See *Guizhou tongzhi* (1987), 638–42; and *Xizong Tianqi shilu*, 14/8a–b. For a firsthand account of the siege, see Liu, *Qiannan shiji, Weicheng rilu*. For additional information on Liu Xixuan, see *Ming shi*, 249/6451–54.

119. Liu, *Qiannan shiji, Weicheng rilu*, 2/5b–9a; *Guizhou tongzhi* (1987), 646–49; *Xizong Tianqi shilu*, 14/16a. The *Tianqi shilu* states that immediately outside Guiyang's city walls there were over forty thousand people residing in makeshift homes.

120. Liu, *Qiannan shiji, Weicheng rilu*, 2/6b–10b.

121. *Guizhou tongzhi* (1987), 646; *Xizong Tianqi shilu*, 13/21a–b.

122. *Xizong Tianqi shilu*, 14/8a–b; Liu, *Qiannan shiji, Weicheng rilu*, 2/10a.

123. *Xizong Tianqi shilu*, 14/25a–b; Liu, *Qiannan shiji, Weicheng rilu*, 2/7a–11b.

124. Liu, *Qiannan shiji, Weicheng rilu*, 2/11b–17a.

125. After making this fateful decision to change tactics, An Bangyan allowed much of his force to return to Shuixi for rest, and as a result a Ming relief force of 20,000 organized by Zhang Yanfang, the garrison commander in Zhenjiang, Huguang, set out for Guiyang. Though Zhang's troops had to fight their way to Guiyang, 5,500 out of the original 20,000 troops were able to make it into Guiyang at the end of the fourth month of the siege. See *Xizong Tianqi shilu*, 15/21a–b; and Liu, *Qiannan shiji, Weicheng rilu*, 2/14a–18b.

126. Liu, *Qiannan shiji, Weicheng rilu*, 2/20b–26b; Xu, "Lun She An shijian," 20–23; Hu, "Yetan She An qiyi de xingzhi," 26–27; Hu, *Ming Qing Yizu shehui*, 93–101.

127. Liu, *Qiannan shiji, Weicheng rilu*, 2/50b–51a; *Xizong Tianqi shilu*, 19/33a.

128. *Guizhou tongzhi* (1987), 646–49; Liu, *Qiannan shiji, Weicheng rilu*, 2/32b–39a.

129. *Guizhou tongzhi* (1987), 642; Liu, *Qiannan shiji, Weicheng rilu*, 2/38b; *Ming shi*, 249/6454–58.

130. *Guizhou tongzhi* (1987), 648–49; *Xizong Tianqi shilu*, 22/8b, 22/10a, 22/11a–12b, 24/6b–7a; *Xi'nan Yizhi*, 328–32.

131. *Guizhou tongzhi* (1987), 643, 649–51; *Xizong Tianqi shilu*, 25/21a–22a, 26/15b–17a, 26/30a–31a, 27/8b–9b, 27/20a–22a, 27/23a–24b, 27/30b–34b, 32/26a–b; *Ming shi*, 249/6457.

132. *Dading fuzhi*, 7/6b; *Guizhou tongzhi* (1987), 650; *Xizong Tianqi shilu*, 32/25b–26a. Yaozhou was the Song dynasty name for Mugebaizhage.

133. *Xizong Tianqi shilu*, 37/26a–27a, 32a–b, 38/1a, 6a–b, 39/9a–10b, 39/12b–14b; *Guizhou tongzhi* (1987), 659; Xu, "Lun She An shijian," 20–23; Hu, "Yetan She An qiyi de xingzhi," 26–27; Hu, *Ming Qing Yizu shehui*, 93–101.

134. *Guizhou tongzhi* (1987), 658–60.

135. *Xizong Tianqi shilu*, 29/12a, 30/31a, 31/5b. In 1628 She Chongming proclaimed himself the "king of Greater Liang" in an attempt to reach across ethnic lines to attract Han Chinese to his cause. In the same year, An Bangyan became the "august elder of the four descendants" (*siyi da zhanglao*) in an appeal to the Nasu in the region.

136. *Xizong Tianqi shilu*, 50/1a–b, 50/2b–3b, 53/2a–3a; *Guizhou tongzhi* (1987), 663–70.

137. *Xizong Tianqi shilu*, 53/2a–3a, 64/27b–28a, 65/37b–38a; *Huaizong Chongzhen shilu*, 2/4b, 2/7a–b; *Guizhou tongzhi* (1987), 700.

138. For information on Zhu Xieyuan, see *Ming shi*, 249/6439–47.

139. *Huaizong Chongzhen shilu*, 2/4b; *Dading fuzhi*, 7/9a–b; *Guizhou tongzhi* (1987), 703.

140. *Guizhou tongzhi* (1987), 703–4.

141. Ibid., 708; Xu, "Lun She An shijian," 20–23; Hu, "Yetan She An qiyi de xingzhi," 26–27; Hu, *Ming Qing Yizu shehui*, 93–101.

142. *Huaizong Chongzhen shilu*, 2/10b, 3/10a–b, 4/3b; *Guizhou tongzhi* (1987), 708–9; Xu, "Lun She An shijian," 20–23; Hu, "Yetan She An qiyi de xingzhi," 26–27; Hu, *Ming Qing Yizu shehui*, 93–101.

143. *Guizhou tongzhi* (1987), 661–63. According to Sichuan Regional Inspector Zhang Lun's detailed accounting of the costs of the rebellion, every year Sichuan authorities assembled over 160,000 troops (some counties sent 4,000 to 5,000 troops into battle, whereas most counties sent 2,000 to 3,000 soldiers), and every day Sichuan spent 4,000 taels in silver and 2,400 *shi* in grain.

144. Ibid., 678, 708–12, 720–26; *Ming shi*, 249/6446–47.

145. *Guizhou tongzhi* (1987), 708–12, 720–26; *Ming shi*, 249/6446–47. By Han Chinese customs, what Zhu Xieyuan was referring to was language, surnames, a Confucian education, and marriage and burial rituals. Zhu believed that only through the judicious use of Chinese law could the "rough behavior" of the people of Shuixi be changed.

146. *Guizhou tongzhi* (1987), 711.

147. *Ming shi*, 249/6446; Zha, *Zuiwei lu*, 34/2805.

148. *Ming shi*, 249/6446; Zha, *Zuiwei lu*, 34/2805.

149. Belief in the ability of the Chinese legal system to influence in a positive manner the behavior of the non-Han Chinese population of Guizhou was more fully explicated in 1659 by the Guizhou governor Zhao Tingchen (d. 1669). According to Governor Zhao, "There is no place where education cannot be used and no village where barbarian customs cannot be enriched. As tricky and greedy as the Miao are, they can be transformed into honest and trustworthy people. To those Miao who create trouble along our main transportation routes, we should control them by establishing the community self-policing organization [*baojia*] in their villages. In those situations when killings result in revenge feuds, we should punish the guilty according to Chinese laws.

The barbarians will then learn that our rewards and punishments are just and reliable" (*Qing Shizu zhang huangdi shilu,* 126/14a–b).

## Chapter 6

1. Struve, "The Southern Ming, 1644–1662," 701.

2. By 1641 there were more than a handful of imperial princes sequestered on large estates throughout the country, but Zhu Changxun was special. Shortly after Zhu's birth in 1586, his father, the Wanli emperor, announced that he had selected Zhu Changxun to be heir to the throne, much to the dismay of the imperial family and court ministers. The rightful heir to the throne was Zhu Changle (1582–1620), Wanli's firstborn son. For fifteen years court life ground to a halt over the right to name the heir apparent. Finally, in 1601, Wanli acquiesced and named Zhu Changle heir apparent. He also gave Zhu Changxun the title "prince of Fu" and granted him vast estates in Henan, although Zhu Changxun remained at his father's side until 1614, when court officials forced Wanli to send his favorite son to his Henan estate. Thus, Li's murder of the prince of Fu sent shock waves that reverberated throughout the entire country. See Atwell, "The T'ai-ch'ang, T'ien-ch'i, and Ch'ung-chen Reigns," 622–23, 635–40; Huang, *1587, A Year of No Significance,* 75–93; Hummel, *Eminent Chinese of the Ch'ing Period,* 176–77; Wakeman, "The Shun Interregnum of 1644," 35–70; and idem, *The Great Enterprise,* 257–66.

3. Atwell, "The T'ai-ch'ang, T'ien-ch'i, and Ch'ung-chen Reigns," 611–38; Hummel, *Eminent Chinese of the Ch'ing Period,* 491–93; Wakeman, *The Great Enterprise,* 257–66.

4. Struve, "The Southern Ming, 1644–1662," 641–726; Hummel, *Eminent Chinese of the Ch'ing Period,* 37–38; Dai, "The Rise of the Southwestern Frontier," 15–33; Struve, *The Southern Ming, 1644–1662,* 38–46.

5. Hummel, *Eminent Chinese of the Ch'ing Period,* 280–81; Parsons, *Peasant Rebellions,* 156–60, 167–78; "The Culmination of a Chinese Peasant Rebellion," 387–400; Dai, "The Rise of the Southwestern Frontier," 18–33; Entemann, "Migration and Settlement in Sichuan," 44–52.

6. Hummel, *Eminent Chinese of the Ch'ing Period,* 489–90, 679; Li, *Wu Sangui dazhuan,* 246.

7. Liu, *Tingwen lu,* 2/1b–3b; *Shizu zhang huangdi shilu,* 66/15; Li, *Wu Sangui dazhuan,* 233; Struve, "The Southern Ming, 1644–1662," 704; Dai, "The Rise of the Southwestern Frontier," 35. The death of Nikan was a major blow to the Manchu imperial family. Nikan was the third son of Cuyen (1580–1615), the eldest son of Nurhaci (1559–1626), and thus the grandson of the founder of the Manchu empire (Hummel, *Eminent Chinese of the Ch'ing Period,* 590–91).

8. The Southern Ming regime was established on December 24, 1646, in Zhaoqing, Guangdong, when the grandson of the Wanli emperor, Zhu Youlang (1623–62), was enthroned as the Yongli emperor (Struve, "The Southern

Ming, 1644–1662," 677–78, 701–2; idem, *The Southern Ming, 1644–1662*, 125–38).

9. Hummel, *Eminent Chinese of the Ch'ing Period*, 679; Struve, "The Southern Ming, 1644–1662," 705–6; idem, *The Southern Ming, 1644–1662*, 73–75, 86–88, 116–19; Wakeman, *The Great Enterprise*, 990, n. 5. The following contemporary description of Guiyang in the 1650s offers a very different perspective of the rebel capital under Sun Kewang's control. "The bund guards in some places had been chased away by tigers, and the mountain slopes from top to bottom were strewn with human bones. There was not a sign of merchants and [other] travelers. All I saw were horsemen flying back and forth [between] clashes. Also, I saw people whose ears and noses had been cut off and some whose arms were gone. But they still [were made to] bear heavy loads for long distances. It was terribly cruel. Even though the scenery was unusually interesting, I could not bear to watch it go by" (Struve, *Voices from the Ming-Qing Cataclysm*, 152–53).

10. Liu, *Tingwen lu*, 3/1a–b; Struve, "The Southern Ming, 1644–1662," 703; idem, *The Southern Ming, 1644–1662*, 73–75, 86–88, 116–19; Dai, "The Rise of the Southwestern Frontier," 35–37.

11. Hong Chengchou, before he was captured by Manchu forces in March 1642, had distinguished himself as a fair and honest Ming official and an exceptional military commander. Throughout the 1630s Hong's troops repeatedly harassed and defeated Li Zicheng's force in Shaanxi. In 1638, Hong's soldiers nearly annihilated Li's gang at an important engagement near Tongguan, Shaanxi, but Li and a few of his followers fled the battle early and made their way deep into the mountains of Shaanxi. Li remained in the mountains for over a year, fearful of attracting Hong's attention. Not until he heard that Hong had been transferred away from Shaanxi in 1639 did Li and his followers come down from the mountains. See Liu, *Tingwen lu*, 3/1a–2b; Hummel, *Eminent Chinese of the Ch'ing Period*, 358–59; Li, *Wu Sangui dazhuan*, 245–48.

12. *Shizu shilu*, 113/7, 12–15; Li, *Wu Sangui dazhuan*, 245–49; Liu, *Tingwen lu*, 3/2a; Struve, "The Southern Ming, 1644–1662," 706; idem, *The Southern Ming, 1644–1662*, 154; Dai, "The Rise of the Southwestern Frontier," 36. Sun Kewang repeatedly requested he be allowed to avenge his enemies and lead an army against Li Dingguo and the Yongli court, but his requests were coldly received. The Qing court was suspicious of Sun, and they watched his every move closely. Sun received the title "righteous king" (*yi wang*), one of only a handful of Chinese ever to receive a title designation of king during the Qing, but this title proved to be little consolation to Sun's bruised ego.

13. *Shizu shilu*, 114/5–6, 116/10, 117/2–6, 119/2; Liu, *Tingwen lu*, 3/2a–3a; *Guizhou shengzhi* (1985), 59–61; Li, *Wu Sangui dazhuan*, 248–60.

14. Liu, *Tingwen lu*, 3/1b–2a; *Shizu shilu*, 123/2b–4a, 124/14b–15a, 137/7b–8a. Shang Kexi was given the title "prince who pacifies the south" in 1649,

when he was charged with conducting the campaign against Ming resistance in Guangdong. Geng Jimao was given the title "prince who tranquilizes the south" in 1651 for participating in attacks against the Ming resistance in Guangdong, but Geng's title, like Shang's, did not specify a sphere of jurisdiction as did the 1658 edict. Geng's father, Geng Zhongming (d. 1649), was originally granted the title "prince who tranquilizes the south" in 1649, and he participated alongside Shang in the Qing campaign against Guangdong. Geng reportedly committed suicide in 1649 as a result of an inquiry that found he had concealed runaway slaves in his army. Geng Jimao was granted his father's title in 1651 despite the fact that he and Shang reportedly executed every adult in Canton following the nine-month siege of the city.

15. *Shizu zhang huangdi shilu*, 113/16–18, 114/7–8, 115/14–15, 116/5–6; *Guizhou shengzhi* (1985), 59–61; *Shengren zu huangdi shilu*, 7/25; Li, *Wu Sangui dazhuan*, 252–61; Struve, "The Southern Ming, 1644–1662," 706–10.

16. Despite Wu Sangui's importance in how the history of early modern China unfolded, we know very little about his family. We do know that Wu had several wives, but we are not sure as to the exact number of his children. It is believed that Wu had only one son, Wu Yingxiong (d. 1674), who was anointed viscount of the third class and married to Princess Kechun (1642–1705), the youngest half sister of the Shunzhi emperor. Wu Yingxiong was married and lived in Beijing, and he had four sons. It is believed that Wu Sangui had six daughters. Four of the daughters traveled to the southwest with him, but all we know about them is their husbands' names: Hu Guozhu, Xia Guoxiang, Guo Zhuangtu, and Wei Po. These sons-in-law were all Wu's trusted confidants. Regarding the other two daughters, one lived in Yangzhou, but we do not know her husband's name. The other daughter lived in Suzhou at Zhuozhengyuan, and her husband was Wang Yongning. Wu Sangui had a nephew named Wu Yingqi, one older brother named Wu Sanfeng, and one younger brother named Wu Sanmei. See Li, *Wu Sangui dazhuan*, 376–93; Hummel, *Eminent Chinese of the Ch'ing Period*, 877–80.

17. Liu, *Tingwen lu*, 3/5b–21b; Li, *Wu Sangui dazhuan*, 329–31.

18. *Shengren zu huangdi shilu*, 7/25; Li, *Wu Sangui dazhuan*, 330–33.

19. *Shengren zu huangdi shilu*, 12/9b. According to another report, in 1664 about 2,457 *qing* (1 *qing* = 100 *mu* or approximately 16.5 acres) of wasteland was reclaimed for cultivation (*Shengren zu huangdi shilu*, 15/10a).

20. *Shengren zu huangdi shilu*, 4/10a–b, 16/2a; Li, *Wu Sangui dazhuan*, 349–51.

21. Liu, *Tingwen lu*, 4/10b–11a, 14a–b; Li, *Wu Sangui dazhuan*, 349–51.

22. Li, *Wu Sangui dazhuan*, 334–35; *Shizu zhang huangdi shilu*, 141/11. The Forward Defense Command regional commander post was filled by Ma Ning; the Rear Defense Command post was filled by Yang Wu; the Left Defense Command post was filled by Shen Yingshi; and the Right Defense Command post was filled by Wang Fuchen.

23. *Shizu zhang huangdi shilu,* 141/11; Liu, *Tingwen lu,* 4/10b–11a; Li, *Wu Sangui dazhuan,* 349–51.

24. Ibid.

25. Liu, *Tingwen lu,* 2/1a–2b, 4/11b–13a; *Shizu zhang huangdi shilu,* 136/22; *Shengren zu huangdi shilu,* 18/7, 21/6, 39/12; Li, *Wu Sangui dazhuan,* 338–40. The political reach of the Army Under the Feudatory's Direct Control was considerable. For example, because of the extended time Wu spent on the Sichuan-Shaanxi border, much of his personal army was made up of individuals from this region. Two individuals particularly close to Wu, Wang Bingfan and Wang Fuchen, were from western Shaanxi, and Wu used their connections in this region to procure Tibetan horses for his personal stable. Reportedly, Wang Bingfan and Wang Fuchen transported as many as three thousand horses to Yunnan every year from the Amdo region of Eastern Tibet (Li, *Wu Sangui dazhuan,* 346).

26. Liu, *Tingwen lu,* 2/1a–2b, 4/11b–13a; *Shizu zhang huangdi shilu,* 133/3; Li, *Wu Sangui dazhuan,* 337–38. On July 29, 1664, Wu ordered his troops in Yunnan to march into Guizhou to attack Shuixi and Wusa.

27. According to the exhaustive study by Li Zhiting, Hu Yun was appointed vice provincial administration commissioner of Yunnan (*Yunnan buzheng shi, canzheng*) and general administrator (*fenshou*) of Jincang circuit; Li Xuan was named assistant administration commissioner of Yunnan (*Yunnan buzheng shi, canyi*) and general administrator of Erhai circuit; He Yuxiu was appointed Yunnan surveillance vice commissioner (*Yunnan ancha shi fushi*) and general administrator of Linyuan circuit; Su Hongmo was named surveillance vice commissioner (*ancha shi fushi*) in charge of Qing post roads; Ma Fengben was appointed Yunnan surveillance vice commissioner in charge of military routes in Lin'an; Ji Yun was named Yunnan supervisor surveillance commissioner (*Yunnan ancha shi jianshi*) in charge of water routes; Ji Yaodian was appointed Yunnan supervisor surveillance commissioner in charge of military routes in Jinteng; Tian Cuizhen became Yunnan surveillance vice commissioner in charge of Erhai circuit; and Lin Yiyuan was named Yunnan surveillance vice commissioner in charge of Qujing circuit (Li, *Wu Sangui dazhuan,* 340–43).

28. Li, *Wu Sangui dazhuan,* 340–45.

29. Liu, *Tingwen lu,* 4/13b–15b; *Shengren zu huangdi shilu,* 7/7a; *Guizhou shengzhi* (1985), 63–64.

30. Li, *Wu Sangui dazhuan,* 346.

31. Liu, *Tingwen lu,* 3/1b–2a; *Shizu zhang huangdi shilu,* 123/2b–4a; Li, *Wu Sangui dazhuan,* 263.

32. Liu, *Tingwen lu,* 3/2a–3b; *Shengren zu huangdi shilu,* 7/7a; *Guizhou shengzhi* (1985), 63; Li, *Wu Sangui dazhuan,* 384.

33. Liu, *Tingwen lu,* 4/2a; *Shengren zu huangdi shilu,* 12/16a–17a; *Guizhou shengzhi* (1985), 63–64; Hou, Shi, and Weng, *Guizhou gudai minzu,* 257–59.

34. *Shengren zu huangdi shilu*, 12/16b.

35. Elliott, *The Manchu Way*, 187–91.

36. Liu, *Tingwen lu*, 4/2a.

37. Ibid.

38. Ma and Luo, *Cuanwen congke*, 142–51.

39. Liu, *Tingwen lu*, 4/1b; Li, *Wu Sangui dazhuan*, 384–85.

40. Liu, *Tingwen lu*, 4/1b; Hou, Shi, and Weng, *Guizhou gudai minzu*, 257–59.

41. Liu, *Tingwen lu*, 4/1b; Li, *Wu Sangui dazhuan*, 385; Hou, Shi, and Weng, *Guizhou gudai minzu*, 257–59.

42. Liu, *Tingwen lu*, 4/1b–2a; Li, *Wu Sangui dazhuan*, 385; Hou, Shi, and Weng, *Guizhou gudai minzu*, 257–59.

43. Liu, *Tingwen lu*, 4/2a–b; Li, *Wu Sangui dazhuan*, 385; Hou, Shi, and Weng, *Guizhou gudai minzu*, 257–59.

44. Liu, *Tingwen lu*, 4/2a–b.

45. Ibid., 4/2b; Li, *Wu Sangui dazhuan*, 385.

46. Liu, *Tingwen lu*, 4/3b–5a; *Shengren zu huangdi shilu*, 15/15; Li, *Wu Sangui dazhuan*, 386–88.

47. Liu, *Tingwen lu*, 4/3b–5a; *Shengren zu huangdi shilu*, 15/15; Li, *Wu Sangui dazhuan*, 386–88.

48. *Shengren zu huangdi shilu*, 16/3, 16/8.

49. Ibid.

50. Ibid., 18/17a–b; *Guizhou shengzhi* (1985), 63–64.

51. *Shengren zu huangdi shilu*, 21/10.

52. Ibid., 12/16–17, 14/12.

53. Hou, Shi, and Weng, *Guizhou gudai minzu*, 257–58.

54. Liu, *Tingwen lu*, 4/5b–11b; Hou, Shi, and Weng, *Guizhou gudai minzu*, 257–58.

55. Wei, *Shengwu ji*, 391–92; Liu, *Tingwen lu*, 4/5b–11b; *Shengren zu huangdi shilu*, 13/19–20, 16/8–9, 18/2, 18/7.

56. Li, *Wu Sangui dazhuan*, 348–50; *Shengren zu huangdi shilu*, 19/19a.

57. *Shengren zu huangdi shilu*, 15/14b, 97/5a–b, 108/16a–17b.

58. Li, *Wu Sangui dazhuan*, 350; *Shengren zu huangdi shilu*, 19/19a.

59. Li, *Wu Sangui dazhuan*, 350; *Shengren zu huangdi shilu*, 19/19a.

60. Li, *Wu Sangui dazhuan*, 348–50; *Shengren zu huangdi shilu*, 19/19a.

61. Li, *Wu Sangui dazhuan*, 348–50; *Shengren zu huangdi shilu*, 19/19a–b.

62. Li, *Wu Sangui dazhuan*, 348–50; *Shengren zu huangdi shilu*, 19/19a–20a.

63. Li, *Wu Sangui dazhuan*, 348–50; *Shengren zu huangdi shilu*, 19/19a–b.

64. Li, *Wu Sangui dazhuan*, 348–50; *Shengren zu huangdi shilu*, 19/19a.

65. Li, *Wu Sangui dazhuan*, 352. Wu Sangui reportedly had plans to confiscate land in a 300 *li* radius around Kunming for the purpose of transforming it into pastureland, but outrage from local officials forced Wu to downsize this plan.

66. Liu, *Tingwen lu*, 4/12a–b; Li, *Wu Sangui dazhuan*, 352–53.

67. Liu, *Tingwen lu*, 4/12b–13a; Li, *Wu Sangui dazhuan*, 355–56.

68. Liu, *Tingwen lu*, 4/13a–15b; Li, *Wu Sangui dazhuan*, 356–58.

69. Dai, "The Rise of the Southwestern Frontier," 87.

70. Li Zhiting argues that many of the petitioners who encouraged the court to reject Wu's request were in some way linked to Wu or associated with persons who sympathized with Wu (*Wu Sangui dazhuan*, 400–401).

71. Li, *Wu Sangui dazhuan*, 401–2.

72. Liu, *Tingwen lu*, 5/1a–b; *Guizhou shengzhi* (1985), 59–61.

73. *Shengren zu huangdi shilu*, 109/2a–b.

74. Liu, *Tingwen lu*, 5/1b–3a; *Shengren zu huangdi shilu*, 109/2a–b, 158/8a–9a, 154/10a; Li, *Wu Sangui dazhuan*, 440–46; *Guizhou shengzhi* (1985), 59–61. Following the defeat of Wu Sangui's rebellion, Kangxi remarked that he had decided at a very young age to eliminate the three feudatories because, as he said, with the passing of time their unchecked military power would pose grave problems for the Qing throne (*Shengren zu huangdi shilu*, 158/8a–9a). According to Wakeman's account of the origins of the rebellion, when Shang Kexi submitted his request to retire to the Qing throne on April 28, 1673, he also sought permission to pass on control of his Guangdong feudatory to his son Shang Zhixin. Kangxi agreed to Shang Kexi's request to retire, but he refused to allow Shang Zhixin to inherit his father's domain. Wu Sangui and Geng Jinzhong submitted their resignations the following August, probably to flush out the throne's true intentions toward the remaining feudatories. Following considerable debate at court, Kangxi decided on September 16, 1873, to accept Wu's resignation, knowing full well that this would precipitate open rebellion (*The Great Enterprise*, 1099–101).

75. The leaders of the three feudatories (*sanfan*) were Wu Sangui in Yunnan and Guizhou, Shang Kexi in Guangdong, and Geng Jingzhong in Fujian.

76. One reason given for why Qing forces did not advance into Sichuan at that time, the summer of 1676, was that Kangxi was concerned about the logistic difficulties of transporting provisions across the mountains that separated Shaanxi and Sichuan, and he did not want his forces stranded in Sichuan without provisions. Although this argument makes perfect sense, an alternative reason can be gleaned from sources that describe Kangxi as irate over the battlefield performance of Manchu and Mongol forces in Shaanxi and deeply concerned about the effectiveness of his commanders in the field. In fact, many of the commanding officers in Shaanxi were ordered back to Beijing following Wang Fuchen's surrender. The failure of Manchu forces to secure control over the northern Sichuan city of Baoning appears to have been the lightning rod for Kangxi's anger. See *Shengren zu huangdi shilu*, 63/18a–19a, 63/19b–20a, 65/19b–20a; Li, *Wu Sangui dazhuan*, 520–37; Wakeman, *The Great Enterprise*, 1109–12.

77. Li, *Wu Sangui dazhuan*, 489–504; Hummel, *Eminent Chinese of the Ch'ing Period*, 228–29; Wakeman, *The Great Enterprise*, 1105–15.

78. Wei, *Shengwu ji*, 2/1a–18b; Li, *Wu Sangui dazhuan*, 461–80; Hummel, *Eminent Chinese of the Ch'ing Period*, 879–80; Wakeman, *The Great Enterprise*, 1119–20.

79. *Shengren zu huangdi shilu*, 91/26a–b; Hummel, *Eminent Chinese of the Ch'ing Period*, 396–97. Jangtai was the great-grandson of Nurhaci and thus a prominent member of the imperial family. Because Jangtai was the commander of Manchu forces in the south, he became the de facto overall commander of the Yunnan campaign.

80. *Shengren zu huangdi shilu*, 91/26a.

81. Hou, Shi, and Weng, *Guizhou gudai minzu*, 257–59.

82. In January 1684, Pingyuan and Qianxi prefectures were reduced to departments and placed under Dading prefecture's jurisdiction. In July 1687, the government reduced Dading prefecture to a department and made Dading, Pingyuan, and Qianxi subordinate to Weining prefecture. In the same month, the Yongning garrison and Puding battalion were combined to make Yongning county, and the Bijie and Chishui garrisons were combined to become Bijie county. Both Yongning and Bijie counties were placed under the jurisdiction of Weining prefecture. According to the report jointly made by the special commissioners to Guizhou, Kulena and Cai Yurong, it was proposed that large *tusi* offices not be restored in Shuixi, because the return of such indigenous officials might pose a threat to the civilian and military officials appointed by the Qing state (*Shengren zu huangdi shilu*, 113/17a, 124/16b–17b).

83. *Shengren zu huangdi shilu*, 106/18b–19a, 124/16b–17b.

84. Ibid., 124/16b–17b.

85. *Guizhou tongzhi* (1741), 35/29b.

86. Herman, "Empire in the Southwest."

87. *Shengren zu huangdi shilu*, 124/17a–b.

## Conclusion

1. Shepherd, *Statecraft and Political Economy*, 4.

2. As Shepherd argues, "the superiority of Chinese military organization and technology in East Asia made the conquest of new territories militarily feasible, but the high cost of financing permanent military and administrative control over distant and unproductive regions often rendered their incorporation undesirable. When the strategy dictated the incorporation of a territory, priority had to be given to minimizing control costs and extracting local revenues to ease the burden of central government finances" (ibid., 4–5).

3. Harrell, *Cultural Encounters*, 4.

4. Wang, "The Chinese Urge to Civilize," 145–64.

5. Millward, *Beyond the Pass*, 241.

6. According to Brook, Zhu Yuanzhang had an idealized vision of a self-sufficient rural community around which Ming society could be structured (*The Confusions of Pleasure*, 17–85).

7. Xu, *Xu Xiake youji*, 621–1121.

# Works Cited

Aibida 愛必達. *Qiannan zhilue* 黔南職略 (An account of government offices in southern Guizhou). 1749. Reprint, Taipei: Zhongwu shuju, 1974.

Allsen, Thomas T. *Mongol Imperialism: The Policies of the Grand Qan Mongke in China, Russia, and the Islamic Lands, 1251–1259.* Berkeley: University of California Press, 1987.

———. "The Rise of the Mongolian Empire and Mongolian Rule in North China." In Denis Twitchett and Herbert Franke, eds., *The Cambridge History of China,* vol. 6, *Alien Regimes and Border States, 907–1368.* Cambridge: Cambridge University Press, 1994.

*Anning zhouzhi* 安寧州志 (Anning department gazetteer). 1710.

Armijo-Hussein, Jacqueline Misty. "Sayyid 'Ayall Shams al-Din: A Muslim from Central Asia, Serving the Mongols in China, and Bringing Civilization to Yunnan." Ph.D. diss., Harvard University, 1997.

Atwell, William. "Notes on Silver, Foreign Trade, and the Late Ming Economy." *Ch'ing-shih wen-t'i* 3.8 (1977): 1–33.

———. "International Bullion Flows and the Chinese Economy, circa 1530–1650." *Past and Present* 95 (1982): 68–90.

———. "Some Observations on the Seventeenth-Century Crisis in China and Japan." *Journal of Asian Studies* 45.2 (1986): 223–44.

———. "The T'ai-ch'ang, T'ien-ch'i, and Ch'ung-chen Reigns." In Frederick W. Mote and Denis Twitchett, eds., *The Cambridge History of China,* vol. 7, *The Ming Dynasty, 1368–1644,* pt. 1. Cambridge: Cambridge University Press, 1988.

Backus, Charles. *The Nan-chao Kingdom and Tang China's Southwestern Frontier.* Cambridge: Cambridge University Press, 1981.

Bai Shouyi 白壽彝. "Mingdai kuangye de fazhan" 明代礦業的發展 (The development of the mining industry during the Ming). In *Zhongguo ziben zhuyi mengya wenti taolun ji* 中國資本主義萌芽問題討論集 (Essays on the buds of capitalism in China). Beijing: Sanlian chubanshe, 1957.

————. "Saidianchi Shansiding zhuan" 賽典赤贍思丁傳 (Biography of Saidianchi Shans al-Din). *Qingzhen yuebao* 青貞月報 (Qingzhen monthly) 31 (1947): 17–22. Reprinted in Li Xinghua and Feng Jinyuan, eds., *Zhongguo Yisilanjiao shi cankao ziliao xuanbian, 1911–1949* 中國伊斯蘭敎史參考資料選編 (China Islamic history reference material selections, 1911–49). Yinchuan: Ningxia renmin chubanshe, 1985.

Bai Shouyi 白壽彝, ed. *Huizu renwu zhi: Yuandai, Saidianchi Shans al-Din* 回族人物志: 元代, 賽典赤 (An account of prominent Muslims [in China]: Sayyid 'Ajall of the Yuan period). Kunming: Yunnan minzu chubanshe, 1981.

Bamo'ayi 巴莫阿依. *Yizu zuling xinyang yanjiu* 彝族祖靈信仰研究 (Research on ancestral-spirit beliefs of the Yi). Chengdu: Sichuan minzu chubanshe, 1994.

Bao Ruji 包汝輯. *Nanzhong jiwen* 南中記聞 (Notes from Nanzhong). 1775–78. Reprint, Taipei: Congshu jicheng, 1968.

Barfield, Thomas J. *The Perilous Frontier: Nomadic Empires and China*. Oxford: Basil Blackwell, 1989.

Beckwith, Christopher I. *The Tibetan Empire in Central Asia: A History of the Struggle for Great Power Among Tibetans, Turks, Arabs, and Chinese During the Early Middle Ages*. Princeton: Princeton University Press, 1987.

Bentley, G. Carter. "Ethnicity and Practice." *Comparative Studies in Society and History* 29.1 (January 1987): 24–55.

*Bijie xianzhi* 畢節縣志 (Bijie county gazetteer). 1834.

Bolanxi 勃蘭盼 et al. *Da Yuan da yitong zhi* 大元大一統志 (Comprehensive gazetteer of Yuan China). Ed. Zhao Wanli 趙萬里. Ca. 1300. Reprint, Shanghai: Zhonghua shuju, 1966.

Boyle, John Andrew. "Dynastic and Political History of the Il-khans." In idem, ed., *The Cambridge History of Iran*, vol. 5, *The Seljuq and Mongol Periods*. Cambridge: Cambridge University Press, 1968.

Bradley, David. *Proto Loloish*. Scandinavian Institute of Asian Studies Monographs Series 39. London: Curzon Press, 1979.

————. "Language Planning for China's Minorities: The Yi Branch." In D. Laycock and W. Winter, eds., *A World of Language: Presented to Professor S. A. Wurm on His Sixty-Fifth Birthday*. Canberra: Department of Linguistics, Australian National University, 1990.

————. "Language Policy for the Yi." In Stevan Harrell, ed., *Perspectives on the Yi of Southwest China*. Berkeley: University of California Press, 2001.

Brook, Timothy. "The Merchant Network in Sixteenth Century China." *Journal of the Economic and Social History of the Orient* 24.2 (1981): 165–214.

————. *Geographical Sources of Ming-Qing History*. Michigan Monographs in Chinese Studies. Ann Arbor: University of Michigan Press, 1988.

———. *The Confusions of Pleasure: Commerce and Culture in Ming China.* Berkeley: University of California Press, 1998.

Brunnert, H. S., and V. V. Hagelstrom. *Present Day Political Organization of China.* Trans. A. Beltchenko and E. E. Moran. Shanghai: Kelley and Walsh, 1912.

Cai Guanluo 蔡冠洛, ed. *Qing shi liezhuan* 清史列傳 (The biographies of Qing history). Taipei: Qiming shuju, 1965.

Cai Yurong 蔡毓榮. *Ping nan jilue* 平南紀略 (A brief account of the campaign to pacify the south). *Qing shi ziliao* 清史資料 (Material on Qing history), no. 3. Taipei: Heluo tushu chubanshe, 1982.

Chan, Hok-lam. "The Rise of Ming T'ai-tsu (1368–98): Facts and Fictions in Early Ming Official Historiography." *Journal of the American Oriental Society* 95.4 (Oct.–Dec. 1975): 679–714.

———. *Legitimation in Imperial China: Discussions Under the Jurchen-Chin Dynasty, 1115–1234.* Seattle: University of Washington Press, 1984.

———. "The Chien-wen, Yung-lo, Hung-hsi, and Hsüan-te reigns, 1399–1435." In Frederick W. Mote and Denis Twitchett, eds., *The Cambridge History of China,* vol. 7, *The Ming Dynasty, 1368–1644.* Cambridge: Cambridge University Press, 1988.

Chang, K. C. *Early Chinese Civilization: Anthropological Perspectives.* Cambridge: Harvard University Press, 1976.

Chao, Emile. "Depictions of Difference: History, Gender, Ritual, and State Discourse Among the Naxi of Southwest China." Ph.D. diss., University of Michigan, 1995.

Chase-Dunn, Christopher, and Thomas D. Hall. *Rise and Demise: Comparing World Systems.* Boulder, CO: Westview Press, 1997.

Chen Ding 陳鼎. *Dian Qian youji* 滇黔遊記 (A record of my journey through Guizhou and Yunnan). 1690.

———. *Dian Qian tusi hunli ji* 滇黔土司婚禮記 (An account of marriage ceremonies among the native officials in Yunnan and Guizhou). 1700.

Chen Guoan 陳國安 and Shi Jizhong 史繼忠. "Shilun Mingdai Guizhou wei-suo" 始論明代貴州衛所 (A preliminary discussion of the Ming *weisuo* system in Guizhou). *Guizhou wenshi luncong* 貴州文史叢刊 (Essays on the literature and history of Guizhou) 3 (1981): 92–101.

Chen Liankai 陳連開. "Zhongguo, Huayi, Fanhan, Zhonghua, Zhonghua minzu—yi ge neizai lianxi fazhan bei renshi de guocheng" 中國·華夷·蕃漢·中華·中華民族——一個在聯系發展被認識的過程 (To make clear the process of interrelated development of such terms as China [Zhongguo], Chinese [Hua] and barbarians [yi], barbarians [fan] and Chinese [Han], China [Zhonghua], China's minority peoples [Zhonghua minzu]). In Fei Xiaotong 費孝通, ed., *Zhonghua minzu duoyuan yiti geju* 中華民族多元一體格局 (The pattern of unity in the diversity of the Chinese nation). Beijing: Zhongyang minzu xueyuan chubanshe, 1989.

Chen Shan 陳單. *Qiannan leibian* 黔南類編 (Guizhou documents). 1537.

Chen Tianjun 陳天君. "Lun Yizu gudai fenqi" 論彝族古代分期 (A discussion of the periodization of ancient Yi history). In He Yaohua 何堯華, ed., *Xi'nan minzu yanjiu: Yizu zhuanji* 西南民族研究: 彝族專集 (Southwest nationalities research: special Yi collection). Kunming: Yunnan minzu chubanshe, 1985.

Chen Ying 陳英. "Guanyu 'Liuzu,' 'Luodian guo' deng wenti de diaocha" 關於 '六祖,' '羅甸國,' 等問題的調查 (An examination of several questions regarding the six ancestors and Luodian kingdom). In Xi Tianxi 西天錫, ed., *Sichuan, Guizhou Yizu shehui lishi diaocha* 四川貴州彝族社會歷史調查 (An examination of the social history of the Yi people in Yunnan and Guizhou). Kunming: Yunnan renmin chubanshe, 1987.

Chen Yuan 陳袁. *Mingji Dian-Qian fojiao kao* 明季滇黔佛教考 (A study of Buddhism in Yunnan and Guizhou in the late Ming). 1940. Reprint, Beijing: Zhonghua shuju, 1962.

Chu, Hung-lam. "The Debate over Recognition of Wang Yangming." *Harvard Journal of Asiatic Studies* 48 (June 1988): 47–70.

———. "Intellectual Trends in the Fifteenth Century." *Ming Studies* 27 (Spring 1989): 1–33.

*Chuxiong fuzhi* 楚雄府志 (Chuxiong prefecture gazetteer). 1716.

Clarke, Samuel R. *Among the Tribes in South-West China*. London: Morgan and Scott, 1911. Reprint, Taipei: Cheng Wen, 1970.

Cleaves, Francis W. "Daruya and Gerege." *Harvard Journal of Asiatic Studies* 16 (1953): 235–60.

———. "The Biography of Bayan of the Barin in the *Yuan shih*." *Harvard Journal of Asiatic Studies* 19 (1956): 185–303.

Crossley, Pamela Kyle. "Thinking About Ethnicity in Early Modern China." *Late Imperial China* 11.1 (1990): 1–35.

*Cuan Youyan bei* 爨尤顏碑 (The stone tablet of Cuan Youyan). 1213. Reprint, Taipei: Huawen shuju, 1967.

Cushman, Richard David. "Rebel Haunts and Lotus Huts: Problems of Ethnology of the Yao." Ph.D. diss., Cornell University, 1970.

*Da Ming huidian* 大明會典 (The collected statutes of the Ming dynasty). Ed. Shen Shixing 申時行 et al. 1587. Reprint, Beijing: Zhonghua shuju, 1989.

*Da Ming yitong zhi* 大明一統志 (Gazetteer of a unified Ming dynasty). Ed. Li Xian 李賢. 1461. Reprint, Taipei: Huawen shuju, 1965.

*Da Qing lichao shilu* 大清歷朝實錄 (The Veritable Records of the Qing dynasty). Tokyo: Okura shuppan kabushiki kaisha, 1937–38. Reprint, Taipei: Huawen shuju, 1964. (*Shizu zhang huangdi shilu* 世祖章皇帝實錄 = Shunzhi reign, 1644–61; *Shengren zu huangdi shilu* 聖仁祖皇帝實錄 = Kangxi reign,

1662–1722; *Shizong xian huangdi shilu* 世宗憲皇帝實錄 = Yongzheng reign, 1723–35; *Gaozong chun huangdi shilu* 高宗純皇帝實錄 = Qianlong reign, 1736–95).

*Da Qing huidian* 大清會典 (The collected statutes of the Qing dynasty). Editions of 1690 (162 *juan*), 1733 (250 *juan*), and 1763 (100 *juan*).

*Da Qing huidian shili* 大清會典事例 (The collected statutes and precedents of the Qing dynasty). 1,220 *juan*. Guangxu edition, 1899.

*Da Qing huidian tu* 大清會典圖 (Illustrations for the collected statutes of the Qing dynasty). 132 *juan*. 1818.

*Da Qing yitong zhi* 大清一統志 (Gazetteer of a unified Qing dynasty). Ed. Jiang Tingxi 蔣廷錫. 1744.

*Dading fuzhi* 大定府志 (Dading prefecture gazetteer). 1850.

*Dading xianzhi* 大定縣志 (Dading county gazetteer). 1855.

Dai, Yingcong. "The Rise of the Southwestern Frontier Under the Qing, 1640–1800." Ph.D. diss., University of Washington, 1996.

*Dali fuzhi* 大理府志 (Dali prefecture gazetteer). 1746.

Dardess, John W. *A Ming Society: T'ai-ho County, Kiangsi, Fourteenth to Seventeenth Centuries*. Berkeley: University of California Press, 1996.

de Beauclair, Inez. "The Keh Lao of Kweichow and Their History According to Chinese Records." *Studia Serica* 2 (1946): 1–44.

———. "Cultural Traits of the Non-Chinese Tribes of Kweichow Province." *Sinologica* 5 (1956): 20–35.

———. "A Miao Tribe of Southeast Kweichow and Its Cultural Configuration." *Bulletin of the Institute of Ethnology, Academia Sinica* 10 (1960): 127–99.

———. *Tribal Cultures of Southwest China*. Asian Folklore and Social Life Monographs, ed. Tsu-k'uang Lou and Wolfram Eberhard, vol. 2. Taipei: Orient Cultural Service, 1970.

de Heer, Philip. *The Caretaker Emperor: Aspects of the Imperial Institution in Fifteenth-Century China as Reflected in the Political History of the Reign of Chu Ch'I-yü*. Leiden: E. J. Brill, 1985.

Dessaint, Alain Y. *Minorities of Southwest China: An Introduction to the Yi (Lolo) and Related Peoples and an Annotated Bibliography*. New Haven, CT: HRAF Press, 1980.

*Dingfan zhouzhi* 定番州志 (Dingfan department gazetteer). 1718.

Dirks, Nicholas B., ed. *Colonialism and Culture*. Ann Arbor: University of Michigan Press, 1992.

*Dongchuan fuzhi* 東川府志 (Dongchuan prefecture gazetteer). 1735.

Doyle, Michael W. *Empires*. Ithaca, NY: Cornell University Press, 1981.

Dreyer, Edward L. *Early Ming China: A Political History, 1355–1435*. Stanford: Stanford University Press, 1982.

Du Yuting 杜玉亭. *Yunnan Menggu zu jianshi* 雲南蒙古族簡史 (A brief history of the Mongols in Yunnan). Kunming: Yunnan renmin chubanshe, 1979.

———. "Yunnan Xiao Liangshan Yizu de nuli zhidu" 雲南小涼山彝族的奴隸
制度 (The Yi slave system in Xiao Liangshan, Yunnan). In *Yunnan Xiao
Liangshan Yizu shehui lishi diaocha* 雲南小涼山彝族社會歷史調差 (Investigations into the history of the Yi society in Yunnan's Xiao Liangshan). Kunming: Yunnan renmin chubanshe, 1984.

Dull, Jack L. "The Evolution of Government in China." In Paul S. Ropp, ed.,
*Heritage of China: Contemporary Perspectives on Chinese Civilization.* Berkeley:
University of California Press, 1990.

*Dushan zhouzhi* 獨山州志 (Dushan department gazetteer). 1769.

E'rong'an 鄂榮安, E'shi 鄂實, E'bi 鄂弼, E'ning 鄂寧, E'xin 鄂忻, and E'mo
鄂謨, eds. *Xiangqin bo E wenduan gong nianpu* 襄勤伯鄂文端公年譜 (The
life chronology of Ortai). Ca. 1748. Reprint, Beijing: Zhonghua shuju, 1993.

Eberhard, Wolfram. *Local Cultures of South and East China.* Leiden: E. J. Brill,
1967.

———. *China's Minorities: Yesterday and Today.* Belmont, CA: Wadsworth,
1982.

Eisenstadt, S. N. *The Political Systems of Empires.* New York: Free Press, 1963.

Elliott, Mark C. *The Manchu Way: The Eight Banners and Ethnic Identity in Late
Imperial China.* Stanford: Stanford University Press, 2001.

Elman, Benjamin A. *From Philosophy to Philology: Intellectual and Social Aspects
of Change in Late Imperial China.* Cambridge: Harvard University Press,
1984.

———. "Changes in Confucian Civil Service Examinations from the Ming to
the Ch'ing Dynasty." In Benjamin A. Elman and Alexander Woodside, eds.,
*Education and Society in Late Imperial China, 1600–1900.* Berkeley: University of California Press, 1994.

Endicott-West, Elizabeth. *Mongolian Rule in China: Local Administration in the
Yuan Dynasty.* Cambridge: Harvard Council on East Asian Studies, 1989.

———. "The Yuan Government and Society." In Herbert Franke and Denis
Twitchett, eds., *The Cambridge History of China,* vol. 6, *Alien Regimes and
Border States, 907–1368.* Cambridge: Cambridge University Press, 1994.

Entemann, Roger E. "Migration and Settlement in Sichuan, 1644–1796."
Ph.D. diss., Harvard University, 1982.

Fan Chuo 樊綽. *Manshu jiaozhu* 蠻書校注 (An annotated edition of the
*Manshu*). Ed. Xiang Da 向達. Ca. 860–73. Reprint, Beijing: Zhonghua
shuju, 1962.

Fang Guoyu 方國瑜. "Guanyu Saidianchi fu Dian gongji" 關於賽典赤撫滇功
績 (A record of Sayyid 'Ayall Shams al-Din's pacification of Yunnan). *Ren-
wen kexue zazhi* 人文科學雜誌 (Humanities) 1 (1958): 7–15.

———. *Yizu shigao* 彝族史稿 (Draft history of the Yi). Chengdu: Sichuan
minzu chubanshe, 1984.

———. *Zhongguo xinan lishi dili kaoshi* 中國西南歷史地理考 (An examination of the history and geography of southwest China). 1987. Reprint, Taipei: Taiwan Commercial Press, 1990.

———. "Shilun Yuan chao zai Yunnan de minzu zhengce" 試論元朝在雲南的民族政策 (A brief discussion of the Yuan government's minority policies in Yunnan). In *Zhongguo minzu shi xuehui* 中國民族史學會 (Studies in the history of China's minority peoples). Beijing: Gaige chubanshe, 1991.

———. "Lun Yuan Ming Qing shiqi xi'nan diqu de wenhua" 論元明清時期西南地區的文化 (An examination of cultural institutions in the southwest during the Yuan, Ming, and Qing dynasties). *Yunnan minzu xueyuan xuebao* 雲南民族學院學報 (Journal of the Yunnan Nationalities Institute) 51.2 (1996): 47–61.

Farmer, Edward L. *Zhu Yuanzhang and Early Ming Legislation: The Reordering of Chinese Society Following the Era of Mongol Rule.* Leiden: E. J. Brill, 1995.

Faure, David. "The Yao Wars in the Mid-Ming and Their Impact on Yao Ethnicity." Paper presented at the conference entitled "Ethnic Identities and the China Frontier: Changing Discourse and Consciousness," Dartmouth College, Hanover, NH, 1996.

Feng Erkang 馮爾康. *Yongzheng zhuan* 雍正傳 (A biography of the Yongzheng emperor). Beijing: Renmin chubanshe, 1985.

Feng Hanyi 馮漢驛. "Yunnan Jinning Shizhaishan chutu tonggu yanjiu" 雲南晉寧石寨山出土銅鼓研究 (Research on the bronze drums excavated from Jinning's Shizhai Mountain, Yunnan). *Kaogu* 考古 (Archaeology) (1963): 319–29.

Feng Hanyi 馮漢驛 and Tong Enzheng 童恩正. "Minjiang shangyoude shiguanzang" 岷江上游的石棺葬 (Stone coffins buried along the upper reaches of the Min River). *Kaogu xuebao* 考古學報 (Studies in archaeology) 2 (1973): 41–59.

Feng, Han-yi, and J. K. Shryock. "The Historical Origins of the Lolo." *Harvard Journal of Asiatic Studies* 3 (1938): 103–27.

———. "The Black Magic Known in China as *Ku.*" *Journal of the American Oriental Society* 55 (1935): 1–30.

Feng Shike 馮士軻. *Dianxing jilue* 滇行記略 (Memories of a trip to Yunnan). 1575.

Feng Su 馮甦. *Dian kao* 滇考 (A study of Dian). 1665.

Feng Yuanwei 馮元蔚, ed. *Le'e teyi* 勒俄特衣 (Hnewo teyy, the book of creation). Chengdu: Sichuan minzu chubanshe, 1985.

Fieldhouse, D. K. *The Colonial Empires.* New York: Delacorte Press, 1967.

Fitzgerald, Charles P. *The Southward Expansion of the Chinese People.* New York: Praeger, 1972.

Franke, Herbert. "Chinese Historiography Under Mongol Rule: The Role of History in Acculturation." *Mongolian Studies* 1 (1974): 15–26.

————. *From Tribal Chieftain to Universal Emperor and God: The Legitimation of the Yuan Dynasty.* Munich: Bayerische Akademie Der Wissenschaften, 1978.

Franke, Herbert, ed. *Sung Biographies.* 4 vols. Wiesbaden: Steiner, 1976.

Franke, Wolfgang. "The Veritable Records of the Ming Dynasty (1368–1644)." In W. B. Beasley and E. G. Pulleyblank, eds., *Historians of China and Japan.* London: Oxford University Press, 1961.

————. *An Introduction to the Sources of Ming History.* Kuala Lumpur: University of Malaya Press, 1968.

Fu Yiling 傅衣凌. "Mingmo nanfang de dianbian, nubian" 明末南方的佃變, 奴變 (Tenant revolts and slave revolts in South China in the late Ming). *Lishi yanjiu* 歷史研究 (Historical research) 5 (1975): 61–67.

————. *Ming-Qing shehui jingji shi lunwen ji* 明-清社會經濟史論文集 (Essays on the social and economic history of the Ming and Qing). Beijing: Renmin chubanshe, 1982.

Furnivall, J. S. *Colonial Policy and Practice.* Cambridge: Cambridge University Press, 1948.

Gao Dai 高代. *Jiaoqing ping Miao* 剿清平苗 (The pacification of the Miao). Ca. 1560.

Gao Gong 高拱. *Jing yi jishi* 靖夷紀事 (A record of the pacification of the barbarians). In Ortai 鄂爾泰, ed., *Guizhou tongzhi* 貴州通志 (Comprehensive gazetteer of Guizhou). 1741. *Juan* 35, 35–42.

Geary, Norman, and Ruth Geary. *Tales Among the Kam.* London: Curzon Press, 2003.

Gernet, Jacques. *A History of Chinese Civilization.* Trans. J. R. Foster and Charles Hartman. Reprint, Cambridge: Cambridge University Press, 1996.

Giersch, Charles Patterson, Jr. "Qing China's Reluctant Subjects: Indigenous Communities and Empire Along the Yunnan Frontier." Ph.D. diss., Yale University, 1998.

————. "A Motley Throng: Social Change in Southwest China's Early Modern Frontier, 1700–1880." *Journal of Asian Studies* 60.1 (Feb. 2001): 67–94.

————. *Asian Borderlands: The Transformation of Qing China's Yunnan Frontier.* Cambridge: Harvard University Press, 2006.

Gong Yin 龔蔭. *Zhongguo tusi zhidu* 中國土司制度 (China's native official institution). Kunming: Yunnan renmin chubanshe, 1992.

*Gongzhong dang Kangxi chao zouzhe* 宮中檔康熙朝奏摺 (Secret palace memorials of the Kangxi period). Taipei: Guoli gugong bowu yuan, 1976–77.

*Gongzhong dang Yongzheng chao zouzhe* 宮中檔雍正朝奏摺 (Secret palace memorials of the Yongzheng period). Taipei: Guoli gugong bowu yuan, 1976–77.

Goodrich, L. Carrington, ed., and Fang Chaoying, assoc. ed. *Dictionary of Ming Biography, 1368–1644.* New York: Columbia University Press, 1976.

Gu Jiegang 顧頡剛 and Li Guangming 黎光明. "Mingmo Qing chu zhi Sichuan" 明末清初之四川 (Sichuan during the Ming-Qing transition). *Dongfang zazhi* 東方雜誌 (East magazine) 31.1 (Jan. 1934): 171–81.

Gu Shanzhen 顧山貞. *Ke Dian shu* 客滇述 (A record of my stay in Yunnan). In *Hukuo Yusheng ji* 虎口餘生記 (A narrative of surviving in the tiger's jaws). Shanghai: Shenzhou guoguangshe, 1951.

Gu Yanwu 顧炎武. *Tianxia junguo libing shu* 天下郡國利病書 (Strengths and weaknesses of the various regions of the realm). 1662. Reprint, Kyoto: Chubun shuppansha, 1975.

———. *Rizhi lu jishi* 日知錄集釋 (A record of knowledge gained day by day, with commentaries). 1834. Reprint, Shanghai: Shanghai guji chubanshe, 1984.

*Guiyang fuzhou* 貴陽府志 (Guiyang prefecture gazetteer). Ed. Zhou Zuoji 周作楫. 1850.

*Guizhou de shaoshu minzu* 貴州的少數民族 (The minority peoples of Guizhou). Ed. Guizhou Nationalities Research Institute. Guiyang: Guizhou renmin chubanshe, 1980.

*Guizhou shengzhi, dili zhi* 貴州省志, 地理志 (Comprehensive gazetteer of Guizhou province, geography section). Ed. Geography Department, Guizhou Normal University. Guiyang: Guizhou renmin chubanshe, 1985.

*Guizhou tongzhi* 貴州通志 (Comprehensive gazetteer of Guizhou province). Ed. Xie Dongshan 謝東山 and Zhang Dao 張道. 1555.

*Guizhou tongzhi* 貴州通志 (Comprehensive gazetteer of Guizhou province). Ed. Xu Yide 許一德. 1597.

*Guizhou tongzhi* 貴州通志 (Comprehensive gazetteer of Guizhou province). 1673.

*Guizhou tongzhi* 貴州通志 (Comprehensive gazetteer of Guizhou province). Ed. Xue Zaide 薛載德 and Fan Chengxun 範承勳. 1692.

*Guizhou tongzhi* 貴州通志 (Comprehensive gazetteer of Guizhou province). Ed. Ortai 鄂爾泰. 1741.

*Guizhou tongzhi* 貴州通志, *qianshi zhi* 前事志 (Comprehensive gazetteer of Guizhou province, records of former events). Guiyang: Guizhou renmin chubanshe, 1987.

*Guizhou tujing xinzhi* 貴州圖經新志 (New illustrated gazetteer of Guizhou province). Ed. Shen Xiang 沈庠 and Zhao Zan 趙瓚. 1502.

Guo, Ji, and Ding, Ha. *Selected Ancient Records of Migrations of the Six Clans of Yi*. Beijing: Central Institute of Nationalities, 1984.

Guo Yingpin 郭應聘. *Xi'nan jishi* 西南紀事 (A record of events in the southwest). Ca. 1585.

Guo Zizhang 郭子章. *Qianji* 黔記 (A record of Qian). 1608.

*Hanshu* 漢書 (History of the Han). Ed. Ban Gu 班固 et al. Ca. 92 CE. Reprint, Beijing: Zhonghua shuju, 1962.

Hargett, James M. *On the Road in Twelfth Century China: The Travel Diaries of Fan Chengda (1126–1193)*. Stuttgart: Franz Steiner Verlag Wiesbaden, 1989.

Harrell, Stevan. "Ethnicity and Kin Terms Among Two Kinds of Yi." In Chien Chiao and Nicholas Tapp, eds., *Ethnicity and Ethnic Groups in China*. Hong Kong: New Asia College, 1989.

———. "Ethnicity, Local Interests, and the State: Yi Communities in Southwest China." *Comparative Studies in Society and History* 32 (1990): 515–48.

———. "The History of the History of the Yi." In idem, ed., *Cultural Encounters on China's Ethnic Frontiers*. Seattle: University of Washington Press, 1994.

———. "Introduction: Civilizing Projects and the Reaction to Them." In idem, ed., *Cultural Encounters on China's Ethnic Frontiers*. Seattle: University of Washington Press, 1994.

———. "Introduction." In idem, ed., *Perspectives on the Yi of Southwest China*. Berkeley: University of California Press, 2001.

Harrell, Stevan, ed., *Cultural Encounters on China's Ethnic Frontiers*. Seattle: University of Washington Press, 1994.

———. *Perspectives on the Yi of Southwest China*. Berkeley: University of California Press, 2001.

Hartwell, Robert M. "Demographic, Political, and Social Transformations of China, 750–1550." *Harvard Journal of Asiatic Studies* 42.2 (Dec. 1982): 365–442.

He Jingwu 何靜梧. "Ming Qing liangdai de Guizhou shuyuan" 明清兩代的書院 (Private academies in Guizhou during the Ming and Qing). *Guizhou wenshi luncong* 貴州文史叢刊 (Essays on the literature and history of Guizhou) 1 (1981): 92–100.

He Qiaoxin 何喬新. *Kanchu Bozhou shiqing shu* 勘處播州事情疏 (An investigation of the Bozhou incident). 1500. Reprint, Beijing: Zhonghua shuju, 1983.

Hechter, Michael. *Internal Colonialism: The Celtic Fringe in British National Development, 1536–1966*. Berkeley: University of California Press, 1975.

Heijdra, Martinus Johannes. "The Socio-Economic Development of Ming Rural China (1368–1644): An Interpretation." Ph.D. diss., Princeton University, 1994.

Herman, John E. "Empire in the Southwest: Early Qing Reforms to the Native Chieftain System." *Journal of Asian Studies* 56.1 (Feb. 1997): 47–74.

———. "The Mongol Conquest of the Dali Kingdom: The Failure of the Second Front." In Nicola Di Cosmo, ed., *Warfare in Inner Asian History*. Leiden: E. J. Brill, 2002.

———. "The Mu'ege Kingdom: A Brief History of a Frontier Empire." In Nicola Di Cosmo and Don Wyatt, eds., *Political Frontiers, Ethnic Boundaries, and Human Geographies in Chinese History*. London: Curzon Press, 2003.

————. "The Cant of Conquest: *Tusi* Offices and China's Political Incorporation of the Southwest Frontier." In Pamela Kyle Crossley, Helen F. Siu, and Donald S. Sutton, eds., *Empire at the Margins: Culture, Ethnicity, and Frontier in Early Modern China*. Berkeley: University of California Press, 2006.

Hill, Ann Maxwell. "Captives, Kin, and Slaves in Xiao Liangshan." *Journal of Asian Studies* 60.4 (Nov. 2001): 1033–49.

Hill, Ann Maxwell, and Eric Diehl. "A Comparative Approach to Lineages Among Xiao Liangshan Nuosu (Yi) and Han." In Stevan Harrell, ed., *Perspectives on the Yi*. Berkeley: University of California Press, 2001.

Ho, Ping-ti. "The Significance of the Ch'ing Period in Chinese History." *Journal of Asian Studies* 26.2 (1967): 189–95.

————. "In Defense of Sinicization: A Rebuttal of Evelyn Rawski's 'Reenvisioning the Qing.'" *Journal of Asian Studies* 57.1 (Feb. 1998): 123–55.

Honig, Emily. *Creating Chinese Ethnicity: Subei People in Shanghai, 1850–1980*. New Haven: Yale University Press, 1992.

Hostetler, Laura. *Qing Colonial Enterprise: Ethnography and Cartography in Early Modern China*. Chicago: University of Chicago Press, 2001.

*Hou Hanshu* 後漢書 (History of the Later Han). Ed. Fan Ye 范曄. 445. Reprint, Beijing: Zhonghua shuju, 1970.

Hou Shaozhuang 侯紹庄, Shi Jizhong 史繼忠, and Weng Jialie 翁家烈. *Guizhou gudai minzu guanxi shi* 貴州古代民族關係史 (History of ethnic relations in ancient Guizhou). Guiyang: Guizhou minzu chubanshe, 1991.

Hsi, Angela. "Wu San-kuei in 1644: A Reappraisal." *Journal of Asian Studies* 34.2 (Feb. 1975): 443–53.

Hsiao, Ch'i-ch'ing. *The Military Establishment of the Yuan Dynasty*. Cambridge: Harvard Council on East Asian Studies, 1978.

Hsiao I-shan (Xiao Yishan) 蕭一山. *Qingdai tongshi* (General history of the Qing period). 5 vols. Taipei: Taiwan shangwu yinshuguan, 1962–63; rev. ed. 1980. Reprint, Beijing: Zhonghua shuju, 1986.

Hu Chengning 胡承寧. "Yetan She An qiyi de xingzhi" 也談奢安起義的性質 (Additional points on the nature of the She-An incident). *Guizhou wenshi congkan* 貴州文史叢刊 (Essays on the literature and history of Guizhou) 69.4 (1996): 34–52.

Hu Naian 胡耐安. "Ming Qing dai tusi" 明清代土司 (Native officials during the Ming and Qing dynasties). *Dalu zazhi* 大陸雜誌 (Mainland magazine) 10 (1959): 1–8.

Hu Qingjun 胡慶鈞. "Songdai Yizu xianmin diqu nuli zhidu de fanrong fazhan" 宋代彝族先民地區奴隸制度的繁榮發展 (The development of a flourishing slave institution among the Yi and the area's earlier inhabitants during the Song dynasty). *Sixiang zhanxian* 思想戰線 (Ideological front) (1980): 31–42.

————. *Ming Qing Yizu shehui shi luncong* 明清彝族社會史論叢 (Collected essays on the history of Yi society during the Ming and Qing dynasties). Shanghai: Shanghai renmin chubanshe, 1981.

Hu Wenhuan 胡文煥. *Huayi fengtu zhi* 華夷風土志 (An account of the customs of Chinese and barbarians). 1614.

Hu Zhaoxi 胡昭曦. "Lun Han Jin de Di Qiang he Sui Tang yihou de Qiangzu" 論漢晉的氏羌和隋唐以後的羌族 (A discussion of the Di-Qiang during the Han and Jin dynasties and the Qiang nationality following the Sui and Tang dynasties). *Lishi yanjiu* 歷史研究 (Historical research) 2 (1963): 153–70.

————. *Zhang Xianzhong tu Shu kaobian—jian xi Huguang tian Sichuan* 張獻忠屠蜀考辨—兼析湖廣填四川 (A study of Zhang Xianzhong's alleged massacre in Sichuan, with an analysis of immigration from Huguang to Sichuan). Chengdu: Sichuan renming chubanshe, 1980.

Huang Bian 黃汴. *Yitong lucheng tuji* 一統路程圖記 (Comprehensive illustrated route book of the empire). 1570.

Huang Fensheng 黃奮生. *Bianjiang zhengjiao zhi yanjiu* 邊疆政教之研究 (Research on political and educational institutions in the frontier). Shanghai: Commercial Press, 1947.

Huang Kaihua 黃開華. "Mingdai tusi zhidu sheshi yu xi'nan kaifa" 明代土司制度設施與西南開發 (The opening of the southwest and the establishment of the native official institution during the Ming dynasty). In She Yize 佘貽澤, ed., *Mingdai tusi zhidu* 明代土司制度 (The Ming native official institution). Taipei: Taiwan xuesheng shuju, 1968.

Huang, Pei. *Autocracy at Work: A Study of the Yung-chung Period, 1723–1735.* Bloomington: Indiana University Press, 1974.

Huang, Ray. "Fiscal Administration During the Ming Dynasty." In Charles Hucker, ed., *Chinese Government in Ming Times: Seven Studies.* New York: Columbia University Press, 1969.

————. *Taxation and Government Finance in Sixteenth-Century Ming China.* Cambridge: Cambridge University Press, 1974.

————. *1587, a Year of No Significance: The Ming Dynasty in Decline.* New Haven: Yale University Press, 1981.

Huang Yuanzhi 黃元治. *Qianzhong zaji* 黔中雜記 (Random notes on Qianzhong). 1683.

*Huangchao wenxian tongkao* 皇朝文獻通考 (General history and examination of Qing institutions and documents). 300 *juan.* 1785. Reprint, 2 vols. Taipei: Taiwan shangwu shuju, 1987.

*Huayang guozhi* 華洋國志 (An account of China and foreign countries). Ed. Chang Qu 常璩. Ca. 265–316. Ba-Shu edition reprint, 1984.

Hucker, Charles O. *The Ming Dynasty: Its Origins and Evolving Institutions.* Ann Arbor: University of Michigan Press, 1978.

———. *A Dictionary of Official Titles in Imperial Times*. Stanford: Stanford University Press, 1985.

*Huguang tongzhi* 湖廣通志 (Comprehensive gazetteer of Huguang). 1592.

Hummel, Arthur W., ed. *Eminent Chinese of the Ch'ing Period*. 2 vols. Washington, D.C.: U.S. Government Printing Office, 1943, 1944.

Humphreys, R. Stephen. *From Saladin to the Mongols: The Ayyubids of Damascus, 1193–1260*. Albany, 1977.

*Hunan tongzhi* 湖南通志 (Comprehensive gazetteer of Hunan). Ed. Zeng Guoquan 曾國荃. 1885.

Isaac, Benjamin. *The Limits of Empire: The Roman Army in the East*. New York: Oxford University Press, 1990.

Jia Jingyan 賈敬顏. "Hanren kao" 漢人考 (An examination of the Han people). In Fei Xiaotong 費孝通, ed., *Zhonghua minzu duoyuan yiti geju* 中華民族多元一體格局 (The multifaceted features of China's minority peoples). Beijing: Zhongyang minzu xueyuan chubanshe, 1989.

Jiang Dexue 蔣德學. "Qingchu Guizhou renkou kao" 清初貴州人口考 (An examination of Guizhou's population during the early Qing). *Guizhou shehui kexue* 貴州社會科學 (Social science in Guizhou) 4 (1982): 50–54.

———. "Shilun Qingdai Guizhou de yimin" 始論清代貴州的移民 (A preliminary discussion of Guizhou's immigrants during the Qing). *Renkou yanjiu* 人口研究 (Population research) (1983): 34–40.

Jiang Yingliang 江應樑. "Liangshan Yizu de nuli zhidu" 涼山彝族的奴隸制度 (The slave system of the Liangshan Yi). *Zhuhai xuebao* 珠海學報 (Zhuhai journal) 1 (1948): 17–53.

———. *Mingdai Yunnan jingnei de tuguan yu tusi* 明代雲南境內的土官與土司 (The *tuguan* and *tusi* offices in Yunnan during the Ming). Kunming: Yunnan renmin chubanshe, 1957.

———. "Mingdai waidi yimin jinru Yunnan kao" 明代外地移民進入雲南考 (Immigration into Yunnan during the Ming). *Yunnan daxue xueshu lunwen ji* 雲南大學學書論文集 (An anthology of scholarly articles from Yunnan University) 2 (April 1963): 1–33.

Jiemei Yixue yanjiu xiaozu 姐妹彝學研究小組 (The three sisters' Yi studies research group). *Yizu fengsu shi* 彝族風俗釋 (Records of Yi customs). Beijing: Central Institute of Nationalities Press, 1992.

Jike'erdazehuo 吉克爾達則伙. *Wo zai shengui zhijian: yige Yizu jisi de zishu* 我在神鬼之間: 一個彝族祭司的自述 (I among the spirits: an autobiography of an Yi priest). Kunming: Yunnan renmin chubanshe, 1990.

*Jiu Tang shu* 舊唐書 (Old history of the Tang). Ed. Liu Xu 劉昫. 945. Reprint, Taipei: Huawen shuju, 1965.

Jjissyt, Dalyt. *Hnewo teyy* 勒俄特衣 (The book of creation). Chengdu: Sichuan minzu chubanshe, 1981.

*Kangxi chao Hanwen zhupi zouche huibian* 康熙朝漢文硃批奏摺彙編 (The collected Chinese-language secret palace memorials of the Kangxi reign). 8 vols. Comp. Number One Historical Archives of China. Ed. Guo Zhulan. Beijing: Dang'an chubanshe, 1984–85.

*Kangxi chao Manwen zhupi zouche quanyi* 康熙朝滿文硃批奏摺全譯 (Complete translation of the Manchu palace memorials of the Kangxi reign). Comp. Number One Historical Archives of China. Ed. Guan Xiaolian and Qu Liusheng. Beijing: Dangan chubanshe, 1996.

Kawahara Masahiro 河原正博. *Kan minzoku Kanan hattenshi kenkyū* 漢民族華南發展史研究 (Research into the history of the development of the southwest by the Han people). Tokyo: Yoshikawa kōbunkan, 1984.

Keightley, David N. *The Origins of Chinese Civilization*. Berkeley: University of California Press, 1983.

Kessler, Lawrence D. *K'ang-hsi and the Consolidation of Ch'ing Rule, 1661–1684*. Chicago: University of Chicago Press, 1976.

Keyes, Charles F. "Toward a New Formulation of the Concept of Ethnic Group." In idem, ed., *Ethnic Change*. Seattle: University of Washington Press, 1981.

Kuang Lu 鄺露. *Chiya* 赤雅 (Uncovered grace). 1635.

Lan Dingyuan 藍鼎元. *Lun biansheng Miao Man shiyi shu* 論邊省苗蠻事宜疏 (A brief discussion of important matters concerning the Miao and Man in border provinces). 1730.

Langlois, John D., Jr. "Chinese Culturalism and the Yuan Analogy: Seventeenth-Century Perspectives." *Harvard Journal of Asiatic Studies* 40 (1980): 355–98.

———. *China Under Mongol Rule*. Princeton: Princeton University Press, 1981.

———. "The Hung-wu Reign, 1368–1398." In Frederick Mote and Denis Twitchett, eds., *The Cambridge History of China*, vol. 7, *The Ming Dynasty, 1368–1644*, pt. 1. Cambridge: Cambridge University Press, 1988.

Lattimore, Owen. *Studies in Frontier History: Collected Papers, 1928–1958*. London: Oxford University Press, 1962.

Lee, James Z. "Food Supply and Population Growth in Southwest China, 1250–1850." *Journal of Asian Studies* 41.4 (1982): 711–46.

———. "The Legacy of Immigration to Southwest China, 1250–1850." *Annales de Démographie Historique* (1982): 279–304.

———. "Ming Qing shiqi Zhongguo xi'nan de jingji fazhan he renkou zengzhang" 明清時期中國西南的經濟發展和人口增長 (Economic development and population growth in southwest China during the Ming and Qing). *Qingshi luncong* 清史論叢 (Essays in Qing history) 5 (1984): 50–102.

———. "The Political Economy of a Frontier: Southwest China, 1350–1850." Ph.D. dissertation, University of Chicago, 1983.

Leng Guangdian 冷光典. *Vonre* (The snow clan). Chengdu: Sichuan minzu yanjiusuo, 1983.

———. *Yi wangxi: yige Yizu tusi de zixu* 彝往昔: 一個彝族土司的自敘 (Retrospection of the past: autobiography of an Yi native official). Kunming: Yunnan renmin chubanshe, 1988.

Leong, Sow-theng. *Migration and Ethnicity in Chinese History: Hakkas, Pengmin, and Their Neighbors.* Ed. Tim Wright. Stanford: Stanford University Press, 1997.

Li Hualong 李化龍. *Bodi shanhou shiyi shu* 播地善後事宜疏 (A record of the events surrounding the reconstruction of Bo territory). In Ortai 鄂爾泰, ed., *Guizhou tongzhi* 貴州通志 (Comprehensive gazetteer of Guizhou). 1741. *Juan* 34, 19a–28b.

———. *Ping Bo quanshu* 平播全書 (The complete story of the Bozhou campaign). In Ortai 鄂爾泰, ed., *Guizhou tongzhi* 貴州通志 (Comprehensive gazetteer of Guizhou). 1741. *Juan* 34, 12b–18b.

Li, Lung-wah. "The Control of the Szechwan-Kweichow Frontier Regions During the Late Ming." Ph.D. diss., Australian National University, 1978.

Li Qing 李卿. "Cong 'Yizu yuanliu' zai lun Yelang guo zushu wenti" 從 "彝族源流" 再論夜朗國族屬問題 (Additional questions regarding Yelang's ethnic classification [following an examination of] "Yizu origins"). *Guizhou wenshi congkan* 貴州文史叢刊 (Essays on literature and history in Guizhou) 3 (1993): 45–52.

———. "Guizhou Yizu tusi yan'ge kao" 貴州彝族土司沿革考 (An examination of the evolution of Yizu native officials in Guizhou). *Guizhou wenshi congkan* 貴州文史叢刊 (Essays on literature and history in Guizhou) 5 (1996): 19–30.

Li Shaoming 李紹明. "Guanyu Qiangzu gudaishi de ji ge wenti" 關於羌族古代史的几個問題 (Several questions concerning the ancient history of the Qiang). *Lishi yanjiu* 歷史研究 (Historical research) 5 (1963): 165–82.

Li Shiyu 李世愉. "Luelun tusi zhidu yu gaitu guiliu" 略論土司制度與改土歸流 (A brief discussion of the native official institution and bureaucratic consolidation). In Ma Dazhang 馬大正, ed., *Zhongguo gudai bianjiang zhengce yanjiu* 中國古代邊疆政策研究 (Research on ancient China's frontier policies). Beijing: Zhongguo shehui kexue chubanshe, 1990.

Li Zhiting 李治亭. *Wu Sangui dazhuan* 吳三桂大傳 (A biography of Wu Sangui). Changchun: Jilin wenshi chubanshe, 1990.

Li Zongfang 李宗昉. *Qian ji* 黔記 (A record of Qian). 1834.

Liang Fangzhong 梁方仲. *Zhongguo lidai hukou, tiandi, tianfu tongji* 中國歷代戶口, 田地, 田賦統計 (Chinese historical statistics on population, land, and taxes). Shanghai: Shanghai renmin chubanshe, 1980.

Lin, Yaohua (Lin, Yueh-hwa) 林耀華. "The Miao-Man Peoples of Kweichow: An Annotated Translation of the Miao-Man Section of the *Ch'ien-nan chih-fang chi-lueh*." *Harvard Journal of Asiatic Studies* 5 (1940): 261–345.

————. *The Lolo of Liangshan*. Trans. Pan Ju-shu. New Haven, CT: HRAF Press, 1961.

————. "Yizu of Liang Shan, Past and Present." In David Maybury-Lewis, ed., *The Prospects for Plural Societies*. Washington, DC: American Ethnological Society, 1984.

Ling Chunsheng 凌純聲. "Tangdai Yunnan de Wuman yu Baiman kao" 唐代雲南的烏蠻與白蠻考 (An examination of the *wuman* and *baiman* of Yunnan during the Tang period). *Renleixue jikan* 人類學記刊 (Anthropology periodical) 1 (1938): 23–41.

*Liping fuzhou* 黎平府志 (Liping prefecture gazetteer). 1845.

Liu Fengyun 劉風雲. *Qingdai sanfan yanjiu* 清代三藩研究 (A study of the San-fan [rebellion] during the Qing). Beijing: Zhongguo renmin daxue chubanshe, 1994.

Liu Jian 劉健. *Tingwen lu* 庭聞錄 (A record of the Qing campaigns against Wu Sangui). 1719. Reprint, Shanghai: Shanghai shudian, 1985.

Liu Xixuan 劉錫玄. *Qiannan shiji* 黔南十記 (Ten records on southern Qian). Ca. 1623.

Liu Yaohan 劉堯漢. *Yizu shehui lishi diaocha yanjiu wenji* 彝族社會歷史調差研究文集 (A collection of papers on historical investigations of Yi society). Beijing: Minzu chubanshe, 1980.

————. *Yizu tianwenxue shi* 彝族天文學史 (A history of Yi astrology). Kunming: Yunnan renmin chubanshe, 1984.

Lo, Winston W. *Szechwan in Sung China: A Case Study in the Political Integration of the Chinese Empire*. Taipei: Chinese Culture University Press, 1982.

Lombard-Salmon, Claudine. *Un exemple d'acculturation chinoise: la province du Guizhou au XVIII siècle*. Paris: Ecole français d'Extrême-Orient, 1972.

Long Xianjun 龍先鈞. *Zhongguo Yizu tongshi gangyao* 中國彝族通史綱要 (A draft history of the Yi nationality in China). Kunming: Yunnan minzu chubanshe, 1993.

Lu Mingzhong et al., eds. *Nanfang minzu gushi shulu* 南方民族古史書錄 (A record of the ancient history of the minority peoples of the southern frontier). Chengdu: Sichuan minzu chubanshe, 1989.

Luo Raodian 羅繞典. *Qiannan zhifang jilue* 黔南職方紀略 (A record of government offices in southern Qian). 1847.

Ma Changshou 馬長壽. *Yizu gudai shi* 彝族古代史 (The ancient history of the Yi). Ed. Li Shaoming 李紹明. Shanghai: Shanghai renmin chubanshe, 1985.

Ma Dazheng 馬大正, ed. *Zhongguo gudai bianjiang zhengce yanjiu* 中國古代邊疆政策研究 (Studies on frontier policy in ancient China). Beijing: Zhongguo shehui kexue chubanshe, 1990.

Ma Dualin 馬端臨. *Wenxian tongkao* 文獻通考 (General history of institutions and critical examination of documents and studies). 1324. Reprint, Beijing: Zhonghua shuju, 1986.

Ma Erzi 馬爾自. "Dui jiu Liangshan Yizu shehui jiegoude zai renshi ji 'Heiyi' 'Baiyi' de bianxi" 對舊涼山彝族社會結構的再認識即 '黑彝''白彝'的辨析 (A reexamination of the social structure of old Liangshan, and the distinction between "Black Yi" and "White Yi"). *Liangshan minzu yanjiu* 涼山民族研究 (Liangshan nationalities research) 2 (1993): 38–48.

Ma Ruheng 馬汝亨 and Ma Dazheng 馬大正. *Qingdai de bianjiang zhengce* 清代的邊疆政策 (The frontier policies of the Qing dynasty). Beijing: Zhonghua shehui kexue chubanshe, 1994.

Ma Ruheng 馬汝亨 and Ma Dazheng 馬大正, eds. *Qingdai bianjiang kaifa yanjiu* 清代邊疆開發研究 (Research on the development of Qing-era frontiers). Beijing: Zhonghua shehui kexue chubanshe, 1990.

Ma Xueliang 馬學良 and Luo Guoyi 羅國義, eds. *Cuanwen congke* 爨文叢刻 (A collection of Cuan [Yi] literature). 3 vols. Chengdu: Sichuan renmin chubanshe, 1986.

Ma Yao 馬曜 et al. *Yunnan jianshi* 雲南簡史 (A brief history of Yunnan). Kunming: Yunnan renmin chubanshe, 1983.

Ma, Yin, ed. *China's Minority Nationalities*. Beijing: People's Publishing Society, 1989.

———— 馬寅. *Zhongguo shaoshu minzu changshi* 中國少數民族常識 (General knowledge of China's minority nationalities). Beijing: China Youth Press, 1984.

*Man shu* 蠻書 (Book of the southern barbarians). Trans. H. Luce. Ed. G. P. Oey. Southeast Asia Program, Cornell University, Data Paper 44. Ithaca, N.Y.: Southeast Asia Program, Cornell University, 1961.

Mao Qiling 毛奇齡. *Mansi hezhi* 蠻司合志 (Collected annals of barbarian offices). 1745. Reprint, Taipei: Guangwen shuju, 1967.

Meng Zhaoxin 孟昭信. *Kangxi dadi quanzhuan* 康熙大帝全傳 (A comprehensive biography of the Kangxi emperor). Changchun: Jilin wenshi chubanshe, 1987.

Meskill, John. *Academies in Ming China: A Historical Survey*. Tucson: University of Arizona Press, 1982.

Millward, James A. "New Perspectives on the Qing Frontier." In Gail Hershatter et al., eds., *Remapping China: Fissures in Historical Terrain*, pp. 113–29. Stanford: Stanford University Press, 1995.

————. *Beyond the Pass: Economy, Ethnicity, and Empire in Qing Central Asia, 1759–1864*. Stanford: Stanford University Press, 1998.

*Ming huiyao* 明會要 (Essential documents of the Ming dynasty). Ed. Long Wenbin 龍文彬. 1887. Reprint, Beijing: Zhonghua shuju, 1956.

*Ming shi* 明史 (The standard history of the Ming dynasty). Ed. Zhang Tingyu 張廷玉. 1736. Reprint, Beijing: Zhonghua shuju, 1974.

*Ming shilu* 明實錄. (Veritable Records of the Ming dynasty). 1418–1661. Reprint, Beijing: Zhonghua shuju, 1987. (*Taizu Hongwu shilu* 太祖洪武實錄 =

Hongwu reign, 1368–98; *Taizong Yongle shilu* 太宗永樂實錄 = Yongle reign, 1403–24; *Yingzong Zhengtong shilu* 英宗正統實錄 = Zhengtong reign, 1436–49; *Yingzong Tianshun shilu* 英宗天順實錄 = Tianshun reign, 1457–64; *Xianzong Chenghua shilu* 憲宗成化實錄 = Chenghua reign, 1465–87; *Xiaozong Hongzhi shilu* 孝宗弘治實錄 = Hongzhi reign, 1488–1505; *Wuzong Zhengde shilu* 武宗正德實錄 = Zhengde reign, 1506–21; *Shizong Jiajing shilu* 世宗嘉靖實錄 = Jiajing reign, 1522–66; *Muzong Longqing shilu* 穆宗隆慶實錄 = Longqing reign, 1567–72; *Shenzong Wanli shilu* 神宗萬曆實錄 = Wanli reign, 1573–1620; *Xizong Tianqi shilu* 熹宗天啓實錄 = Tianqi reign, 1621–27; *Huaizong Chongzhen shilu* 懷宗崇禎實錄 = Chongzhen reign, 1628–44).

Miyazaki, Ichisada. "The Confucianization of South China." In Arthur F. Wright, ed., *The Confucian Persuasion*. Stanford: Stanford University Press, 1960.

Morgan, Lewis Henry. *Ancient Society*. Cambridge: Belknap Press of Harvard University Press, 1964.

Mote, F. W. "The T'u-mu Incident of 1449." In Frank A. Kierman, Jr., and John K. Fairbank, eds., *Chinese Ways in Warfare*. Cambridge: Harvard University Press, 1974.

Mu Jihong 木霽弘 et al. *Dian, Zang, Chuan da sanjiao wenhua tanmi* 滇藏川大三角文化探秘 (An exploration of the cultures in the area of the great delta of Yunnan, Tibet, and Sichuan). Kunming: Yunnan daxue chubanshe, 1992.

Mu Qin 沐芹, ed. *Nanchao yeshi* 南詔野史 (An unofficial history of the Nanzhao kingdom). Kunming: Yunnan renmin chubanshe, 1990.

Nan Bingwen 南炳文. *Nan Ming shi* 南明史 (A history of the Southern Ming). Tianjin: Nankai daxue chubanshe, 1992.

Nishida Tatsuo. *A Study of the Lolo-Chinese Vocabulary Lolo I-yu*. Kyoto: Shokadō, 1979.

Okada Koji 岡田宏二. *Chūgoku Kanan minzoku shakaishi kenkyū* 中國華南民族社會史研究 (Research on minority societies in southern China). Tokyo: Kyūko shoin, 1993.

Parsons, James B. "The Culmination of a Chinese Peasant Rebellion: Chang Hsien-chung in Szechwan, 1644–1646." *Journal of Asian Studies* 16.3 (May 1957): 387–400.

———. "The Ming Dynasty Bureaucracy: Aspects of Background Forces." In Charles Hucker, ed., *Chinese Government in Ming Times: Seven Studies*. New York: Columbia University Press, 1969.

———. *The Peasant Rebellions of the Late Ming Dynasty*. Tucson: University of Arizona Press, 1970.

Perdue, Peter C. *Exhausting the Earth: State and Peasant in Hunan, 1500–1850*. Cambridge: Council on East Asian Studies, Harvard University, 1987.

———. *China Marches West: The Qing Conquest of Central Eurasia*. Cambridge: Belknap Press of Harvard University Press, 2005.

Petech, Luciano. *China and Tibet in the Early Eighteenth Century: History of the Establishment of a Chinese Protectorate in Tibet.* Leiden: E. J. Brill, 1972.

———. *Central Tibet and the Mongols: The Yuan-Sa-skya Period of Tibetan History.* Rome: Instituto Italiano per il medio ed estremo oriente, 1990.

Peterson, Willard. *Bitter Gourd: Fang I-chih and the Impetus for Intellectual Change.* New Haven: Yale University Press, 1979.

*Pingba xianzhi* 平壩縣志 (Pingba county gazetteer). 1931.

*Pingyi xianzhi* 平夷縣志 (Pingyi county gazetteer). 1705.

*Pingyuan zhouzhi* 平遠州志 (Pingyuan department gazetteer). 1848.

Pollard, Samuel. *Tight Corner in China.* London: Henry Hooks, 1919.

———. *In Unknown China: A Record of the Observations, Adventures, and Experiences of a Pioneer Missionary During a Prolonged Sojourn Amongst the Wild and Unknown Nosu Tribe of Western China.* London: Seeley, Service, and Co., 1921.

Polo, Marco. *The Travels of Marco Polo.* Trans. R. E. Latham. Ca. 1310. Reprint, New York: Viking Penguin, 1986.

Pomeranz, Kenneth. *The Great Divergence: Europe, China, and the Making of the Modern World Economy.* Princeton: Princeton University Press, 2000.

Prakash, Gyan, ed. *After Colonialism: Imperial Histories and Postcolonial Displacements.* Princeton: Princeton University Press, 1995.

Pratt, Mary Louise. *Imperial Eyes: Travel Writing and Transculturation.* London and New York: Routledge, 1992.

Pu Tongjin 普同金. "Yizu xinyang de bijiao" 彝族信仰的敎 (The bi[mo] religion of the Yi). *Yunnan minzu xueyuan xuebao* 雲南民族學院學報 (Journal of the Yunnan Nationalities Institute) 3 (1996): 66–72.

*Puan zhouzhi* 普安州志 (Puan department gazetteer). 1758.

*Qian Hanshu* 前漢書 (History of the Former Han). Ed. Ban Gu 班固. 92 CE. Reprint, Taipei: Huawen shuju, 1968.

*Qianxi zhouzhi* 黔西州志 (Qianxi department gazetteer). 1835.

*Qinding gujin tushu jicheng* 欽定古今圖書集成 (Imperially approved synthesis of books and illustrations past and present). Ed. Chen Menglie 陳夢雷. 1726–28.

*Qinding xuezheng quanshu* 欽定學政全書 (Imperially authorized compendium of records on education policy). Ed. Tong Huang 童璜 et al. 1812.

*Qingdai renwu zhuangao* 清代人物傳稿 (Draft biographies of Qing figures). Ser. 1. 5 vols. Beijing: Zhonghua shuju, 1985–88.

*Qingshi gao* 清史稿 (Qing history drafts). 529 *juan*. 48 vols. Ed. Zhao Erxun 趙爾巽. 1928. Reprint, Beijing: Zhonghua shuju, 1976–77.

*Qingshi liezhuan* 清史列傳 (Qing history biographies). 80 *juan*. 1928. Reprint, Beijing: Zhonghua shuju, 1987.

*Qingshi ziliao* 清史資料 (Materials on Qing history). 7 vols. Comp. Chinese Academy of Social Sciences, Institute of History, Qing History Research Department. Beijing: Zhonghua shuju, 1981–89.

Qu Jiusi 瞿九思. *Wanli wugong lu* 萬歷武功錄 (A record of the military successes during the Wanli reign). 1612. Reprint, Taipei: Yiwen yinshuguan, 1980.

Quan Hansheng 全漢昇. "Qingdai Yunnan tongkuang gong" 清代雲南銅礦工 (The copper mining industry in Yunnan during the Qing). *Journal of the Institute of Chinese Studies of the Chinese University of Hong Kong* 7.1 (1974): 157–82.

———. "Ming-Qing shidai Yunnan de yinke yu yin chan e" 明清時代雲南的銀課與銀產額 (Silver levies and silver production quotas in Yunnan during the Ming and Qing periods). *Xinya xuebao* 新亞學報 (New Asia journal) 11.1 (March 1976): 61–88.

Rawski, Evelyn Sakakida. "Presidential Address: Reenvisioning the Qing: The Significance of the Qing Period in Chinese History." *Journal of Asian Studies* 55.4 (Nov. 1996): 829–50.

Rock, Joseph F. *The Ancient Na-khi Kingdom of Southwest China.* 2 vols. Cambridge: Harvard University Press, 1947.

Rossabi, Morris. "The Tea and Horse Trade with Inner Asia During the Ming." *Journal of Asian History* (Weisbaden) 4.2 (1970): 135–68.

———. *Khubilai Khan: His Life and Times.* Berkeley: University of California Press, 1988.

———. "The Reign of Khubilai Khan." In Denis Twitchett and Herbert Franke, eds., *The Cambridge History of China,* vol. 6, *Alien Regimes and Border States, 907–1368.* Cambridge: Cambridge University Press, 1994.

Rowe, William T. "Education and Empire in Southwest China: Ch'en Hungmou in Yunnan, 1733–38." In Benjamin Elman and Alexander Woodside, eds., *Education and Society in Late Imperial China, 1600–1800.* Berkeley: University of California Press, 1994.

———. *Saving the World: Chen Hongmou and Elite Consciousness in Eighteenth Century China.* Stanford: Stanford University Press, 2001.

Ruey Yih-fu 芮逸夫. "Boren kao" 僰人考 (An examination of the Bo people). *Zhongyang yanjiuyuan Yuyan yanjiusuo jikan* 中央研究院語言研究所紀刊 (Journal of the Language Research Institute of the Academia Sinica) 23 (1951): 245–78.

———. "Liao ren kao" 僚人考 (An examination of the Liao people). *Zhongyang yanjiuyuan Lishi yuyan yanjiusuo jikan* 中央研究院語言研究所紀刊 (Journal of the Institute of History and Philology of the Academia Sinica) 28 (1956): 727–70.

————. "Nanzhao shi" 南昭史 (The history of the Nanzhao). In Yih-fu Ruey, ed., *China: The Nation and Some Aspects of Its Cultures: A Collection of Selected Essays with Anthropological Approaches*. Taipei: Yee Wen, 1972.

Sahlins, Peter. *Boundaries: The Making of France and Spain in the Pyrenees*. Stanford: Stanford University Press, 1989.

*Sanguo zhi* 三國志 (Record of the Three Kingdoms). Ed. Chen Shou 陳壽. 297. Reprint, Taipei: Huawen shuju, 1965.

Schafer, Edward H. *The Vermilion Bird: T'ang Images of the South*. Berkeley: University of California Press, 1967.

Scott, Margret Inver. "A Study of the Ch'iang with Special Reference to Their Settlements in China from the Second to the Fifth Century." Ph.D. diss., University of Cambridge, 1953.

Shaughnessy, Edward L. *Sources of Western Zhou History*. Berkeley: University of California Press, 1991.

She Yize 佘貽澤. *Zhongguo tusi zhidu* 中國土司制度 (China's native official institution). 1944. Reprint, Shanghai: Shangwu shuju, 1947.

Shen Xu 申旭 and Liu Zhi 劉雉. *Zhongguo xi'nan yu dongnan ya de kuajing minzu* 中國西南與東南亞的跨境民族 (Border minorities in southwest China and Southeast Asia). Kunming: Yunnan minzu chubanshe, 1988.

Shepherd, John R. *Statecraft and Political Economy on the Taiwan Frontier, 1600–1800*. Stanford: Stanford University Press, 1993.

*Shiji* 史記 (Records of a historian). Ed. Sima Qian 司馬遷. Ca. 145–86 BCE. Reprint, Taipei: Taiwan Shangwu Yinshuguan, 1983.

Shin, Leo Kwok-Yueh. "Tribalizing the Frontier: Barbarians, Settlers, and the State in Ming South China." Ph.D. diss., Princeton University, 1999.

*Sichuan tongzhi* 四川通志 (Comprehensive gazetteer of Sichuan province). Ed. Huang Tinggui 黃廷桂. 1736.

*Sichuan tongzhi* 四川通志 (Comprehensive gazetteer of Sichuan province). Ed. Yang Fangcan 楊芳燦. 1816. Reprint, Chengdu: Sichuan renmin chubanshe, 1984.

*Sinan fuzhi* 思南府志 (Sinan prefecture gazetteer). 1537.

*Sizhou fuzhi* 思州府志 (Sizhou prefecture gazetteer). 1722.

Skelton, R. A., trans. *The Vinland Map and the Tartar Relation*. New Haven: Yale University Press, 1965.

Smith, Anthony D. *The Ethnic Origins of Nations*. New York: Blackwell Publications, 1987.

Smith, Kent Clarke. "Ch'ing Policy and the Development of Southwest China: Aspects of Ortai's Governor-Generalship, 1726–1731." Ph.D. diss., Yale University, 1970.

Smith, Paul J. "Taxing Heaven's Storehouse: The Szechwan Tea Monopoly and the Tsinghai Horse Trade, 1074–1204." Ph.D. diss., University of Pennsylvania, 1983.

Song Lian 宋濂. *Yangshi jiazhuan* 楊氏家傳 (A chronology of the Yang family). 1887.

*Song shi* 宋史 (History of the Song). Ed. Tuotuo (Toghto) 脫脫 et al. 1345. Reprint, Beijing: Zhonghua shuju, 1977.

Song Shikun 宋世坤. "Kele kaogu zaji" 可樂考古雜記 (Random notes on the Kele archaeological site). *Guizhou wenwu* 貴州文物 (Guizhou's cultural relics) 1 (1982): 3–8.

———. "Qingdai Guizhou shaoshu minzu de fengsu hua" 清代貴州少數民族的風俗化 (The changing customs of the national minorities in Guizhou during the Qing). *Wenwu yuekan* 文物月刊 (1988): 82–90.

Spence, Jonathan D., and John E. Wills, eds. *From Ming to Ch'ing: Conquest, Region, and Community in Seventeenth-Century China.* New Haven: Yale University Press, 1979.

Spenser, J. E. "Kueichou: An Internal Colony." *Pacific Affairs* 13 (1940): 162–72.

Struve, Lynn A. *The Southern Ming, 1644–1662.* New Haven: Yale University Press, 1984.

———. "The Southern Ming, 1644–1662." In Frederick Mote and Denis Twitchett, eds., *The Cambridge History of China,* vol. 7, *The Ming Dynasty, 1368–1644,* pt. 1. Cambridge: Cambridge University Press, 1988.

———. *The Ming-Qing Conflict, 1619–1683: A Historiography and Source Guide.* Ann Arbor, Mich.: Association for Asian Studies, 1998.

———. *Voices from the Ming-Qing Cataclysm: China in the Tigers' Jaws.* New Haven: Yale University Press, 1993.

Su Jianling 蘇建靈. "Lun Mingdai Guangxi dongbu de tusi" 論明代廣西東部的土司 (A discussion of the native official offices in eastern Guangxi during the Ming). *Sixiang zhanxian* 思想戰線 (Ideological front) 6 (1986): 27–33.

———. "Qin Han shiqi de Lingnan junxian—qian lun Lingnan tusi zhidu de yuanyuan" 秦漢時期的嶺南郡縣—兼論嶺南土司制度的淵源 (The commanderies and districts of Lingnan during the Qin and Han—with a discussion on the origins of *tusi* offices in Lingnan). *Guangxi minzu yanjiu* 廣西民族研究 (Collected papers on Guangxi's minority population) 1 (1989): 5–23.

———. "Yuandai Guangxi de tuguan zhidu" 元代廣西的土官制度 (The *tusi* institution in Guangxi during the Yuan period). *Guangxi minzu yanjiu* 廣西民族研究 (Collected papers on Guangxi's minority population) 2 (1988): 53–59.

Su Tongbing 蘇同炳. *Mingdai yizhan zhidu* 明代驛站制度 (The imperial post system of the Ming dynasty). Taipei: Zhonghua congshu bianshen weiyuanhui, 1969.

*Sui shu* 隋書 (History of the Sui). Ed. Wei Zheng 魏徵. 636. Reprint, Taipei: Huawen shuju, 1965.

Sun, E-tu Zen. "The Copper of Yunnan: An Historical Sketch." *Mining Engineering* (July 1964): 118–24.

Tan Qixiang 譚其驤. "Zhongguo neidi yimin shi—Hunan pian" 中國內地移民史—湖南偏 (The history of internal migrations in China—Hunan). *Shixue nianbao* 史學年報 (Historical studies) 1.4 (1932): 47–104.

Tan Qixiang 譚其驤, ed. *Zhongguo lishi ditu ji* 中國歷史地圖集 (The historical atlas of China). 8 vols. Shanghai: Ditu chubanshe, 1987.

Teng, Emma Jinhua. *Taiwan's Imagined Geography: Chinese Colonial Travel Writing and Pictures, 1683–1895.* Cambridge: Harvard University Asia Center, 2004.

Tian Rucheng 田汝成. *Yanjiao jiwen* 炎缴紀聞 (A record of the southern frontier). 1560.

Tian Wen 田雯. *Qian shu* 黔書 (A book on Qian). 1690.

Tong Enzheng 童恩正. "Sichuan xi'nan diqu Dashimu zushu shitan" 四川西南地區大石墓族屬試探 (More on the people of Dashimu in the southwest portion of Sichuan province). *Kaogu* 考古 (Archaeology) 2 (1978): 104–10.

———. "Jinnianlai Zhongguo xi'nan minzu diqu Zhanguo, Qin, Han shidai de kaogu faxian jiqi yanjiu" 近年來中國西南民族地區戰國秦漢時代的考古發現及其研究 (Recent research on archaeological discoveries in China's southwest minority areas dating from the Warring States, Qin, and Han periods). *Kaogu xuebao* 考古學報 (Studies in archaeology) (1980): 417–42.

Tong, James. *Disorder Under Heaven: Collective Violence in the Ming Dynasty.* Stanford: Stanford University Press, 1991.

*Tongren fuzhi* 銅仁府志 (Tongren prefecture gazetteer). 1614.

Treistman, Judith. *The Early Cultures of Szechwan and Yunnan.* Cornell University East Asia Papers. Ithaca, N.Y.: Cornell University China-Japan Program, 1974.

*Tuguan dibu* 土官底簿 (A record of native official offices). Ca. 1520. Reprint, Taipei: Shangwu yinshuguan, 1986.

Twitchett, Denis, and Tilemann Grimm. "The Cheng-t'ung, Ching-t'ai, and T'ien-shun Reigns, 1436–1464." In Frederick W. Mote and Denis Twitchett, eds., *The Cambridge History of China*, vol. 7, *The Ming Dynasty, 1368–1644*, pt. 1. Cambridge: Cambridge University Press, 1988.

Vial, Paul. *Les Lolos—histoire, religion, moeurs, langue, écriture* (The Lolos—history, religion, customs, language, writing). Etudes sino-orientales (Sino-Oriental studies), pt. a. Shanghai: Imprimerie de la Mission catholique, 1898.

———. "A travers la Chine inconnue: chez les Lolos" (Traveling across unknown China: among the Lolos). *Les missions catholiques* 49 (1917): 537–38, 254–57.

von Dewall, Magdalene. "The Tien Culture of South-west China." *Antiquity* 41 (1967): 8–21.

von Glahn, Richard. *The Country of Streams and Grottoes: Expansion, Settlement, and the Civilizing of the Sichuan Frontier in Song Times*. Cambridge: Council on East Asian Studies, Harvard University, 1987.

———. *Fountain of Fortune: Money and Monetary Policy in China, 1000–1700*. Berkeley: University of California Press, 1996.

Wade, Geoff. "The Ming *shi-lu* (Veritable Records of the Ming Dynasty) as a Source for Southeast Asian History, Fourteenth to Seventeenth Century." Ph.D. diss., University of Hong Kong, 1994.

———. "Some Topoi in Southern Border Historiography During the Ming (and Their Modern Relevance)." In Savine Dabringhaus and Roderich Ptak, eds., *China and Her Neighbors: Borders, Visions of the Other, Foreign Policy, Tenth to Nineteenth Century*. Wiesbaden: Harrassowitz Verlag, 1997.

Wakeman, Frederic, Jr. "The Shun Interregnum of 1644." In Jonathan D. Spence and John E. Wills, eds., *From Ming to Ch'ing: Conquest, Region, and Continuity in Seventeenth-Century China*. New Haven: Yale University Press, 1979.

———. *The Great Enterprise: The Manchu Reconstruction of Imperial Order in Seventeenth-Century China*. 2 vols. Berkeley: University of California Press, 1985.

Waldron, Arthur. *The Great Wall of China: From History to Myth*. Cambridge: Cambridge University Press, 1990.

Wang Guifu 王桂馥 and Chen Ying 陳英. "Yizu liuzu yuanliu ji qi niandai wenti" 彝族六祖源流及其年代問題 (The origins of the six ancestors of the Yi nationality and questions on successive generations). In Xi Tianxi 西天錫, ed., *Sichuan Guizhou Yizu shehui lishi diaocha* 四川貴州彝族社會歷史調查 (An examination of the history and society of the Yi nationality in Sichuan and Guizhou). Kunming: Yunnan renimin chubanshe, 1986.

Wang, Gungwu. "The Chinese Urge to Civilize: Reflections on Change." In Gungwu Wang, ed., *The Chineseness of China*. Hong Kong: Oxford University Press, 1991.

Wang Jichao 王繼超 and Wang Ziguo 王子國, trans. *Yizu yuanliu* 彝族源流 (The origins of the Yi nationality). Guiyang: Guizhou minzu chubanshe, 1997.

Wang Mingke 王明珂. "Zhongguo gudai Jiang, Qiang, Diqiang zhi yanjiu" 中國古代姜, 羌, 氐羌之研究 (Research on China's ancient Jiang, Qiang, and Diqiang peoples). Master's thesis, National Taiwan Normal University, 1983.

Wang Ningsheng 汪寧生. *Yunnan kaogu* 雲南考古 (Yunnan archaeology). Kunming: Yunnan renmin chubanshe, 1980.

Wang Shi 王軾. *Ping Man lu* 平蠻錄 (An account of the pacification of the Miao). Ca. 1450.

Wang Shixing 王士性. *Guangyou zhi* 廣遊記 (My travels through Guang). Ca. 1590.

———. *Qian zhi* 黔志 (A record of Qian). Ca. 1590.

Wang Shouren 王守仁. *Yangming quanshu* 陽明全書 (A complete account of the life of Wang Yangming). 1572. Reprint, Taipei: Zhonghua shuju, 1965.

Wang Shuwu 王叔武, ed. *Dali xingji jiaozhu Yunnan zhilue jijiao* 大理行記校註 雲南志略輯校 (An edited version of "A Record of [My] Journey to Dali," with footnotes, in the edited collection "The Annals of Yunnan"). Kunming: Yunnan renmin chubanshe, 1986.

Wang Yangming 王陽明. *Wang Yangming quanji* 王陽明全集 (The collected works of Wang Yangming). 1547. Reprint, Taipei: Huawen shuju, 1964.

Wang Yuquan 王毓銓. *Mingdai de juntun* 明代的軍屯 (Military colonies during the Ming era). Beijing: Zhonghua shuju, 1965.

Wei Qingyuan 韋慶遠. *Mingdai huangce zhidu* 明代黃冊制度 (The yellow register system of the Ming dynasty). Beijing: Zhonghua shuju, 1961.

Wei Yuan 魏源. *Shengwu ji* 聖武記 (A record of military achievements). 14 *juan*. 2 vols. 1844. Reprint, Beijing: Zhonghua shuju, 1984.

Wiens, Herold J. *China's March Toward the Tropics*. Hamden, CT: Shoe String Press, 1954.

Wilhelm, Helmut. "On Ming Orthodoxy." *Monumenta Serica* 29 (1970–71): 1–26.

Wilkinson, Endymion. *Chinese History: A Manual*. Cambridge: Harvard University Asia Center, Harvard University Press, 2000.

Wolf, Eric R. *Sons of the Shaking Earth*. Chicago and London: University of Chicago Press, 1962.

Wu, Gu. "Reconstructing Yi History from Yi Records," In Stevan Harrell, ed., *Perspectives on the Yi of Southwest China*. Berkeley: University of California Press, 2001.

Wu Heng 吳恒 and Long Pingping 龍平平. "Guizhou Dafang xian Yizu lishi wenwu diaocha" 貴州大方縣彝族歷史文物調查 (An examination into the history and cultural artifacts of the Yi nationality in Guizhou's Dafang County). In *Sichuan Guizhou Yizu shehui lishi diaocha* 四川貴州彝族社會歷史調查 (An examination of the history and society of the Yi nationality in Sichuan and Guizhou). Kunming: Yunnan renmin chubanshe, 1987.

Wu, Jingzhong. "Nzymo as Seen in Some Yi Classical Books." In Stevan Harrell, ed., *Perspectives on the Yi of Southwest China*. Berkeley: University of California Press, 2001.

Wu Yongzhang 吳永章. *Zhongguo tusi zhidu yuanyuan yu fazhan shi* 中國土司制度淵源與發展史 (The origins and historical development of China's native official institution). Chengdu: Sichuan minzu chubanshe, 1988.

Wu Yongzhang 吳永章, ed. *Zhongnan minzu guanxi shi* 中南民族關係史 (A history of minority relations in southern China). Beijing: Minzu chubanshe, 1992.

Wyatt, David K. *Thailand: A Short History*. New Haven: Yale University Press, 1984.

Xi Tianxi 西天錫, ed. *Sichuan Guizhou Yizu shehui lishi diaocha* 四川貴州彝族社會歷史調查 (An investigation into the social history of the Yi nationality in Sichuan and Guizhou). Kunming: Yunnan renmin chubanshe, 1987.

Xie Guozhen 謝國楨. *Ming Qing zhi ji dangshe yundong kao* 明清之際黨社運動考 (Study of partisan movements in the Ming and Qing periods). Shanghai: Shangwu yinshuguan, 1934.

———. *Nan Ming shilue* 南明史略 (A brief history of the Southern Ming). Shanghai: Shanghai renmin chubanshe, 1957.

*Xi'nan Yizhi* 西南彝志 (A record of the Yi in the southwest). *Juan* 5–6. Guiyang: Guizhou renmin chubanshe, 1991.

*Xi'nan Yizhi* 西南彝志 (A record of the Yi in the southwest). *Juan* 7–8. Guiyang: Guizhou renmin chubanshe, 1994.

*Xi'nan Yizhi xuan* 西南彝志選 (Selections from *A Record of the Yi in the Southwest*). Guiyang: Guizhou renmin chubanshe, 1982.

*Xin Tang shu* 新唐書 (New history of the Tang). Ed. Ouyang Xiu 歐陽修 and Song Qi 宋祁. 1060. Reprint, Beijing: Zhonghua shuju, 1975.

Xu Mingde 徐明德. "Lun She An shijian zhi qiyin ji qi yingxiang" 論奢安事件之起因及其影響 (A discussion on the origins of the She-An Incident and its impact). *Guizhou wenshi congkan* 貴州文史叢刊 (On literature and history in Guizhou) 69.4 (1996): 5–14.

Xu Xiake 徐霞客. *Xu Xiake youji* 徐霞客遊記 (The travel diaries of Xu Xiake). Ed. Zhou Ningxia 周寧霞. Ca. 1641. Reprint, Shanghai: Shanghai guji chubanshe, 1997.

Xu Zanzeng 徐贊鎮. *Dianxing jicheng* 滇行紀程 (A record of my trip to Yunnan). 1680.

———. "Tangdai Dian Yue tongdao kao" 唐代滇越通道考 (A study of the communications between Yunnan and Vietnam during the Tang dynasty). *Journal of the Institute of Chinese Studies of the Chinese University of Hong Kong* 8.1 (1976): 38–51.

Yang, Lien-sheng. "Historical Notes on the Chinese World Order." In John K. Fairbank, ed., *The Chinese World Order*, 20–33. Cambridge: Harvard University Press, 1968.

———. "Ming Local Administration." In Charles Hucker, ed., *Chinese Government in Ming Times: Seven Studies*. New York: Columbia University Press, 1969.

Yang Shen 楊慎. *Sheng'an quanji* 升菴全集 (The complete writings of Yang Shen). 1582. Reprint, Taipei: Shangwu yinshuguan, 1968.

Yang Xiaoneng. *The Golden Age of Chinese Archaeology: Celebrated Discoveries from the People's Republic of China*. New Haven: Yale University Press, 1999.

*Yizu jianshi* 彝族簡史 (A short history of the Yi). Kunming: Yunnan renmin chubanshe, 1987.

*Yizu yuanliu* 彝族源流 (Origins of the Yi nationality). Guiyang: Guizhou renmin chubanshe, 1997.

*Yongning zhouzhi* 永寧州志 (Yongning department gazetteer). 1837.

*Yongzheng chao Hanwen zhupi zouzhe huibian* 雍正朝漢文硃批奏摺彙編 (Collected Chinese-language palace memorials of the Yongzheng reign). 33 vols. Beijing: Number One Historical Archives and Jiangsu guji chubanshe, 1989–91.

*Yongzheng zhupi yuzhi* 雍正硃批諭旨 (Vermilion rescripts [and palace memorials] of the Yongzheng period). Taipei: Wenhai chubanshe, 1965.

You Faxian 猶法賢. *Qian shi* 黔史 (A history of Guizhou). 1889.

You Zhong 尤中. *Nanzhao shihua* 南昭史話 (A history of the Nanzhao kingdom). Kunming: Yunnan renmin chubanshe, 1962.

———. *Yunnan gudai minzu* 雲南古代民族 (The minority peoples in ancient Yunnan). Kunming: Yunnan minzu xueyuan, 1978.

———. *Zhongguo xi'nan de gudai minzu* 中國西南的古代民族 (The minority peoples in the early history of China's southwest). Kunming: Yunnan renmin chubanshe, 1980.

———. *Zhongguo xi'nan minzu shi* 中國西南民族史 (A history of the minority peoples of southwest China). Kunming: Yunnan minzu chubanshe, 1985.

———. "Yuan, Ming, Qing shiqi Yizu shehui de fazhan yanbian" 元、明、清時期彝族社會的發展演變 (Change and development in Yi society during the Yuan, Ming, and Qing periods). In You Zhong 尤中, ed., *Xi'nan minzu yanjiu* 西南民族研究 (Southwest nationalities research). Kunming: Yunnan renmin chubanshe, 1987.

Yu Hongmo 余宏模. "Mingdai Guizhou xuanweishi 'cixing An shi' lizheng" 明代貴州宣慰使 '賜姓安氏' 例証 (An illustration of the "imperially bestowed surname An" of the Guizhou pacification commissioner during the Ming). *Guizhou wenshi congkan* (1998) 1: 5–7.

Yu Hongmo 余宏模, An Wenxin 安文新, and Li Pingfa 李平凡, eds. *Guizhou Yixue* 貴州彝學 (Yi studies in Guizhou). Guiyang: Guizhou minzu chubanshe, 1993.

Yu Ying-shih. "Han Foreign Relations." In Denis Twitchett and Michael Loewe, eds., *The Cambridge History of China*, vol. 1, *The Ch'in and Han Dynasties, 221 BC–AD 220*. Cambridge: Cambridge University Press, 1986.

*Yuan shi* 元史 (Yuan history). Ed. Song Lian 宋濂 et al. Ca. 1381. Reprint, Beijing: Zhonghua shuju, 1976.

*Yunnan tongzhi* 雲南通志 (Comprehensive gazetteer of Yunnan province). 1574.

*Yunnan tongzhi* 雲南通志 (Comprehensive gazetteer of Yunnan province). Ed. Yin Jishan 尹繼善 et al. 1736.

*Yunnan zhi* 雲南志 (Gazetteer of Yunnan province). 1553.

Zha Jizuo 查繼左. *Zuiwei lu* 罪惟錄 (Record [written in] cognizance [that it may bring my] indictment). 1676.

Zhang Fu 張福, ed. *Yizu gudai wenhua shi* 彝族古代文化史 (The history of ancient Yi culture). Kunming: Yunnan jiaoyu chubanshe, 1999.

Zhang Hong 張泓. *Nan Yi ji* 南夷記 (A record of the southern barbarians). 1733.

Zhang Huang 章潢. *Tushu bian* 圖書編 (A collection of books and illustrations). 1613. Reprint, Taipei: Chengwen chubanshe, 1971.

Zhang Xuejun 張學君 and Ran Guangrong 冉光榮. *Ming Qing Sichuan jing yan shigao* 明清四川井鹽史稿 (A draft history of the salt industry in Sichuan during the Ming and Qing periods). Chengdu: Sichuan renmin chubanshe, 1984.

Zhang Yurong 張瑜榮. "Guanyu Qingdai qianqi Yunnan kuangye de ziben zhuyi mengya wenti" 關於清代前期雲南礦業的資本主義萌芽問題 (Incipient capitalism in the mining industry of Yunnan before the Qing dynasty). *Xueshu yanjiu* 學書研究 (Scholarly research) 3 (1963): 37–44.

Zheng Xiao 鄭曉. *Huang Ming siyi kao* 皇明四夷考 (An examination of the four barbarians during the Ming). 1564. Reprint, Taipei: Huawen shuju, 1967.

Zhou Hongmo 周洪謀. *Zhishi yuwen* 知識語文 (Sundry things I have heard on governing the realm). 1521. Reprint, Beijing: Zhonghua shuju, 1985.

Zhuge Yuansheng 諸葛遠升. *Dianshi* 滇史 (A history of Yunnan). 1618.

Zhu Mengzhen 朱孟震. *Xi'nan yi fengtu ji* 西南夷風土記 (Customs of the non-Han in the southwest). 1600.

Zhu Xieyuan 朱燮元. *Shushi jilue* 蜀事記略 (Record of events in Sichuan). 1622.

Zhu Yuanzhang 朱元章. *Ming taizu ji* 明太祖記 (The writings of the founding Ming emperor). Ed. Hu Shi'e 胡士萼. Hefei: Huangshan shushe, 1991.

*Zizhi tongjian* 資治通鑑 (Comprehensive mirror for aid in government). Ca. 1300. Reprint, Beijing: Zhonghua shuju, 1995.

# Character List

Acha 阿察
Agengawei 阿更阿委
Ahua 阿畫
Aicui 靄翠
Ailu 愛魯
Ajia 阿架
An Bangyan 安邦彥
An Bupa 安卜葩
An De 安的
An Guan 安觀
An Guirong 安貴榮
An Guoheng 安國亨
An Jiangchen 安疆臣
An Ju 安聚
An Kun 安坤
An Longfu 安隴富
An Ren 安仁
An Wanquan 安萬銓
An Wanyi 安萬鎰
An Wanzhong 安萬鍾
An Wei 安位
An Yaochen 安堯臣
An Zhong 安中
An Zuo 安佐
*anfu si* 安撫司
Annan 安南
Anshun 安順

Anzhuang 安庄
Awangren 阿旺仁
Ayong 阿永
Azhe 阿哲

Babai xifu 八百媳婦
Bafan 八蕃
*baihu suo* 百户所
*baiman* 白蠻
*bao* 堡
*baojia* 保甲
Bei Pan 北盤 River
*bianjun* 邊郡
Bijie 畢節
*bingbu* 兵部
Bo 僰
Bole 播勒
Bozhou 播州
*bu* 部
*buzheng si* 布政司

Cai Yurong 蔡毓榮
*canjiang* 參將
Caoni 草泥
Caotang 草塘
Cheli 車里
Chen Youliang 陳友諒

Chengdu 成都

Chengfan 程番

*chengxiang* 丞相

Chishui 赤水

Chongqing 重慶

*chuang jiang* 闖蔣

*chuang wang* 闖王

*cishi* 刺史

Cuan 爨

Dading 大定

Dafang 大方

*dafu huguo daiwei qinjun du zhihui Bafan yanbian xuanwei shi* 大夫護國待衛親軍都指揮八蕃延邊宣慰司

Daguzhai 大鼓寨

Dali 大理

*dao* 道

*daogeng huozhong* 刀耕火種

Daxi 大西

*daxing* 大姓

Dedu 的都

Degai 得蓋

Dian 滇

*dian* 殿

Dingfan 定蕃

*dingkou* 丁口

Dongchuan 東川

*du zhihui si* 都指揮司

Duan Xingzhi 段興智

*dudu fu* 都督府

*duhu fu* 都護府

Dumu 篤慕

Duoni 朵你

Dushan 獨山

Duyun 都勻

Fagua 法卦

*fanluo* 蕃落

Fengning 豐寧

*fu* 府

Fu Youde 傅友德

*fuxin* 符信

*fuzi lianming* 父子連名

*gaitu guiliu* 改土歸流

Gao Yingxiang 高迎祥

*gaochi* 誥敕

*gaoming* 誥命

Geng Jimao 耿繼茂

Geng Jingzhong 耿精忠

*Geya yidao* 閣鴉驛道

Gong 龔 (Qianxi 黔西)

*gong* 貢

Gu Yanwu 顧炎武

*guandai* 冠帶

*gui* 鬼

*guide jiangjun* 歸德將軍

*guihua wang* 歸化王

*Guizhou fangyu shi* 貴州防禦使

*guizhu* 鬼主

Guo Zizhang 郭子章

Guoyongdi 果雍地

*guozi jian* 國子監

*Han jian* 漢奸

*Han-tu* 漢-土

Hankou 漢口

Hao 郝 (Zhijin 織金)

He Qiaoxin 何喬新

Hezhang 赫章

Hong Chengchou 洪承疇

Hongwu 洪武

*huangce* 黃冊

Huangping 黃平

*hufu* 虎符

Hui 暉 (Zhijin 織金)

Jangtai 彰泰

Jiale 架勒

Jian 犍 (northeast of Dafang 大方)

Jiang Dongzhi 蔣東知

Jiaozhi 交趾

jimi fuzhou 羈縻府州
jingnan wang 靖南王
jiuche 九擒
jiuxi shiba dong 九溪十八洞
jiuzong 九縱
Ju 矩 (Guiyang 貴陽)
jun 軍
junhu 軍戶
junmin zongguan fu 軍民總管府
juntun 軍屯
junxian 郡縣

Kaili 凱里
Kangxi 康熙
Kong Youde 孔有德
kou 口
Kunming 昆明
Kunzhou 昆州
kuqiao 苦蕎

Li Dehui 李德輝
Li Dingguo 李定國
Li Hualong 李化龍
Li Zicheng 李自成
libu 吏部
limu 吏目
Liping 黎平
Liu Jichang 劉繼昌
Liu Shuzhen 劉淑貞
Liu Xixuan 劉錫玄
Liumu 六慕
liyi 禮儀
Long Shou 龍壽
Long Yanyao 龍彥瑤
Long Zheng 龍徵
Longchang 龍場
longhu da jiangjun 龍虎大將軍
Longkua 隴垮
Lu 祿 (Bijie 畢節)
lu 路
Lu(zhou) nan yijie duda jiangjun 瀘(州)南夷界都大將軍

lu zongguan fu 路總管府
Luchuan 麓川
Luodian junzhang 羅甸君長
Luoluosi 玀玀司
Luoshi gui guo 玀氏鬼國
Luzhou 瀘州

Ma guo 馬國
Ma Hua 馬驊
man 蠻
Mangbu 芒部
manyi zhangguan si 蠻夷長官司
mayi 禡喬
Mian 緬
Miao 苗
Milu 米魯
mingde furen 明德夫人
minhu 民戶
mintun 民屯
Mopoleipo 莫波雷波 (Zhijin 織金)
mu 畝
Mu Sheng 沐盛
Mu Tianbo 沐天伯
Mu Ying 沐英
Mu'ege 慕俄格
Mugebaizhage 慕格白扎戈
Mujiji 慕濟濟
Mukua 慕胯
muzhuo 穆濯

na 那
Nanzhong 南中
neidi 內地
ningyuan da jiangjun 寧遠大將軍

Ortai 鄂爾泰

paizi 牌字
Panxian-Puan 盤縣-普安
Pi Luoge 皮邏閣
Pianqiao 偏橋

Pingba 平壩
Pingchiande 屏池安的 (Qianxi 黔西)
*pingman jiangjun* 平蠻將軍
*pingnan wang* 平南王
*pingtian dawang* 平天大王
*pingxi da jiangjun* 平西大將軍
Pingyuan 平遠
Pingyue 平越
Pu 濮
*pu* 舖
Puan 普安
Puding 普定
Pugui 普貴

Qian 黔
*qian* 簽
*Qian xibei Luoshi guiguo shouling* 黔西北玀氏鬼國首領
Qiang 羌
*qianhu suo* 千户所
Qianxi 黔西
Qianzhong 黔中
Qingzhu 清諸 (Qingzhen 清鎮)
Qujing 曲靖
*quna* 曲那

Saiyid 'Ajall Shams al-Din (Sai-dianchi) 賽典赤
*sanfan zhi luan* 三藩之亂
*sanzhu hufu* 三珠虎符
Shanchan 善單
Shang Kexi 尚可熹
*shao* 哨
She Chongming 奢崇明
She Xiang 奢香
She Xiaozhong 奢效忠
*sheng* 生
*shexue* 社學
Shi Yongan 石永安
Shibing 施秉
Shilong 石龍

*shu* 熟
Shu wang 蜀王
*shuguo* 屬國
Shuidong 水東
Shuixi 水西
Shuiyan-Tianwang 水鹽天望
Shuizhu 水著
*shujie* 鼠街
*shunde furen* 順德夫人
Shunyuan 順元
Shunyuan-Bafan 順元-八蕃
*Shunyuan jun Luodian guo* 順元軍羅甸國
Si Jifa 思機發
Si Lunfa 思倫發
Sinan 思南
Sizhou 思州
Song Qin 宋欽
Song Tianfu 宋添富
*sugie* 朔杰
Sun Kewang 孫可望

Tanzhou 潭州
Tangwang 溏望 (Bijie and Shui-cheng 水城 area)
*tianxia du zhaotao bingma da yuan-shuai* 天下都招討兵馬大元帥
*tidu junwu* 提督軍務
*tixing ancha si* 提刑按察司
Tongren 銅仁
*toumu* 頭目
*tu zhifu* 土知府
*tu zhixian* 土知縣
*tu zhizhou* 土知州
*tuguan* 土官
*tumu* 土目
*tun* 屯
*tuntian* 屯田
Tuoazhe 妥阿哲
*tuqiu weiguan* 土酋爲官
*tushe* 土舍
*tusi* 土司

Uriyangqadai (Wuliang hetai)
兀良合台

wang 王
Wang Ji 王翼
Wang Sanshan 王三善
Wang Shouren 王守仁
wanhu fu 萬户府
wei shihui shi 衛指揮使
Wei Wengtong 韋翁同
Weining 威寧
weisuo 衛所
Wu Sangui 吳三桂
Wu Shifan 吳世璠
Wuana 勿阿納
wujing dafu zhongzhou cishi 武經
大夫忠州刺史
wuman 烏蠻
Wumeng 烏蒙
Wusa 烏撒

xian 縣
Xiang 湘
xiang 降
Xibao 西堡
Xie Yuanshen 謝元深
xi'nan fanbu da xunjian shi 西南
蕃部大巡檢使
xi'nan fan wuyi dafu 西南蕃五夷
大撫
xing zhongshu sheng pingzhang
zhengshi 行中書省平章政事
xinzhi 信紙
Xiongsuo 雄所
xixuan 西選
xuanfu shi 宣撫使
xuanfu si 宣撫司
xuanwei shi 宣慰使
xuanwei si 宣慰司
xunjian 巡檢

Yachi 鴨池 River

yanfang si 驗放司
Yang Ai 楊愛
Yang Hui 楊輝
Yang Wanba 楊萬霸
Yang Yinglong 楊應龍
Yang You 楊友
Yao 姚 (Dafang 大方)
Yaocihai 藥刺海
Yaozhou 姚州
Yelang 夜郎
Yesudinger 也速頂兒
Yi 義 (northeast of Qianxi 黔西)
yidao 驛道
yinxin 印信
yinzhang 印章
yitiao bianfa 一條變法
Yixibuxue 亦溪不薛
yixu 裔續
yizhan 驛站
Yizhu 以著
Yongle 永樂
Yongli 永曆
Yongning 永寧
Yongzheng 雍正
Yude 于的
Yushi 于矢

Zangge 牂牁
zesu 則蘇
Zewo 則窩
zexi 則溪
Zhang Changqing 張常慶
Zhang Xianzhong 張獻忠
zhangguan si 長官司
Zhao Tingchen 趙庭臣
zhaotao si 招討司
zhaoyong da jiangjun 昭勇大將軍
Zhenning 鎮寧
Zhenyuan 鎮遠
zhou 州
Zhou Hongmou 周洪謀
Zhu Changxun 朱常洵

Zhu Xieyuan 朱燮元
Zhu Yuanzhang 朱元章
Zhuge Liang 諸葛亮
*zhusha* 硃砂
*zimo* 茲莫

Ziqi 自杞
*zongguan dudu* 總官都督
*zongling* 總領
*zu* 族
Zunyi 遵義

# Index

## Harvard East Asian Monographs
(*out-of-print)

*20. Toshio G. Tsukahira, *Feudal Control in Tokugawa Japan: The Sankin Kōtai System*

*21. Kwang-Ching Liu, ed., *American Missionaries in China: Papers from Harvard Seminars*

*22. George Moseley, *A Sino-Soviet Cultural Frontier: The Ili Kazakh Autonomous Chou*

23. Carl F. Nathan, *Plague Prevention and Politics in Manchuria, 1910–1931*

*24. Adrian Arthur Bennett, *John Fryer: The Introduction of Western Science and Technology into Nineteenth-Century China*

*25. Donald J. Friedman, *The Road from Isolation: The Campaign of the American Committee for Non-Participation in Japanese Aggression, 1938–1941*

*26. Edward LeFevour, *Western Enterprise in Late Ching China: A Selective Survey of Jardine, Matheson and Company's Operations, 1842–1895*

27. Charles Neuhauser, *Third World Politics: China and the Afro-Asian People's Solidarity Organization, 1957–1967*

*28. Kungtu C. Sun, assisted by Ralph W. Huenemann, *The Economic Development of Manchuria in the First Half of the Twentieth Century*

*29. Shahid Javed Burki, *A Study of Chinese Communes, 1965*

30. John Carter Vincent, *The Extraterritorial System in China: Final Phase*

31. Madeleine Chi, *China Diplomacy, 1914–1918*

*32. Clifton Jackson Phillips, *Protestant America and the Pagan World: The First Half Century of the American Board of Commissioners for Foreign Missions, 1810–1860*

*33. James Pusey, *Wu Han: Attacking the Present Through the Past*

*34. Ying-wan Cheng, *Postal Communication in China and Its Modernization, 1860–1896*

35. Tuvia Blumenthal, *Saving in Postwar Japan*

36. Peter Frost, *The Bakumatsu Currency Crisis*

37. Stephen C. Lockwood, *Augustine Heard and Company, 1858–1862*

38. Robert R. Campbell, *James Duncan Campbell: A Memoir by His Son*

39. Jerome Alan Cohen, ed., *The Dynamics of China's Foreign Relations*

40. V. V. Vishnyakova-Akimova, *Two Years in Revolutionary China, 1925–1927,* trans. Steven L. Levine

41. Meron Medzini, *French Policy in Japan During the Closing Years of the Tokugawa Regime*

42. Ezra Vogel, Margie Sargent, Vivienne B. Shue, Thomas Jay Mathews, and Deborah S. Davis, *The Cultural Revolution in the Provinces*

43. Sidney A. Forsythe, *An American Missionary Community in China, 1895–1905*

*44. Benjamin I. Schwartz, ed., *Reflections on the May Fourth Movement.: A Symposium*

*45. Ching Young Choe, *The Rule of the Taewŏngun, 1864–1873: Restoration in Yi Korea*

46. W. P. J. Hall, *A Bibliographical Guide to Japanese Research on the Chinese Economy, 1958–1970*

47. Jack J. Gerson, *Horatio Nelson Lay and Sino-British Relations, 1854–1864*

126. Bob Tadashi Wakabayashi, *Anti-Foreignism and Western Learning in Early-Modern Japan: The "New Theses" of 1825*

127. Atsuko Hirai, *Individualism and Socialism: The Life and Thought of Kawai Eijirō (1891–1944)*

128. Ellen Widmer, *The Margins of Utopia: "Shui-hu hou-chuan" and the Literature of Ming Loyalism*

129. R. Kent Guy, *The Emperor's Four Treasuries: Scholars and the State in the Late Chien-lung Era*

130. Peter C. Perdue, *Exhausting the Earth: State and Peasant in Hunan, 1500–1850*

131. Susan Chan Egan, *A Latterday Confucian: Reminiscences of William Hung (1893–1980)*

132. James T. C. Liu, *China Turning Inward: Intellectual-Political Changes in the Early Twelfth Century*

*133. Paul A. Cohen, *Between Tradition and Modernity: Wang T'ao and Reform in Late Ching China*

134. Kate Wildman Nakai, *Shogunal Politics: Arai Hakuseki and the Premises of Tokugawa Rule*

*135. Parks M. Coble, *Facing Japan: Chinese Politics and Japanese Imperialism, 1931–1937*

136. Jon L. Saari, *Legacies of Childhood: Growing Up Chinese in a Time of Crisis, 1890–1920*

137. Susan Downing Videen, *Tales of Heichū*

138. Heinz Morioka and Miyoko Sasaki, *Rakugo: The Popular Narrative Art of Japan*

139. Joshua A. Fogel, *Nakae Ushikichi in China: The Mourning of Spirit*

140. Alexander Barton Woodside, *Vietnam and the Chinese Model: A Comparative Study of Vietnamese and Chinese Government in the First Half of the Nineteenth Century*

*141. George Elison, *Deus Destroyed: The Image of Christianity in Early Modern Japan*

142. William D. Wray, ed., *Managing Industrial Enterprise: Cases from Japan's Prewar Experience*

*143. T'ung-tsu Ch'ü, *Local Government in China Under the Ching*

144. Marie Anchordoguy, *Computers, Inc.: Japan's Challenge to IBM*

145. Barbara Molony, *Technology and Investment: The Prewar Japanese Chemical Industry*

146. Mary Elizabeth Berry, *Hideyoshi*

147. Laura E. Hein, *Fueling Growth: The Energy Revolution and Economic Policy in Postwar Japan*

148. Wen-hsin Yeh, *The Alienated Academy: Culture and Politics in Republican China, 1919–1937*

149. Dru C. Gladney, *Muslim Chinese: Ethnic Nationalism in the People's Republic*

150. Merle Goldman and Paul A. Cohen, eds., *Ideas Across Cultures: Essays on Chinese Thought in Honor of Benjamin L Schwartz*

151. James M. Polachek, *The Inner Opium War*

152. Gail Lee Bernstein, *Japanese Marxist: A Portrait of Kawakami Hajime, 1879–1946*

Harvard East Asian Monographs

203. Robert S. Ross and Jiang Changbin, eds., *Re-examining the Cold War: U.S.-China Diplomacy, 1954–1973*

204. Guanhua Wang, *In Search of Justice: The 1905–1906 Chinese Anti-American Boycott*

205. David Schaberg, *A Patterned Past: Form and Thought in Early Chinese Historiography*

206. Christine Yano, *Tears of Longing: Nostalgia and the Nation in Japanese Popular Song*

207. Milena Doleželová-Velingerová and Oldřich Král, with Graham Sanders, eds., *The Appropriation of Cultural Capital: China's May Fourth Project*

208. Robert N. Huey, *The Making of 'Shinkokinshū'*

209. Lee Butler, *Emperor and Aristocracy in Japan, 1467–1680: Resilience and Renewal*

210. Suzanne Ogden, *Inklings of Democracy in China*

211. Kenneth J. Ruoff, *The People's Emperor: Democracy and the Japanese Monarchy, 1945–1995*

212. Haun Saussy, *Great Walls of Discourse and Other Adventures in Cultural China*

213. Aviad E. Raz, *Emotions at Work: Normative Control, Organizations, and Culture in Japan and America*

214. Rebecca E. Karl and Peter Zarrow, eds., *Rethinking the 1898 Reform Period: Political and Cultural Change in Late Qing China*

215. Kevin O'Rourke, *The Book of Korean Shijo*

216. Ezra F. Vogel, ed., *The Golden Age of the U.S.-China-Japan Triangle, 1972–1989*

217. Thomas A. Wilson, ed., *On Sacred Grounds: Culture, Society, Politics, and the Formation of the Cult of Confucius*

218. Donald S. Sutton, *Steps of Perfection: Exorcistic Performers and Chinese Religion in Twentieth-Century Taiwan*

219. Daqing Yang, *Technology of Empire: Telecommunications and Japanese Expansionism, 1895–1945*

220. Qianshen Bai, *Fu Shan's World: The Transformation of Chinese Calligraphy in the Seventeenth Century*

221. Paul Jakov Smith and Richard von Glahn, eds., *The Song-Yuan-Ming Transition in Chinese History*

222. Rania Huntington, *Alien Kind: Foxes and Late Imperial Chinese Narrative*

223. Jordan Sand, *House and Home in Modern Japan: Architecture, Domestic Space, and Bourgeois Culture, 1880–1930*

224. Karl Gerth, *China Made: Consumer Culture and the Creation of the Nation*

225. Xiaoshan Yang, *Metamorphosis of the Private Sphere: Gardens and Objects in Tang-Song Poetry*

226. Barbara Mittler, *A Newspaper for China? Power, Identity, and Change in Shanghai's News Media, 1872–1912*

227. Joyce A. Madancy, *The Troublesome Legacy of Commissioner Lin: The Opium Trade and Opium Suppression in Fujian Province, 1820s to 1920s*